A Counter-History of Composition

Pittsburgh Series in Composition, Literacy, and Culture

David Bartholomae and Jean Ferguson Carr, Editors

A COUNTER-HISTORY
OF COMPOSITION

TOWARD

METHODOLOGIES

OF COMPLEXITY

BYRON HAWK

UNIVERSITY OF PITTSBURGH PRESS

Published by the University of Pittsburgh Press, Pittsburgh PA 15260

Copyright © 2007, University of Pittsburgh Press

Manufactured in the United States of America

Printed on acid-free paper

10 9 8 7 6 5 4 3 2 1

ISBN 13: 978-0-8229-5973-1

ISBN 10: 0-8229-5973-9

Library of Congress Cataloging-in-Publication Data

Hawk, Byron.

  A counter-history of composition : toward methodologies of complexity /
Byron Hawk.

    p. cm. — (Pittsburgh series in composition, literacy, and culture)

  Includes bibliographical references and index.

  ISBN-13: 978-0-8229-5973-1 (pbk. : alk. paper)

  ISBN-10: 0-8229-5973-9 (pbk. : alk. paper)

  1. English language—Rhetoric. I. Title.

  PE1404.H394 2007

  808'.042—dc22

                        .2007025337

CONTENTS

Acknowledgments   vii

Introduction: From Vitalism to Complexity   1

1. Mapping Rhetoric and Composition   12

2. Cartography and Forgetting   49

3. Remapping Method   86

4. A Short Counter-History   121

5. Technology-Complexity-Methodology   166

6. Toward Inventive Composition Pedagogies   207

Afterword: Toward a Counter-Historiography   259

Notes   275

Bibliography   291

Index   303

ACKNOWLEDGMENTS

I would like to thank those at the University of Texas at Arlington who influenced this book and my desire to become someone who writes such books: Victor J. Vitanza for providing the space to think and write and for stepping in at just the right moments when intervention was crucial to forward movement; Luanne Frank for teaching me to read, write, and perhaps most importantly to listen; Hans Kellner for always being willing to sit and chat about many vital topics and proffer insightful responses; Audrey Wick and Nancy Wood for pedagogical thinking that I still use today. Thanks must also go to a cadre of alumni without whom this book would not exist: Michelle Ballif, Diane Davis, Lorie Goodman, Cynthia Haynes, Lisa Hill, and Lynn Worsham for building the initial conceptual and social ecologies from which this book emerged; Sarah Arroyo, Jennifer Bay, Collin Brooke, Matthew Levy, Thomas Rickert, David Rieder, and Alan Taylor for all the conversations and thoughtful provocations. Special thanks go to Thomas Rickert for telling me what books I *have* to read and for always being right, and Collin Brooke for reading *everything* and then putting it out into the ecology for the rest of us.

Many colleagues in the field also contributed a great deal to the book. Thanks go to David Blakesley for limitless support, David Bartholomae and Jean Ferguson Carr at the University of Pittsburgh for seeing potential in this project and providing exacting feedback, Jenny Edbauer for exposing the field to vitalist thought, Paul Kameen for feedback and encouragement, Jeff Rice for making technology more than a tool, Geoffrey Sirc for always being willing to call the field on its assumptions, Gregory Ulmer for writing books with infinite inventive potential, Chris Venner for helpful discussions about Deleuze and Guattari. And to *JAC, Technical Communications Quarterly,* and *Pedagogy* for reprint rights to material from previously published articles. Special thanks go to the blind reviewers who clearly read the manuscript carefully and provided insightful commentary that reshaped the final manuscript.

Thanks should also go to my colleagues at George Mason University: Don Gallehr, Jim Henry, E. Shelley Reid, Chris Thaiss, and Terry Zawacki. I have learned a lot about our field from the ecology they have created. Special thanks go to Chris, Jim, and Denise Albanese for being willing to slug through early drafts of articles and provide important feedback. And to George Mason for a semester of research leave that allowed me to formulate key elements of the book's argument.

Finally, I would like to thank my parents for enabling my extended adolescence by providing continued financial support for a struggling assistant professor, Susie for emotional support above and beyond the call of duty, and Alex for the ultimate motivation.

A Counter-History of Composition

INTRODUCTION

From Vitalism to Complexity

COMPOSITION HAS BEEN HAUNTED BY an unseen ghost. Since the 1970s, its disciplinary discourse has been operating on assumptions that have gone unquestioned. Coded under the umbrella of romanticism—a category often used in the discipline for identifying and excluding particular rhetorical practices—vitalism has been mischaracterized and left out of most scholarship in the field. So in order to bring vitalism as a distinct theoretical body to light, this book literally begins from the margins, from two footnotes in Paul Kameen's "Rewording the Rhetoric of Composition" and one footnote in Victor Vitanza's "Three Countertheses." Kameen points out that Richard Young's interpretation of Samuel T. Coleridge and vitalism in his seminal essays "Invention: A Topographical Survey" and "Paradigms and Problems" is grounded in his student

Hal Rivers Weidner's unpublished dissertation, "Three Models of Rhetoric: Traditional, Mechanical, and Vital." The issue for Kameen is that "Weidner posits the causal link between Coleridge and 'vitalism' with an argument more often based on a presumption of what Coleridge said than on an interpretation of actual texts" (91–92n10). The problem is not only that Young uses Weidner's work to ground his arguments in these key essays but also and more importantly that these essays provide a critical basis for the development of the discipline, which dismisses Coleridge's method due to a questionable reading. Even though Young characterizes his own approach as rhetorical, Kameen argues that inventional procedures such as tagmemics are grounded on a universal, positivist epistemology and that Coleridge's proto-phenomenological method is actually more attentive to an open encounter with rhetorical situations (92n11).

Likewise, Vitanza sees a problem with the way the discipline has characterized vitalism and used the term rhetorically. Weidner's reading of Coleridge, Vitanza argues, has problems that scholars of rhetoric and composition have yet to acknowledge. The result is the "unfortunate historiographical terministic screen" that sets up the categorical distinction between classicism and romanticism and the limited notion of what counts as inventional strategies that follows (171n14). The question of romanticism's relationship to the discipline goes at least as far back as the early debates between Janice Lauer and Ann Berthoff regarding the nature of inventive thinking and how it should be theorized and taught in rhetoric and composition. Berthoff becomes coded as a "romantic" who denies the "teachability" of invention by leaving it up to chance, to the imaginations of geniuses. Even though this is a mischaracterization of Berthoff's position, this rhetorical maneuver is extended by Young, who conflates this notion of romanticism with vitalism and juxtaposes it with directly teachable, heuristic approaches to rhetoric. The binary heuristics/chance excludes the possibility that there can be heuristics based on aleatory procedures or methods. As Vitanza notes, "neither Young nor Weidner takes nontechnological thinking (i.e., nonsystematic heuristics) seriously, and each cavalierly dismisses it as vitalism or mere Romanticism" (171n14). The further conflation of romanticism (an eighteenth- and nineteenth-century philosophical and literary discourse), expressivism (an approach to composition pedagogy that, according to James

Berlin, began in the 1920s and became prominent in the 1960s), and vitalism (a set of philosophical and scientific theories that extends from Aristotle to the twentieth century) does not allow the possibility of method as a nonsystematic heuristic to be seen or valued.

One only needs to look at uses of vitalism in rhetoric and composition to note the exclusionary terministic screen enacted through the term. Compositionists use vitalism as a term that denotes an "anything-goes" approach to writing and thinking, as an ahistorical category that subsumes multiple divergent practices, and as an assumed negative counterpart to preferred rhetorical practices that establishes a binary between rhetoric and poetics. In the *Encyclopedia of Rhetoric and Composition,* for example, Gideon Burton uses this rhetorical move in his entry on Rousseau: "Rousseau also gave impetus to the subjective epistemologies of his century, favoring private, expressive, and intuitive models of discourse over formal, social, or artificial ones (the 'vitalists' of twentieth-century composition still bear this influence)" (644–45). Ross Winterowd also utilizes an equally general category in his book *The English Department: A Personal and Institutional History:* "Both current-traditionalism and expressivism (vitalism, Neo Romanticism) resulted from the rationalistic rhetoric of the Enlightenment and Romanticism" (2). He goes on to discuss romantic idealism in relation to English studies in general and rhetoric and composition in particular, but nowhere does he question this conflation of expressivism, vitalism, and neo-romanticism much less its assumed negative connotation and connection to current-traditional rhetoric.

Perhaps one of the most noteworthy uses of vitalism is George Kennedy's response to Vitanza's essay "Critical Sub/Versions of the History of Philosophical Rhetoric." Kennedy characterizes "Vitanzan Vitalism" as a type of "linguistic herpes" that comes and goes, "the historical tendency of rhetoric to slip from oral, civic, and rational discourse into written, poetic, composition with an emphasis on style" that privileges "expression over analysis" ("Some Reflections" 231). Throughout his response, Kennedy equates neomodernism, neo-romanticism, vitalism, and postmodernism. His entire critique rests on all of these being equivalent to the narrow, ahistorical notion that vitalism equals a subjectivism based on genius and irrationalism, as opposed to The New Rhetoric, which is "a rhetoric for the real world, and as such teachable" (231). Kennedy is deflecting an argument by situating it within an oversimplified category that for him and much of the emerging disciplinary audience carries a negative connotation—a maneuver that, as Vitanza notes in "Three Countertheses," is related to most uses of vitalism in the discipline. All of these uses assume an overly general category and fail to question the divergent historical perspectives at play within these oppositional arguments.

It is fascinating that such emotionally charged rhetoric can grow out of a dissertation that few in the field have even read. That emotional fallacies such as associating someone with herpes come from deep-seated assumptions is perhaps not that surprising. But the fact that a marginalized discourse such as the dissertation can have such a wide-reaching and unseen impact on the field is. Perhaps it is just such a marginalized status that gives the idea its impact. Kameen remarks that he is "reluctant to explore [Weidner's] argument in depth because it remains in the peculiar semi-public realm of dissertation publication. But its influence is, through others, becoming so widespread—its conclusions cited as if they were facts—that a thorough critique may well be in order soon" (91–92n10). Kameen is prophetic in one sense: this use of vitalism is problematic, taken for granted in the discipline, and on the verge, as of 1980, of being spread by Young, Winterowd, and those who operate under the emerging categories for composition theories and pedagogies. On the other hand, more than twenty-five years after Kameen's insight there is still no critique of Weidner or analysis of vitalism. Given that in those twenty-five years this categorical confusion has implicitly had such a large impact on rhetoric and composition, this book takes up Kameen's call and seeks to analyze vitalism outside of its assumed history. From these marginal points I look to disconnect vitalism from its placement with romanticism and expressivism and examine its relevance to contemporary pedagogies of invention.

While vitalism has romantic variations, at its roots it is theoretically and historically distinct. The fundamental question that cuts across all vitalisms is "What is life?" Each episteme, period, or paradigm answers the question of life differently according to its own situation and within its own discourse, but they are all trying to come to grips with what drives self-organization and development in the world. Historically, the general answers have ranged from an animistic, abstract, or mystical power that exists outside of and operates on the world, to an evolutionary and physico-chemical process that operates in the world, to a complex combination of material, biological, historical, social, linguistic, and ultimately technological processes that produce emergence. Life is situated in the relationships among these bodies and their forces. Rather than seeing life as an autonomous force, or as caused by physico-chemical or purely biological processes, this latter view situates life within complex, ecological interactions. I see in each of these answers two key assumptions: that life is fundamentally complex (and that complexity must be accounted for or addressed) and that life is fundamentally generative (force, energy, will, power, or desire is central to this complexity). These key assumptions hold together the larger category of vitalism even as each period, paradigm, or even person provides a different answer. Vitalism is certainly tied to the complexities within romanticism—a category as diverse as romanticism makes it easy to find vitalist variations—but reducing all vitalisms to this one period, or one particular answer in that period, ignores its larger philosophical and scientific history and keeps vitalism from entering into our disciplinary conversations.

To move toward a new articulation of this larger history, I break vitalism down into subgroups that designate three types of responses to the question of life: oppositional, investigative, and complex. Oppositional vitalisms in the early nineteenth century see polarity as the primary force of life. Initially, this force is conceptualized as existing prior to the animated body and draws upon earlier models of animism and certain late-eighteenth-century idealisms. Isaiah Berlin looks at the roots of romanticism in selected eighteenth-century reactions to the Enlightenment (such as Johann Georg Hamann's), many of which are caught up in mysticism, myth, and spiritualism as a way to counter emerging scientific dominance. He calls this "mystical vitalism" (*Roots* 48–49). To be sure, this reactionary element in the eighteenth century influences the vitalist qualities of some romanticisms, which are of course a part of the general "oppositional" tenor of the times. But vitalism writ large cannot be reduced to this one early "romantic" reaction to the Enlightenment. Linking some elements of romanticism to emerging scientific theories, as Coleridge does in the early nineteenth century, transforms the more mystical oppositional vitalism into a power produced through the engagement of oppositional forces and engenders the movement into investigative vitalism.

The emergence of investigative vitalisms appears in the later nineteenth century with the development of scientific disciplines and the attempt to (re)define life. Michel Foucault argues in *The Order of Things* that before the modern episteme life did not exist—only living beings existed. During this episteme (which Foucault assembles out of the nineteenth century) both scientific and philosophical discourses began to investigate life as a scientific and philosophical principle from Hans Driesch's investigation of biological cells up to Henri Bergson's phenomenological investigation of movement and time. These phenomenological inquiries culminate in Heidegger's attempt to combine being and time into a more ecological and complex view of life, which sets the stage for understanding the emerging technological era. Complex vitalisms extend these investigations into the middle and late twentieth century, developing into systems and complexity theory in scientific disciplines and work such as Foucault's, Gilles Deleuze's, and N. Katherine Hayles's in the humanities. Thinkers such as Deleuze look to merge scientific theories with work in the humanities in an attempt to understand and map out the complexities of contemporary life. Many of these thinkers look to the body and to desire within material organizations as a connecting force within the emergence of complex systems. Rooted in biology and materiality, such an approach is far removed from mysticism and romanticism but is genealogically linked through the same grounding question and key assumptions.

In short, this book argues that transforming rhetoric and composition's image of vitalism from mysticism to complexity provides a basis for thinking about rhetoric and pedagogy that is more attuned to contemporary contexts. While much of this book examines the historical background in the field to unpack the unseen assumption upon which the discipline is built, the purpose of the book is to argue for a new category or paradigm through which figures such as Aristotle, Kameen, Deleuze, or Vitanza and practices such as Berlin's heuristic or Gregory Ulmer's method can be read in a new way. Though some of these rereadings have their beginnings in this book, my hope is that many more will be taken up and extended by others in the field. Many theorists and practices associated with rhetoric and composition need to be read outside of the classicism/romanticism dichotomy that has grounded the discipline. A more complex view of writing and rhetoric seen from this expanded perspective on vitalism would equally set aside the arguments that result from the opposition between expressivism and social-epistemic rhetoric and attempt to see writing processes as appropriately complex; the binaries teachable or unteachable, rhetorical or poetic, social or personal all reduce the complexity of writing. A new paradigm built around complexity could produce a post-dialectical understanding of contemporary pedagogies of invention for the emerging scene produced by digital technology.

In order to establish the rhetorical context around this refiguring, this book is centered on 1980 as a key transitional year and focuses on three significant articles: Young's "Arts, Crafts, Gifts, and Knacks," James A. Berlin's "The Rhetoric of Romanticism," and Kameen's "Rewording the Rhetoric of Composition." All three appear in 1980 and turn the arguments surrounding romanticism and vitalism toward three different paths. While Young's position emerged in the 1970s, it became dominant in the 1980s, resulting in dismissals such as Kennedy's. Berlin's categories emerge in the 1980s and become dominant in the 1990s with the rise of cultural studies and the loss of vitalism from the discipline's view. Kameen's position, however, has been largely unacknowledged. This book argues that its time is finally emerging along with complexity theories as technology alters the historical and rhetorical contexts in which life operates.

Chapter 1, "Mapping Rhetoric and Composition," centers on the work of Young, who excludes vitalism and romanticism in favor of a particular notion of rhetoric and rhetorical invention that operates on a strict notion of method. In the 1970s, compositionists such as Lauer, Frank D'Angelo, Weidner, Young, and Winterowd worked to find a solid basis for rhetoric and composition's disciplinary status. Young's "Arts, Crafts, Gifts, and Knacks" sums up these developments in the 1970s, solidifies the exclusion of method and vitalism, and establishes the dominance of (neo)classical approaches to process-based pedagogies. Coleridge emerges as a central figure in this debate (and in this book) because he was the primary person labeled a vitalist in the 1970s, and this categorization led to the exclusion of vitalism and romanticism among rhetoricians for the next twenty-five years. Young divides method into informal and formal categories, paradoxically characterizes Coleridge's method as both overly formalist and dominated by mystical genius, and labels this paradox vitalism. The problem is that this mapping gives rhetoric and composition an incomplete picture of invention that excludes more informal methods as relevant factors in pedagogies of invention. Consequently, this chapter begins the movement of Coleridge from the discipline's narrative of retreat and return to an eventual placement in a narrative of vitalism's emergence.

Chapter 2, "Cartography and Forgetting," centers on Berlin, who rereads romanticism and method more explicitly in terms of dialectics but continues to exclude vitalism. Having attended Young's 1978 National Endowment for the Humanities seminar, Berlin accepts Young's articulation of current-traditional rhetoric and folds vitalism into this category while at the same time revaluing Coleridge. Berlin's "The Rhetoric of Romanticism" recognizes Weidner's problematic reading of Coleridge but interprets Coleridge's method in terms of dialectical methods and turns it toward what will become social-epistemic rhetoric. The effect of this new cartography is that vitalism almost disappears from the discourse of rhetoric and composition in the 1980s via the development and dissemination of Berlin's categorical mappings of the field. Vitalism remains only as a scapegoat term equated with mysticism and expressivism. Though initially valued, Coleridge's method ultimately disappears as well because Berlin synthesizes it with a more Hegelian or Marxist dialectical method. As Berlin accepts a Marxist framework for his politics and writing pedagogy, language and ideology become a more central element in his epistemological maps, a turn that ultimately excludes vitalist or bodily epistemologies in favor of more mind-centered pedagogies that focus on unmasking false consciousness.

The issue of method continues in chapter 3, "Remapping Method," which centers on Kameen. In the 1990s, cultural studies led the expanding field of rhetoric and composition and extended the categorical exclusion of vitalism and romanticism. Consequently, most of the subsequent attempts to revisit Berlin's categories do so within the context of his mappings and fall short of reimagining the field in a way that addresses the changing historical context.

This chapter reads Kameen's attempt to chart a path for Coleridge and method in "Rewording the Rhetoric of Composition" as a new conceptual starting place. Operating from a basis in Heideggerian phenomenology, Kameen looks to establish a new space for reading Coleridge, dialectics, and method that emphasizes the explicit as well as intuitive relation between a body and a situation. This position opens the way for a third reading of method and a rereading of vitalism. It articulates an epistemology beyond those established in Berlin's categories and sets the stage for an expanded notion of method and more possibilities for composition pedagogies.

This book then begins to turn from historical context to the development of an ulterior paradigm with chapter 4, "A Short Counter-History," which expands the concept of vitalism that is implicit in Kameen. After tracing vitalism's beginning with Aristotle, the chapter details the three vitalist subgroupings—oppositional, investigative, and complex—that have emerged since the late eighteenth century. The corresponding philosophies of Coleridge, Bergson, and Deleuze are set in the historical context of science and the emergence of complexity theory. The chapter argues that throughout its history, vitalism as a philosophy has always existed in concert with science and has evolved along with it into contemporary models of complexity. This work reinserts Coleridge into more a contemporary context to show an alternative genealogy that breaks the old categorical placements with romanticism and rhetoric's narrative of retreat and return. Rather than read Coleridge from a classicism/romanticism binary, I place Coleridge into a new grouping with figures from Aristotle to Deleuze. As the chapter attempts to show, however, there are genuine historical reasons to read Coleridge this way given the multifaceted nature of romanticism and the emergence of investigative vitalism.

Chapter 5, "Technology-Complexity-Methodology," examines the shifting cultural context in the 1990s and links method not to traditional method or dialectics but to this ulterior history of vitalism. Young's attempt to turn method toward *technê* operates on a more strict art-versus-method divide that ultimately leans technê more toward rigid, formalist practices. Berlin's sense of method opens it to dialectical procedures, but Berlin's historical moment and narrow disciplinary focus keep him from seeing that technology is beginning to reshape the larger rhetorical landscape. Network culture puts the importance of ecology and immersion in sharp relief, making Berlin's mind-centered epistemological categories much less relevant and Kameen's phenomenological approach much more significant. The chapter extends Kameen's emphasis on Heidegger into the issue of technology and shows how viewing technê in the context of complexity can provide a new basis for rhetoric and a new sense of method. Reconfiguring technê from the perspective of embodiment and complexity explores what Vitanza might mean by "nontechnological thinking" and "nonsystematic heuristics." Vitanza is typically seen as someone who views technê as purely mechanical and to be avoided, which simply places him in the generic "vitalist" category. But Vitanza is not really against the mechanical or technological. He questions their instrumentalist underpinnings that work to exclude the body and all of its possible combinations with the world. Seen from the perspective of complex vitalism, this position opens up invention and rhetoric to multiple methods, techniques, and practices.

Chapter 6, "Toward Inventive Composition Pedagogies," examines the pedagogies of Berlin, Kameen, and Ulmer, and investigates how this newer model of method and technê impacts invention. Berlin, like Young, ultimately reduces rhetorical invention to pre-established heuristics. Kameen's and Ulmer's pedagogical methods, however, emphasize linking individual bodies to particular local contexts. In contradistinction to Berlin's mind-centered heuristics, their pedagogical methods situate student bodies in complex ecological environments as an epistemological basis for invention. Particular heuristics are seen as parts of these larger constellations rather than abstracted general procedures. This more open method fits our current electronic context and the complex ecologies in which students write and think and situates these practices within a contemporary vitalist paradigm of complexity.

At its core, this book seeks nothing more than to enact the ancient practice of *dissoi logoi*, making the weaker argument the stronger. Once a way of thinking becomes so ingrained that no one bothers to question it, the most effective way to make it show up is to attempt the opposite argument that no one would even consider investigating. Such a strategy reopens the question and provokes renewed consideration. It may be the case that there are plenty of historical reasons to hold on to the discipline's typical view of vitalism. But as my short afterword on historiography attempts to show, counter-histories can always be drawn, and new groupings of texts, events, and practices can always be articulated. The goal of such a historiography is not simply to arrive at a more accurate image of the past but to create a particular affect in the present. If it is the case that exposing the specter of vitalism does nothing more than garner negative criticism from traditional historical and theoretical perspectives, then I hope that my arguments will elicit more detailed and considered responses than the typical uncritical rhetoric of exclusion that has surrounded it. This rhetorical outcome would, I hope, be enough to move discussions of contemporary composition theories from currently accepted categories toward new models for invention and pedagogy.

MAPPING RHETORIC

AND COMPOSITION

IN THE HISTORY OF RHETORIC and composition, the year 1980 is unique: it solidified one historical trajectory, started another, and covered over a third. Throughout the 1970s, rhetoric and composition was growing as a discipline: theories from the history of rhetoric were coming back to inform composition and composition was developing its own knowledge base through scholars' cognitive and ethnographic research on writers. By 1980, Richard Young had summed up these developments and set the tone for their expansion in his article "Arts, Crafts, Gifts, and Knacks." But also in 1980, James Berlin wrote "The Rhetoric of Romanticism," which, unbeknownst to many, started the disciplinary movement toward cultural rather than cognitive investigation. While these two histories are largely known, even though Berlin's article typically is not, another historical trajectory began in 1980 but is just now (re)emerging. Paul Kameen's article "Rewording the Rhetoric of Composition," also published in 1980, questions these two histories of the field even before they begin to dominate the landscape. While most maps of rhetoric and composition acknowledge the work of Young and Berlin, Kameen's position has been largely overlooked. This chapter begins the process of remapping rhetoric and composition to bring Kameen's ulterior position to the surface by examining Young's drive for disciplinarity. Young's categorical mapping, and the areas of investigation that lead up to and follow his grounding assumptions, excludes issues that can be important for invention—most notably an acceptance of a broader notion of method as an acceptable model for rhetorical invention.

The desire to map the field of rhetoric and composition comes from its inception as a discipline.[1] In his essay "Freshman English, Composition, and CCCC," David Bartholomae locates this desire in the dichotomy of the two opening plenary speeches of the Conference on College Composition and Communication (CCCC) in 1949. He casts Richard Weaver as the emblematic figure in English studies that CCCC was established to question: Weaver's speech promoted the belief in a unified culture, a morality, and a truth that language must represent. Bartholomae sees James McCrimmon as the new voice: McCrimmon's speech set the tone for what would become a new emphasis on rhetoric that would inform the development of rhetoric and composition. This oppositional debate establishes a tension that drives early mappings of the field. Virginia Anderson notes in "Property Rights: Exclusion as Moral Action in 'The Battle of Texas'" that "[t]he tensions of these social relations can be read in the pages of *College Composition and Communication* (*CCC*). From its earliest days in the 1950s, contributors constructed and then reconstructed a changing set of conceptual Venn diagrams positioning rhetoric, linguistics, science, social science, and especially literature in relation to composition" (451). The debates revolve around how much influence these disciplines should be allowed to have on composition and which disciplines should be excluded from composition.

As the discipline develops and searches for an identity all its own, it invariably (perhaps necessarily) falls into various categorical mappings and polemic narratives that emerge from the two positions established at the first CCCC. The situational need to delineate a territory for rhetoric and composition (to define a *them* to exclude and an *us* to identify with) fed into a narrative of retreat and return. The early nineteenth century, as the story was and is told, saw the devaluation of rhetoric due to the Enlightenment elevation of logic, the value of romantic individualism, and the rise of national literatures throughout the nineteenth century. To fill the void left by rhetoric's displacement, composition emerged in the late nineteenth century largely due to a literacy crisis that provided the exigence for what has become first-year composition. But the separation of composition from literature through the development of a separate conference in 1949 allowed a space for rhetoric's return.

The combination of mapping via categorical distinction and a narrative of rhetoric's retreat and return sets the disciplinary context for Daniel Fogarty's *Roots for a New Rhetoric* (1959). Fogarty is credited with naming current-traditional rhetoric as the paradigm that develops from the institutional structure of first-year composition as well as sounding a call for a new rhetoric in opposition to the outmoded current-traditional approach.[2] All the now-classic current-traditional characteristics are present in Fogarty's categorization: the focus on grammar, mechanics, syntax, spelling, and punctuation; the focus on the four modes; the focus on clear and coherent style; the division of texts/discourse into paragraphs, sentences, and words; and the naive empirical epistemology. Fogarty constructs this current traditionalism category explicitly to situate the "new rhetoric" exemplified in the work of I. A. Richards, Kenneth Burke, and the General Semanticists. To assess their potential importance for improving the first-year course, Fogarty charts Aristotelian rhetoric, outlines current-traditional rhetoric, and displays them adjacent to a diagram of the ideas of Richards, Burke, and the General Semanticists. In short, to discover the new rhetoric he has to delineate the old rhetorics.

The first thing Fogarty sees in this map is a distinction between teaching rhetoric and the philosophy of rhetoric. This distinction is important in two respects: first, it shows that current-traditional rhetoric is "still largely Aristotelian in its basic philosophy" but has new formal elements that "time and expediency have added to the teaching of rhetoric" (120), and second, it shows a similarity among Richards, Burke, and the General Semanticists—they all want to extend their philosophies of rhetoric into their teaching rhetorics. For Fogarty, all three look to make this move because "the new sciences had given them a new consciousness of the all-pervading importance of language for any study in any field. And language has provided multiple problems never adequately faced before" (121). This situation calls for these issues to be raised in the composition classroom if the students are going to be equipped to deal with language use in the cultural context of the late twentieth century. Fogarty imagines that in Aristotle's time, and in the times of the trivium and quadrivium, students studied both philosophy and rhetoric. But in his day, "the average college student may never make the connection between his philosophy and his composition" (122).

Roots for a New Rhetoric provides a basis for two important developments in rhetoric and composition: first, it sets up current-traditional rhetoric as a category to be mapped and argued against, providing rhetoric and composition with an exclusionary term and scapegoat category and a them/us, old/new mapping strategy, and second, it provides a foundation for Berlin's social-epistemic rhetoric.[3] For the moment, the former is central because Fogarty sees current-traditional practice as an extension of Aristotelian classical rhetoric (hence the name current-*traditional*), rather than seeing a distinction between classical rhetoric and current-traditional rhetoric. Much of the "new rhetoric" in the 1960s explicitly brought back classical themes (e.g., C. H. Perelman and L. Olbrechts-Tyteca's *The New Rhetoric: A Treatise on Argumentation*), which is a much different approach to "new rhetoric" than Fogarty's emphasis on Burke, Richards, and the Semanticists.[4] For Fogarty, current-traditional rhetoric's philosophical basis is Aristotelian, even though that basis has been largely forgotten under the pressure for more direct pedagogical application. Fogarty's new rhetoric does not bring back Aristotle but looks to contemporary theorists to build a new philosophy for the development of new practices.

Nevertheless, major figures in the field, including Young, set up current-traditional rhetoric in opposition to new classical rhetorics, which supports a narrative of retreat and return: classical rhetoric retreats during the dominance of current-traditional practices but is returning in the late twentieth century. A corresponding move seeks to link literature and romanticism to current-traditional rhetoric and early approaches to composition. Historically these moments do happen in conjunction, but their articulation in early arguments for the return of rhetoric function predominantly in the service of polemics and a rhetoric of exclusion. In the 1970s, and up through the 1980s, compositionists such as Janice Lauer, Frank D'Angelo, Hal Rivers Weidner, Young, and Ross Winterowd worked to find a solid basis for rhetoric and composition's disciplinary status and generally did so at the expense of some scapegoat category, whether it is characterized as current-traditional rhetoric, literature, romanticism, expressivism, vitalism, or articulated in some amalgamation of these discourses. The combination of categorical exclusion and narrative retreat and return establishes specific disciplinary roots for rhetoric and composition that ground attempts to map out disciplinary territory and continue to influence the field today.

Romanticism and the Case against Vitalism

Fogarty's oppositional approach to mapping the emerging discipline is extended to other debates as new classical approaches face challenges. Some of the early debates surrounding romanticism centered on an exchange in 1971–72 between Janice Lauer and Ann Berthoff. The exchange began with Lauer's "Heuristics and Composition" (1970) a bibliography of work in psychology on creative problem solving, which was taken from her dissertation. For Lauer, these investigations held great promise for those "interested in identifying the stages of creativity, defining heuristics and locating its place in the creative process" (397), which were some of the main goals of scholars looking to make rhetoric and composition a discipline. Ann Berthoff, however, sees a potential problem with "converting English composition itself to a problem" ("The Problem of Problem Solving" 237). In other words, the problem is the reduction of creative thinking in general to problem solving in particular. In her response to Berthoff, Lauer claims that she does not reduce creativity or heuristics to problem solving, even though many of the psychologists she includes call creativity "creative problem solving." In her mind, problem solving as a heuristic is "effective guessing," not limited but "open-ended" ("Response" 208–209). Berthoff, however, in her own "Response," notes, "Adding 'creative' to 'problem solving' doesn't really solve the problem" (404). It does not address the reduction of thinking and heuristics to a specific conception of problem solving.

One of the primary problems in the exchange between Lauer and Berthoff is epistemological: for Berthoff, as for Fogarty, language is more than a signal code as the psychologists conceive it. Rather than relying on experts in psychology, she argues that a method of creative thinking with a coherent epistemology based on language and a corresponding, sound pedagogical history exists in English studies in the "legacy of the Romantic Movement" ("Response to Janice Lauer" 415). For her, Coleridge's method is developed around the creative person as artist, not as problem solver. She points to Melville: "a careful disorderliness is the true method"; to Whitehead: "a state of imaginative, muddled suspense . . . precedes any successful inductive generalization"; and to Klee: "I begin with chaos; it is the most natural start" (415). For her, Coleridge's method works with thinking that is "something other than effective guessing" (415). But most importantly she states that artists use their minds—they do not simply *express* themselves—and she goes on to list all of the things a writer can develop through practice and learning. In her mind, these are the things that can be taught in composition, and they are all beyond the things that psychologists can reduce to sub-abilities so they can make laws out of them.

As the debates between heuristics, specific procedures for the process of invention, and method, a more open-ended procedure for addressing situations, heat up, their importance becomes clearer. In these debates, Berthoff, along with others, is labeled a "new romantic" who believes that writing cannot be taught, a position she shows in her "Response" that she does not hold.

The term "new romanticism" is coined and defined by Frank D'Angelo in his book *A Conceptual Theory of Rhetoric* (1975):

> The importance of these new approaches to writing [that focus on creative expression and on personal writing] is that they provide a healthy balance to the rational, systematic approaches to writing which have long dominated the classroom. These new approaches emphasize feeling rather than intellect, exploration and discovery rather than preconceived ideas, the imagination,

creativity, free association, fantasy, play, dreams, the unconscious, nonintel-
lectual sensing, the stream-of-consciousness, and the self. . . . This new emphasis on writing which is relatively free of control and direction may be
termed the new romanticism. It holds that not all of our mental processes
are rational. It denies that the intellect is more in touch with reality than the
imagination or other non-logical process. (159)

D'Angelo's characterization may seem innocent enough. But unfortunately the
binary that is created between problem solving or heuristics, on the one hand,
and new romantics, on the other, becomes drastically polarized into those who
see invention—and by extension writing—as teachable via heuristics, and those
who have no method at all and leave invention up to subjective genius and
feeling, seeing it as unsusceptible to being taught. The result is that Berthoff,
and anyone associated with other versions of romanticism, is relegated to this
reductive notion of new romanticism. But Berthoff is not a romantic in this
particular, expressivist sense. She never espouses genius without any method
but rather works for a method that utilizes the mind, language, and the world.
Eventually James Berlin comes to this understanding and claims that Berthoff
is a "new rhetorician," but the general category of new romanticism becomes
the new scapegoat for new classical rhetorics.

     After their lively exchange, Lauer continued to work with cognitive psy-
chology and heuristics, while Berthoff focused on Coleridge and method.
These two points of departure go on to develop into two different trajectories,
and the con-flation and confusion on which they are built continue on through
Young and into the field. One of the most important events in the rhetoric/ro-
mantic debates is how vitalism gets connected to romanticism in the field. In
the mid-1970s, Weidner set the precedent for the dismissal of vitalism as a productive part of rhetoric and composition's history in his dissertation "Three
Models of Rhetoric: Traditional, Mechanical and Vital" (1975), which was directed by Young. Most problematic is Weidner's conflation of vitalism with the
general category of new romanticism outlined by D'Angelo. In his dissertation,
Weidner uses Coleridge as the vitalist-romantic who is the archetypal adversary
of rhetoric and all future teachers of writing. Weidner claims that Coleridge
had no principle or method of origination, no method of inventing the sub-

stance of his poetry. But as Kameen points out, Weidner depends on certain assumptions about vitalism as a whole in his reading and subsequent categorization of Coleridge. Unfortunately, Young popularizes, through his own work and that of many of his students, much of what Weidner claims as being the case against vitalism. The result for rhetoric and composition as a discipline is a widespread and unnoticed confusion of intellectual and historical categories.

In his dissertation, Weidner examines rhetoric's treatment in the hands of scientists and romantics in England between 1750 and 1850. To do so, he sets up an opposition between science and philosophy. For him, science subordinates rhetoric and commonplaces to experiment, while romantic philosophy subordinates rhetoric and commonplaces to insight: "In either case, it is thought that an art is no longer needed for mediating between the formal systems of theory and the applied principles of practice. In both the scientific and romantic movements, it is believed that 'facts' alone, either objectively or subjectively discerned, are wholly sufficient for the effective government of human life" (6). They both see nature, the material world or the world of the mind, respectively, "as the living corpus of truth"; therefore, they have no need for rhetorical "artifice" (6). Weidner's distinctions among art, science, and philosophy set up a clash of epistemologies between classical rhetoric, the enlightenment, and romanticism. He examines the clash by choosing one work from one author to represent each of the three models: Aristotle, traditional; Campbell, mechanical; Coleridge, vital. He acknowledges that it is a shortcut to treat one historical work as a paradigm, qualifying his results as tentative. Nevertheless, the real problem with his mapping is that he never addresses his use of the term vitalism as a synonym for romanticism. For him, "Coleridge is, in England, one of the vitalistic movement's most articulate literary philosophers and surely its strongest opponent of mechanism. Most of his ideas are shared to a greater or lesser degree by authors labeled by literary historians as 'romantic'" (190).

And with that claim, Weidner lumps all vitalists and romanticists together under the category "anti-mechanism"—a category that creates a genus/species problematic. If a category is broad enough, vastly different species will be able to fit under its umbrella. Weidner claims that "Romantic theory in general and

Coleridge's metatheory in particular are both essentially vitalistic" (211) and elevates this to a general category, which is historiographically problematic: the general categories simply fit into slots in the narrative of retreat and return, which sidesteps a closer examination of vitalism.

One of Weidner's problems in this regard is that at crucial moments in his argument, where Coleridge is linked to a conception of vitalism, he relies too heavily on other readings of Coleridge rather than his own. He does quote Coleridge's texts quite often, but when vitalism and its conflation with romanticism comes up he appeals to someone else for validation. For example, he turns to Jacques Barzun's *Classic, Romantic, Modern* for a critical point. For Barzun, vitalism implies "that life is an element and not merely a combination of dead parts. It implies organic structure and organic function. It implies that the primary reality is the individual and not either the parts of which is made or the artificial groupings which they enter into. This in a word is individualism" (quoted in Weidner 211). Weidner then quotes an extended definition of vitalism from Arthur Berndtson's entry in *A History of Philosophical Systems* that is fair enough. But he bases his reading of Berndtson's philosophical definition of vitalism on Barzun's literary interpretation, claiming, "To [Berndtson's] concept of vitalism Coleridge's theory *adds* a concept emphasizing man's uncommonly powerful creative potential, directed by a universal spirit with whom man communicates by means of feeling. This capacity of the individual to directly apprehend truth frees him from conventions: social, intellectual, or linguistic" (212; emphasis added).

What Weidner fails to recognize is that this addition makes Coleridge's theory something other than vitalism: if romanticism can be added to vitalism, then they are not necessarily equivalent and it opens the question of the nature of vitalism as distinct from romanticism. As I will argue, vitalism in most of its forms does not subscribe to subjectivism, individualism, or an individual will. This position is a product largely of the romantic period, though Hegel's romanticism can be read as acknowledging the individual's dialectical relationship to the social whole—an understanding that can be seen in Coleridge as well. But the problem is that these historically specific discourses are applied to all vitalisms and romanticisms. Vitalisms in other periods display different epistemic characteristics. As rhetoric and composition scholars chart out the discipline's paradigms, this historical difference gets forgotten and vitalism's relationship to art, method, situation, and ultimately rhetoric is obscured.

The Problem with Paradigms

In 1978–79, Young directed a National Endowment for the Humanities postdoctoral seminar, "Rhetorical Invention and the Composing Process," at Carnegie Mellon University (CMU) that became a foundational moment for the discipline. The seminar was attended by many people who went on to become key figures in the field. It exposed these people to the practice of mapping the field, and its content drew directly from Fogarty, the Berthoff/Lauer debate, and Weidner. The seminar was attended by Sharon Bassett, James Berlin, Lisa Ede, David Fractenberg, Robert Inkster, Charles Kneupper, Victor Vitanza, Sam Watson, Vickie Winkler, and William Nelson. Speakers or visitors to the seminar included Linda Flower (who was teaching writing in the business college at CMU and gave protocols to many of the participants that she and Dick Hayes used as a basis for their early research on the composing process), Richard Ohmann, Alton Becker (of Young, Becker, and Pike), Bill Coles (University of Pittsburgh), A. D. Van Nostrand (Brown University), Richard Enos (who was interviewed for a position at CMU), Otis Walter (University of Pittsburgh, Department of Speech), Janice Lauer (University of Detroit), and Henry Johnstone (an editor of the journal *Philosophy and Rhetoric*).

Since many of the participants had degrees in literature rather than rhetoric —generating one of the primary needs for the seminar—Young exposed them to many maps of the field as a way of orienting them to composition: Fogarty's Aristotle, current-traditional, and new rhetorics; James Kinneavy's expressive, persuasive, referential, and literary; Frank D'Angelo's logical (static, progressive, repetitive) and nonlogical (imagining, condensation, symbolizing, displacement, free association, transformation, nonlogical repetition); Weidner's traditional, mechanical, and vital; Stephen Pepper's formalism, mechanism, organicism, and contextualism; Northrop Frye's comedy, romance, tragedy, and irony (satire); and M. H. Abrams's pragmatic, mimetic, expressive, and objective. In addition to reading Fogarty's book, the participants read three important dissertations: Albert Kitzhaber's dissertation (1953) in which he examines the pedagogical practices Fogarty later calls current-traditional from which Kitzhaber initially published the bibliography; Janice Lauer's dissertation (1967) from which she also published the bibliography that initiated the early debates with Ann Berthoff; and Weidner's dissertation (1975) that laid the basis for rhetoric and composition's dismissal of vitalism.[5]

The NEH seminar was largely based on Young's articles "Invention: A Topographical Survey" (1976) and "Paradigms and Problems: Needed Research in Rhetorical Invention" (1978). "Paradigms and Problems" provided a basis for the seminar by establishing an image of rhetorical invention that is informed by Fogarty's notion of current-traditional rhetoric, Weidner's use of vitalism, and Lauer's take on rhetorical invention. In the article, Young uses Thomas Kuhn's concept of the paradigm as "disciplinary matrix" to argue that Fogarty's current-traditional rhetoric is the dominant paradigm in composition. Young argues that current-traditional rhetoric has been operating in the mode of normal science—using the assumptions of a paradigm without questioning them. But as Kuhn notes, this period of stability rarely endures. At some point a problem arises that the paradigm cannot account for. In Young's mind, the discipline is confronting such a crisis in the late seventies because current-traditional rhetoric does not properly account for rhetorical invention.

Following Weidner, Young argues that the current-traditional paradigm rests on "the vitalist assumption that creative processes : . . are not susceptible to conscious control by formal procedures" ("Paradigms and Problems" 32) and therefore excludes the formal arts of invention from composition practice. Current-traditional rhetoric relies on other disciplines for content and the production of knowledge, while vitalism relies on a collection of informal methods of invention—using lists of topics to elaborate on by looking up references, writing from experience, reading essays and applying their ideas, or using look-think-write procedures based on images (33). Composition begins to use these informal methods, according to Young, because relying on other disciplines was not working. But he also sees informal approaches as insufficient because they assume invention cannot be taught directly. Informal methods only try to set up conditions so the habits of inventive thinking can be learned, and, perhaps more importantly for Young, such methods do not address the need for invention as critical thinking or analytical problem solving. Consequently, the discipline needs new research in formal rather than informal inventional practices so scholars can judge the old current-traditional paradigm as problematic and develop the basis for a new rhetorical paradigm.

To establish this opposition between current-traditional and rhetorical paradigms, Young reenacts two of Weidner's categorical moves. Weidner conflates romanticism and vitalism and puts them in opposition to mechanism or scientific formalism but then connects romantic philosophy and scientific method and opposes them to rhetoric as art. Young follows both of these curious moves. Though Young does not use the term romanticism in "Paradigms and Problems," his reading of vitalism has questionable supports. One says the individual writer is not in control of invention (32) and the other says some aspects of invention cannot be taught and exist in the writer (32n5). Both positions may have associations with some romantic philosophies, but neither has any clear connection to vitalism. Young is assuming Weidner's conflation (as Kameen notes ["Rewording" 91n10], Weidner's thesis is listed in the bibliography of "Paradigms and Problems" but is not cited directly). Young also follows Weidner in connecting science and romanticism/vitalism in opposition to rhetoric as art or technê. By reducing rhetorical invention to D'Angelo's logical/nonlogical (formal/informal) dichotomy, Young can group oppositional approaches such as current-traditionalism and vitalism together as informal. It is odd, however, to place current-traditional rhetoric in the informal category. The connection between science as a strict, formal method of invention and current-traditional rhetoric as formal methods of arrangement and style makes sense. But the connection to "vitalist" informal methods makes less sense. When Young calls for research into formal arts of invention, he is linking art to science and current-traditional rhetoric. The connection is between current-traditional rhetoric and classical rhetoric, not current-traditional rhetoric and vitalism or romanticism. Unwittingly, perhaps, this categorical sleight of hand reduces art or technê to a brand of formalism. In valuing scientific and ethnographic research—over and above his call for metarhetorical, philosophical, and historical research—Young is turning rhetoric toward the scientific and the formal.

By following Weidner's categorical moves and trying to reduce them to formal and informal categories, Young essentially covers over the connection between Aristotle's rhetoric and current-traditional rhetoric established by Fogarty. Sounding much like Fogarty, Young argues that "an important educational, and social, need is not being met" by current-traditional rhetoric ("Paradigms and Problems" 34). But unlike Fogarty, Young links current-traditional practice to scientific method and romantic philosophy rather than Aristotelian philosophy. Seeing that current-traditional, formalist practice is grounded on Aristotelian philosophy, Fogarty calls for the development of a new philosophical basis for the new twentieth-century rhetorics and the extension of this philosophy into the production of a prose communication course. Young, however, accepts a particular version of classical rhetoric as his philosophical foundation and calls for the scientific study of formal arts of invention to support and extend that philosophy rather than for a contemporary philosophy of rhetoric and hence a new teaching rhetoric.

The emphasis on scientific study of formal arts of invention rather than on philosophical foundations leads Young into a form/content distinction. Young wants rhetoric and composition to develop formal heuristics that would enable students to derive content. The form/content binary is still there. Rather than develop a philosophical basis to displace current-traditional formalism, Young is actually extending formalism into invention and inadvertently extending current-traditional rhetoric. His conflation of vitalism (Weidner) and current-traditional rhetoric (Fogarty) under the rubric of informal inventional procedures that cannot be taught (D'Angelo) may allow him to see the need for research into invention, but it also keeps him from seeing that classical rhetoric and current-traditional rhetoric can be classified together under formalism. Perhaps one of the reasons Young and others do not follow up on Fogarty is that his call for a new rhetoric is emphatically interdisciplinary and Young's real goal is to establish rhetoric and composition as a discipline, not prose communication as a course. This would account for the fact that Young dismisses Fogarty's recognition of the collusion between Aristotelian rhetoric and current-traditional rhetoric—Young needed classical rhetoric as an authoritative basis for the discipline.

There are two keys things to take away from "Paradigms and Problems." First, the issue of vitalism's historical and theoretical nature is directly linked to issues of inventional methods. Vitalism is seen as leaving invention up to a mystical process, whether in the world or the mind, that writers cannot consciously control or account for. In this sense, the term is used almost analogically or metaphorically rather than to designate a historical theory or philosophy. Second, the enduring problem is that this negative use of vitalism excludes informal methods (or habitual and contextual learning) in favor of formal procedures for the ultimate goal of disciplinarity rather than learning. Research into formal procedures can provide a stronger justification for claiming that rhetoric and composition is a research-based discipline with its own knowledge base, but in the long run it loses sight of pragmatic classroom practice by reducing what counts as rhetorical invention.

Arts, Crafts, Gifts, Knacks

Perhaps in response to these categorical difficulties, Young tries to refine his position in "Arts, Crafts, Gifts, and Knacks: Some Disharmonies in the New Rhetoric" (1980), which establishes the distinctions and solidifies their extension into the discourse of the field. In "Paradigms and Problems" no mention is made of romanticism or expressivism, only vitalism. But in "Arts, Crafts, Gifts, and Knacks," Young works from Weidner's position that vitalism is synonymous with romanticism to extend D'Angelo's characterization of new romanticism, indicate its connection to vitalism, and establish rhetoric as a middle-ground option between the formal methods of science and current-traditionalism and the informal methods of romantic-vitalism. To do so, Young makes a number of Platonic, species/genus moves that are difficult to follow. He establishes two sets of categorical distinctions and attempts to integrate them. In the first, he sets up the binary of current-traditional rhetoric and new rhetoric and then divides new rhetoric into new romantic and new classical versions. Both new rhetorics are reactions to current-traditional rhetoric, but for Young a new romantic approach to invention and the composing process is problematic. To make this argument he uses a second set of distinctions among art (heuristics to aid in the discovery of content), craft (the emphasis on form and surface features of a text), gift (innate natural talent), and knack (something learned through habit or practice). The subtle interconnections of these two categorical sets ultimately establish the basis for the misplacement of Coleridge and the devaluing of vitalism.

Young begins by making the distinction between current-traditional rhetoric and new rhetoric, selecting the nineteenth-century rhetorician John Genung, whom he cites in "Paradigms and Problems" as one of his vitalist examples, to represent current-traditional rhetoric and mid-1960s compositionist Gordon Rohman to represent new rhetoric. Genung recognizes that rhetoric as an aspect of literature cannot be reduced to "mere grammatical apparatuses or [equated] with Huxley's logic engine" because real authorship must also be concerned with "the whole man, his outfit of conviction and emotion, imagination and will, translating himself . . . into a vital and ordered utterance" (quoted in Young, "Arts, Crafts" 53). But even so, the teaching of rhetoric does not include invention. The teachable aspect of rhetoric is craft—modes, genres, structures of discourse, and norms of style and usage. Thinking, invention, and creativity are left up to the more mysterious powers of gifted individuals. Current-traditional rhetoric, in the example of Genung, combines the formal study of craft with the vitalist approach to invention that leaves it up to natural genius. Young then describes Rohman as claiming that the new rhetoric of the twentieth century encompasses the entire writing process, including invention. For Rohman, invention entails "an active, not passive enlistment in the 'cause' of an idea. . . . [It is] essentially the imposition of pattern upon experience" (quoted in "Arts, Crafts" 54). Following compositionists such as Rohman, new rhetoric seeks to include the structure of thinking and invention among the teachable elements of rhetoric and thus combines the formal study of craft with explicit approaches to teaching the art of invention.

However, there is disharmony in the new rhetoric. Young's next move is to distinguish between two movements within new rhetoric: new romanticism and new classicism. Young claims that new romanticism is "a reaffirmation of vitalist philosophy" that argues the composing process should be free of control, believes the rational is no more in touch with reality than nonrational processes, sees the composing process as a mysterious and unconscious growth, and insists on the "primacy of the imagination" (55). Quoting James Miller's position that teaching orderly processes does not result in good writing but in dehumanized and unreadable writing, Young concludes that new romantics leave the teacher with nothing to teach but the mystery of the process of imagination. Even though Young makes the initial distinction between current-traditional rhetoric and new romanticism, he reestablishes their connection. Citing William Coles as an example of a contemporary new romantic, Young argues that, like Genung, Coles believes the art of composing cannot be taught even though craft can. But unlike Genung, this does not mean that invention must be ignored. For Young, the new romantic writing instructor is "no longer a purveyor of information about the craft of writing but a designer of occasions that stimulate the creative process" (55). Essentially Young is reasserting his formal/informal distinction. Whereas current-traditional rhetoric contrasts craft with gift and emphasizes teaching craft, new romanticism contrasts craft with art as the mysterious powers of creative invention and emphasizes creating situations in which it can be learned informally.

New classicists, on the other hand, are those who see art as technê—"knowledge necessary for producing preconceived results by conscious directed action" (56)—thus making writing and invention teachable. According to Young, this notion of art contrasts with knack—"a habit acquired through repeated experience" (56). Basing the distinction on Aristotle, Young sees artists as people who have a theory of what they have learned through experience, which enables them to teach others the skill. This distinction is an attempt to code new romantics who teach via creating contexts as only allowing their students to acquire habits. Even though Young, following Aristotle, recognizes that both "the man who has knack and the man who has art can carry out that activity" (56), he disregards the fact that habit can work for students who are not going to be teachers and privileges technê as habit turned into a system via the knowledge of causes. To avoid the charge that this form of Aristotelian philosophy is falling back into the formalism of current-traditional rhetoric, he makes yet another distinction: his position espouses a heuristic system ("explicit strategies for effective guessing") rather than a rule-governed system ("a finite series of steps that can be carried out consciously and mechanically without the aid of intuition or special ability, and if properly carried out always yields a correct result") (57). Young wants to position heuristics as a middle-ground option between unconscious knack and craft as a near-algorithmic emphasis on form. Not only do heuristics more easily avoid becoming algorithmic by producing provisional results, according to Young, but they also avoid becoming merely habitual because they are used consciously and systematically—they are generic and rationally directed.

These slippery categorical distinctions ultimately generate problems for the field of rhetoric and composition. Young makes a crucial statement regarding new romanticism: "Though we lack the historical studies that permit generalizing with confidence, the position [of the new romantics] seems not so much an innovation in the discipline as a reaffirmation of the vitalist philosophies of an old romanticism enriched by modern psychology" (55). It is precisely the lack of historical studies of romanticism and vitalism in rhetoric and composition that allows Young to claim that new romanticism is a vitalist philosophy based on mystery and genius. And it is precisely this lack of historical basis that allows both of Weidner's curious moves to disseminate through the discipline. First, even though in "Arts, Crafts, Gifts, and Knacks" Young mentions Coleridge only once, as someone who grapples with the same issues surrounding art, the connection between Coleridge and romanticism is so widespread that the additional connection to vitalism that Weidner assumes and Young extends through his characterization of new romanticism continues to stick. This is especially so with regard to issues surrounding method and its formal or informal status. Second, these historical and categorical confusions also lead to unnecessary distinctions and debates over what constitutes art. Aristotle recognizes the validity of both knack and techné. Arbitrarily dividing them based on the need to assert disciplinary status only hurts the teaching of invention in the end. Young's attempt to establish his position as the middle-ground option does nothing to keep the application of heuristics from generating what are really just new forms of formalism.

It is in fact this complicated relationship between Aristotle's basic philosophy, current-traditional formalism, and vitalism that is at issue. Even though Young attempts to shift the formalism that Fogarty sees in Aristotle's basic philosophy over to vitalism and romanticism, his understanding of technê is grounded in a commonsense, empirical notion of cause and effect.

Young privileges technê as habit turned into a system via the knowledge of causes. By labeling vitalism as naive genius and excluding new romantic informal methods as inadequate for learning to operate in systems, Young's work closes off the ability to see vitalism, and ultimately Aristotle, differently. As I argue in chapters 4 and 5, complex vitalism looks to articulate a more complex notion of system beyond basic cause and effect, which can be used to enhance the practice of contextual teaching. This notion of vitalism will not only ultimately allow for a different perspective on informal methods in relation to invention but also create a space for looking at Aristotle in a way that goes beyond a more commonsense, empirical philosophy.

Romanticism as Current-Traditionalism

Young's attempt to delineate both the connection and distinction between current-traditional rhetoric and new romanticism is grounded in Weidner's elevation of Coleridge to the archetypal anti-rhetorical vitalist through assumptions about Coleridge's relationship to formal scientific method and romantic individualism. This complex categorical connection to Coleridge is built on rhetoric's traditional narrative of retreat and return. Vasile Florescu, for example, in "Rhetoric and Its Rehabilitation in Contemporary Philosophy" (1970), outlines a typical genealogy for connecting scientific method to individual expression. The reduction of rhetoric as a focus of study begins, for him, with Bacon and Descartes. Bacon supplements Aristotelian syllogistic logic, the primary mode of inquiry in the Renaissance, with inductive logic. But the increasing value of inductive logic results in a devaluing of rhetoric, seen as another form of deductive inquiry. For Florescu, Descartes's attempt to provide a method founded on something other than scholastic logic proves even more damaging to rhetorical study. Descartes's utilization of self-evidence as the criterion for clear and distinct ideas denounces scholastic logic as sterile. Essentially, Descartes is condemning all art, technê, and heuristics in favor "not [of] divine inspiration, but the simple natural talent" of the inquirer (197).

For Florescu, this slippage from formal method to individual talent for perception is pushed further by German romanticism. Influenced by the Reformation, this individual talent gains prominence primarily through the theological mysticism of the time and culture expressed in the works of Kant and Hegel, among others. Florescu sees the culmination of this line of thought in Benedetto Croce. In *Estetica come scienza dell'expressione e linguistica generale* (1902), Croce's coupling of intuition and expression resulted "in eliminating rhetoric from the esthetic problematic" (Florescu 202). From this point of view, "an idea is born with its expression"; therefore, "every work of art is a unique phenomenon," which "signifies the denial of all the theory of specialized arts" (203). Art in this narrative moves from rhetorical technê to scientific method to natural talent, resulting in the loss of rhetoric.

Two scholars in rhetoric and composition—Sharon Crowley and Ross Winterowd—have situated Coleridge at the center of this movement from rhetorical invention to formal method to romantic individualism. In *The Methodical Memory: Invention in Current-Traditional Rhetoric* (1990), Crowley notes the basis of current-traditional rhetoric in Cartesian philosophy. To show that all knowledge comes from direct experience of the world, Descartes has to assume that all experience is accurately coded into memory and that a precise method would allow any individual to accurately remember experiences and record them in language. Crowley argues that the "big three" eighteenth-century rhetoricians—George Campbell, Hugh Blair, and Richard Whately—transfer rhetorical forms into this sense of formal method. Aristotelian *topoi* and tropes are shifted to associational psychology or put into style and arrangement. In each case, authority is turned from the rhetorical tradition to scientific method (either forms in the mind or in the text). Crowley extends her reading of Descartes and formal method into a reading of Coleridge's method. For Crowley, Coleridge sees method as a combination of unity and progression—method unifies disparate material by focusing it toward a common end. The individual mind establishes the purposive goal through initiative or intention. If the mind follows a properly methodical path, it can operate in line with natural and metaphysical laws. This synthesis goes beyond the basic empiricism of Locke and Hume to establish the mind, rather than the rhetorical tradition or scientific method, as the primary determinant in discursive or artistic acts. The individual mind does not simply reflect nature but unifies and thus forms it (42–43).

By the mid-nineteenth century, this shift from rhetoric to method turns decidedly toward texts and textbooks and produces what compositionists now call current-traditional rhetoric. For current-traditional rhetoric, a clear, ordered text not only shows that the writer has employed the proper method but also ensures the text's validity. Thus, current-traditional textbooks focused on punctuation, grammar, economy, and clarity to the detriment of invention and audience. Most compositionists see current-traditional rhetoric as an extension of the work of Peter Ramus—a rhetoric with no theory of invention. For Crowley, current-traditional rhetoric does have invention, but it had to be redirected into the mind or the text (a position that generates the research paper as an inventional device—writers are to discover the arguments in other texts) in order to correspond to the empirical epistemology of the day. This displacement of rhetoric and invention generates the notion of romantic genius when shifted into the mind and the notion of composition when shifted into the text. This is part of the reason the term composition developed in the late nineteenth century to take the place of rhetoric—composition is an analogue for arrangement.

While Crowley abstains from turning this analysis into a denunciation of romanticism, Ross Winterowd, in *The English Department: A Personal and Institutional History* (1998), carries this reading of current-traditional rhetoric more vigorously into romanticism and the individual. In a discussion of Crowley's book, Winterowd reads romantic "method" as Crowley sees Cartesian "method." Enlightenment mentalism sees the mind as the accurate, passive receiver of the objective world but gives way to a romantic mentalism that sees the structure of the individual mind as the active agent in perception. In each case, mentalism becomes what Winterowd calls "methodism": "That methodism was a major force shaping current-traditional rhetoric is beyond doubt, but it was also a prime element in romantic rhetoric, and for evidence we can turn to Coleridge and Emerson" (49). He bases this claim on his reading of Coleridge's imagination as "split" into "two or more subfaculties" (51). He is referring of course to Coleridge's now (in)famous distinction between primary imagination, secondary imagination, and fancy. Winterowd's subsequent reading of these distinctions is a fairly standard, hierarchical one. Primary imagination is passive perception (Enlightenment mentalism), secondary imagination is the active, creative mind (romantic mentalism), and fancy is everyday cultural commonplaces (traditional rhetoric). Coleridge and romantics, as Winterowd and others argue, privilege secondary imagination as the genius of the creative artist, which for Winterowd is "an innate, mysterious power" (53). Art in this schema is a product of methodism—the primary imagination photographs objective reality, and secondary imagination turns these photographs into ideas to be called up later in memory and reshaped by creative genius into artistic works, most notably poetry.

For Winterowd, "the solipsism became total with Coleridge" (58), and the ultimate result is the devaluation of rhetoric as fancy. The creative genius is the person who can unify universal law (mind) and natural law (world) through intuition without the intervention of fancy (culture or tradition). For Winterowd, this "'method' is simply introspection" (123). Descartes's formal method follows strict, rational, linear rules. But according to Winterowd's readings, Coleridge's methodism is ultimately a method of no method at all: it turns formal, objective method into arbitrary, subjective impulse. For Cowley, formal scientific method is still present in Coleridge. But Winterowd's reading is much more value laden. He argues that Coleridge dismantles formal method, leaving only individual intuition, which ultimately even devalues informal method. What is natural talent in Florescu and methodical synthesis in Crowley becomes natural genius in Winterowd's reading. This is not an innocent term. Genius carries with it a much more caustic and evaluative tone, and it is this term that, despite even Winterowd's use of the term methodism, is seen as completely arbitrary and free of method.

Crowley links Coleridge to the history of method, and Winterowd links Coleridge to individual genius. It is Coleridge's position at this intersection of current-traditional formalism and romantic individualism that Weidner and Young mischaracterize as vitalism. There are two fundamental problems with this placement. What allows the conflation of romanticism and vitalism is the problematic nature of defining romanticism. Romanticism is much too large for one definition to cover. Isaiah Berlin, in *The Roots of Romanticism,* provides a dizzying catalogue of definitions and characteristics of romanticism that provide a wealth of conflicting if not contradictory elements from valuing life to valuing death, from individualism to the dissolution of the individual, from the retreat to the primitive to the call for a new future through revolution (14–18). Likewise, in "On the Discrimination of Romanticisms," Arthur Lovejoy opens with another dizzying list of different origins and descriptions as well as offspring of romanticism, the result of which, for him, is "a confusion of terms and of ideas" (232). For Lovejoy, there are a number of romanticisms in operation historically: Germany in the 1790s (which, for Lovejoy, is most legitimately called Romanticism), England in the 1740s, France circa 1801, France from 1810 to 1820 (which adopted the German concept of romanticism that carried almost the opposite meaning of the 1801 version), and the works of Rousseau and a number of other writers and thinkers (235–36). These romanticisms cover a broad range of characteristics: a revolt against neo-classical aesthetics, an admiration of Shakespeare, a push toward independence from artistic rules, a distinction between nature and art that values the natural, the value of the savage over the cultural. But the term nature in particular is also complex and shifting.[6] In earlier romanticisms it connotes the value of the simple, naive, unsophisticated, and primitive. Later romanticisms see in nature the value of the complex, wild, spontaneous, and irregular to the point that later German romanticism promoted conscious art over mere nature (241). All of these ideas can rightly be called romanticism but should not be confused or conflated.

The other problem with Weidner's and Young's mislabeling is that, in the discourse of rhetoric and composition, both Coleridge and vitalism get caught up in this categorical confusion. Coleridge gets wrongly associated with a naive approach to natural genius rather than method and complexity. Coleridge follows this more complex trajectory of romanticism espoused by the later Germans and should not be thought of as standing for irrationalism, or a "natural" genius devoid of method. Genius in Coleridge is not simply genetic and left up to the subjective mind but is taught and methodical, a product of education. In the disciplinary discourse of rhetoric and composition, however, all romanticisms have come to be seen as merely subjective—left up to the mysterious gift of geniuses. A similar problem exists in terms of method. Coleridge's sense of method should not be read strictly in terms of Cartesian method and current-traditionalism. As I argue in chapters 2 and 3, James Berlin reads Coleridge's method in terms of Hegelian and Marxist dialectics, and Kameen reads it as an attempt that goes beyond formal scientific logic and epistemology to engage with rhetorical situations. These readings ultimately problematize the generalizing categorical move that links current-traditional rhetoric, romanticism, and vitalism.

Lovejoy's conclusion is that "any attempt at a *general* appraisal even of a single chronologically determinate Romanticism . . . is a fatuity. . . . It will, no doubt, remain abstractly possible to raise the question whether the preponderant effect, moral or aesthetic, of one or another large movement which has been called by the name was good or bad. But that ambitious inquiry cannot even be legitimately begun until a prior task of analysis and detailed comparison . . . has been accomplished" (252). In short, one cannot make definitive good or bad evaluations based on overly general categories. Such a move is at root uncritical. Ironically, those who charge Coleridge and, by association, vitalism with anti-intellectualism are operating historiographically and argumentatively with a form of anti-intellectualism. In the end, Coleridge cannot stand as a metonym for the intersection of all of these elements that make up the ahistorical category of vitalism as it is used rhetorically in rhetoric and composition. What I am trying to do is read Coleridge outside of this narrative of retreat and return, with its built-in scapegoat category for the demise of rhetoric, and instead read him from an ulterior narrative—the history of vitalism as a distinct paradigm. Rather than equate vitalism with a naive approach to nature, I build a new series of categorizations for it that follow its genealogy from Aristotelian theories of nature through the complexities of German romanticism to contemporary theories of complexity.

Disciplining Rhetoric and Composition

Despite this categorical complexity, Young follows Weidner by conflating the notion of current-traditional rhetoric with new romanticism under the guise of vitalism, and he uses it as a straw man against which to define a new disciplinary paradigm. In the 1950s and on through the 1960s, there were two dominant pedagogical approaches in composition classrooms: current-traditionalism (based on formalism and craft) and expressivism (based on gift and knack). Geoffrey Sirc, in his essay "Never Mind the Tagmemics, Where's the Sex Pistols?" discusses expressivist pedagogies of the late sixties as a reaction to the focus on objective, formal writing. In order to offset the sterile compositions being produced by the students, these pedagogies "preached sincerity and relevance at the expense of rules" (11) and used popular culture as the primary content for writing. In the general context of anti-establishment sentiments, the classroom became a place for the teacher to create a happening—a situation that stimulates or fosters invention. But as Sirc notes, "gradually such dreams were abandoned in favor of righting writing; traditional, determinate goals were re-affirmed. Writing could no longer *be,* it had to be a certain way" (11). For those who were invested in creating a discipline, the classroom situation had become quite undisciplined. If a new paradigm was going to be established, there had to be general, easily communicable, and transferable strategies that were grounded in institutional values; there had to be *discipline.*

Young opens "Arts, Crafts, Gifts, and Knacks" with the claim that "to understand the new rhetoric . . . we *must* see it as a reaction to an earlier rhetoric" (53; emphasis added). This mandate is a rhetorical response to these two dominant pedagogies that were still holding sway in the 1970s. In order to valorize the new rhetoric, Young conflates current-traditionalism and expressivism by arguing that they both rest on the same assumption—writing and invention cannot be taught. For Young, both epistemologies ignore the social and the teachable, one in favor of objectivity, the other in favor of subjectivity. If invention is unproblematic as in objective, current-traditional methods, or is left up to the realm of chance, intuition, or genius as in new romantic or expressivist pedagogies, then the only thing left to teach is the surface features of arrangement and grammar—not the directed origination or discovery of content. So if current-traditional rhetoric continues to dominate writing instruction, or if expressivism becomes the predominant theoretical model for composition pedagogy, there is no research object or practice that can serve as a basis for the discipline. There is no justification for claiming that composition is worthy of disciplinary status. Rhetorically, Young has to group current-traditionalism and expressivism together because they are the forces to be reckoned with if he wants to establish rhetoric as a new disciplinary paradigm. Rhetoric can provide a deeper historical legacy to justify composition's status as a unique discipline, and rhetorical invention can be examined by the methods of other more contemporary science-oriented fields to ground disciplinary research.

In order to draw upon these two institutional values for establishing a discipline—history and science—Young works toward developing rhetorical heuristics that are based on scientific research. This project began as early as Young's textbook with Alton Becker and Kenneth Pike, *Rhetoric: Discovery and Change* (1970). The book draws upon the more scientific disciplines of linguistics and psychology to produce a structured procedure that could apply to a large array of situations. Young, Becker, and Pike argue that people deal with the chaos of life (external reality) via three cognitive processes: (1) they categorize perceptions by comparison/contrast with other perceptions, (2) they determine differences among perceptions within the same category, and (3) they look at the way these perceptions are distributed in their experience. In each of these activities, the object under examination can be seen as (1) an isolated particle, (2) a dynamic wave, or (3) a field of relations. This produces nine possible ways to examine an object or topic and a nine-celled grid with corresponding heuristic questions.[7] This generic template can be applied to a wide array of writing situations to produce content on almost any topic. The heuristic is formal but also open to chance connections a student may make.

This type of research program accomplished what Young hoped—it extended into the 1970s and influenced research into the cognitive aspects of the composing process, composition's unique research object and disciplinary center. However, it did have unintended effects. *Rhetoric: Discovery and Change* was published in 1970, just before the Berthoff/Lauer debates, and set the stage for privileging one side of this debate over the other. At least as early as "Arts, Crafts, Gifts, and Knacks" (1980), Young does attempt to place rhetoric (art) in the middle-ground position between current-traditionalism (craft) and new romanticism (gift and knack). He writes that heuristics such as Francis Christensen's generative rhetoric of the sentence and tagmemics "[do] not insist on the primacy of reason, nor . . . repudiate non-rational activity; instead [they] assume a subtle and elaborate dialectic between the two" (58). This dialectical middle way makes perfect sense theoretically, but it does not necessarily play out in the influence of Young's position on disciplinary discourse and pedagogical practice. Research on invention continues to value science over the humanities.

As late as 1994, in their introduction to *Landmark Essays on Rhetorical Invention in Writing,* Young and coauthor Yameng Liu try to heal the opposition that still lingers from the Berthoff/Lauer debates by positing the distinction between discovery (science) and creation (humanities) and then posing invention (rhetoric) as a synthesis of the two. For them, invention means heuristics, which they define as "explicit strateg[ies] for effective guessing which enables the writer to bring principles of invention to bear in composing by transforming them into questions or operations to be performed" (xvi). The types of strategies commonly associated with invention—using clustering or mapping to produce a visual representation of content, using commonplaces or topoi as generic forms of argument, freewriting or keeping a journal to collect ideas, or answering journalistic questions or questions based on the tagmemic grid to generate material—are largely acontextual. This is what it means to be heuristic—"applying an art of rhetorical invention which is simultaneously heuristic and managerial, giving the rhetor both a universal capacity to define issues in indeterminate situations and a receptivity to the particularities of individual situations" (xiv).

However, what this does is create a gap between the universal and the particular. The two are not really integrated—one is *applied* to the other: the heuristic predetermines what can be seen (or not seen) in the situation. For Young and Liu, this is what gives heuristics their teachability. However, this opposition merely upholds the problematic binary at play in the field. Young and Liu reiterate the argument that invention (or heuristics) produces a dialectical relation between the "reason" of the "new classicists" and "the imagination" of the "new romantics" (xvi). But requiring invention to be generalizable—directly teachable and applicable—actually upholds the division. A heuristic may be somewhat open-ended with regard to student responses but remain instrumental in its operation, its application. In the end, the subtitle of Young's earlier textbook, *Rhetoric: Discovery and Change,* belies the emphasis on science and discovery rather than rhetoric and invention.

In his quip "never mind the tagmemics," Sirc is in some ways reacting to the irony that it is current-traditionalism and expressivism that get conflated and not current-traditionalism and Young's rhetorical approach. In "Arts, Crafts, Gifts, and Knacks," Young indicates that he wants writing instructors to be able to teach increased control over rhetorical invention. But he recognizes that "the great danger of a technical theory of art . . . is and has been in the past that it may over rationalize the composing process. In their preoccupation with analysis and method, those holding the theory may ignore our non-rational powers, inadvertently trying to turn heuristic procedures into rule-governed procedures and devising strategies for carrying out processes that are better dealt with by the unaided mind" (59). This is indeed the danger. It is the connection between current-traditional practice and the Aristotelian philosophy that Fogarty recognized early on. And as Crowley's analysis implies, it is the commonsense physics and rhetorical topoi of Aristotle that get transferred into current-traditional texts via the scientific paradigm, not the supposedly irrational individualism of Coleridge. The devaluation of art and technê that Florescu attributes to Descartes is not a denunciation of Aristotle but a transfer of Aristotle from inventional forms, to formal method, to formal texts. This connection is played out in the attempts to put tagmemics into practice. *The Bedford Bibliography for Teachers of Writing* notes that Young, Becker, and Pike's textbook, *Rhetoric: Discovery and Change,* was "seldom used in undergraduate courses" (86). The process of using the heuristic was overly formalized and too difficult to implement widely. To Young's credit the heuristic is trying to tackle complexity, but it is too rigid and attempts to control and direct the invention process too much. Its basis in scientific research justifies disciplinary status but does not necessarily play out pedagogically.

Some Categorical Consequences for Invention

Despite the categorical confusion and ultimately exclusionary effect of Young's species/genus analytics, the implicit scientific, and essentially political, value continues to influence the way invention, and in particular research on invention, is conceptualized and discussed. Janet Atwill traces similar historical territory regarding invention in her introduction to *Perspectives on Rhetorical Invention* (2002). Going back to the Berthoff/Lauer debates, Atwill argues that Berthoff is trying to defend the humanities from the sciences and critiques her for reducing the issue to politics (xiv). But Lauer is equally trying to save composition from literature, stating that it is "time for writing teachers to 'break out of the ghetto'" (quoted in Atwill xiii). It is hard to see Lauer's position as apolitical. Both Lauer and Weidner were Young's students, and it seems clear that disciplinary politics is at the root of their collective efforts. Richard Enos, who worked with Young at Carnegie Mellon, indicates as much in his foreword to *Inventing a Discipline*. He writes, "Young's vision was no less ambitious than to change the landscape of the field of English studies. Young's effort was not merely to 'reclaim' rhetoric for English but to reconceptualize what rhetoric is and, in doing so, change forever our idea of what English is, does, and offers" (viii). The issue for both Lauer and Berthoff is the defense of disciplinary territory and the humanities/science, literature/composition divide. Lauer invokes the contemporary authority of science and links it to rhetoric in order to defend rhetoric against the domination of literature in the English department. Berthoff is trying to link rhetoric to the humanities in order to establish rhetoric as a traditional part of the English department and keep science at bay. Even though they both appeal to rhetoric, the result of the debate is the solidification of the new romantic category and its opposition to new classical approaches, each with its own image of rhetoric.

One consequence of the categorical history, then, becomes a dispute over the definition of rhetoric—is it more of a general theory (like a science) or is it an artistic practice (like most of the humanities)? Lauer sees rhetoric and invention as a general theory. As Atwill puts it, "the very purpose of inventional strategies is to enable practice across rhetorical situations" (xvi). Rhetoric, in this case, is a generalization from empirical studies that can be applied to a variety of contexts. Lauer is following a particular reading of the Aristotelian tradition that seeks to generalize from actual practitioners so those generalizations can be applied to other situations. But there are other rhetorical traditions. Rhetoric is also the *kairotic* development of discursive strategies out of specific situations, not just their extraction and later application. Atwill proffers Stanley Fish's argument that practice is so situation-bound that a general theory does not apply as the typical postmodern anti-invention stance, arguing that this strict theory/practice division "challenges" rhetorical invention, putting it on the "defensive" (xvi). Fish's proposition, however, can be read as calling for a continued, ongoing practice/art of invention. Theory in this case is always being invented out of practice rather than extracted ahead of time and then applied —various theories and practices come together in a particular situation and a new theory for dealing with that situation comes out of the mix. Rather than being applied, a general theory or heuristic is one element of a more complex situation. Atwill is still operating on a model that splits invention along these competing notions of rhetoric and privileges a scientific notion of invention over humanistic approaches—a position that allows Atwill, who is following Lauer, to argue that "research" on invention was declining during the 1990s in favor of theory (xi), a position that undervalues all of the ways invention was talked about and practiced during that decade.[8]

For me, this is the second legacy of "Arts, Crafts, Gifts, and Knacks": dividing and categorizing arts, crafts, gifts, and knacks ultimately leads to overvaluing some elements and undervaluing others. All four are important to invention as a practice rather than a research object, and even though Young seeks to make invention/rhetoric a mediating principle between science and the humanities, the categories involved set up valuations and exclusions when it comes to inventional procedures. Though he includes James Britton's essay in the *Landmark Essays* collection, for example, Young still codes Britton's "spontaneous inventiveness" as "romantic" (xxii), and in doing so he sets it up to be of less value. The roots of this devaluation lie in the use of vitalism as a rhetorical figure in the narrative of rhetoric's retreat and return. When Young follows Weidner in labeling the conflation of current-traditionalism and new romanticism "vitalism" as a way to devalue his competition, he cannot go back and try to mediate these categories. Once vitalism is established as a trope for the "earlier rhetoric" that has to be excluded in order to define the new rhetoric, the die is cast. The whole notion of heuristics as the ultimate value in invention cannot be cleanly separated from the context of exclusion.

The long-term consequences of this definitional and categorical divide effect a number of issues surrounding the concept of invention: expanding the definition of method as well as art, theorizing affect and the body, and developing situation-specific heuristics or methods. The short-term issue that grounds these long-term consequences is the problematic reading of Coleridge as the archetypal representative of the conflation of current-traditional rhetoric and romanticism under the moniker of vitalism. Undoing Coleridge's function as a rhetorical trope in the metanarrative of rhetoric's retreat and return opens up a space for valuing invention in the context of pedagogy rather than research.

Genius, Talent, Sense, and Cleverness

Despite, or because of, the dominance of the narrative of retreat and return as the grounding metanarrative for the rise of the discipline, rhetoric and composition is doing well, as Winterowd indicates at the end of his book (*English Department* 203–4). Consequently, rhetoric and composition scholars do not necessarily need to talk in terms of disciplinarity anymore. The historical distance now exists for an examination and reconsideration of this rhetorical approach. And this reconsideration needs to begin with Coleridge, who is situated at the center of these mappings of the field. In Young's desire to categorize rhetorics, two terms get caught up in the battle and coded in specific ways. Art comes to stand for natural genius at the expense of technê, and method comes to stand for rigid formalism at the expense of heuristics. Both of these terms, obviously connected with romanticism and current-traditionalism, get connected to Coleridge's placement in rhetoric's narrative of retreat and return. Coleridge is seen as promoting the idea that artistic geniuses naturally employ proper formal method. However, Coleridge's sense of art cannot be reduced to natural genius, and his sense of method cannot be reduced to scientific formalism. Separating Coleridge from these assumptions opens the way for re-evaluating his relationship to rhetoric.

Rather than leave genius up to natural ability or a mystical spontaneity, Coleridge seeks to ground it in an education based on method and situated-ness. In "Essays on the Principles of Method," Coleridge notes that one of the distinguishing characteristics of educated people is their speech, which is "grounded on the habit of foreseeing in each integral part, or (more plainly) in every sentence, the whole that he intends to communicate" (449). This di-alectical "habit" does not just exist in a person as a gift but is the result of the study of method, which he argues is "a manifestation of intellect, and not a spontaneous and uncertain production of circumstances" ("Treatise on Method" 630). As Coleridge sees it,

> The habit of Method, should always be present and effective; but in order to render it so, a certain training, or education of the mind, is indispensably necessary. Events and images, the lively and spirit-stirring machinery of the external world, are like light, and air, and moisture, to the seed of the mind, which would else rot and perish. In all processes of mental evolution the ob-jects of the senses must stimulate the mind; and the mind must in turn as-similate and digest the food which it thus receives from without. Method, therefore, must result from the due mean, or balance, between our passive impressions and the mind's re-action on them. (634)

The mind is not passive, merely accepting the chaos of images inductively with-out placing an ordering principle on them. But neither should an ordering principle be placed randomly or deductively on the world. To employ method, one has to examine the material context closely and tailor the arrangements of it to the conditions of possibility it offers. Consequently, genius is largely the result of a proper education in the dialectical relationship between part and whole, mind and world. Coleridge states explicitly that "we may define the ex-cellence of [a text's] method as consisting in that just proportion, that union and interpretation of the universal and the particular, which must ever pervade all works of decided genius and true science" ("Essays" 457).

The term genius here should not be misconstrued, however. In a short essay entitled "Genius, Talent, Sense, and Cleverness," from *The Friend*, Coleridge sets out to define precisely what he means when he employs these terms. He

notes that they are often used synonymously, which leads to misunderstand-
ings of his usages. For him, genius is "the faculty which *adds* to the existing
stock of power, and knowledge by new views, new combinations. . . . [It is]
originality in intellectual construction: the moral accompaniment, and actu-
ating principle of which consists, perhaps, in the carrying on of the freshness
and feelings of childhood into the powers of manhood" (419). Rather than
something left up to chance, genius is a studied critical faculty that allows one
to see outside of commonplace forms of thought and bring fresh perspectives
and connections to a topic. It is, in short, a capacity for critical thinking and
invention. Talent is "the comparative facility of acquiring, arranging, and applying the stock furnished by others and already existing in books or other
conservatories of intellect" (419). This is a skill of *arrangement* and *style*: being
able to see the relationships between existing knowledges and to link and order
them in insightful ways. Coleridge sees sense as a skill for balance and judgment: it is "to the judgment what health is to the body" (419). The relationship
between the mind and the body is important: "The mind seems to act *en masse*,
by a synthetic rather than analytic process: even as the outward senses, from
which the metaphor is taken, perceive immediately, each as it were by a peculiar
tact or intuition, without any consciousness of mechanism by which the perception is realized" (419). Intuition, sense, is something learned, absorbed from
one's environment. It is knowledge at the level of the body. In addition to
knowledge from the material environment, sense is in accord with the cultural
environment, or cultural *memory*, and leans toward balance and compromise.
Coleridge notes, "If Genius be the initiative, and Talent the administrative,
Sense is the conservative, branch, in the intellectual republic" (420). Lastly,
cleverness is "a comparative readiness in the invention and use of means, for
the realizing of objects and ideas" (420). Cleverness can take the ideas developed by the other skills and make them happen, put them into action. "In
short," for Coleridge, "Cleverness is a sort of genius for instrumentality" (420).
In terms of the rhetorical canons, cleverness would amount to *delivery*, or the
ability to deliver.

All of these aspects can have elements of innate ability, and they can all be
enhanced and developed through the study and practice of method. Young
recognizes that the conflict between art as gift and art as technê goes back to

Greece, the eighteenth century, and "romantics like Coleridge": "It reemerges every time men think seriously about the discipline" ("Arts" 59). But it is precisely this emphasis on discplinarity that Coleridge does not share. In order to support composition as a research discipline, Young has to emphasize the fact that writing can be objectified. In order to support composition as an institutional course, Young has to emphasize the fact that writing can be taught. Gift and knack have to be devalued in favor of arts as explicitly identifiable and teachable. Coleridge has no such rhetorical or institutional exigence. Though Coleridge does value a particular conception of genius, he does not devalue talent, sense, or cleverness. All of these rhetorical capacities are important to education. As Coleridge notes, all ideas are based in experience and instincts: "the boy knows that his hoop is round, and this, in years after, helps to teach him, that in the circle, all the lines drawn from the centre to the circumference, are equal" ("Treatise" 633). Inborn capacities, bodily habits acquired through experience, and explicit instruction in methods through language are all important aspects of educational development. If the goal is rhetorical pedagogy and invention rather than disciplinary research and justification, all of these elements should be valued and utilized.

The Methodical Middle Way

This misreading of Coleridge's concept of genius as purely natural extends to his concept of method as purely formal. Sharon Crowley recognizes the pliability of the term in *The Methodical Memory:* "The term method has been used since classical times to designate any orderly or systematic procedure, and it continues to be used in this loose sense. However, an important technical use of the term *method* began to emerge among the generations of scholars who immediately preceded Descartes. Walter Ong defines this historical use of method to mean 'a series of ordered steps gone through to produce with a certain efficacy a desired effect—a routine of *efficiency'*" (33). It is the difference between this informal rhetorical sense of method and the formal scientific sense of method that produces different readings and valuations of Coleridge and causes confusion among terms and categories. In "On the Origin and Progress of the Sect of Sophists in Greece," Coleridge explicitly juxtaposes his method with the reductive formalism of the sophists, who use overly simple forms to pretend to teach truth and wisdom. For Coleridge, the term sophist originally signified "one who professes the power of making others wise, a wholesale and retail dealer in wisdom," and it is for this, "not their abuse of the arts of reasoning," that sophism should be dismissed (436). The issue for Coleridge is that they instructed the young in simplistic, acontextual forms rather than in moral and philosophical inquiry (a position not dissimilar to Fogarty's call for the development of a contemporary philosophical basis for rhetoric and composition rather than current-traditional formalism). Rather than conceptualize method in the strict scientific sense of his day, Coleridge looks back to the Greek sense of method to pose an alternative to sophistic formalism.

In "Treatise on Method" Coleridge traces the term method back to its Greek origins. In the Greek, method "literally means a way, or path, of transit" (630). This implies that method is concerned with a transition from one point in a process to another. For Coleridge, this movement is not a random or passive acceptance of circumstances but the ability of the mind to see the steps in a process as connected to a whole or larger goal. The initiative of the process, then, comes from a goal or purpose that is then set in relation to circumstances. The object of methodical thinking is not things or ideas, but relations—relations of things with each other, relations of ideas with each other, and the relations of things and ideas with each other. The ability to see these complex interactions is what enables a thinker to move toward the goal or purpose. Such a way or path is not a strict, formalist sense of method that when employed will always lead to the same end. It is both designated by the intentions of the educated mind and the conditions of possibility that the material situation sets up. Consequently, the force of genius or the limits of empiricism cannot determine the path. This middle way can unfold only through dialectical interaction. The key to method, then, is following all of an initial goal's ramifications so that sometimes the mind will wander to divergent paths that are then retraced in order to set out on "a new departure" (633). This recursive process is essentially an artistic practice that Coleridge places at the intersections of philosophy and science, between the dialectical method of Plato and the empirical method of Bacon. Art as a middle-ground method draws on these other methods but places them within a communicative situation. As he notes, "Method . . . demands a knowledge of the relations which things bear to each other, or to the observer, or to the state and apprehension of the hearers" (650).

In addition to being a product of a full education rather than reductive forms, this sense of method is also a rhetorical art. Coleridge uses the archetypal example of Shakespeare to show that genius is not purely natural or formal but founded on method. There are those who have been taught that Shakespeare is "immethodical"—a natural genius who works at random. In Coleridge's mind, "Shakespeare was not only endowed with great native genius (which he is commonly allowed to have been), but what is less frequently conceded, he has much acquired knowledge" (649). Through his education, Shakespeare learned a great deal of information—facts, law, and culture—all of which appears in the detail of his characters and plots. The archbishop of Canterbury's speech in *Henry V*, for example, required a man of knowledge to produce. Most importantly for Coleridge, all of Shakespeare's reading, information, and knowledge were not a rough, unordered mass of things. Shakespeare's use of this knowledge demanded an understanding of the relation among all of that information, the observer, and the hearers. Coleridge cites two examples: a passage by Mrs. Quickley in *Henry IV* and one by Hamlet. Coleridge notes that if we examine only the form, both would be "immethodical." Mrs. Quickley merely restates from her memory the random chain of events, no matter how disconnected. Hamlet, however, organizes, reconfigures, and recontextualizes the information in light of the whole, and with regard to material circumstances and the friend to whom it is communicated. In each case, the relationship to method in these characters is deliberate on Shakespeare's part. The relationships are aspects of the characters' minds, their experience of the world, and their levels of methodical education and show Shakespeare's methodical understanding of the characters' places within a rhetorical situation.

Coleridge argues that most critics of his day completely missed this aspect of Shakespeare: Shakespeare did not apply simple formalisms to his works any more than he operated randomly with no method but contemplated ideas and their relationship to the world. Coleridge quotes A. W. Schlegel's note that Shakespeare "*lays open to us, in a single word, a whole series of preceding conditions*" (quoted in "Treatise" 654; emphasis by Coleridge). Coleridge sees in

Shakespeare a methodical mind that contemplated ideas in their full complexity, "in which alone are involved conditions of consequences *ad infinitum*" (654). The problem, as Coleridge sees it, is that most critics focus on finding some formal disproportion or discontinuity in Shakespeare, rather than the methodical examination of situatedness. Coleridge posits two possible responses to these critics: either Shakespeare understood the workings of language and passion better than his critics, or he "was pursuing two methods at once: one poetical, the other psychological" (655). But even this dual approach does not grasp all of what is going on in Shakespeare's works. Coleridge goes on to remark, "We said that Shakespeare pursued two methods. Oh! He pursued many, many more" (655). Method is multiple and situational. To write about ships requires knowledge of the oar, the sail, the helm, the stars, the artillery. Writing is not the application of simple formalisms to all occasions. It requires a broad-based education and being open to the multiple paths that can emerge out of any given rhetorical situation. For Coleridge, this is something a critic, with his "scalping knife and tomahawk," would never recognize (656).

Far from espousing a reliance on art as natural genius, method as pure formalism, and poetry as superior to rhetoric, Coleridge is arguing against those who, in his time, held such positions. All of this comes down to the nature of art. All works of philosophy, science, and art become "poetry" as long as they display method. In the "meditative observation" of scientists such as Humphry Davy, William Wollaston, Charles Hatchet, and John Murray, Coleridge finds poetry. For him, "[t]his consideration leads us from the paths of physical science into a region apparently very different. Those who tread the enchanted ground of Poetry, often times do not even suspect that there is such a thing as *Method* to guide their steps. Yet even here we undertake to show that [poetry] not only has a necessary existence, but the strictest philosophical application; and that it is founded on the very philosophy which has furnished us with the principles already laid down" (649). Far from reducing poetry to natural genius or the adherence to linguistic form, poetry is grounded in philosophy and method. Coleridge states explicitly that "Plato was a poetic philosopher, as Shakespeare a philosophic poet. In the poetry, as well as in the philosophy, of both, there was a necessary predominance of ideas; but this did not make them regardless of the actual existences around them. They were not visionaries or mystics; but dwelt in 'the sober certainty' of waking knowledge" (660). From this perspective, poetry becomes "all works of the higher imagination" that display method, regardless of medium, including all of what we typically consider the fine arts and humanities (658). When Weidner, Young, and others claim that for Coleridge poetry devalues rhetoric, they are not looking at this expanded definition, which can include works of rhetoric, and which can no longer be said to be immethodical or only left up to chance or natural genius. The only way Coleridge can be seen as devaluing rhetoric is if his notion of rhetoric is reduced to sophism. But the reduction to formalism he is against can be seen in all of these disciplines just as method can. It is not restricted to the discipline of rhetoric.

Young looks to place rhetoric as the mediating principle between subjective and objective principles. But this is precisely where Coleridge places art and method—potentially all forms of the arts and sciences, including rhetoric. Rather than seeing Coleridge as the enemy of rhetoric, as Weidner, Winterowd, and others do, I would argue that it becomes more profitable to place him in the context of an approach to rhetoric that values dialectic and situatedness. If rhetoric is defined by the social-scientific production of heuristics, Coleridge may have little value. But if rhetoric is defined as seeing the available means of persuasion and action in a given situation, then Coleridge should be seen as a precursor to contemporary rhetorics who had a method for theorizing situatedness. This move would make Coleridge part of rhetoric's return rather than retreat or would at least question the notion of a complete retreat. And it is just such a perspective that James Berlin and Kameen explore. Berlin reads Coleridge's method in terms of dialectics, and Kameen reads it in terms of phenomenological engagement with situations. These readings ultimately problematize the generalizing categorical move that links current-traditional rhetoric, romanticism, and vitalism. I extend Berlin's and Kameen's work by taking Coleridge out of the narrative of retreat and return and placing him into a vitalist history. Coleridge's vitalism emerges out of his study of scientific theories rather than an adherence to "romantic" individualism, which takes him away from vitalism as natural genius or mystical spontaneity. Instead, a more in-depth understanding of life becomes a key aspect of a methodical practice within complex contexts.

2

CARTOGRAPHY

AND FORGETTING

FOLLOWING RICHARD YOUNG'S 1978 NEH seminar, James Berlin accepts Young's articulation of current-traditional rhetoric and folds vitalism into this category while at the same time revaluing Coleridge. In three articles that appeared in 1980, Berlin establishes his debt to the seminar but also turns the discourse of the field away from the more social-scientific basis that Young uses to ground the discipline. Initially, Berlin reads the concept of vitalism as natural genius and moves it from romanticism to current-traditional rhetoric via the work of Hugh Blair and Richard Whately. Though he starts out using the term vitalism in conjunction with genius, it quickly disappears from his texts altogether. What remains of it is the concept of genius, which simply becomes an aspect of an early current-traditional rhetoric. But in the 1980s as he moves on to develop new maps in his two-book-length histories of writing instruction, Berlin recognizes that this genius can no longer function within current-traditional rhetoric, which by the late nineteenth century is dominated by empiricism and positivism. So in his discussion of the twentieth century, genius resurfaces in his map within subjective rather than objective theories. Berlin shifts the disappearance of vitalism from current-traditional rhetoric to romanticism and then expressivism. The effect of this new cartography is that vitalism almost disappears from the discourse of rhetoric and composition in the 1980s via the development and dissemination of Berlin's categorical maps of the field. Vitalism is forgotten, remaining only as a scapegoat term equated with mysticism and expressivism. Though initially valued, Coleridge's method ultimately disappears as well because Berlin synthesizes it with a more Hegelian or Marxist dialectical method. As Berlin accepts a Marxist framework for his politics and writing pedagogy, language and ideology become a more central element in his epistemological maps, which ultimately exclude vitalist or bodily epistemologies in favor of more mind-centered pedagogies that focus on unmasking false consciousness.

Two of Berlin's articles from 1980, "Current-Traditional Rhetoric: Paradigm and Practice," with Robert Inkster, and "Richard Whately and Current-Traditional Rhetoric," accept the notion of current-traditional rhetoric that Young derived from Fogarty and presented as the nemesis against which he needs to map the field. In the first article, Berlin and Inkster cite Young's characterization of the current-traditional paradigm with the intention of bringing out the current-traditional assumptions in four composition textbooks in use during the 1970s. The article exhibits several characteristics that provide the basis for most of Berlin's later work: the importance of examining epistemological assumptions behind rhetorical and pedagogical practices; the importance of *evaluating* these assumptions and practices rather than just dissecting them; the use of James Kinneavy's communications triangle—author, audience, text, world—as a map for evaluating discourses and practices; the importance of transaction among these elements and the social; and the recognition that epistemological differences have "profound ramifications that are ethical, social, and political" (14).

By reading these textbooks across the elements of the communications triangle, Berlin and Inkster expose the commonsense epistemology that they
trace back to George Campbell (1776), Hugh Blair (1783), and Richard Whately
(1828). This commonsense epistemology sees a direct and unproblematic correspondence between world, mind, and language. One outcome of this method
of analysis is that it leads Berlin and Inkster to accept Young's conflation of
current-traditional rhetoric and vitalism with romanticism. The "vitalist" notion that leaves invention up to individual genius or to research and reading is
also seen as direct and unproblematic. They point out that an algorithmic emphasis on style and form and an aleatory emphasis based on genius that rejects
"all methodical procedure" are polar opposites but that they both "converge on
the underlying philosophical issues" (13). Each position ignores the problematic and transactional nature of knowledge and meaning. The problem Berlin
and Inkster identify is the same one Fogarty recognizes: writing teachers should
not be using a rhetoric that has the late eighteenth and early nineteenth centuries as its cultural context—using it pretends that "Freud, Einstein, and
Heisenberg" never happened. Following Weidner and Young, Berlin and
Inkster call this emphasis on genius "Romantic" (2), demonstrate that we are
in the midst of a current-traditional "crisis," and pose heuristic procedures as
the best transactional middle ground (13).

In "Richard Whately and Current-Traditional Rhetoric," Berlin steps away
from attributing the reliance on natural, subjective genius to romanticism.
Rather than trace vitalism back to Coleridge and romanticism, he traces it back
to Blair, Campbell, and Whately. Berlin argues that current-traditional rhetoric
finds its "immediate sources" in "two late nineteenth-century classroom
rhetorics: A. S. Hill's *The Principles of Rhetoric* (1878) and J. Genung's *The Practical Elements of Rhetoric* (1886)" (11), both of which are more influenced by
Whately, who is responding to and extending Campbell and Blair, than by
Coleridge or the English Romantics. Whately's real contribution, according to
Berlin, is that he extends issues of commonsense epistemology into practical
application, which serves as a primary prototype for Hill and Genung. This
movement from philosophy to pedagogy is outlined in Fogarty's distinction
between Aristotelian rhetoric and current-traditional practice. The correspon-

dence epistemology is there in both, but it is removed from consideration in current-traditional rhetoric, which focuses solely on pedagogical formalisms.

Most interesting for this discussion, though, is how vitalism fits into the picture Berlin is painting in this article. He traces the reduction of invention to genius back to Blair, who conflated rhetoric and literary criticism. The result for Berlin is a devaluation of rhetoric: "from this point of view, to learn to criticize is to learn to compose," which "tended to make invention in rhetoric as mysterious and unique a process as it was thought to be in poetry and fiction" (13).[1] Berlin flatly calls this a "vitalist theory of invention" without ever really addressing what vitalism is. Berlin is attempting to show the influence that Blair and Campbell have on Whately: Blair providing the vitalism, Campbell providing the commonsense epistemology based on "a simple, mechanical congruence between the external world and the faculties of the mind" (13). Both of these perspectives come together in Whately: from Blair he accepts the role of genius, which leaves invention to chance or mystery and reduces rhetoric to a rule-governed procedure of arrangement and style; from Campbell he accepts the basic correspondence of mind and world, which leaves discovery up to science and reduces rhetoric to a managerial art.

These elements come together specifically in Whately's pedagogical prescriptions. Berlin states that "Whately's managerial discovery procedures are divided into classifications of the various forms arguments may assume and advice on applying these forms to particular situations" (14). He also notes that Whately sees his formal pedagogy as being in the tradition of Aristotle—the connection Fogarty noted between Aristotelian rhetoric and current-traditional rhetoric. But what is important for Berlin is how Whately differs: his pedagogy removes invention from the domain of rhetoric, whereas Aristotle did not. For Berlin, Whately is actually the first to conflate current-traditional rhetoric and vitalism. His work influences Genung and Hill, who influence the textbooks of the late nineteenth century, which form the basis for twentieth-century current-traditional rhetoric. In short, Berlin accepts Young's definition of vitalism and its conflation with current-traditional rhetoric while questioning the way that Weidner and Young link it to Coleridge and romanticism.

In "The Rhetoric of Romanticism: The Case for Coleridge," the third of Berlin's articles from 1980, he extends this reading of romanticism and sets out to detail the problems with Weidner and Young's claim that Coleridge makes a distinctive split between rhetoric and poetics that damages rhetoric. In addition to being non-Aristotelian, Berlin argues, Coleridge's rhetoric cannot be considered derivative of the eighteenth century, a move Young attempts to make by linking romanticism with current-traditional rhetoric under the category "writing cannot be taught." Berlin is "convinced" that "the conflation of Coleridge with the eighteenth-century rhetorics of Smith and Blair has . . . led Young and Weidner astray" (63). Coleridge opposes the collapsing of the subject into the object in eighteenth-century empiricism because this ignores the necessary dialectic of the two in any process of understanding or interpretation. What is most important to Berlin in his reading of Coleridge is the emphasis on dialectics, or what Coleridge calls "polarities" (65). It is the placing of things or ideas in relation to other things or ideas that produces a dialectical movement toward more understanding.

This dialectical process can take two possible forms: poetic or rhetorical. Argument as a form is meant to communicate information to readers. Verse as a form is meant to induce pleasure in readers. Both are designed to reveal error, but argumentation can be disturbing to the audience if its members have to question their commonplace beliefs directly. Verse aims for the same end but does so in a less confrontational, more pleasurable way. Consequently, Coleridge values poetic form because he thinks it is more rhetorically effective. Readers will return to poetry again and again because it is pleasurable. However, Coleridge makes the important distinction between poetry and a poem. A poem is a specific type of form with rhyme and meter; poetry is the enactment of a dialectical, methodological search. Berlin notes that for Coleridge it is the primary imagination that produces a dialectical path on the journey to truth, while the secondary imagination produces the form of a poem or argument. Therefore poetry as a function of the primary imagination can be found in rhetorical prose as well as poetic verse. Arguments might be dead and mechanical, but they also might display the art of method. Poems might display the art of method, but they can also be dead and mechanical. Both rhetorical forms and poetic forms require imagination as the impetus for dialectical movement if they are to be valued. For Berlin, such a perspective on rhetorics and poetics does not automatically damage rhetoric. According to Berlin, it is the eighteenth-century rhetorics, not Coleridge or romanticism, that create a hierarchy between rhetoric and poetics that leads to the disappearance of invention in nineteenth-century rhetoric and composition texts..

Mapping Epistemologies

These three key articles from 1980 establish current-traditional rhetoric as a scapegoat paradigm and separate romanticism from vitalism's focus on genius. The term expressivism begins to appear in Berlin's maps in "Contemporary Composition: The Major Pedagogical Theories" (1982), which is, in part, a response to Richard Fulkerson's essay "Four Philosophies of Composition" (1979).[2] In this essay, Fulkerson bases his map of composition philosophies on M. H. Abrams's *The Mirror and the Lamp* (1953). Abrams identifies four prevailing theories in literary criticism: pragmatic (theories that focus on the reader or the effect literature has on the reader), mimetic (theories that make the universe the primary element), expressive (theories that emphasize the personal views of the artist, "such as in the Romantic period, [which] Abrams labels the expressive position"), and objective (theories that emphasize the internal relationships within a text) (Fulkerson 3). Fulkerson re-inscribes these categories to correspond to four predominant philosophies of composition: he keeps the term *expressive* for philosophies that emphasize the writer and *mimetic* for philosophies that focus on correspondence with the world, while calling philosophies that focus on the reader *rhetorical* and philosophies that emphasize the text *formalist*. Both Abrams's and Fulkerson's categorizations correspond to James Kinneavy's aims (persuasive, referential, expressive, and literary) outlined in *A Theory of Discourse* (1971), which also function as elements in the communications triangle and utilize the term expressive for a focus on the writer.

Fulkerson does not assess each element and identify a preferable aim. His main thesis is that "there is nothing wrong with an expressive philosophy, but there is something seriously wrong with classroom methodology which implies one variety of value judgment when another will actually be employed" (7). His primary concern is that teachers unconsciously give an assignment that asks the student to write in one mode, and then they evaluate the student's paper from the perspective of another mode. Assigning an expressive paper but grading it across formal concerns "is modal confusion, mindlessness" (7). He sees his map as a useful tool that will keep teachers from making this pedagogical mistake but emphasizes that there is "nothing wrong" with any mode as long as it is applied consistently.

Berlin disagrees with this claim. He also sees the dominant models in composition textbooks as separating the elements in the communications triangle but to the detriment of writing theory and instruction. In "Contemporary Composition," Berlin produces his first full map of rhetoric and composition across the complex relations among audience, reality, writer, and language and the epistemologies that ground each one.[3] Those epistemologies are neo-Aristotelian (classical), emphasizing logic as the primary means through which the mind reasons and produces knowledge with the goal of persuading an equally rational audience; positivist (current-traditional), emphasizing the world as the seat of knowledge based on a commonsense realism that posits a direct relationship between the world and the individual mind as tabula rasa, where knowledge is attainable in the sciences through scientific method and in the arts through genius; neo-Platonic (expressive), emphasizing the writer who is cut off from truth and must use dialectical method in the form of dialogue with others through speech or dialogue with the self through writing to remove error in personal vision in an attempt to move closer to transcendent knowledge; new rhetoric (epistemic), emphasizing the social, seeing knowledge and truth as transactional, created through the dialectical intersection of all the elements of the communications triangle. The dialectical method in this group utilizes language and communication to negotiate relations among writers, audiences, and the world in order to produce temporary knowledges.

Using epistemology in conjunction with the communications triangle has implications for both Fogarty's and Fulkerson's categories. Whereas Fogarty sees Aristotelian philosophy as the basis of current-traditional rhetoric, Berlin makes a clear separation between the two. Berlin implicitly addresses Fogarty when he states that "my main purpose in starting with the [neo-Aristotelians] is to show that many who say they are followers of Aristotle are in truth opposed to his system in every sense" ("Contemporary Composition" 767). Fogarty's argument is that there is no philosophy expressed in current-traditional rhetoric because it unconsciously presumes an Aristotelian base. Using epistemology, rather than philosophy, allows Berlin to imply that there is no philosophy expressed there because the epistemology is one of commonsense realism—no philosophy is needed because knowledge is unproblematic. This epistemological distinction allows Berlin to recognize that the modal confusion Fulkerson sees in pedagogical practices exists at a theoretical level as well. Most textbooks claiming to be Aristotelian are actually operating within the current-traditional paradigm (768–69). Epistemology also provides Berlin a perspective from which to evaluate these differing discourses—a possibility not available through Fulkerson's emphasis on pedagogical aims. Berlin can then argue that there is something wrong with classical, current-traditional, or expressive approaches —they are epistemologically unsophisticated at best, epistemologically irresponsible at worst.

This turn allows us to examine more closely what happens to vitalism. In "The Rhetoric of Romanticism," Berlin notes Young's use of the term vitalism in "Paradigms and Problems" and attributes Young's position on vitalism and Coleridge to Weidner, but he does not make a point of dealing with its problematic use. The term vitalism is absent from "Contemporary Composition," but it shows up implicitly in Berlin's positivist category under the guise of genius. In current-traditional rhetoric, "[t]ruth is to be discovered outside the rhetorical enterprise—through the method, usually the scientific method, of the appropriate discipline, or, as in poetry and oratory, through genius" (769–70). This is his only mention of genius in the article, but the implication in the light of his article on Whately is clear: as noted above, he directly links genius to vitalism and its conflation with current-traditional rhetoric.

A crucial new move is being made, however, with his construction of the neo-Platonic and new rhetoric categories that goes back to "The Rhetoric of Romanticism," where Berlin wants to separate Coleridge's romanticism from Young's ahistorical romantic category that links romanticism with vitalism and current-traditionalism. Berlin makes a further distinction among romanticisms. He states that expressivism is based in Plato, Emerson, and romanticism, and he places William Coles in this neo-Platonic category, claiming that Coles sees writing as "an unteachable act . . . that can be learned but not taught," so "his pedagogical role is to provide a classroom environment in which the student learns to write . . . through dialectic" (772). This is precisely the way Young characterizes Coles in "Arts, Crafts, Gifts, and Knacks." But in new rhetoric, yet another form of romanticism shows up under the figures of Ann Berthoff and I. A. Richards, who are explicit Coleridgeans. Characterizing the new rhetoric as placing "language . . . at the center of [the] dialectical interplay between individual and world" (774) allows Berlin to put these Coleridgeans in the same category with Young, a characterization Young would likely disagree with after Weidner's characterization of Coleridge as the supreme vitalist.

What is happening in Berlin's continued attempt to recuperate Coleridge is the desire to articulate varying dialectical methods. As Berlin argues in "The Rhetoric of Romanticism," "Coleridge's dialectic is clearly not Plato's" (68). Plato's dialectic is primarily dialogue. Coleridge's is primarily polarity—the synthesis of opposing forces in the world and dialectical oppositions in the mind. So dialectical method in the expressive category of Plato, Coles, and at this point Emerson, is dialogue for the removal of error from the mind so it can see truth and knowledge. Coleridge's dialectic, however, is based on language and is creative; it is generative of reality. For Berlin, Coleridge's rhetoric does have an inventional system "since the dialectical process itself becomes a heuristic device" (71). Therefore it has to be placed in new rhetoric given Berlin's epistemological distinctions in "Contemporary Composition." In this mapping Berlin is unknowingly making the distinction between mystical vitalism in current-traditional rhetoric and oppositional vitalism in Coleridge's dialectical polarities. He is using Coleridge's oppositional vitalism to ground his own dialectical model. This distinction, however, is lost in Berlin's mappings. The turn toward evaluation and the reduction of vitalism to genius perpetuates the stereotype and its negative assessment in rhetoric and composition, allowing its history to disappear from disciplinary discourse.

The Politics of Mapping

Berlin grounds his maps of the field in epistemology because it allows him to engage in disciplinary politics. I see three ways his map in "Contemporary Composition" is political. On one level, Berlin is making a political move in relation to key players in the discipline. His map is not just about situating composition theories; it is about situating himself in relation to Young and Fulkerson. He both aligns himself with and distinguishes himself from them. Berlin is aligning himself with Young by placing him in the epistemic or new rhetoric category and privileging this category epistemologically. But he is separating himself from Young by leaving vitalism in current-traditional rhetoric, putting expressivism with Plato and Emerson's romanticism, and assigning Coleridge's romanticism (via Berthoff) to epistemic rhetoric. Berlin is acknowledging an element of romanticism in expressivism while at the same time showing that there is more than one romanticism. Berlin is also aligning himself with Fulkerson by acknowledging the importance of Fulkerson's map and even generally agreeing with his descriptions of each philosophy; Fulkerson notes that Abrams connects romanticism with expressivism, and Berlin shows that he agrees via his neo-Platonic category. At the same time, however, Berlin is showing that these philosophies can be evaluated and these maps can be rearticulated. Berlin essentially folds formalist approaches to texts into a mimetic model of the world so he can reformulate the emphasis on language as dialectically engaged with the other three elements of the communications triangle. Berlin creates his categories by identifying the epistemology that values one element of the communications triangle over the others but then looks at how writer, audience, language, and world function within each category.

This leads to a second political level: describing philosophies of composition epistemologically allows Berlin to establish a political subject by examining the role of the writer in each new category. In positivist current-traditionalism, the writer is effaced. By viewing himself or herself as a tabula rasa, as purely a filter for induction, the subject has no (political) agency. In neo-Platonic expressivism, the writer is at the center but is cut off from the community, the social. Even though the writer has the capacity for agency, it is only applicable to his or her own self-development and knowledge. The agency does not extend to the world. In neo-Aristotelian classicism, the writer is at the center but is limited by the emphasis on logic and the enthymeme. The social is only engaged through the rational minds of the audience. The world is static rather than changed through new knowledge. In new rhetoric, the writer is "a creator of meaning, a shaper of reality" ("Contemporary Composition" 776). The writer has agency within a transactional relationship with language and the social, historical context to produce knowledge about the world and therefore shape that world. So Berlin concludes, "In teaching writing, we are not simply offering training in a useful technical skill that is meant as a simple complement to the more important studies of other areas. We are teaching a way of experiencing the world, a way of ordering and making sense of it" (776). This fact has definite political consequences for Berlin: the textbooks and the teachers who accept them unproblematically are politically irresponsible because they are creating particular kinds of passive or ineffectual subjects. Berlin wants to create rhetorically and politically active subjects.

A third political level operates by enacting change within the discipline as a whole. If the subject can change the world via language, then Berlin's ever-shifting maps are meant to, and ultimately do, change the way the discipline views itself. Berlin wants rhetoric and compositionists to see the discipline as politically engaged and therefore valuable. If Young wants to establish disciplinary credibility through a basis in science and history, Berlin wants to create it through a basis in critical, rhetorical, and literary theory. This would place the field more squarely on the values of English as a discipline and move rhetoric away from the science/humanities divide that Berthoff wants to overcome through an emphasis on Coleridge. In many ways, Berlin's maps do accomplish this goal. As one of the most widely read rhetoricians of the 1980s, he contributes greatly to the shift in the field toward cultural studies. To accomplish this rhetorical goal, however, Berlin is always changing his maps in successive articles and books, often with no direct explanation. (Later, in *Writing Instruction in Nineteenth-Century American Colleges,* for example, Berlin brings Emerson out of the Platonic/expressivist realm and puts him in the New Rhetoric/epistemic category without referring to his earlier categorization of him in "Contemporary Composition"). This basic maneuver is important for the first political reason—Berlin is subtly realigning himself and does not want to call attention to it. But more importantly, even though Berlin acknowledges open dialectics in his historiography, he always writes his histories as if his maps are total. Presenting the face of totality is one thing that makes his maps persuasive.

A simple, clear, and stable map of the field is one that will be easily understood and therefore more likely to be taught, adopted, and disseminated. In short, it is more politically effective.

The outcome of this totalizing approach to writing histories is ultimately exclusion, as I discuss later. As Berlin points out, a way of seeing is a way of not seeing. And what increasingly is not seen by Berlin is vitalism as a distinct philosophical and epistemological perspective, as something with a history far beyond the simple notion of natural genius. His mappings in these early articles on current-traditional rhetoric and Whately reduce vitalism to natural genius, equate it with current-traditional rhetoric, and then drop the term altogether, leaving genius as the sole explicit vestige of vitalism in his work, with oppositional vitalism remaining only implicit in his work with Coleridge. Ultimately, vitalism is the repressed content, the spectre, of Berlin's maps. His continual mappings of the field that rearticulate romanticism, expressivism, and social-epistemic rhetoric seal the disappearance and forgetting of vitalism.

Rewriting Romanticism

With *Writing Instruction in Nineteenth-Century American Colleges* (1984) and *Rhetoric and Reality: Writing Instruction in American Colleges, 1900–1985* (1987), Berlin's more synchronic categories in "Contemporary Composition" are turned toward larger historical periods. In both books, Berlin is essentially tracing the split between expressivism and romanticism in more historical detail, allowing him to develop epistemic rhetoric out of a particular form of romanticism. With a focus on the nineteenth century in *Writing Instruction,* Berlin alters his previous map—neo-Aristotelian (classical), positivist (current-traditional), neo-Platonic (expressivist), and new rhetoric (epistemic)—to exclude new rhetoric and expressivism, both twentieth-century manifestations. His map in *Writing Instruction*—classical rhetoric (Aristotle and others), psychological-epistemological rhetoric (Campbell, Blair, Whately, and others), and romantic rhetoric (Ralph Waldo Emerson, American Transcendentalists, and Fred Newton Scott)—extends the arguments in his early articles. Berlin is continuing to make a distinction between current-traditional or vitalist approaches and romanticism, essentially extending his reading of Coleridge to Emerson and Scott.

In his new set of categories, the term vitalism disappears along with genius and a new one is connected to current-traditional rhetoric, now called psychological-epistemological. Berlin makes the claim that "Common Sense Realism locates reality in two distinct realms, the spiritual and the material, and posits a set of separate and likewise discrete mental faculties constituted so as to apprehend each" (*Writing Instruction* 6). Everyone has the faculty to perceive spiritual truths, but these are left up to the individual and his or her relationship with God and cannot be defined externally. Likewise with the material realm: everyone has the faculties to perceive reality "unencumbered by the interpretations of others" (6). Berlin is again linking current-traditional rhetoric and implicitly vitalism with a Cartesian epistemology—the same kind of move made by Young, Ross Winterowd, and Crowley, as noted in chapter 1. But the disappearance of vitalism into genius is now concealed further by the disappearance of both into the "spiritual." The appearance of this term is the result of further historicizing. For Berlin, rhetorics and poetics rise or fall due to social circumstances. The term spiritual arrives in his text because he is arguing that the commonsense realism of the eighteenth century corresponds epistemologically to the nineteenth-century materialistic bent in both economics and science following materialism's rejection of Aristotle and scholasticism, Protestantism's primary status in America and its rejection of Catholicism in favor of individual unmediated interpretation of the Bible, and the corresponding American value system based on the individual (33). The result of this historical congruence, however, is the further repression of oppositional and investigative vitalisms via an implicit linking of all vitalisms with mystical vitalism in the form of spirituality.[4]

In *Writing Instruction*, Berlin favors romantic rhetoric over psychological-epistemological rhetoric. He makes an argument for Emerson similar to the one he made for Coleridge in "The Rhetoric of Romanticism": for Emerson, knowledge, truth, and reality are only attainable through a dialectic among writer, reality, the social, and language (46–47). To argue for this specific type of romanticism, Berlin directly argues against the ahistorical romanticism typically used in the discipline to fit into the narrative of retreat and return. For Berlin, "It is a commonplace of contemporary discussions of rhetoric to regard the romantic frame of mind as staunchly anti-rhetorical. . . . The romantics, with their insistence on the private and personal in discovering and communicating truth, deny the inherently communal nature of art, thereby abolishing rhetoric's reason for being" (42). Again noting Young as someone who holds this position, Berlin posits Emerson as one of the best arguments against this commonplace. In order to shift Emerson from retreat to return, Berlin puts into practice a critical observation in Fulkerson's take on categorization.

Fulkerson acknowledges the problems of trying to place theorists and practices definitively in one category as opposed to another. He points out that different aims show up in unexpected places, often making theorists difficult to categorize. In *The Contemporary Writer* (1975), for example, Ross Winterowd —a person who later comes to devalue expressivism—actually promotes expressivism: "There's a very good chance that learning to do self-expressive writing will constitute the greatest benefit that you can gain from *The Contemporary Writer*" (quoted in Fulkerson 5). Fulkerson also found Peter Elbow's *Writing without Teachers* (1973) tough to classify. Elbow's pedagogy seems to put him with expressivists, but his application of them "at least in 1968" was rhetorical. In Elbow's article "A Method for Teaching Writing" (1968), he "explained that his theories of freewriting, collaborative criticism, and audience adaptation are really classical theories masquerading as modern theories" (Fulkerson 6). Fulkerson also notes that he uses journals, but for a mimetic end rather than an expressive one. A particular pedagogy or a particular person cannot be simply equated with one category in an abstract sense. Theorists change over time, and pedagogical practices can change aim in different contexts. For Fulkerson, the fact that aims are not mutually exclusive "leads to both theoretical and practical problems, not the least of which is that it gives us no direction in selecting which writing types merit greater emphasis in our courses" (7). But for Berlin, this openness to difference enables him to make finer distinctions that ultimately allow him to evaluate the epistemological bases for practices.

In "Contemporary Composition," for example, Emerson appears in the Platonic-expressivist category and Coleridge (via Berthoff) is in the new rhetoric-epistemic category. But in *Writing Instruction,* Berlin puts forward two readings of Emerson; one emphasizes his individualistic and Platonic texts and the other, his social, democratic, and rhetorical texts. He argues that the individualistic reading has been the prevailing, popular reading, which ignores Emerson's works that deal with the individual as "the center of political and social action" (43). Berlin cites Roberta Ray as an example of one who advocates a Platonic reading of Emerson. Ray places Emerson in an idealist tradition that sees reality and truth in an ideal, spiritual realm that provides a basis for material existence. The material world is only valuable as a source for metaphor, which allows the individual access to spiritual existence—God or the Over-soul, which embodies goodness, truth, and beauty. Ray places Emerson in this tradition because Emerson makes "ideal truth the product of inspiration, a gift" (45). For Berlin, Ray's position essentially overlooks Emerson's later social and political concerns. Berlin acknowledges that Emerson did have an early affinity with the works of Blair and the belles lettres tradition, but later he rejected the "commonsense" basis of Blair's work and developed his own theory and practice that is not in the Platonic tradition. He posits William Tacey as a prime example of this second reading of Emerson. From this perspective, Emerson "locates the real in the fusion of the sensual and the ideal. Reality is a human construction, joining the world of ideas to the material object in an act of creative perception" (46).[5] The ideal and the real form a polarity that functions as the source of agency carried out in the social sphere through language.

In order to further lay out his position as an extension of Tacey's, Berlin cites Richard Weaver as someone who sees this double reading in Plato, not just in Emerson. Weaver posits the potential for a public rhetoric in the *Phaedrus,* where the rhetorician as lover of the good uses dialectic and analogy to "modulate by the peculiar features of an occasion" (quoted in Berlin, *Writing Instruction* 49). But Weaver's reading of Plato does not completely equate with Berlin's reading of Emerson: "The important difference is that Emerson erects his system on a post-Kantian epistemology and a democratic egalitarianism" (49). For Plato, reality is the ideal. For Emerson, reality exists in the fusion of material and ideal across language. Contra Plato, Emerson does not see the material world as mere flux or illusion. This view denies its reality. The ideal is something the individual brings to the material world, and correspondingly, nature provides individuals with symbols of the divine. Hence, knowledge functions through this dialectic: a perceiver bringing the ideal to his or her perceptions and in return deriving the ideal from nature. As with Plato, this interaction can happen only through language, symbol, and metaphor. But for Emerson, metaphor is not the exception utilized by the philosopher, who thinks truth can be approached only through metaphor. Instead, metaphor is the norm; it is the way all language works. In "Eloquence," for example, Emerson turns this perspective on language to the functioning of democracy in America. For him, the courts, the pulpit, journalism, and town hall meetings mean that the ability to use language and analogy is necessary for citizenship in a democracy. The use of dialectic goes beyond removal of error to the relationship between idea and object, speaker and event, and differing political opinions. Through dialectic, language produces consequences in the world, not just in the mind, and becomes a form of social action (55). Though Emerson comes out of a Platonic tradition, he updates it in the light of a more modern epistemology and a more democratic social context.

These two readings of Emerson come to stand as the basis for Berlin's distinction between psychological-epistemological rhetoric (founded on the individualist reading of Plato) and romanticism (founded on a transformation of Platonic dialectics into a method of social engagement and agency). While discussing Blair earlier in his book, Berlin makes an important distinction: "Blair repeatedly emphasizes the role of genius in literature, making it the source of invention in poetry. He is *not*, however, speaking of the exalted, creative faculty of the romantics" (27; emphasis added). Blair's use of genius is something more along the lines of natural talent, a talent that is given to the individual as a gift. The romantic, creative faculty, however, is a capacity or agency that results from the dialectical interaction with the world. In the light of his new work on Emerson, Berlin can begin to make the distinction between expressivism as a function of Blair's genius and romanticism as a function of Emerson's agent.

At the end of *Writing Instruction*, in "Postscript on the Present," Berlin's map—classical (Aristotelian rhetorics such as the one John Quincy Adams published in 1810), psychological-epistemological (the eighteenth-century rhetorics of Blair, Campbell, and Whately, which influenced late-nineteenth-century current-traditional rhetoric), and romantic (rhetorics based on Emerson and Thoreau, who saw the interaction of observer and observed at the center of knowledge)—is transformed into a new map for the twentieth century. As deliberate alternatives to current-traditional rhetorics, Berlin sees three approaches working today: classical, expressive, and new rhetorical. Expressivists—William Coles, Ken Macrorie, J. Miller and S. Judy, and Donald Stewart—follow from the subjective reading of Plato, emphasizing dialogue to correct individual error and emphasizing metaphor to find fresh personal vision and expression. Rhetors in this category posit a continual dialogue but with the goal of the individual's private struggle. New rhetoricians—Peter Elbow, Ann Berthoff, and Richard Young, who are the "rhetorical descendants of Ralph Waldo Emerson and Fred Newton Scott" (90)—are read as following a social or rhetorical development that moves beyond Platonic idealism, and they are placed in the epistemic category. Berlin notes that expressivists see themselves as coming out of a romantic tradition and often invoke figures such as Emerson as precursors, but he argues that "[a]lthough expressionists commonly call upon nineteenth-century romantic rhetoric—the examples of Emerson and Thoreau—they are in my view closer to a Platonic rhetorical tradition in their theory and practice" (88). The distinction between expressivism as its own category and romanticism as a subset of new rhetoric echoes his work in "Contemporary Composition" and sets the stage for his next book.

The Emergence of Expressivism

In Berlin's next historical book, *Rhetoric and Reality,* which is devoted to the twentieth century, he traces the linear development of both expressive and epistemic rhetorics as reactions to the current-traditionalism of the late nineteenth century—even as current-traditional rhetoric continued to dominate during the twentieth century. To manage an analysis of these developments, Berlin breaks the century into twenty-year blocks and breaks his map into three primary categories: objective theories, subjective theories, and transactional theories. Under the genus objective theories, Berlin charts the continuance of current-traditional rhetoric and the development of behaviorist, semanticist, and structural linguistic approaches to rhetoric.[6] The twentieth century also sees the expansion of subjective theories via the development of expressivism in the form of liberal rhetorics, American Freudian and post-Freudian psychologies, and the growing dominance of expressive approaches to writing. Within transactional theories, Berlin posits three species: classical, cognitive, and epistemic. In order to continue following the disappearance of vitalism, it is necessary to focus on the development of subjective theories with an eye toward epistemic rhetorics.

The dual reading of Emerson in *Writing Instruction* allows Berlin to make more detailed historical distinctions between expressivism and romanticism in *Rhetoric and Reality*. Emerson now shows up in Berlin's initial description of subjective theories: "The most obvious historical precedents for this approach are in Plato, and, more recently, in one of the strands of Emerson's thought on rhetoric" (11). The implication of course is that there is more than one strand of Emerson's thought. At this juncture, Berlin posits two subjectivist readings based on Plato: an idealist reading coming out of Blair and a more social reading coming out of Weaver. Berlin brings up Emerson while discussing subjective theories not because he thinks Emerson himself belongs in this category but because romantic critics in the twentieth century invoke him as a precursor. When they do, according to Berlin, they are invoking either the Blairian idealist reading or Weaver's social reading. Both readings lead to subjective theories, however, because the epistemology of each is based on the individual. Weaver's reading allows positive knowledge through metaphor, not just the ability to correct error. But even though positive knowledge is now partially communicable to an audience, knowledge still rests with the individual, who in the first version must discover truth and, in the second reading, must confirm truth "through a private act of intuition" (*Rhetoric and Reality* 13).

Rather than appear in conjunction with current-traditional positivism, genius and spirit are now taken up by various subjective theories advocated by domesticated Freudianism, aesthetic expressivism, and aristocratic/liberal culture. Berlin reads Freud's unconscious as mutating into a popular form of philosophical idealism. The unconscious functions as the spiritual, pre-linguistic ground of the individual. When transferred to literary and composition practice, unconscious methods focus on the individual, chance, and metaphor. This watered-down Freud works its way into literary and writing theory via liberal culture and a general sentiment of aesthetic expressivism. Berlin begins his discussion of liberal culture in his analysis of 1900 to 1920 by quickly establishing his objective, subjective, transactional map: current-traditionalism is objective, positivistic, and democratic in a way—it opens education to middle and lower classes—but ultimately supports meritocracy; liberal culture is subjective, focuses on individual genius, emphasizes writing for the goal of self-cultivation (52), and is fundamentally aristocratic; and progressive movements are largely transactional and democratic, focusing on the social as both ends and means.

The important category in terms of Berlin's placement of vitalism is liberal culture. With its aristocratic bent, this approach to education sought to foster a "few geniuses" who were "gifted" (43). And, the goal was to make these men more "spiritual" (44). The belles lettres tradition of Blair resurfaces in liberal culture, which is founded on what Berlin terms "Brahminical romanticism" (44). This is Berlin's first mention of this species of romanticism. Deriving the name from Brahma—Hindi for the ultimate ground of all being—Berlin claims this version of romanticism holds "that all material reality has a spiritual foundation" (44) and that the goal of this approach to education and art is to get from the material to the spiritual. Art and literature take over the job of religion —to create a "soul state" or a particular type of subjectivity. This brand of romanticism redeploys older forms of mystical or idealist vitalism—the type of vitalism Berlin argued that Coleridge never ascribed to, especially in terms of gift and genius, as I argue in chapter 1. Berlin simply created another term for it in order to begin a move away from the term romanticism altogether.

Berlin clearly sees liberal culture founded on Brahminical romanticism as the basis for the development of expressivism. He writes, "The educational ideal of liberal culture did not survive as a major force, despite its outspoken proponents at some of the most prestigious schools in the nation," and he mentions Glenn Palmer of the University of Kansas, the Yale model, the Harvard plan, Charles

Osgood of Princeton, Hiram Corson and Lane Cooper at Cornell, William Phelps at Yale, and Frank Aydelotte at Indiana (46). Liberal culture had successors, including American Critical Idealism and elitist New Humanism, but it "also maintained the academic tie with romantic thought—however Brahminical the version—and this had its effects on an egalitarian conception of expressionistic rhetoric that appeared in the twenties" (46). In his analysis of 1920 to 1940, Berlin reiterates this connection: the liberal culture of 1900 to 1920 that focused on the aristocracy, genius, and retirement from active life to contemplation created the climate for the expressivism of the next twenty-year period. Earlier radical and political uses of art gave way to subjective, expressive, and aesthetic uses and values. To designate this shift, Berlin brings in two new terms—mandarin and patrician—to add further distinctions from Brahminical romanticism. Berlin writes, "Liberal culture helped create a climate in which expressionistic rhetoric could develop, but the sources of expressionism are far from a nineteenth-century mandarin romanticism" (73). Mandarin—a person of position or influence in a literary circle—must refer to Coleridge and Emerson. His statement connotes a development away from the nineteenth-century romanticisms of Coleridge and Emerson and into liberal culture and then expressivism.

Liberal culture is not the only precursor to expressivism. In the context of 1920 to 1940, Berlin argues, "[t]he origin of [expressionistic] rhetoric can [also] be found in the postwar, Freudian-inspired, expressionistic notions of childhood education that the progressives attempted to propagate" (73). These pedagogies combined doctrines of self-expression, liberty, iconoclastic individualism, psychological adjustment, and social reform. Children were encouraged to develop their own ideas and potential free from intervention.[7] Popular Freudianism encouraged the recognition of the unconscious as the source of truth, arguing for the necessity to throw off repression. For Berlin, both the aesthetic and psychoanalytic dimensions of this pedagogy aimed for individual rather than, or as a means of, social transformation. Expressivism, then, comes out of "an unlikely union of patrician romanticism, aesthetic expressionism, and a domesticated Freudianism" (74). Berlin slips this distinction in as well, linking this type of romanticism to the aristocratic person of cultivation espoused by liberal culture; he claims earlier that if we democratize Brahminical romanticism, "we are in the realm of expressionistic rhetoric" (73), and his exposition shows that this elitist notion of the literary life has become the desired norm for all schoolchildren.

Poetics and Pedagogy

In the rest of *Rhetoric and Reality,* Berlin extends this new map through the twentieth century up to 1975. Expressivist rhetoricians of the twenties such as Raymond Weaver, Allan Gilbert, Calvin Johnson, Adele Bildersee, and others espouse genius, personal expression, and writing as art and mystery, all of which, for Berlin, leads to the rise of creative writing (79). The development of New Criticism plays an important contribution to the rise of poetics in the form of expressivism. Joel Spingarn, who relies largely on Benedetto Croce's idealism, opposes historical and philological literary criticism in a lecture entitled "The New Criticism," delivered in 1910. In it, he calls for critics to examine literary works of art without any preconceptions, as one creative mind to another. This method relies on intuition and private vision, "providing a counterpart in poetic to the expressionistic rhetoric of the period" (Berlin 81). From 1940 to 1960, New Criticism provided an approach to literary criticism and the teaching of literature that functioned as a basis for literary studies as a discipline. English departments began to argue against any form of teaching writing that did not involve the study of literature. Many argued that since English teachers were teaching composition, the course should focus on literature since it is the basis of their scholarship. Others argued that "writing about social or political essays . . . resulted in superficiality" (108). But Berlin argues that this move is, at least in part, a function of the time period. A new critical focus on the text itself in literature and composition courses was "safe." The call for linking literature and composition rather than addressing social issues is obvious in the context of the 1950s: academics did not want to call for social solutions and appear soft on communism (109–10). Thus they argue against the communications emphasis and the social rhetoric of the 1920s through 1940, which focused on understanding propaganda in the light of the war.

This poetic legacy, according to Berlin, is bequeathed to the expressivism of the 1960s and early 1970s. Berlin continues his dual reading of Plato—one subjective, the other more social—into this period. Each version, as noted earlier, still shares the same epistemology: truth is discovered by the individual through an examination of his or her inner life. The world is lifeless matter, the social a force that coerces the individual's apprehension of truth. For Berlin, the excesses of this expressivist epistemology lead to an anarchistic extreme. Domesticated Freudianism and Brahminical romanticism develop into a writing pedagogy that espouses unlimited freedom and the usurpation of all convention, all in the name of the individual. Berlin cites S. I. Hayakawa's analogy between the classroom and group psychotherapy, and his recommendation of freewriting as practiced by surrealist poets. The view of writing as art emphasizes art as original expression that defies traditional, community commonplaces. In each composition theorist Berlin cites—Margaret Blanchard, Harold Simonson, Leslie Fiedler, Ken Macrorie, Lou Kelly—expression is always self-expression.

In the late 1960s, this expressive tradition of teacherless pedagogy turns political. One version, for Berlin, comes out of an extreme individualist and subjective reading of Plato, which fosters the emergence of "composition as a happening" (150). Composition pedagogues such as Charles Deemer, Leo Hamilton and James Hatch, and William Lutz advocate the breaking down of authority in the classroom by creating scenes in which the students would participate. The goal is to shock students out of their complacency by staging a scene—having discussions in the dark, making students speak to the wall, listening to music during discussions or listening to music in different settings—then having students write about their experience of it. Their responses were intended to be aleatory, and thus any grading system had to be disregarded. The other extreme, coming out of Weaver's reading of Plato, consists of a few expressivists who are close to transactional theories and epistemic rhetoric. For Berlin, "[t]hese rhetoricians see reality as arising out of the interaction of the private vision of the individual and the language used to express this vision" (146). These rhetorics fall short of being epistemic because the dialectic they support does not involve all the elements of the communications triangle. Or in Berlin's words, they deny "the place of intersubjective, social processes in shaping reality" (146).

In the other version, figures such as Walker Gibson, William Coles, Donald Murray, and Peter Elbow—whom Berlin characterized as epistemic at the end of *Writing Instruction*—attempt to take the social into consideration while avoiding the "excesses" of solipsism and anarchy. Murray argues that individualism and freedom should be valued without rejecting teacher and student responsibility. Coles emphasizes a literary self rather than a political self, and for Berlin the "emphasis on the place of language in shaping the self does save Murray and Coles, as well as a number of other leaders of their group, from some of the excesses of their contemporaries" (152). Considering language to be an important element in the shaping of the individual generates a more rigorous analysis and utilization of language and dialectics, not only between the individual and language but also between the individual and peer review groups. The premise behind both the open-ended pedagogies and the language-based pedagogies is that the personal is already a function of the political, so to change the person is to effect political change. But in the end, for Berlin, this focus on the personal devalues teaching and the social. In short, he judges it insufficient because its epistemology is not fully transactional.

Berlin's new distinctions between mandarin romanticism, Brahminical romanticism, and patrician romanticism allow him to separate Coleridge and Emerson from these later historical developments into twentieth-century expressivisms.[8] It is Blair's subject that influences twentieth-century romanticism and expressivism, not Coleridge's or Emerson's. In twentieth-century expressivisms, the subject is passive to nature, spirit, or the unconscious. It is the active, creative subject that grounds the historical movement into transactional and epistemic rhetoric. Because *Rhetoric and Reality* focuses on the twentieth century, Coleridge and Emerson do not figure prominently. But the link back to their romanticism is made through Fred Newton Scott, who is both a late-nineteenth- and an early-twentieth-century figure. In Berlin's *Writing Instruction in Nineteenth-Century American Colleges*, Scott is the rhetorician who extends Berlin's dialectical reading of Emerson into the American pragmatism of William James and the educational theories of John Dewey. Berlin reads Scott as one of the primary people trying to pose pedagogical alternatives to current-traditional rhetoric. The key difference is that each has a different metaphor for the mind: current-traditional rhetoric sees the mind as a machine, while Scott's romanticism functions on an organic metaphor. Rather than a machine with parts that make up a mechanistic whole, "meaning grows, with a variety of mental operations occurring simultaneously, as the perceiver, a unique whole, brings all of his past experiences to the particular situation" (84). As Berlin notes, quoting Gertrude Buck, this is a "vital process"—"a living product of an active creative mind" (84). It is Scott who brings this other romantic tradition into the twentieth century and engenders the genealogical path Berlin traces into epistemic rhetoric in *Rhetoric and Reality*.

It should be clear at this point that the histories Berlin wants to trace out of Coleridge can be read as a particular kind of vitalism, and not one necessarily grounded in natural genius. Berlin makes these distinctions in detail, but it is the connection to vitalism that gets lost in his articulations of expressivism and development of epistemic rhetoric. Berlin's mapping of expressivism is trying to deal with the shifting complexity of romanticisms, but vitalism, even in its mystical form, gets excluded. Vitalism shifts from a function of current-traditionalism, to Brahminical and patrician romanticism, to expressivism, and it is essentially excluded from his examination of transactional rhetorics. Because vitalism is disregarded as a term, and especially as a historical development, its evolution from oppositional, to investigative, to complex is forgotten—it has no place in Berlin's cartography.

History and Dialectics

After following Berlin's histories that shift mystical vitalism into current-traditional rhetoric and then into expressivism in order to separate it from the romanticism of Coleridge, Emerson, and Scott, it is clear that this particular form of romanticism grounds his future work, most specifically his concept of dialectics. There are a number of possible ways to read Coleridge's dialectics: as Platonic, as Cartesian, as Coleridgean, or as Hegelian. Berlin makes it clear that he sees Coleridge's dialectical method as something more than a reiteration of Plato or reduction to Descartes. While it is tempting to conflate Coleridge's method with the prevailing scientific method of his day, this clearly ignores the fact that Coleridge sees his method as a dialectic between Plato's more idealist model and Bacon's more empirical one. Likewise, while it is clear that Coleridge is a Platonist of sorts, a reduction of his model to Plato ignores the way he updates Plato. In "The Rhetoric of Romanticism," Berlin intermixes his reading of Coleridge's dialectics with Owen Barfield's reading. In *What Coleridge Thought*, Barfield notes that the "polarity between subject and object, which is at the base of Coleridge's system, is nowhere to be found in Plato" (125). Plato's dialectic is essentially a function of the dialogue between two people. Coleridge's dialectic is between a person's mind and the world expressed primarily through language, art, writing—poetry in Coleridge's sense. Berlin is interested in the way Coleridge's method is continually generative of the subject through interpretation. But the more open-ended, organic aspects of Coleridge's dialectical model fall away in favor of a synthetic, Hegelian reading as Berlin begins to apply this dialectical model to history and his emerging political and pedagogical interests.

In the same year *Rhetoric and Reality* was published (1987), Berlin's "Revisionary History: The Dialectical Method" appeared in *Pre/Text*. This article identifies his historiography as revisionary and situates this approach as a three-way dialectic among history, language, and the subject. On the one hand, Berlin accepts the fact that historical context has a primary influence on events. He states explicitly in *Writing Instruction in Nineteenth-Century American Colleges* that the book is predicated more on "attending to the social conditions that made one kind of rhetoric possible and another kind inevitable" to buffer his "predilection for romantic rhetoric" (12). On the other hand, Berlin's emphasis on epistemic rhetoric is ultimately grounded in language, since all the elements are, at least in part, verbal constructs. Berlin writes, "In epistemic rhetoric there is never a division between experience and language, whether the experience involves the subject, the subject and other subjects, or the subject and the material world. All experiences, even the scientific and the logical, are grounded in language, and language determines content and structure. And just as language structures our response to social and political issues, language structures our response to the material world" (*Rhetoric and Reality* 16). Language, discourse, and ideology necessarily frame the historian's response to historical conditions. However, in "Revisionary History" the subject becomes the center of the dialectic. For Berlin, subjects are "as much determined by their own historical moment as they are determiners of it" (55). Individual participants can determine history because they are interpreters of it through language. For Berlin, historians have the agency to rationally and consciously understand their ideological, interpretive framework, to state it up front in their analyses, and to choose which historical elements to include and which to exclude: revisionary historians need "to choose rather than passively be chosen—to be dialectically engaged subjects rather than simple interpellated subjects" (58). The call is clearly for the Emersonian subject who has the agency to engage and create the social as opposed to the Blairian subject who is passive to the world.

This emphasis on the subject, however, begins moving Berlin's approach toward a more Hegelian dialectic in a subjective, objective, and teleological sense. William Desmond, in *Beyond Hegel and Dialectic,* sees subjectivism as another aspect of Hegelian ontology; he writes, "I find a certain logic in Hegelian thinking that repeats itself throughout the entirety of the system; this is the logic of what I call 'dialectical self-mediation,' . . . [which] includes a reference to what is other, but also always ends by including that other as a subordinate moment within a more encompassing self-mediating whole" (2). In Hegel, all mediation is self-mediation. Berlin's attempt to balance opposing, conflicting concepts and worlds also falls back on the personal, individual consciousness of the mediator, even though it is tempered by language and history. As Desmond puts it, "The thought of everything other to thought risks getting finally reduced to a moment of thought thinking itself" (7). Berlin's use of dialectics and mapping is also susceptible to this charge. Everything the historiographer attempts to mediate is reduced to that historiographer's framework. In thinking his or her Other—history—the active, engaged historiographer is thinking himself or herself. This folding back onto the self, this inability to finally attend to the Other, creates the inevitable blind spot as a result of Berlin's mapping. Dialectics is always self-dialectics: the self's interpretive framework is always to a certain degree reductive to that particular perspective; Berlin's maps will let him see only what he wants to see and, therefore, will necessarily forget the Other, history.

Berlin's dialectical method can also toggle over and succumb to objectivity. The primary political goal in this revisionary historiography is to bring to the surface excluded rhetorics and rhetoricians. The dominant rhetorics in any period emerge as winners of past historical, social, and economic forces, but these struggles always produce resistant rhetorics as well that are covered over, lost through the production of dominant histories. In order to create political effects in the present, the revisionary historian must go back and bring these histories to light. Berlin calls for plurality because it makes possible a better understanding of competing ideologies at any historical moment: "plurality will lead to clarification" ("Revisionary History" 57). His claim is that stating the interpretive framework up front and acknowledging a plurality of rhetorics will make it clear that histories are not objective. But his call to openness implies a unity and synthesis. In working for more inclusion, he is working for historical accuracy, for a history that is more objective, even though he claims that complete objectivity can never finally be achieved. This end-goal is actually at the heart of Berlin's historiography and politics. He still believes we can get to a better place—a "better judgment," "enlightenment," (58) or "better classes," or a "better body politic" (60). The path, the dialectic, is not completely open. Berlin falls into his own brand of enlightenment idealism: "Out of the competing versions will come enlightenment about the ideological nature of rhetoric" (58). Through active, subjective agency Berlin is touting objectivity—both objective, historical facts, and an objective, a teleological goal.

The real problem with Berlin's dialectical model is its teleological movement toward reification, which brings an open-ended interpretation of Coleridge's dialectic to a halt. In theory, Berlin is working with an open Coleridgean dialectic. But in practice, both historiographically and pedagogically, a synthetic Hegelian dialectic is also at work. He is working toward a better history, toward a better pedagogy, toward social-epistemic rhetoric. This dialectic of open/closed dialectics appears implicitly in the construction of *Rhetoric and Reality*. At the level of species, within the epistemic category, a Coleridgean dialectic is privileged. But at the level of genus, the book is constructed across a definite Hegelian model—objective, subjective, transactional. The implication is that the teleological movement is toward improvement, toward epistemic rhetoric. His way of dealing with this "paradox" of competing dialectics—of arguing for openness and totality, of arguing against objectivity, then calling for it—is not surprisingly to imply a dialectic of dialectics. Berlin closes "Revisionary History" with a crucial claim about interpretive frameworks. He calls upon T. W. Adorno's notion of negative dialectics in order to argue that the dialectic of historiography must "see the individual from the perspective of the whole, the concrete through the concept—in other words, [it must] offer a totalizing perspective, an account that purports to cover everything, leaving nothing unexplained" (58). But Adorno recognizes "that no version of the total can ever stand unquestioned, that no formulation of whole . . . can ever be reliable" (58). New historical facts can always overturn the previous conception of the whole. Nevertheless, the subjective history must operate as if it were objective.

The problem is that even if historians take this stance—realizing that in theory their maps are not total while using them *as if* they are—in practice readers can and will take the maps as total. Many teachers and scholars in the discipline of rhetoric and composition have imagined that Berlin's categories correspond to the territory of the field, even though Berlin knows they do not. As he notes, "The new historian must resist the urge to reduce all rhetorics to a master template . . . that is, to a few dominant patterns inevitably present in every time and place" (56). But this is precisely what happens to his maps. As a general acceptance of Berlin's maps by a majority of teachers and researchers in rhetoric and composition takes hold, the function of historical context gets lost. Berlin's maps change because the historical period he is examining changes, and teachers in the discipline tacitly accept his categories—no matter how generalized—because they do, in part, correspond to practices being advocated and practiced in the discipline at particular times. But just as pedagogical practices become reified by the time they make their way into textbooks, Berlin's maps become reified as they are generally accepted by the discipline. And the same thing happens to Berlin himself. Though his earlier maps trace diverse historical practices and their bases in epistemology, they lead him to a preferred position and definitive determinations: this epistemology is bad and this one is good, this politics is bad and this one is good, this pedagogy is bad and this one is good, regardless of the historical context. And once that position is clearly delineated in his mind, he turns from his historical mapping toward pedagogical implementation of his program, removing the possibility that his thought would continue an open historical development.

The Turn to Social-Epistemic Rhetoric

Berlin's final map, of the 1980s, appears just after *Rhetoric and Reality* and turns his work from history toward pedagogy and politics. As Berlin is working out his historiography, he writes "Rhetoric and Ideology in the Writing Class" (1988), in which he designates rhetoric—the central mediating principle of a dialectic between material forces and individuals—as the realm of the ideological, turning the dialectic to focus on language. Following Goran Therborn's *The Ideology of Power and the Power of Ideology,* Berlin situates both rhetoric and power within ideology and posits ideology as the discursive space where we formulate what exists, what is good, and what is possible through a dialectical/social exchange. Berlin's objective, subjective, transactional map from *Rhetoric and Reality* is represented in the three rhetorics he chooses to examine: cognitive psychology, expressivism, and social-epistemic rhetoric. By shifting his primary term from epistemology to ideology, Berlin now has a new position from which to judge rhetorics, one that is decidedly political. For Berlin, an objectivist stance such as that exhibited in cognitive psychology "encourages discursive practices that are compatible with the dominant economic, social and political formations" ("Rhetoric and Ideology" 478). Expressivist rhetorics oppose the scientism of objective rhetorics, but because they focus on the individual as the seat of power they are also open to supporting capitalism. Social-epistemic rhetoric, however, makes ideology the center of the classroom and thus provides a self-corrective, dialectical element that allows it to avoid such co-option.

This essay is the first time Berlin sets up the term or category social-epistemic after having set up epistemic in *Writing Instruction* and the genus transactional in *Rhetoric and Reality.* By adding the social to epistemic, Berlin is distinguishing himself from the other rhetorics that he has previously included in the epistemic category: he is refining his epistemic category politically—rather than epistemologically—to place value on a particular type of epistemic rhetoric. In Berlin's usage, social has three meanings, each moving from general to particular: (1) social context (the general condition that makes a dialectic among the elements of the communications triangle possible—the basis of epistemic rhetoric), (2) social construction (the next level of specificity that recognizes language as the central, determining element in the communications triangle), and (3) socialist politics (the specific political agenda that comes from placing ideology at the center and recognizing language's use as a political tool).

This last perspective sets the groundwork for Berlin's pedagogy. Berlin's social-epistemic pedagogy focuses on the subject, who is a "social construct that emerges through the linguistically circumscribed interaction of the individual, the community, and the material world" ("Rhetoric and Ideology" 489). It is important to note that each of these elements is its own entity but is set in a "social" relationship to the others. Consequently, "this is not to say that individuals do not ever act as individuals. It is to assert, however, that they never act with complete freedom" (489). Each element has an effect on the other elements. Each individual element is a source of agency. This is the agency Berlin wants to awaken in his students. For him, social-epistemic rhetoric offers explicit critiques of economic, political, and social orders, and he posits Ira Shor as his primary example of social-epistemic pedagogy. Shor argues that teachers must make students aware of the ways they are controlled and denied their "full humanity" in a way that would empower "students to be their own agents for social change, their own creators of democratic culture" (quoted in Berlin 490).

Following Paulo Freire and the so-called Hegelian Marxists of the Frankfurt School, Berlin argues that the goal of such a pedagogy is to "externalize false consciousness" (491). The students are to be exposed to an epistemological awakening from reification, pre-scientific thinking, acceleration, and mystifications. Social-epistemic pedagogy sets out to persuade students that change is possible, that their identities and social positions are neither fixed nor natural, that luck and chance are not the source of social arrangements, that the sensory bombardment of urban life and popular entertainment disrupts critical thinking, and that, despite being told they live in a free country, they are "systematically denied opportunities" arbitrarily (490–91). Berlin imagines the teacher and student in a mutual dialogue, participating as equals working toward a "liberatory classroom" (491) via the creation of a "liberated consciousness" (492). For Berlin, "self-autonomy and self-fulfillment are thus possible not through becoming detached from the social, but through resisting those social influences that alienate and disempower" (491).

Basing social-epistemic rhetoric on a socialist ideology, Berlin wants to replace current-traditional and expressive pedagogies with a heuristics that focuses on enlightening students and bringing them out of false consciousness. But in "Freirean Pedagogy in the U.S.: A Response" (1992) Berlin explicitly shows his ideological wares in a way that, at least potentially, exposes him to critique from his own position. For him, "[t]he codes, scripts, or terministic screens that define individuals as helpless ciphers can be replaced by narratives that enable democratic participation in creating a more equitable distribution of the necessities and pleasures of life" (415). Here Berlin exposes his desire to interpellate students into his own ideology. He wants to replace narratives of cynicism with narratives that position the students to *believe* they can change the world. However, his blanket belief in consciousness over history creates problems. Berlin has yet to explain how this change is possible. He says it is possible through dialectic but does not explain how the use of dialectic can create a predictable historical outcome—a particular change in students or their life conditions. By touting an uncritical progressivism, Berlin is interpellating his students into an ahistorical belief. In the 1960s, students believed they could change the world and they did—even though some would argue that the change was only slight or temporary. This belief made them mobilize and come together as a group, rather than as individuals, to call for change. But this belief cannot be a general principle: it cannot be generalized into a method that is not tied to a particular historical time and place. This belief worked in the sixties because particular circumstances set the stage for it. But if historical circumstances are such that this belief in and of itself is not enough to generate change, students can come to believe that they cannot change the world to correspond to their desire. In practice, Berlin's position has the potential to transform itself into its opposite—cynicism.

In their introduction to *Cultural Studies in the English Classroom* (1992), Berlin and Michael Vivion posit another claim that privileges consciousness over history, rationality over nonrationality. For them, "teaching students the methods of critical inquiry peculiar to cultural studies while expecting them to arrive at predetermined conclusions offers only the pretense of critique" (xv). This assertion is troubling in two related ways. First of all, if teachers do as Berlin suggests and lay bare their ideological wares at the beginning of a course, they are prefiguring the types of conclusions they expect their students to reach once the students have done their semiotic analyses. Whether consciously or unconsciously, explicitly or implicitly, teachers are telling students exactly what Berlin is telling all of rhetoric and composition when he maps out the field: here are your positions, and here is my position, and I am going to persuade you to adopt my position. This is a closed system: the end result is a predetermined progress toward a better class, or a better pedagogy, or a better subjectivity, or a better politics. This is a teleological system. However, the second problem lies in the acceptance of Berlin's words here. Even if we take Berlin's call to openness at face value, what will be the outcome? If teachers do not have predetermined positions for their students, if they are not trying to change students politically, then students will often continue to believe what they believed before the course began. Hence, Berlin feels that he must state his ideological position up front if he hopes to persuade the students. But this "openness" establishes a predetermined, desired conclusion—it can close off other possible outcomes, close off invention.

Berlin has to state his position up front and he has to put faith in the power of rationality and the free individual: if teachers display rational readings of injustice for their students, he surmises, surely they will be persuaded by the just. For his pedagogy to work, rationality has to overcome the historical and cultural position of the students and their irrational desires.[9] But he does not take into account the fact that justice is also situational, and, yes, irrational. Just because teachers point out sexism in our culture to a sexist male student does not mean that he will then become less sexist. He does not necessarily have an investment in women's struggles, since he is male; if feeling threatened, he might become defensive and even more sexist. Furthermore, social-epistemic composition teachers can also become frustrated because they cannot rationally change these students. Again, cynicism may be the outcome of Berlin's theory as it is put into practice. Teachers cannot predict the outcome of their pedagogy any more than historiographers can predict history. Remember that Fulkerson recognizes the problem with evaluating practices: the aims are not mutually exclusive, a fact that "leads to both theoretical and practical problems, not the least of which is that it gives us no direction in selecting which writing types merit greater emphasis in our courses" ("Four Philosophies" 7). Berlin's use of (synchronic) epistemology rather than (diachronic) pedagogy initially allows him to bypass the problem of evaluating practices based on ends. But when he comes to call for his own pedagogy, the problem returns: he can no longer unproblematically ignore the arbitrary outcomes of aims. These are in the realm of complexity and context, not teleology and progress.[10] Berlin begins with an emphasis on history and language. But once he shifts his emphasis to the subject and pedagogy, history is forgotten. And more specifically, the history of vitalism beyond Coleridge is excluded, with all its developing philosophies of flow, time, movement, and complexity.

Forgotten History

The problem is that Berlin's first-year pedagogy cannot account for the complexity of change, of history. In "Rhetoric and Ideology in the Writing Class," Berlin adopts the position on ideology proffered by Goran Therborn. But Berlin does not clarify and adopt Therborn's theory of change to show how this applies to his composition pedagogy. Therborn, in *The Ideology of Power and the Power of Ideology,* attempts to take Louis Althusser to task for his deterministic, scientific view of Marxism (Berlin makes a similar critique of Foucault in "Revisionary History"). In some senses, Therborn is with Althusser in that he sees ideology as creating our potential subject positions. But he harkens back to a historical materialism that attempts to deal with historical change. Therborn characterizes Althusser's model as positing four stages: interpellation, subjection, recognition, guarantee. Therborn sees the problem in the last step. For him, even if individuals are hailed, there is no guarantee they will be "qualified" to heed the call. Therborn's first move is to make a distinction between personality and subjectivity. Personality is the set of characteristics a person develops from childhood through libidinal energies, a pre-subjectivity. Subjectivity is the social position that society constructs for a person to occupy. This allows Therborn to posit a theory of change based on a rather basic Hegelian dialectic. *Thesis:* a person is hailed and his or her personality is adequate to fit with the subject position. *Antithesis:* due to historical, social, or economic reasons either an individual's personality changes so that it is no longer compatible with the subject position, or the society changes and that role becomes obsolete. Either way, for Therborn, there can be a disjunction between personality and subjectivity based on historical developments. *Synthesis:* this disjunction results in a shift in subject position for which an individual will be qualified.

Though Berlin does not discuss or explain this theory of change, I surmise that he wants his pedagogy to do one of two things: raise the student's consciousness in a way that creates a disjunction between personality and subjectivity, allowing him or her to recognize the possibility of choosing among a set of already multiple subject positions, or raise the consciousness of the student so he or she can choose to band together collectively to change the historical conditions, thereby creating a disjunction between personality and subjectivity. In either case, Berlin is sidestepping Therborn's recognition that it is historical or social change that creates the disjunction. And each case assumes a liberal, humanist subject free of historical forces and able to choose.

Instead of Therborn's dialectic, Berlin opts to focus on Therborn's notion of the possible. In this matrix of subjection-qualification, Therborn sees three predominant ideological questions as constituting the workings of ideology: what exists, what is good, and what is possible. For him, liberal humanists tend to focus on what is good, while Marxists tend to focus on what exists and what is good. Neither, he claims, focus on what is possible. His primary example of how these ideological questions work within his dialectic is generational change. If material conditions do not change, parents will raise the next generation on what is good and the children will assume the subject positions of the previous generation. However, if conditions change, the second generation will focus on what exists and what is possible. They will recognize the existing disjunction between their personalities and the roles provided and attempt to adjust accordingly, either dropping out or adopting new, possible personalities. What is possible is clearly tied to the historical and material conditions that exist. Therborn goes on to map what he sees as the primary possible subject positions for (practically) every society in a somewhat complex matrix, and he seems to assume that this charts the territory. But again, Berlin opts to sidestep the historical role in the process of change that is explicit in Therborn's theory. Instead, Berlin wants to replace narratives of what exists with what is possible. And for Berlin, it is possible to choose otherwise.

I am anticipating Berlin at this point. He does not discuss Paul Smith's notion of the subject until "Postmodernism, Politics, and Histories of Rhetoric" (1990)—two years after "Rhetoric and Ideology in the Writing Class." Following Smith, Berlin comes to see the subject as already divided and multiple and therefore it is always possible to choose a different subject position.[11] This theory of the subject, then, circumvents Therborn's emphasis on material, historical change as the catalyst for changes in subjectivity. The individual is not completely free and ideology still designates subject positions, but for Berlin the individual is free within a set of given possible subject positions regardless of history.

In "Determinacy and Indeterminacy in the Theory of Ideology," Nicholas Abercrombie, Stephen Hill, and Bryan Turner review Therborn's book. While they applaud his attempt to deal with change, they critique him for turning ideology into what amounts to sociological role theory. They claim this really reduces the force of his historical materialism. For them, Therborn never really discusses resistance (i.e., what the power of ideology really is). Therborn is working with a materialist approach, at least on one level. But their most pertinent critique is that Therborn does not see in his personality/subjectivity distinction that these personalities and subjectivities have *bodies*. This is the kind of materialism they say Therborn cannot account for. He cannot really deal with something like Foucault's medicalization.[12] His fairly simplistic dialectic reduces the ideological complexity that puts bodies into a matrix of power/ knowledge to regulate it, normalize it, and monitor it. In other words, Therborn posits an individual subject to historical forces but unconstrained by complex disciplinary forces on bodies. Berlin's theory avoids this as well. In order to promote his socialist ideology—what is good—Berlin has to make his students believe that change is possible, that they have free individual agency regardless of history and disciplinarity. In the process, historical and social complexity is forgotten and is repressed in favor of possibility and progress—the interpretation of Coleridge's dialectic moves from an open-ended and continual dialectical development of the subject in relation to the world to the development of the social toward specific utopian possibilities.

In her essay "Composition's Ethic of Service, the Universal Requirement, and the Discourse of Student Need," Sharon Crowley, citing Michael Murphy's "After Progressivism," points out that Berlin's "progressivist baggage" makes it easy for social-epistemic rhetoric to be co-opted by institutional forms of ideology (quoted in Crowley 251). This co-option is ironic because it is Berlin's charge against expressivist rhetorics in "Rhetoric and Ideology in the Writing Class" (487). Because Berlin is invested in the idea that we can teach change in the composition classroom, he cannot see that the first-year course and current-traditional rhetoric are forces that cannot be changed so easily. The first-year composition course is fully entrenched in the institution, thanks in part to the strong ethic of service in composition studies. Berlin does not take into account the fact that his site of resistance has full institutional legitimacy. Rather than being persuaded by social-epistemic rhetoric, composition teachers are caught in the historical and institutional forces that support current-traditional rhetoric. They are regulated by the discipline and disciplined by the institution and course. Social-epistemic rhetoric, rather than winning over composition teachers and students, is assimilated into the first-year course and reified just like current-traditional rhetoric. Berlin's adherence to progressivism (his belief in teleological change for the better) and his forgetting of history and disciplinarity keep him from seeing that social-epistemic rhetoric cannot defeat current-traditional rhetoric, according to Crowley, as long as he continues to promote the first-year course. He needs first-year composition to stage his ideological clash, to set up a dialectic, but because of the first-year course he cannot overcome its predominant rhetoric.

By believing he can persuade teachers and students to adopt social-epistemic rhetoric via social-epistemic rhetoric despite institutional and historical forces, Berlin has to forget history, forget disciplinarity, and forget his own unconscious, nonrational pedagogical desire in order to focus solely on individual, rational consciousness. Given this pedagogical, ideological desire, he forgets, or never fully sees, vitalism as a theory of complexity and bodily (tacit/unconscious) knowledge. Just as Young reduces vitalism for the sake of disciplinarity,

Berlin forgets it for the sake of politics. When Berlin turns to his pedagogical and ideological maps, he remains stuck in the nineteenth century with Coleridge, Hegel, and Marx. Despite the fact that Berlin bases his entire project on Daniel Fogarty's articulation of current-traditional rhetoric and call for developing a new rhetoric based on a philosophy for contemporary times, Berlin's philosophical basis never moves beyond the nineteenth century. Even though he argues for contemporary science over positivism and commonsense realism, invoking Einstein and Heisenberg, his predilection for nineteenth-century philosophy keeps him from moving into complexity.[13] This grounding in a particular constellation of nineteenth-century theorists leads him to privilege the conscious mind over a more complete understanding of learning that includes bodily epistemologies and their complex relationships with the world. By accepting Young's reduction of vitalism to mystical genius, Berlin fails to see an alternative reading of Coleridge as an oppositional vitalist. Such a reading engenders an ulterior genealogy that can extend the philosophical basis of Berlin's work into the twentieth century. The move to begin this new genealogy starts with Paul Kameen's reading of Coleridge in "Rewording the Rhetoric of Composition," another work that appeared in 1980.

REMAPPING

METHOD

Because he was teaching at the University of Pittsburgh at the time, Paul Kameen was a part of the academic milieu surrounding Richard Young's NEH seminar at Carnegie Mellon University in 1978. William Coles and Otis Walter, also from the University of Pittsburgh, were guests at the seminar, and Kameen was very much aware of their work regarding the composing process and rhetorical invention. Like James Berlin, Kameen was wary of the dubious connection between Coleridge and the characterization of vitalism that Young was putting forward in the seminar. Kameen also published a key article in 1980 that put forward his reading of Coleridge and its relationship to rhetoric, invention, and the composing process. Unlike Berlin, however, Kameen did not move on to build a publishing career around "Rewording the Rhetoric of Composition," as Berlin had done with his own piece, "The Rhetoric of Romanticism: The Case for Coleridge." Berlin developed a clear end-goal for his overall research trajectory. His emphasis on persuading the discipline to adopt a particular socio-political program was unwavering and kept him on a single path. One can read this approach into Berlin's reading of Coleridge, which ultimately emphasizes the aim for unity as a central component of his dialectical method. Kameen, on the other hand, reads Coleridge's method differently, and as a result his research practice resembles the desire for ongoing invention, leaving the question open, rather than setting out a clear and stable end-goal. And because the negative reading of Coleridge and vitalism dominated the 1980s, Kameen was often left to publish his work in more obscure settings or not at all.[1] But the changing historical context of the 1990s opened the way for revisiting his position and examining the possibility that his work can lead us to ulterior narratives for the field beyond the retreat and return of rhetoric and ulterior categories beyond current-traditionalism, expressivism, and social-epistemic rhetoric.

The 1980s witnessed the proliferation of taxonomies in rhetoric and composition. In addition to James Berlin's divisions along epistemological and ideological lines, Patricia Bizzell (1982) divides the discipline into inner- and outer-directed theories; Lester Faigley (1986) classifies composing processes into cognitive, expressive, and social approaches; and Stephen North (1987) maps the profession into researcher, scholar, and practitioner methodologies. If the dichotomies of the 1970s are needed to provide a basis for disciplinarity, the cartographies of the 1980s are needed to make sense of the proliferation of knowledge produced by the discipline. By 1990, however, these categories had become more than ways to deal with an expanding field of knowledge. Despite declarations by many of the cartographers that the maps are of heuristic value only, the dissemination of the models both through expanding Ph.D. programs as well as textbooks and conferences solidified the categories into dichotomies once again. As Kate Ronald and Hephzibah Roskelly argue in *Farther Along: Transforming Dichotomies in Rhetoric and Composition* (1990), "[O]nce these perspectives are named, they tend to evolve into positions that require defending or attacking" (3). Their book ushers in a decade that sees two competing developments: the extension of Berlinian forms of cultural studies to a place of prominence in the discipline and an increasing call to question the divisions that had become reified ideological strongholds.

In the early to mid-nineties, many were looking to defend an established category. For Ronald and Roskelly, the early eighties had been marked by James N. Britton's *Language and Learning*, which continued to be cited in an array of articles centered on expressive writing and practices (*Farther Along* 5). But the desire for credibility and political stature in English departments led rhetoric and compositionists to return to scientific methods or bring in literary and social studies, both of which rose to prominence in congruence with the mappings of the field in the late eighties. Though Ronald and Roskelly see the paradox between the rise of social construction and dialogism and the fact that "taxonomies don't permit argument, aren't designed for dialectics" (3), they still want to work for new dialectical relations between subjective and transactive models rather than the oppositional relationship created by the reification of the dominant categories.

Similarly, Stephen Fishman and Lucille McCarthy look to recuperate expressivism. In "Is Expressivism Dead?: Reconsidering Its Romantic Roots and Its Relation to Social Constructionism" (1992), they defend Peter Elbow against social constructionist charges that he follows the romantic ideal of the isolated writer. Fishman, who pens the first half of the article, charges social constructionists such as Bizzell, Berlin, and John Trimbur with reducing expressivists to a "naïve view of the writer as independent, as possessing innate abilities to discover truth" (648). Fishman argues that "although Elbow shares with eighteenth-century German romanticism a reverence for personal experience, it is not experience leading to isolation. Rather, by reinserting personal experience into interactions, Elbow, like Johann Gottfried Herder and other German romantics, hopes to increase our chances for restructuring community. To understand romanticism as championing the artist as lonely, spontaneous genius is to adopt too narrow a view of romanticism" (648–49). Romantic poets reacted against the professionalization and commodification of writing that forced writers to cater to audiences, but this isolation was not an elevation of the isolated individual.[2] Herder saw all thought as social, and called for the integration of "personal life and public expression" (651). Fishman concludes that from Herder onward, romantics looked for a transformational discourse as opposed to a transactional one—a discourse that transforms the individual's relationship to the social.[3]

In *Romancing Rhetorics: Social Expressivist Perspectives on the Teaching of Writing* (1995), Sherrie Gradin puts forth a book-length critique of the standard anti-romantic narrative and an analysis of expressivism's link to the social. Like Fishman and McCarthy, she seeks to re-historicize the overly general notions of expressivism, but she goes back to British romanticism rather than German romanticism. While recognizing the limitations of an article-length study, she also feels that Fishman and McCarthy give a reductive reading of social construction, which she attempts to rectify with her book in order to highlight the shared history between social-constructivist theories and expressive theories—her goal being to delineate a social-expressivism. Gradin draws on Jacques Barzun, who argues that "much of the aversion to romanticism . . . seems based on caricatures of the romantic poets . . . either by the poets themselves or by the satirical portraits of romantic contemporaries" (6). These caricatures laid the groundwork for the anti-romantic rendering of expressivism—the myth of inspiration, anti-intellectualism, and lack of social connection. She argues against the denigration of expressivism based on these misconceptions and shows that social-expressivism has been in the discourse all along but has remained invisible due to the exclusionary nature of the categories established in the discipline. Thus, Gradin seeks to "reclaim what anti-expressivists have left out in their versions and narratives of expressivism" (xviii).[4] Sounding similar to Berlin's attempt to recoup romanticism, Gradin sees social expressivism as asking writers to discover their own beliefs and selves, but these beliefs and selves are created via negotiation within a social system—they act on the environment and their environment acts on them.[5]

As late as 1997, Robert Connors even steps in to question the characterization of current-traditionalism. In *Composition-Rhetoric,* he argues against the reified notion of current-traditional rhetoric popularized by Young. According to Connors's analysis, Young substitutes Fogarty's "rhetoric" with "paradigm" and uses the category as a "default term" for "a classroom tradition he disliked" (4–5).

The paradigm, then, "became a convenient whipping boy, the term of choice after 1985 for describing whatever in nineteenth- and twentieth-century rhetorical or pedagogical history any given author found wanting" (5). Connors posits the term "composition-rhetoric" as a way to revalue rhetorical writing pedagogies of the nineteenth and twentieth centuries, and he maps composition-rhetoric into four "eras"—early American, postwar, consolidation, and modern—in order to historicize it and bring it back from its de-historicized distinction as a paradigm (a rhetorical move similar to the one I carry out in this book with regard to vitalism).

The Calls for Remapping

While many in the early 1990s questioned Berlin's categories and attempted to recoup a category he found wanting, by the mid-1990s many scholars were calling for more open remappings of the field. In Lynn Bloom's conclusion to *Composition in the Twenty-First Century*, "Mapping Composition's New Geography" (1996), she argues that compositionists need a new map for the changing territory of the field, which has become multidisciplinary, eclectic, and more inclusive. Following Anne Ruggles Gere, Bloom defines the field not as "a bounded territory, one that can be distinguished and set apart" but as "a complex of forces . . . a kind of charged space in which multiple 'sites' of interaction appear" (quoted in Bloom 274). In short, rhetoric and composition has moved from a discipline that needs a restricted territory, unique object, and restrictive research practices (a hierarchical, institutional category) to a field that is a cluster of related issues, texts, theorists, and practitioners (a flat, nonhierarchical surface that links to subfields in other disciplines), which carries with it a wide variety of possible combinations or assemblages. This new, evolving complexity makes the field difficult to map and requires that any map be "continually redrawn." For Bloom, "even the familiar questions cannot be asked in the old ways, nor can we expect familiar answers" (274).

Stephen North echoes this diversity in his contribution to *Composition in the Twenty-First Century*, "The Death of Paradigm Hope, the End of Paradigm Guilt, and the Future of (Research in) Composition" (1996), by linking the need for new mappings to the waning of the scientific basis for disciplinarity. North argues that the research paradigm established by Richard Braddock, Richard Lloyd-Jones, and Lowell Schoer in *Research in Written Composition* (1963) is far too restrictive for the complexity of the field today. That book calls for composition to become a disinterested, positivist science that would include "only work on written composition; only studies in which 'some actual writing was involved'; and only research 'employing scientific methods'" (198). Such a research agenda was meant to establish the foundation for a modern discipline, but it inevitably excludes a great deal of work done in rhetoric and composition, not the least of which is historical (206n3).[6] The new paradigm that North outlines is eminently local: "it will . . . be both far less transportable and . . . far more disposable" (205). As he puts it, studies for writing at SUNY Albany will be far less relevant to the needs of Georgia State or Cal State Northridge. The scientific paradigm, he argues, requires composition as an object to be general enough to cut across specific situations. Such a requirement is ultimately conservative, supporting general current-traditional forms and general heuristics derived from empirical research and ignoring the significance of local writing situations.

The reality of this changing situation grounds Louise Wetherbee Phelps, Mark Wiley, and Barbara Gleason's *Composition in Four Keys: Inquiring into the Field* (1996). It is precisely the "sprawling exuberance, bewildering variety, ill-defined edges, and overlaps with other fields" that create both the desire for "simple schemes" to deal with complexity and the need to critique those schemes by regularly building new ones (1). Any map is a construct that "has important limitations and blind spots" that create open spaces and the conditions of possibility for new mappings (10). As a strategy to counteract the almost ubiquitous practice of reading Berlin's work for graduate training in the discipline, which contributes to the reification of his maps, the book by Phelps et al. grows out of a graduate course that takes advantage of these blind spots and makes remapping the fundamental aim of the course.

In order to encourage the creation of new maps, Phelps and her coauthors include a number of strategies to facilitate alternative mappings. They use categories as a mapping strategy but call them "keys" (after Susanne Langer) to imply that there is a mutual interrelationship among the discourses that operates more like musical modes than species/genus analytics. They begin with four primary keys—nature, art, science, and politics—and group a number of essays in each key, provide introductory material to frame the keys, and ask students to read beyond the book in order to problematize the given categories. They base the readings primarily on work in the 1970s and 1980s that highlights issues that arose during the emergence of the field; by doing so they open the possibility of a new cartography appropriate to the 1990s and the first decade of the new century. And they ask students to set up a "wild card" category to collect material that does not fit into one of the pre-established categories. In their original course, for example, they began with nature, science, and art and developed the key of politics through the process. This experience will gradually make the initial scheme "more complex and qualified" (2), perhaps leading to the invention of new keys or even the abandonment of the categories altogether. For them, this mapping process should enable the student-cartographer to contextualize articles and books outside of the anthology, recognize divergence from the categories and their tentative nature, and create new maps for material that does not fit the scheme (9).

This background of category critique and calls to produce new maps sets the stage for my investigation into the issue of vitalism. Ronald and Roskelly, Fishman and McCarthy, Gradin, and Connors all try to recoup or synthesize categories, leaving them intact for all practical purposes. Bloom, North, and Phelps et al. call for opening up the field to new mappings, but they do not provide a new category to compete with the dominant categories. Patricia Roberts-Miller's "Post-Contemporary Composition: Social Construction and Its Alternatives" (2002), for example, keeps a more open approach but also leaves the reified categories intact, posing no alternative that can challenge the status quo. Roberts-Miller provides an important critique of social construction, noting that it can argue against the other categories, but cannot hold up to the critiques it makes of other epistemologies and practices. If the options are only subjective, objective, and transactional, and the first two are shown wanting, then transactional can be the default preference without having to hold up to scrutiny. For her, epistemology is still an open issue. Her call to open up possibilities rings true, but her example of Habermas as an alternative proves to be less compelling: Habermas himself cannot provide a categorical alternative for rhetoric and composition in general and invention in particular.

While a more open approach to mapping the field is the only position to take in *general,* in the particular rhetorical situation that rhetoric and composition faces today, a clearly articulated paradigmatic alternative needs to be posed in order to break the reification of objective, subjective, and transactional models. Perhaps it is the case that the basic objective (current-traditional), subjective (expressive), transactional (social-epistemic) map does, at a fair level of generality, describe real theoretical and pedagogical distinctions within the field. But if the old typology has closed down the conversation, a new paradigm is needed to open it up again. A new model can provide a conceptual starting place outside the old typology that allows the more multidisciplinary and eclectic directions the field is taking to be connected to the emerging practices that do not fit within the old borders. Many of these new practices are responses to a changing technological and rhetorical landscape that could not have been anticipated by a typology developed in the 1980s. Consequently, a more extensive categorical alternative that challenges the dominant models but continues to call for more mappings of the field can begin to lay the groundwork for conceptualizing the contemporary development of the field.

Another Reconsideration of Coleridge

To initiate an alternative genealogy to the ones traced by Young and Berlin, I start with Kameen's reading of Coleridge's method. In "Rewording the Rhetoric of Composition," Kameen maps the field into three fairly typical categories— formalist, self-expressivist, and audience-based approaches—arguing that "[e]ach is both created and bounded by the particular metaphors that function as analogies for the writing process" (73–74). Formalists such as Frank D'Angelo argue that topoi—cause and effect, whole and part, similarity and difference— are built into the mind. This conception of thinking creates a rigid split between mind and world and fosters a very formulaic metaphor for the writing process: writing is the application of mental constructs that mirror the world.

Self-expressivists such as James Miller and Stephen Judy conceptualize thinking as self-discovery. For Kameen, "Miller and Judy have delivered the writer out of the bondage of formal structures which D'Angelo imposes over intentionality. Yet they have delivered him into an equally confining world wherein the motivation to write must arise mysteriously from 'inner sources'" (76–77). This model is also based on a split between mind and world, but the emphasis on thinking as self-discovery creates an idiosyncratic metaphor for the writing process: writing is whatever the individual mind engenders. Audience-based approaches, such as Linda Flower's problem solving, are against this type of reductive self-expressivism but are still predicated on the separation of writing, the mind, and the world. Confining thinking to problem-solution heuristics, dividing the writing process into stages, and claiming that writers should know the rhetorical problem and the audience before they start writing creates a metaphor for the writing process that detaches writing from the rhetorical situation: writing is only a way to communicate the problem, not discover it.

For Kameen these images of the writing process essentially exclude language as an element of invention, and he puts forward Coleridge's method as an alternative approach that views the communications triangle as a complex, interdependent system centered on writing. Kameen chooses Coleridge partly because "his rhetoric is one of the most widely misunderstood" in composition theory (74).[7] Most self-based rhetoricians abandon Coleridge's balancing of self and world across language, and most new classical rhetoricians attempt to reduce Coleridge to a purely self-expressive discourse, which in no way identifies Coleridge's position: "It is such reductive misstatements of Romantic theory that the 'new' classical rhetoricians call 'vitalism,' wrongly attributing it to Coleridge" (78). Kameen cites Young in this regard and sets out to counter such readings. Far from reducing writing or thinking to a function of gift or genius, Coleridge is focused acutely on the relation between subject and object and views the composing situation as a whole whose parts are interdependent. Kameen writes,

> Discourse is not grounded in forms or experience or audience; it engages all
> of these elements simultaneously. And the locus of this synthesis is the text
> itself, which both enacts and creates our intentions, our voices, and our au-

diences. As Coleridge suggests, writing is neither process nor product, it is both in the continual act of becoming one another; writing is neither self nor world, it is both in the continual act of becoming one another; writing is neither information nor expression, it is both in the continual act of becoming one another. Writing is, most simply, the potential of language being explored under the mutual guidance of writer and reader. It is work and play with words. (82)

Coleridge does not recommend that writers depend only on inspirational gifts. Writers are to "reflect phenomenologically on the relations that exist among all aspects of the writing process" (78). Rather than knowing their differences before writing, writers are to work through their interdependent relationships through writing.

This kind of situational complexity is often lost on critics of Coleridge. In his essay "Coleridge, the Return to Nature, and the New Anti-Romanticism: An Essay in Polemic," Seamus Perry traces the dialectical paradox of mind and world back to Coleridge—he is both dreamy idealist and partisan of the concrete. Coleridge is one of the first to critique the concrete, corporeal aspects of Wordsworth's poetry and to place himself on the side of idealism in the dispute with mechanistic philosophies. That Coleridge was an idealist is widely acknowledged. But the opposite is also true of Coleridge. As Perry notes, a "magically responsive realism" is one of Coleridge's dreams for Shakespeare—"an art that becomes the thing contemplated."[8] Consequently, there is no straightforward connection between Coleridge and idealism.

Coleridge does not want to choose between idealism and realism: he wants reconciliation. Perry concludes, "We can perhaps see Coleridge's theoretical orientation as rather more complicated than the traditional anti-romantic case generally has it."[9] Rather than freeze Coleridge into an idealist position as many critics do, John Beer is someone who recognizes the way Coleridgean argument "'seems to be pointing firmly in one direction [but] turns out to contain within itself a statement which acts as a counter-current, suggesting somewhere an alternative motion of the mind'" (quoted in Perry). This is Coleridge's dialectic at work. Coleridge uses writing as a way to work out these complex relationships —at one point emphasizing the mind, at another emphasizing the world. This dialectic appears again and again in his work—at one point touting concrete experience as the basis of knowledge, at another emphasizing books and education. Perry locates the Coleridgean tradition in the affirmation of these opposites.

This complexity is what allows critics like Young to dismiss Coleridge.[10] The fact that these two elements are a part of Coleridge's thinking allows critics to place him in a subjectivist category, an objectivist category, or in a third that conflates the two and is mislabeled vitalism. But these moves that isolate and freeze one moment in Coleridge's thinking ignore his conception of method as a continual act, an alternative motion. Much of this characterization so far sounds reminiscent of Berlin's reading. Berlin views dialectics as a toggling back and forth between dialectical poles that places language and writing at the intersection of self and world. But a closer look at Kameen's interpretation of Coleridge reveals some very clear differences. Coleridge's method is in constant movement. It is a continually recursive approach to thinking that puts forward a very different metaphor for the writing process than the typical approaches of the late 1970s and early 1980s that dominate the discipline. Looking more closely at Kameen's reading of Coleridge's dialectics actually points a way toward a post-dialectical model. It is the first step along the path to the ulterior genealogy from the oppositional vitalism of Coleridge, to the investigative vitalism of Bergson, to the complex vitalism of Deleuze.

Imagination and Dialectics

"Rewording the Rhetoric of Composition" is primarily centered on re-establishing imagination as a key term for rhetoric and composition. As Kameen notes in "Coleridge: On Method" (1986), he embarks on a more detailed look at method as a key concept because it "draws into unison" the three aspects of Coleridge's theory of imagination that have been inappropriately seen as distinct. In order to ground my discussion of his arguments in those two essays, I want to begin with a close look at Coleridge's theory of imagination not only because it is where Berlin puts much of his emphasis when he reads Coleridge's dialectics across the idea of polarity but also because it allows for a greater distinction between Berlin's and Kameen's readings. Berlin's emphasis on the subject draws him more toward primary imagination and its relationship to dialectics. Kameen's emphasis on invention draws him more toward the secondary imagination and its dialectical relationship to the world. These two aims create two different readings of Coleridge and two different theoretical trajectories.

It is no accident that Coleridge opens chapter 13 of *Biographia Literaria* with a discussion of polarity. Coleridge cites Kant's recognition that there are two kinds of opposites, logical and real. Logical opposites are incompatible and contradictory: "a body, at one and the same time in motion and not in motion, is nothing, or at most, air articulated into nonsense" (298). Real opposites, however, are not contradictory: "a motory force of a body in one direction, and an equal force of the same body in an opposite direction is not incompatible, and the result, namely rest, is real and representable" (298). Coleridge links this idea to transcendental philosophy (e.g., Fichte, Schelling [299n1]), claiming that these two forces are "prior to all direction, nay, as the primary forces from which the conditions of all possible directions are derivative and deducible" (299) and that these two forces are infinite and indestructible. The aim, for Coleridge, is to investigate the finite results or products of these oppositional forces. Coleridge then cuts to the fictitious letter, written by himself, that asks him not to publish this work because it will not be received well due to its lack of clarity. Tacked on to the end of the letter is the famous passage distinguishing primary imagination, secondary imagination, and fancy. In form this appears completely "immethodical." But thinking in terms of polarity as the dynamic force that propels thinking forward, always engendering a recursive move to set thinking on a new departure, it seems clear that the idea of polarity enables him to start again with the primary product of the polarity of subject and object, the imagination.

Coleridge's primary imagination is subjective, but it happens in the active mind. In Coleridge's one sentence on the primary imagination, it is clear that this principle is much more than passive perception or even the organizing principle of Kant's categories: "The primary Imagination I hold to be the living Power and prime Agent of all human Perception, and as a repetition in the finite mind of the eternal act of creation in the infinite I am" (304). Because

Berlin is primarily interested in subject formation, he emphasizes this aspect of the imagination's agency. Through the primary imagination, the individual becomes a subject by becoming an object to itself. Berlin quotes Coleridge: "In other words, it is a subject that becomes a subject by the act of constructing itself objectively to itself; but which never is an object except for itself, and only so far as by the very same act becomes a subject" ("Rhetoric of Romanticism" 64). In objectifying itself to itself, the individual recognizes its own subjectivity and in doing so recognizes dialectic as the principal nature of truth. This discovery of *dissoi logoi* cannot be taught, but it can be alluded to via language, which lays the intuitive groundwork for the future conscious understanding and implementation of dialectics. Similarly, the force generated by the polarity of subject and object creates the condition of possibility for secondary imagination—people must recognize their own active subjectivity and its dialectical relationship to the world before they can perform secondary imagination (hence, primary imagination's designation as primary).

The secondary imagination is "an echo of the former, co-existing with the conscious will, yet still as identical with the primary in the *kind* of its agency, and differing only in *degree,* and in the *mode* of its operation" (*Biographia* 304). This conscious form of the primary imagination gives unity to differences observed in the world. Coleridge's famous passage notes that secondary imagination "dissolves, diffuses, dissipates, in order to re-create; or where this process is rendered impossible, yet still, at all events, it struggles to idealize and to unify. It is essentially *vital,* even as all objects (*as* objects) are essentially fixed and dead" (304). Secondary imagination is essentially vital not because it is mystical but because it is active. But the key, of course, is that this active principle must be based on a dialectical relationship between subjective categorization and objective reality that is played out in language. Rather than create subjectivity, the secondary imagination writes new metaphors, new images of the world. As Kameen characterizes it, the imagination can be read as the ability to create new commonplaces. The unifications it produces result in new metaphors (not yet common commonplaces) that will not necessarily follow from standard heuristics. These metaphors are not a window to reality but provide an interpretive image of truth, just as Nietzsche's notion of truth and language is extra-moral.[11]

In his passage, Coleridge gives us perhaps even less indication of the nature of fancy. He states that it "has no other counters to play with, but fixities and definites. The fancy is indeed no other than a mode of Memory emancipated from time and space; and blended with, and modified by that empirical phenomenon of the will, which we express by the word Choice. But equally with the ordinary memory it must receive all its materials ready made from the law of association" (305). Setting aside a lengthier discussion of his arguments against David Hartley and associationism, Coleridge's point here is that fancy does not have the same kind of agency as secondary imagination, which is an agency that associationism cannot account for. If the secondary imagination is a will to unify via method, the movement of intuitive knowledge toward conscious theory, then fancy can choose only to arrange bits and pieces immethodically. Fancy brings together images, words, or thoughts that have no dialectical relationship but are nevertheless put together by a writer. Since it reiterates commonplaces or dead metaphors rather than creates new ones, it cannot move a listener closer to a new truth. All fancy is also metaphoric—as language it hints at truth rather than mirrors truth—but as a reified commonplace it gets interpreted as representative or mimetic.

As Kameen indicates in his brief nod to the imagination in "Coleridge: On Method," these three operations of the mind form their own dialectic, which is neither Plato's dialogue nor Hegel's synthesis. The unity of a polarity is more a balance or relationship than a dialectical movement of sublation (*Aufhebung*).[12] The teleology is set aside for an ongoing relationship between polarities. Owen Barfield cites Coleridge's use of the image of water as an illustration of this point (*What Coleridge Thought* 31): hydrogen and oxygen together constitute water, but neither is overcome in a linear sense. Rather, they form an assemblage. They remain in their entirety, even though together they comprise a third entity. The whole is greater than the sum of the parts, but the parts persist alongside the whole. Paraphrasing Coleridge, Barfield points out that "polarity is dynamic, not abstract. It is not 'a mere balance or compromise,' but 'a living and generative *interpretation.*' Where logical opposites are contradictory, polar opposites are generative of each other—and together generative of a new product" (36). Coleridge's notion of dialectic does not have a thesis and antithesis that are overcome. In Hegel, previous moments are negated when they are integrated. In Coleridge, polarities are integrated but not negated. The polarity must remain intact to produce the active, generative movement. There is a balance that is more than a mere balance: each aspect folds over the other to become the condition of possibility for each other.

Just as primary imagination provides a condition of possibility for secondary imagination, fancy performs a similar function. Secondary imagination dissolves, diffuses, and dissipates the fixities and definites that fancy can only rearrange. But fancy must perform those arrangements for secondary imagination to break them down, dialectically connect them to the world in new ways, and then unify them. Coleridge does indicate in chapter 13 of *Biographia Literaria* that fancy can be active: fancy can in fact *choose*. When fancy chooses to replicate dead metaphors, the mind is more passive. When fancy begins to rearrange the fixities, it becomes more active. Secondary imagination needs fancy as much as it needs the primary imagination. It needs disparate fixities to unify as much as it needs the recognition of subjectivity to willfully unify. Just as there is a polarity of subject and object in primary imagination that constitutes it, there is a polarity of subject (active choice) and object (passive choice) in fancy that constitutes it. And at a larger level, these two elements of the imagination form a polarity of subject (primary imagination) and object (fancy) that constitutes secondary imagination. Primary imagination is hydrogen; fancy is oxygen; secondary imagination is water. Method is progressive in the sense that these polarities produce movement, action, and thought, but there is no teleological process, no ascent to absolute knowledge.

Imagination and Invention

While Berlin's interest in Coleridge's imagination zeros in on the dialectical formation of the subject in the primary imagination, Kameen's focus seems to center more on secondary imagination and its implications for rhetorical invention. In "Rewording the Rhetoric of Composition," Kameen argues that the term imagination has taken on a colloquial meaning that Young and others wish to elevate to a critical meaning, which has allowed invention to replace imagination as a key concept in composition theory. Coding imagination as the product of natural genius allows more generic models of invention to dominate by default. If imagination is seen as a product of nature and thus unteachable, it is automatically disregarded without further critical attention. But closer examination of Coleridge's conception of the imagination shows that it warrants more consideration than would ordinarily be given to mystical genius. In the light of such a perspective, Kameen wants to renovate the term for rhetorical study because "it allows us to say some things about thinking, knowing, and writing that are otherwise almost unsayable" (85). The dialectical movement that grounds the production of knowledge should not be excluded from thinking about invention, the composing process, or epistemology.

For Kameen, the application of formal structures in order to invent material, the solipsistic look into the self and personal experience as the source of invention, and the use of heuristics to invent material for moving between a predetermined problem and solution all reduce the imagination's role in the production of knowledge. Rather than reduce invention to particular points in a process, imagination expands invention to become the entire process. As Kameen puts it, "[T]o begin to write, to begin to think about writing, to think about thinking, to think about, to perform any of these basic acts is to have already begun a composition; and the arena of this composition is language" (82). In addition to forecasting language as the primary element of social construction that Berlin and so many others tap into in the 1980s, Kameen is appealing to the Heideggerian and Derridian emphasis on the etymological roots of terms and their ability to reveal and conceal meanings and ways of seeing the world. Language is not the primary determinant, as many in the eighties interpreted such a statement. It can only construct knowledge through a dialectical development with the world. In this dialectical model, there is no language/world split: "To dwell in language is to dwell in a world" (83). To cut off language's role in the imagination is to cut inquiry off from the other elements of the dialectical production of knowledge: writers construct themselves, understand their world, and engage their audiences through a common social language. This model of the imagination does not express a self but expresses the dialectical interrelationships of a world. As Kameen notes, without this approach to language as metaphors that unite self, world, and hearer, "rhetoric is reduced to craft, persuasion to technique" (84).

The problem with excluding this larger role of the imagination is that it reduces thinking to generic inventional strategies that are then plugged into a linear and acontextual model of the composing process. Invention in the three models Kameen examines becomes overly pre-directed and does not allow the mind to fully address and express the specifics of a situation. Writers will discover what the heuristic allows them to discover, covering over many of the new possibilities that a rhetorical situation may open up. Kameen argues that inventional devices give the writer a "very clear idea of what he is searching for, [so] he can make and execute plans to find it, and it is the only thing he will find given the goal-directed framework that pre-constitutes his search. It is on this point that invention and imagination part company. For the imagination is more like an explorer than a chaser; its mission is not to find a pre-designed something, but to discover the best of what is there to find, to creatively shape that which fills the needs of [Coleridge's] 'forethoughtful query'" (86). Coleridge's notion of forethoughtful query is a central element of his method and does not easily fit into the 1970s model of the composing process. Rather than pre-determine the path of inquiry, it continually sets that inquiry in motion.

Kameen does not elaborate on the concept of "forethoughtful query" in "Rewording" but gives it ample treatment in his follow-up essay, "Coleridge: On Method." For Kameen, "the question . . . is not so much what method is, but how it is enacted" (n.p.), and he situates forethoughtful query at the center of this enaction. Borrowing the concept from Bacon, Coleridge sees it as both the motive and guide of any philosophical investigation. As motive it is before thought, "a kind of urgency towards truth that both initiates thinking and draws it purposively along." As guide it is a carefully constituted point of departure, "a question which results from thoughtful activity and creates a *context* and the *occasion* for subsequent inquiry" (Kameen, "Coleridge: On Method"). Like a hermeneutic circle, inquiry starts from the emergence of an intuition expressed through immersion in a world that suggests a question may be answerable. This possibility motivates the initial conscious formulation of a research question. But these two elements do not pre-constitute the path or the answer. The path is revealed only through a dialectical relation with the world, which then prepares the ground for the next step in the process. The writer comes back to the initial question in the light of the new information or experience of the world, only to resume the search from this new position. This circuit is repeated again and again. A writer may cut the circuit short and turn in the paper or abandon the search, but at any point the search could be renewed and moved forward, as with Coleridge's return to the "Treatise on Method" and its revision into "Essays on the Principles of Method." Thinking never arrives at a final or ultimate conclusion because forethoughtful queries are intimately tied to rhetorical situations that set the conditions of possibility within which thought can proceed. As the circumstances constantly evolve, so does the thinking. From this conception of enaction, method cannot be a general technique, strategy, process, or heuristic: since each step sets the context for the next step, the specific route of the inquiry cannot be pre-established, "cannot be mapped *a priori*." The path "must be discovered as it is traversed" (Kameen, "Coleridge: On Method").

Kameen concludes "Rewording" with an explicit connection to epistemology. Rather than the positivist, mimetic epistemology that grounds formalist, expressivist, and audience-based rhetorics, Kameen seeks a holistic model that includes nondiscursive as well as discursive elements in this methodical movement. The crucial problem is that the use of invention rather than imagination as the primary metaphor for thinking excludes insight, intuition, and nondiscursive thought as the polar counterpart to rational, knowable, discursive thought. In this regard Kameen cites Susanne Langer, who posits both discursive and nondiscursive thinking as phenomenologically inseparable: "they are both present in almost every act of cognition. Just as it is futile to divide the mental life into sense, emotion, and reason, . . . so it is bootless to dichotomize into intellect and intuition, one of which excludes the other" (quoted in "Rewording" 87). Though Kameen reads Coleridge as clearly privileging imagination, imagination can be understood only in the context of method's complex dialectical movement that includes these nondiscursive elements of thinking in every discursive act. Kameen recognizes that both Coleridge and Langer "share the same epistemology: to know is to interpret; to interpret to make meaning; and to make meaning is to recognize on the phenomenal level the unity and integrity of the creative human experience" (87). Kameen concludes that the exclusion of imagination from formalisms, the relegation of it to sub-jectivism in expressivism, and its predetermination under heuristic models de-nies complex, dialectical thinking a constitutive role in composition and thus damages our discipline both philosophically and pedagogically.

Intuition and Method as Movement

In the light of the expanded discussion of Coleridge's imagination, Kameen's argument in "Rewording" can be read as emphasizing secondary imagination's function within the dialectical polarity of primary imagination's unconscious, instinctual knowledge and fancy's conscious, linguistic knowledge, while em-phasizing their nonhierarchical relations.[13] The secondary imagination dialec-tically brings together, in Lev Vygotsky's terms, the complex thinking of participating in the world and the conceptual thinking of participating in culture ("Rewording" 88). While Berlin initiates his notion of dialectics with Coleridge's imagination and method, imagination ultimately gets reduced to the primary imagination's production of the subject and method gets reduced to dialectical interchange among static points on the communications trian-gle—author, reader, language, and world. This move does not see the body as being immersed in a world, reducing the author to a mind that makes rational choices based on an ethic or ideology. Kameen's investigations of Coleridge's method, however, recognize that a mind dwells in a body and a body dwells in a real-world situation. This embodied life grounds dialectics and extends it to the full range of human thought: the primary imagination's instinct and intu-ition, the secondary imagination's will or desire, and fancy's choice. A closer look at Coleridge's method reveals the centrality of intuition as the driving force of methodical movement.

In keeping with method as a way or path, Coleridge wants to move away from the examination of things, which leads to dead classifications, toward re-lations of things, which leads to a continuous transition and reciprocity.[14] For Coleridge, "as soon as the mind becomes accustomed to contemplate, not things only, but relations of things, there is immediate need of some path or way of transit from one to the other of the things related;—there must be some law of agreement or of contrast between them; there must be some mode of comparison; in short, there must be Method" ("Treatise on Method" 631). Intuition charts this path. To illustrate this movement, Coleridge makes the distinction between two kinds of relations: relations of law and relations of theory. Law lays down a rule both moral and intellectual, as in the pure sciences, to which all must conform. These moral (metaphysical) and intellectual (mathematical) laws exist for the mind. Theory, on the other hand, consists of the laws of nature, and since natural laws are "discovered by observation," nature "suggest[s] a given arrangement to the mind" (632). Laws, such as those in mathematics, do not change: the definition of a circle makes the object. But in theory such a perfect idea cannot be supplied by generalization alone. It must be continuously tested against the world. Theory must be representative of the relations in nature and continuously progress and change with them. From the perspective of relations, a person can have an instinct or intuition about a (natural) law before it has been tested and turned into theory (648). From this perspective, relations in nature, not subjective genius, drive intuition. Relations are felt intuitively first, which establishes the conditions of possibility for the path or way of invention. Method begins in embodiment.

Just as law and theory follow intuitive, methodical paths, the fine arts flow from embodied intuition. Visual art and musical art both have their own senses of method "dependent on the external objects of sight and sound" (632). Laws of taste, Coleridge claims, are not based on acculturation as much as "the body of the sound . . . or that effect which is derived from the materials, [which] encroaches too far on the effect derived from the proportions of notes, which proportions are in fact laws of the mind, analogous to the laws of Arithmetic and Geometry" (632). Law in the system of musical notation, for example, is based on the natural arithmetic within the relationships among sound waves (notes), the physical characteristics of the instrument, and the resonance of sound in the human body, while still relying on cultural taste to recognize the laws of notation and tone in the same way a person relies on the understanding of method to grasp the laws of mathematics or the theories of nature. Coleridge makes the distinction between instinct and clear and distinct ideas, but rather than simply privilege one over the other he sees instinct in relation to ideas as on the way to an idea. All of our ideas begin as instincts. As an example, he describes the image of the passage from childhood to adulthood: knowing intuitively that his hoop is round will help a boy learn later that a circle has lines from the center to the circumference that are equal. Instinct, then, is "a vague appetency toward something which the mind incessantly hunts for but cannot find." Coleridge claims that "this distinction between the instinctive approach to an idea, and the idea itself, is of high importance in methodizing art and science" (633).

For Coleridge, this is the principle of progression—progress as path, way, or movement, not eschatology. The body hears or feels that something about a piece of music sounds bad or good, and later, based on that experience, it can learn the method behind that intuition, but only by "following it out through all of its ramifications. It requires, in short, a constant wakefulness of mind; so that if we wander but in a single instance from our path, we cannot reach the goal, but by retracing our steps to the point of divergency, and thence beginning our progress anew. Thus, a ship beating off and on an unknown coast, often takes, in nautical phrase, 'a new departure'" (633). For Kameen in "Rewording," this is the primary function of writing. He wants to ground invention and the composing process on the metaphor of exploration rather than problem solving. As Coleridge explains explicitly and shows implicitly in his texts, writing and thinking are always on the way, in mid-process, always setting out on a new departure, operating on instincts and working to form them into ideas. If one looks merely at the form of his texts, they are often "immethodical." But they are methodical in the traveling of the mind from an intuition *toward* an idea that has yet to be fully articulated—this movement is method.

In "Treatise on Method," Coleridge brings up the discovery of electricity as a movement from intuitions about it—that it was a function of fluids, chemistry, or matter—to "the idea of *two—opposite—forces,* tending to rest by equilibrium" (641–42). His initial point is to show how methodical progress can move over time from accident, to intuition, to theory, and then to law. But he goes on to say that there is "in all electrical phaenomena the operation of a law which reigns through all nature, viz: the law of *polarity,* or the manifestation of one power by opposite forces" (642). Reaching this law may seem like the methodical search has come to a universal conclusion about electricity and then stopped. But this moment only folds back to serve as a new departure. The idea of polarity becomes a new basis for understanding nature and by implication the mind. Given the importance Coleridge places on the balance between nature and the mind in method, method can be read as the dialectical movement between a material and a mental process that both function through the power of polarity. Seen from the analogy with polarity and force in electricity, readers can get an intuitive sense of what the driving force of method might be. Polarity is the force that creates the generative power and movement of method. And as two forces of the same power, embodiment cannot be divorced from thinking.

Toward a Counter-Method

Kameen's take on Coleridge and a closer look at Coleridge's texts lay the groundwork for remapping method. Reading Coleridge's method as a reiteration of Descartes or Plato clashes with almost everything he says about method. The mind is neither passive as in current-traditionalism nor determinative as in expressivism. For Coleridge, both Bacon and Plato "saw that there could be no hope of any fruitful and secure method, while forms, merely *subjective,* were presumed as the pure and proper moulds of *objective* truth" ("Essays on the Principles of Method" 490). And conversely, both Bacon and Plato saw that truth "may indeed be revealed to us *through* and *with,* but never *by* the senses" (492). Coleridge's method is concerned with the relations among the extremes of current-traditional and expressive positions. But it is also difficult to place his sense of method in social-epistemic rhetoric. Intuition is not some mysterious, subjective phenomenon, but it is also more than a dialectic among static points on a communications triangle or a reduction to the social-construction of knowledge via language. Intuition is grounded in the body and its complex relations with the world as they unfold with material situations. This position also extends beyond the boundaries of social-expressivist attempts to recuperate expressivism or romanticism. What is important is not the retrieval of Coleridge or romanticism but to see how this conception of method develops in the twentieth century. As Ann Berthoff notes in her introduction to *Richards on Rhetoric*, "Richards said of his discussions of Coleridge, the aim is not to establish *what he thought*, but to provide occasions to explore *what we might do with what he said*" (xiii). Exploring recent attempts to articulate a sense of counter-method lays the groundwork for what we might do with what Coleridge said: articulate a new paradigm beyond Berlin's maps that can account for both the methodology and epistemology that grows out of Kameen's reading of Coleridge.

In the years since the publication of Kameen's "Rewording the Rhetoric of Composition" in 1980, both Louise Wetherbee Phelps and E. C. White have addressed the question of method in the context of rhetoric and composition. In *Composition as a Human Science,* Phelps also looks to overcome the subjectivist/objectivist opposition within the discipline by enacting a metamethod for mediating the differing methods this polarity creates. Working out of a phenomenological and hermeneutic tradition, she argues that Paul Ricoeur's dialectical method poses a "third way" to mediate "living tensions" (190). Counter to most readings of Hegelian dialectics, Ricoeur posits an infinite postponing of synthesis as a way to look at each side of a polarity more critically and come to a new understanding. Ricoeur begins by assuming one side of the polarity. In this case, according to Phelps, he begins subjectively with phenomenology, which grounds understanding in the "complex wholes of living experience" and the "prereflective belonging of humans to the world" (192). He then introduces an objectivist counter-method, such as structuralism, and uses it to take a critical stance on the initial method. Positing both discourse (as phenomenologically temporal, open, and creative) and system (as structurally static, closed, and prescriptive) as equally true leaves him with the need to find a third term, something that participates in both opposing views. He finds the word, which occurs both phenomenologically in speech and abstractly in language as a system. Like the note in jazz improvisation, the word operates as the intermediary between system and performance, theory and practice. A full synthesis never happens—the two methods of the polarity continuously operate in a productive tension, one shedding light on the other. Method and counter-method form a dialectic for the development of new knowledge.[15]

Similarly, E. C. White reintegrates the concept of ground into method via *kairos*. In *Kaironomia: On the Will-to-Invent*, he reads *kairos* as "a passing instant when an opening appears which must be driven through with force if success is to be achieved" (13). Since circumstances, grounds, are always changing, there can never be more than a "provisional management" of these opportune moments. Invention becomes more like jazz improvisation than scientific method. Music theory forms a system, but that system must always be interpreted in, reinvented in, and adapted to evolving, newly emergent musical circumstances. White associates this practice with Gorgias, who sees rhetoric and invention as a process of adjusting to the situation but also of creating the situation through interaction with it. Such a model comes from *dissoi logoi*, or the tension and force created through the contrary of rhetor and situation.

Like Phelps's take on Ricoeur's dialectic, this tension produces movement and active thought. But White seeks a proliferation of methods and a more intense sense of situatedness that he also sees in Coleridge's take on method:

> No single "method" is privileged . . . over all others. Coleridge can speak of the philosophic method of Plato, the scientific method of Bacon, and the poetic method of Shakespeare without implying a hierarchical ranking among philosophy, science, and poetry. Consistent with the view that no discourse provides more than a temporarily adequate account of reality, *Coleridge argues in effect for a proliferation of methods.* If the meaning of the world must be renewed at every occasion, then the efficacy of method is not given once and for all but depends instead on the creative intervention of the speaker. (58; emphasis added)

Such a view of creative intervention and proliferation not only opens method to the moment but also means that method is not something that pre-exists and then mediates subject and object as a third term. Rather, subject and object are interanimating and interdependent. Method does not create the interdependence but operates through this interanimating ground. As White puts it, "Knowledge is produced not by a process of gradual approximation to a pre-existent truth [or method], but in response to the speaker's present situation, whose endless novelty insures [*sic*] that our experience of the world will never finally be resumed in the nets of language" (60). Method, or language, is not something that is to be imposed on the world. A generative, evolutionary development drives creative intervention, and method responds to and operates within this development.[16]

This more intense sense of situatedness is reminiscent of Paul Feyerabend's work in the 1970s. In *Against Method*, Feyerabend turns this kairotic situatedness toward science, innovation, and a more complex sense of method. For Feyerabend, science is inherently anarchic. There is not one monolithic science but many sciences and subfields with varied theories, methods, and objects. Experiments, observations, and facts mean something different in each specific disciplinary and historical context. Therefore, there can be no general scientific method. Given the specificity of history and the complexity of reality, the only way to be a successful scientist is to "adopt whatever procedure seems to fit the occasion" (10). Abstract general rules or methods that appeal to rationality or reason are often set aside when scientists confront a concrete problem. Because no particular research situation is the same as another, a certain amount of methodological openness is required. Quoting Lenin, Feyerabend argues that those who want to create change "must be able to understand, and to apply, not only one particular methodology, but any methodology, and any variation thereof [they] can imagine" without exception or exclusion (10). Operating on the basis of inclusion means that researchers should try to improve rather than discard past views. A theory that is discredited in one context might turn out later to be the foundation for a new paradigm.[17] Similarly, just as no theory should be excluded, no form of knowledge should be excluded. "Intuitive plausibility," Feyerabend writes, "was once thought to be the most important guide to truth" (150). But as education in science increasingly began to develop and privilege formal, abstract methods, intuition as an important connection to experience and experiment is shut down.

In order to create an open context of investigation and inclusion, Feyerabend recommends the procedure of setting up counter-rules that oppose the familiar rules of science. There will always be circumstances in which ignoring the rules or even enacting the opposite of the rules can lead to new insights. Thus, scientists should develop hypotheses that are inconsistent with accepted theories and/or facts. This practice expands the possible "empirical context" by initiating a "pluralistic methodology" (20). Feyerabend directly links this counter-method to *dissoi logoi:* this activity should "make the weaker argument the stronger, as a sophist said, and thereby... sustain the motion of the whole" (21). But importantly, Feyerabend is not attempting to propose a new methodology that would replace a rationalist methodology. Rather than universalizing the method of *dissoi logoi,* he is advocating a notion of paratactic aggregate, oper-ating by addition rather than subtraction, negation, or sublation (synthesis): "the elements of such an aggregate are all given equal importance, the only re-lation between them is sequential, there is no hierarchy, no part is presented as being subordinate to and determined by others" (173). Because no one method could ever uncover all the facts within a situation, the constant addition of new perspectives is the only general principle commensurate with scientific discovery. The sequential addition of new perspectives moves thinking forward and ensures that one methodology never assumes a hierarchical and exclu-sionary position.

Berlin might place Phelps's reading of dialectics in social-epistemic rhetoric, but it is less clear where a figure like White or Feyerabend fits into his scheme. Whereas Phelps's approach to method does a better job of integrating a phe-nomenological perspective than Berlin's, it still relies on method as a form of interpretation and mediation of subject and object, which is more reminiscent of Berlin. Phelps's approach is also less geared toward invention: phenome-nology and structuralism already exist to be used as counter-methods. As in Berlin's view, method is for creating critical distance, not for addressing rhetor-ical situations with an eye toward inventing more methods. White and Feyer-abend, on the other hand, turn method more explicitly toward invention. Rather than apply a method to a situation to generate material, as with Berlin's heuristic, method is a part of the situation and is co-developed through that situatedness. Feyerabend's "anarchistic methodology" selects from all possible methodologies, connects bits and pieces of them to an immediate context, and looks to build and invent new methods from this situationally specific aggre-gate. Such a position is not a metamethod—not a method for negotiating methods—but a paratactic aggregate that is open to using methods that intu-itively seem reasonable or workable. If they do not work out in practice, then one can invent a new aggregate and test it within a context. This more kairotic approach to method shifts from being dialectical to post-dialectical and consequently it has no place in Berlin's categorical scheme. When confronted with thinkers such as Derrida or Deleuze who push the bounds of complexity, Berlin often forces them into a subjectivist category. And in the case of Foucault in particular, Berlin tries to recoup some elements of his thinking for social-epistemic rhetoric but then excludes other elements that do not neatly fit into the framework of the paradigm. Rather than generating a sense of uninterrupted openness, Berlin's dialectical method is ultimately used to close off counter-methods and the model of epistemology that emerges with them.

Mapping Epistemology beyond Berlin

Berlin's epistemological categories for composition theories have no place for the kinds of complex situatedness initiated in Coleridge's method. Berlin draws the epistemological distinctions this way: in classical rhetoric, truth and knowledge are in the rational minds of both author and the audience and the logic that connects them; in current-traditional rhetoric, truth and knowledge are in the individual's clear perception of the world; in expressivism, truth and knowledge are in the individual's understanding and exploration of self; and in social-epistemic rhetoric, truth and knowledge are transactional—developed in a dialectical relation between individual/mind, social/world, and linguistic/texts. In the other categories, truth exists prior to knowledge. In social-epistemic rhetoric, truth arises from the production of knowledge. The dialectic behind social-epistemic rhetoric wants to see the subject in relation to the elements of the communications triangle but can only imagine, ironically, a more mystical notion of this relationship. Hayden White says of the syllogism, "[T]he move from the major premise (All men are mortal) to the *choice* of the datum to serve as the minor (Socrates is a man) is itself a troplogical move, a 'swerve' from the universal to the particular which logic cannot preside over, since it is logic itself that is being served by this move" (*Tropics of Discourse* 3). This same problematic operates in Berlin's dialectics, which cannot map the complexity of such dialectical turnings and therefore must assume its own moves. Berlin does attempt to make the subject more complex through fragmentation, but his adherence to dialectics continues to rest on the grounds of such a choice, or more specifically a theory that makes such a choice conscious and rational.

It is easy to see why Berlin has mystical vitalism in expressivism or current-traditional rhetoric as positing a prior unknown force that informs the world. In doing so, however, he misses not only complex vitalism's post-dialectical approach to complex interrelationships but also the notion of bodily experience and knowledge as being the local moment out of which more complex understanding is connected and initiated. By emphasizing a subject's conscious, rational choice, Berlin loses the complexity of the local, of the way the body is connected to its social, cultural, historical, and technological environments. But because Berlin rests on dialectics as the sole means to understand transaction among the elements of the communications triangle, he cannot theorize an epistemology that is more complex than a dialectic among static points on the triangle.

Many thinkers who could be considered vitalist attempt to theorize and map such spaces rather than leave them up to mystery. Henri Bergson, for example, argues that the spatializing and differentiating of the world, as in the communications triangle, is a product of our attempt to conceptualize it, to find a language to represent experience. Berlin writes, "In epistemic rhetoric there is never a division between experience and language, whether the experience involves the subject, the subject and other subjects, or the subject and the material world. All experiences, even the scientific and the logical, are grounded in language, and language determines content and structure. And just as language structures our response to social and political issues, language structures our response to the material world" (*Rhetoric and Reality* 16). Berlin has to conflate experience and language in order to understand experience semiotically and dialectically. Bergson, on the other hand, recognizes that the body can know and understand the world prior to conscious linguistic understanding. Bergson makes the distinction between analysis and intuition. Analysis is the procedure of science that divides time into space so it can be conceptualized. It is propositional and based on experiment, which results in the creation of generalizations. Intuition is Bergson's method of philosophy that approaches time as a whole so it can be experienced. It is nonlinguistic and based on embodiment, which sees things as individual or particular in the context of the individual's life history, its entire relationship to the world. This is not simply an opposition but a complex movement. Instinct is a feeling of life for life that drives practical relations to the world; intelligence is the conscious faculty for manufacturing objects in the world; intuition is the becoming of the former into the latter. Intuition is a process of living in the complex, evolving interplay of body, mind, and the world.

For Bergson, the epistemological distinction between mind and body is something like the difference between knowing Paris from books and photographs and the "*awareness* of Paris possessed by someone who has really been there and so has had an intuition of the place as a unified whole" (Matthews 17). Even this more commonplace sense of intuition exemplifies why a more comprehensive theory of epistemology should consider how conscious knowledge emerges from complex embodied situatedness. This position deviates from Plato (expressivism) as well as Descartes (current-traditionalism) by positing a continuum between mind and body rather than a split. For Bergson, "Perception is never a mere contact of the mind with the object present; it is impregnated with memory-images which complete it as they interpret it" (*Matter and Memory* 133). Perception is never outside the body's entire life history. The existence of mind and body can be understood only as the unfolding of this history in the complexity of duration—Bergson's philosophy of time as the lived experience of the whole of past, present, and future rather than time as divided into minutes and hours. The personal, therefore, is not an insulated mind, as Berlin would have it, but the most concrete level of existence: it is where bodies perform actual actions in specific situations. Thoughts, feelings, perceptions, and desires flow into each other to the point that the whole of subject and object, mind and body, is there in intuitive motion. We know something all at once, kairotically and concretely. From such a perspective, language cannot represent or determine the body's experience of the world: it becomes a part of that experience; it enacts movements with/in the world.

Berlin ultimately categorizes the concept of intuition as a purely individual, subjective matter: expressivism ultimately must confirm truth "through a private act of intuition" (*Rhetoric and Reality* 13). But this allows Berlin to exclude critical elements of knowledge production. In *Spinoza: Practical Philosophy*, for example, Deleuze argues that we do not need to know every proposition in Spinoza's work in order to have an intuition of what we might do with his work—how we might plug it into an assemblage or create a composition with it. From this perspective, Bergson's "[i]ntuition is neither a feeling, an inspiration, nor a disorderly sympathy, but a fully developed method, one of the most fully developed methods in philosophy" (Deleuze, *Bergsonism* 13). Just as Coleridge's method attempts to account for the entire movement of thinking, Bergson's method is a perpetual, lived process that takes place simultaneously at the level of tacit, bodily knowledge as well as conscious, linguistic knowledge. Humans, for example, know how to act in a given (social) situation by acquiring that knowledge unconsciously through repetition and enculturation. There is nothing particularly personal or subjective about this level of bodily knowledge: it is like the acquisition of a primary language—a person's ability to speak a language, or act according to a social code, is generally no different from that of other members of that particular culture. Intuition, then, is not some faculty or genius. Both body and mind are used to navigate our environment in an intuitive and holistic way that is far from belonging to scientific objectivism or subjective romanticism.

Berlin's desire to link intuition and private experience obscures its relation to the world, its role in the production of knowledge, and its potential relation to heuristics. In *Heuristic Research,* Clark Moustakas argues that the key heuristic element in any research project is immersion in the world. Heuristic thinking, for him, is a process of discovery that can only begin through an immersion in a topic, its literature, and its way of being experienced. Following Michael Polanyi, among many others, Moustakas examines tacit knowing and intuition in the context of indwelling and immersion. Polanyi's approach to epistemology makes the distinction between subsidiary (conscious) and focal (unconscious) levels of knowledge that are linked through a "tacit capacity" to construct a coherent image or concept of something from snapshots or parts. For Polanyi, "*We can know more than we can tell.* . . . Take an example. We know a person's face, and can recognize it among a million. Yet we usually cannot tell how we recognize a face we know . . . this knowledge cannot be put into words" (quoted in Moustakas 20). This excess of conscious, linguistic knowledge requires intuition to link "personal" focal knowledge to conscious, subsidiary application. Moustakas sees "the bridge between the explicit and the tacit [as] the realm of the between, or the intuitive" (23). All conscious knowing rests on tacit knowing and our capacity for intuition—linking the tacit and the conscious. Such intuition requires immersion—"to understand something fully, one dwells inside the subsidiary and focal factors to draw from them every possible nuance, texture, fact, and meaning" (24). To attain bodily or personal knowledge requires practice, study, and long-term immersion in a body of language and the contexts of its use. Michael Polanyi's books *Personal Knowledge* and *The Tacit Dimension* were well-known and oft-cited works in rhetoric and composition during the 1960s and 1970s, but they fell out of favor and use during the 1980s and 1990s, when the concept of social construction was most dominant. Social-epistemic rhetoric ultimately excludes bodily knowledge and the entire context of tacit knowing that serves as the contextual ground for any heuristic discovery.

Epistemology, the Body, and the Virtual

Thinkers such as Deleuze and Brian Massumi extend these phenomenological models of Bergson and Polanyi into a more detailed look at the body and the ways it is connected to the world. In his book *Parables for the Virtual,* Massumi discusses epistemology from the perspectives of the sensible concept and the virtual. In one chapter Massumi discusses the artist Stelarc's work with the body when it is plugged into a network of relations in order to produce what Stelarc had termed a "'physical experience of ideas'" (89). Massumi uses as an example one of Stelarc's early performances in which the audience is asked to wear goggles that scramble binocular vision by emulating the eye of an insect. The bodily experience of a change in perception produces what Massumi calls a sensible concept. The concept that Stelarc is after is not just that perception is relative but that different bodies have different capacities for relations to the world. A bee's body allows it to interact with a flower by engaging in certain actions—drinking nectar, spreading pollen. A human's body allows it the capacity to create pharmaceuticals from flowers or write poetry about flowers (each of which also ensures the flowers' continued reproduction and survival). Perceptions, then, are not merely conceptual—they are potential bodily actions and relationships. An object, such as a flower, is never outside the set of these potential relations (there is no thing-in-itself). Saying that something exists outside potential relations is itself adopting a particular kind of relation to the thing. An objective stance attempts to generalize potential bodily relations into concepts, "stockpiling for future use of the possible actions relating to a thing" (94). The possible is quantifiable, general, and potential is qualitative, intimately particular. An objective relation to a thing makes possible relations more anticipatable, which paradoxically opens up more potential connections. Thus perception (potential bodily relations) and thought (possible conceptual relations) form a feedback loop.

For Massumi, the overall epistemological process or movement of this reciprocal relation between the potential and the possible is intelligence, and intelligence invents concepts or objects that precede their utility. Massumi argues that "[a]n invention is something for which a use must be created." As a "trial and error process" for creating new relations, invention is the production and enaction of "a sensible concept that precedes and produces its own possibility" (96). An invention, whether it is a concept or an object, must be plugged in to a system of real-world potential relations in order to enable the production of abstract possible relations, and only then can it yield real-world useful relations. Stelarc's goggles, for example, enacted such a sensible concept but are still waiting for a practical use. Nevertheless, we "can't begin to know what bug goggles can do until" they are invented and we put them on; "[y]ou have to experience them even to begin to imagine a use for them, and what your body is with them" (97). Knowledge, both abstract and practical, can emerge only through this larger feedback loop between bodily potential and conceptual possibility.

This qualitative potential within particular relations or events is the virtual. Massumi cites an experiment as emblematic: electrodes were implanted in the cerebral cortex and placed on the skin of human patients. When mild electrical impulses were given to the cortex and also to the skin, the stimulation was felt only if it lasted more than half a second (28). The missing half a second, Massumi asserts, is the realm of the virtual—this is the realm of tacit bodily knowledge. The virtual is something that happens beyond the human brain's ability to perceive it consciously—"something that happens too quickly to have happened, actually" (30). The virtual is like bullet time in *The Matrix*. The effect is a key point in cinema because prior to this spectators have seen only stasis points, not movement. They see a shot from a gun and someone being hit. With bullet time, viewers see the trajectory, the movement of the bullet, slowed down, intensified, so they can get a sense of that movement, which is a primary form of reality beyond static points of visual perception. As Stelarc's goggles attempted to show, human bodies are set up to perceive some potentialities that are in excess of the brain's conscious perception. Even though brains cannot consciously perceive virtual events, bodies can sometimes feel, sense, or intuit them. Since there is something material there to feel, sense, or intuit— the bullet physically moves through space and time—virtual space is not empty. The brain cannot perceive it precisely because it is an excess of reality beyond our bodies' perceptive capacity. So the virtual and the actual are part of the same real-world continuum, the same feedback loop, that affects the body.

Internet readers, for example, experience virtual affects during their movement through the Web. Whether boredom or engagement, Web surfing is compelling through the accumulation of affect, or the momentum that carries the surfer from link to link (the same feeling that makes channel surfing on TV so enthralling): the surfer moves from one link or channel to the next but with each move the vagueness of the experience changes, the difference keeping us connected and moving; then one sensation may stand out; "the vagueness may sharpen into a . . . clarity of thought that strikes the foreground of consciousness in a flash of sudden interest or even revelation" (Massumi 140); or, "link after link we click ourselves into a lull" (139)—boredom; but the useless boredom may still set the stage for further movement toward future usefulness. Whether one experiences boredom or engagement, the affective sensation of surfing enacts potential. The possibility stored in the digital 1s and 0s relies on this affective potential within the virtual. The digital has to circuit through bodies—in the case of digital music, for example, a human body has to enact the sound to record it digitally and then plug in a digital device to hear it. For Massumi, "To look only at bodies and objects is to miss the movement" (136), the process of such a circuit. The analog embodies this movement from the virtual to the actual and back to the virtual—a movement or circuitry that fuels invention. The digital and its structure do not set the possible or potential into motion. Potential and the possible can emerge only through the experiential relays of analog reception and enaction of the body. Experiential, bodily knowledge happens via affect and the virtual and grounds all possible conscious knowledge.[18]

Berlin concludes his final book, the posthumously published *Rhetorics, Poetics, and Cultures,* by arguing that both rhetoric and poetics teachers and classes create student subjectivity. So he wants to position his ideological subject at the forefront of both rhetorical and poetics instruction. He calls for teachers to state their ideology up front and for both rhetoric and poetics instructors in English departments to form a "collaborative effort" (180) in the project of foregrounding a subject consistent with social-epistemic rhetoric. But Berlin misses the entire body of work that deals with bodily, tacit knowledges, which would fundamentally change his view of the subject and its relationship to language. In *Gilles Deleuze: Vitalism and Multiplicity,* John Marks discusses subjectification as the multiple forces of life that pass through us. This model of subjectivity is not about creating the subject through language and argument but about "inventing new possibilities of life . . . 'a vitalism rooted in aesthetics'" (Deleuze quoted in Marks 1). The subject is not about ideological construction at the level of rational, conscious debate in the classroom. A body's agency is not the universal aspect of a sovereign subject but a matter of what bodies can do, their capacity to affect other bodies by entering into relations with them. For Aurelia Armstrong, "[t]he growth of agency is shown to consist in a process of *becoming-active,* in the increase and enhancement of 'individual' powers through their combination with the powers of other, compatible individuals and things" ("Some Reflections" 50). For Deleuze, the art of "organizing good encounters, composing relations, forming powers, [and] experimenting" follow rules that promote action, not rules that constrain action (quoted in Armstrong 50). In short, the kind of heuristic pedagogy Berlin establishes cannot achieve its ends if it ignores the centrality of the body and its levels of connectedness to specific, lived situations.

It is toward this more complex understanding of situatedness and its connections to invention that Coleridge's method points. This more developed concept of intuition that extends through Bergson, Polanyi, and Deleuze complicates Coleridge's assumed connection to a mystical vitalism. Either Coleridge is not a vitalist, as Berlin wants to claim, or he is a vitalist of some quite different sort. If the latter is assumed, then it begs the question, what sort of vitalist is he? What vitalist tradition beyond mysticism is he connected to? And more specifically, what impact could answering this question have on thinking about invention and pedagogy in the more complex technical environments in which today's students live? For Young and Berlin, heuristics are primarily seen as functioning in conjunction with the mind. But Kameen's reading of Coleridge opens the path for thinking about the ways heuristics might function as an aspect of a larger method that is interested in seeing a constellation among heuristics, minds, bodies, texts, and contexts. As Kameen writes, such a "circuit" of thought is more than a recursive process: "Methodical thinking is site-dependent—i.e., the subject or situation or set of circumstances will inscribe the limits within which thought can and should proceed; and the structure of thought will change or vary as one changes or varies the subject, situation, or circumstances. Method, in short, is not the form of, or for, thoughts; it is the texture of thinking. Any heuristic can, of course, become its instrument; method is in fact, the engine that makes heuristics work" ("Coleridge: On Method"). Heuristics and method are not necessarily in opposition. Method is the ground and the force behind the invention and use of heuristics. Heuristics do not function in a vacuum; they function within complex and specific rhetorical situations. Importantly, the body is the critical, epistemological link between situation and invention. It is the interface, the one that Berlin's taxonomy cannot see. The rest of this book sets out to establish a historical and theoretical foundation for thinking about this potentiality.

4

A SHORT

COUNTER-HISTORY

RATHER THAN PLACE COLERIDGE IN the narrative of rhetoric's retreat and return, either in retreat as Richard Young does or in return as James Berlin does, Paul Kameen's reading seems to place Coleridge elsewhere. Certainly Kameen is interested in the ways Coleridge can expand the field's conceptions of rhetorical invention and the composing process, but his rearticulation of Coleridge goes beyond the revaluation of the romantic individual. If Coleridge is read as espousing a complex relationship among the world, the body, the mind, and writing, then his importance clearly goes beyond mystical genius. But simply placing Coleridge into the return of rhetoric limits an understanding of his thinking to particular readings of dialectics or invention. Kameen's reading ultimately begs the question of what historical narrative or paradigmatic discourse would open a space for extending the insights he gains from reading Coleridge. As I have been indicating in this book, a more detailed historical understanding of vitalism provides a new narrative for understanding Coleridge's contribution to the field, one that does not recuperate him but extends his line of thinking to today's complexity theories. The problem surrounding vitalism in rhetoric and composition is that the discipline has selected one definition, equating it with romantic genius and individual expression, excluded vitalism from the discourse of the field based on this definition, and thus covered over the possibility of seeing what vitalism has become. This forgotten history has been missing from the historical debate about Coleridge, but more importantly the debate has excluded an entire line of thinking from deepening our understanding of what rhetoric and invention can become.

In order to lay out a short history of vitalism beyond its association with mysticism, I begin with Aristotle, who is much more than his traditionally interpreted positions on rhetoric and technê. Much of his work on physics and metaphysics actually establishes a starting point for vitalist theories of life that try to account for action, development, evolution, movement, and self-organization. In the years since Aristotle's lifetime, astrology, alchemy, and animism have dominated theories of life and led to vitalism's association with mysticism. But once the modern episteme began to emerge in the early nineteenth century, vitalist perspectives began to integrate with contemporary notions of science and philosophy. I detail these rearticulations through three modes of vitalism: oppositional, investigative, and complex. These distinctions are at root a fluid continuum, but they show clear historical variation in the modern period. Oppositional vitalisms look to notions of electromagnetic force in the sciences and notions of polarity in philosophy. Investigative vitalisms examine evolution and cell theory in the sciences and phenomenology and time in philosophy. Complex vitalisms ultimately turn the opposition of mechanical and vital theories into a cooperative system, turning force in the sciences and power in philosophy into complex, co-emergent phenomena. Such a position expands knowledge, thinking, and invention beyond Berlin's individual expressivism and social-epistemic rhetoric into Deleuze's expressionism and complexity theory. This ulterior historical development does not retrieve rhetoric and establish its return but expands rhetoric and extends its scope. In the words of Paul Feyerabend, such a counter-history is an additive paratactic aggregate rather than a recuperative maneuver.

Beginnings in Aristotle

Even though vitalism has been associated with romanticism, genius, and creativity devoid of technê, going against all the grounding principles of rhetoric, most histories of vitalism begin with Aristotle. Writing before the exclusive linking of vitalism to romanticism and the opposition of both to new classicism, Richard Hughes argues that the "modern" Aristotle is based on contemporary criticism and misses the historical Aristotle's basis in vitalism. In "The Contemporaneity of Classical Rhetoric" (1965), he discusses vitalism as the foundation of Aristotle's system matter-of-factly rather than seeing it as something to be excluded. Hughes argues that there are three key components to Aristotle: his vitalism, his concept of argument, and his concept of the topics. For him, vitalism grounds the other two:

> The first, the vitalism, is the most important, for this is the root and cause of argument and topic. By *vitalism* I mean that assumption, ubiquitous in Aristotle's writings, springing from his concern for entelechy, that all the arts are generative. His biological studies predisposed him to see reality as the end product of form evolving into its ideally realized material structure. As there is an embryo, an evolution and finally a status in the biological kingdom, so too in the intellectual kingdom. The literal *life-ness* of the arts, and particularly the language arts, is at the heart of Aristotle's rhetoric. Realities, verities, concepts, attitudes are not thought of as static but as dynamic, as continually evolving to a point of status.... Rhetoric is one art of moving an idea from embryo to reality. It is, consequently, an art which rests not at the end of the intellectual process, but an art which is *within* the process. There is no hyperbole, but only a sound literalism, in calling Aristotle's rhetoric a *creative* rhetoric. (37–38)

Hughes exhibits a more inclusive perspective that does not prejudge vitalism as nonrhetorical. Instead, he articulates a link between art and nature, rhetoric and vitalism. Aristotle posits the concept of entelechy as the driving force of art's creative power, one that establishes his theory of causes as the ground for his theory of rhetoric.

Aristotle articulates the first scientific, or at least naturalistic, notion of vitalism in his concept of entelechy. The prefix *ent* means within, *telos* means goal, *ech* means to have, and *y* denotes process. Entelechy, then, is the process of development through having the goal within. Aristotle associates entelechy with his theory of causes. Every thing has four causes: (1) material cause—what the thing is made of; (2) efficient cause—the agent, beginning, or source that brings the thing into existence; (3) formal cause—the thing's abstract structure or design; and (4) final cause—the thing's purpose or aim, or the object toward which it is developing. A house, for example, would have a material cause (bricks), efficient cause (builder), formal cause (blueprint), and final cause (house). The sum total of material reality sets the conditions for what can emerge out of it. All the physical characteristics of bricks and mortar and wood enable them to produce a functioning building. Efficient cause generally resembles basic notions of cause and effect, where motion requires an outside agent. Aristotle, however, argued that in many cases motion is inherent within the object. Though he got the notion of formal causes from Plato's forms, he sees the forms in nature rather than in some abstract or heavenly space. Looking at biological organisms, he thought that they had to possess the form or plan for their development internally. In order for organic development to occur without an external agent, the thing had to have the formal cause within itself as the final cause in miniature. The formal cause creates the self-motivation to strive toward its final completion, to play out its potential. The prime examples are the seed that develops into a tree or the embryo that develops into an animal. No outside agent such as a gardener or geneticist is necessary for its development. The potential in organic nature provides its own source for purposive action. Nature has its own agency by encompassing all four causes.

It is the inherent power or capacity to move from potentiality to actuality in nature that makes Aristotle's theory of entelechy more vitalistic than mechanistic. Aristotle makes a key distinction between potentiality and actuality. Potentiality resides in the existence of the four causes. Actuality is the enaction of this potential, its motion toward an end. This distinction creates three possible kinds of motion-related existence: (1) that which is in the process of motion toward an end, (2) that which has the potential of motion but which is not now in process, and (3) that which is in the process of motion toward one end but also has the potential of motion toward an end which is not now in process (Lindsay 38–39). A seed, for example, might be in the process of becoming a tree but it also carries the potential to become a house, a chair, or home to a bird's nest. This third mode of existence points to a more complex notion of entelechy. Not only are there multiple potentialities that may or may not be in motion or ever realized but there are also multiple factors needed to set them in motion or freeze them in potential. Kenneth Burke, in *The Rhetoric of Religion*, writes, "The Aristotelian concept of 'entelechy,' as an aim contained within the entity, is essentially a biological analogy. It is the title for the fact that the seed 'implicitly contains' a future conforming to its nature, if the external conditions necessary to such unfolding and fulfillment occur in the right order. Were you to think of the circumstances and the seed together, as composing a single process, then the locus of the entelechy could be thought of as residing not just in the nature of the seed, but *in the ground of the process as a whole*" (246–47). So when Aristotle identifies entelechy as internal, this statement contains the potential to move beyond internal to the seed to internal to the situation. A seed is not just the beginning of a process but also the end of a previous tree's development. Link these two processes together and there is an ongoing process of becoming. Link that process to the myriad processes and potential processes within a ground or circumstance and the overall movement becomes a complex ecology. It is a complex arrangement of causes that goes beyond simple mechanistic cause and effect to become the vital ground for rhetoric.

Aristotle's theory of entelechy provides a framework for seeing rhetoric in the context of such ecological processes. For Aristotle, technê works material into a form. The difference between nature and art is that the design is internal to natural objects whereas artificial objects come into being through a design enacted by an artist. But for Aristotle, an object, because of its material and formal causes, would have the same process or final cause whether being created naturally or artificially. David Channell, in *The Vital Machine,* makes the connection to genetics. In order for humans to impose their design on genetic development, they mimic nature's process. Learning the form of DNA allows us to intervene in the process. But in order to produce a particular animal, the same genetic form has to come together, either by nature or through art. All arts, for Aristotle, are similarly modeled on nature by realizing the potential form that is inherent in the material used and the contextual constraints. In cases such as building a house, human agents enact a potential that is there in the wood that nature cannot enact. But the artist does so by mimicking processes and forms in nature: "the craftsman takes a form that exists in nature, abstracts it from its natural material, and realizes it in some new material of his art" (70). The craftsman might get the idea of a house from a stone cave, but the attempt to enact that form through new material will create new material conditions and thus a different form than the cave. Thus, nature provides the forms for technology to imitate, and technology helps complete new forms that nature does not materially enact on its own.

This dual movement of nature and technology creates a larger ecological context in which humans and rhetoric operate. The basic logic of entelechy is that the overall configuration of any situation, including both natural and human acts and forms, combines to create its own conditions of possibility that strive to be played out to completion. The combination of the four causes in nature is not just a push from behind but also a pull toward the future, the striving to develop potential. In more contemporary evolutionary terms, an ecological situation produces the structural conditions for certain types of plants or animals to develop and thrive and they strive to fill those gaps, to enact that potentiality. Humans as an efficient cause cannot be abstracted from this larger contextual ground set up by the other causes and the ecology or potentiality they enact. A human might have an internal, psychological, or intellectual motive, but a huge variety of cultural, linguistic, and material factors help create and enact that motive. As part of nature, humans can help realize the situational potential via the techné available to them through the complex ecological arrangement, and it is in this larger movement that rhetoric operates. Hughes goes on to link this generative power to argument and the topics: "The essential items in Aristotle's concept of argument are the gradual evolution of a judgment out of disparate and embryonic evidence, the formulation of the realized judgment in the rhetor's own mind, and the propagating of that realized judgment in whatever structures will lead to a duplication of his discovery in the mind of his audience. . . . . Argument, then, is a generative process. . . . It has a clear contact with the vitalism of Aristotle's attitude toward all the arts. The *topics* of Aristotle are in turn connected with the evolutionary nature of argument" (38). The whole rhetorical process is about this movement. The rhetor assesses a rhetorical situation and determines the right forms, or topoi, that will initiate the movement from situational conditions to audience adherence. To separate rhetoric from vitalism is to cut it off from its circumstantial context and the very grounds and processes that make it possible.[1]

Astrology, Alchemy, Animism

From Aristotle onward, vitalism is any attempt to theorize a self-organizing or self-motivating system. As Greek philosophy developed up to the Renaissance, it paradoxically combined Aristotle's more material answer to this problem with mystical connotations. This connection laid the groundwork not only for the link between vitalism and mysticism but also for modern scientific ideas and practices. After Aristotle, the Stoics operated from a form of determinism that believes the world functions according to laws. But rather than lead to a mechanistic philosophy, it led to astrology based on an ecological congruence between celestial and terrestrial events. Atomists such as Democritus and Epicurus believed that natural order occurs by chance or random interaction, but the Stoics argued that something else more material had to create order in the universe. They called this other entity *pneuma* and saw it as a mixture of earth, air, fire, and water, essentially a gas (*spiritus*), that spreads through the organized system and holds bodies together. It came to be seen as the basic principle of life, what the Greeks called *psyche*. In the Roman period, both animate and inanimate objects in nature were seen in the context of psyche, which is the source of both individuals as well as planets. This connection between the universe and smaller parts of it led to the development of astrology. Because the World Soul, or psyche, was the source of the pneuma for individuals as well as stars and planets, which all function according to deterministic laws, the attempt to harness those laws for the sake of humans became a reasonable endeavor.

Alchemy took this position more directly to the problem of creation. As far back as Aristotle, all matter was seen as being delivered from one fundamental substance. Earth, air, fire, and water developed from this *prima materia* when acted upon by qualities such as wetness, dryness, heat, or cold. Since all elements have this original source, it was thought that some process similar to chemistry could transform one substance into another through the manipulation of these qualities. Artisans working with metal—blacksmiths, miners, and metallurgists—all followed a form of vitalism that associated these inorganic elements with Aristotle's biological analogy and considered them to be alive, like an embryo or egg. Analogically, Mother Earth was considered the womb and source of everything alive, and since metal goes through a process of development within the earth there arose a theory that metal was moving through a process or stages similar to an embryo's development; thus, base metals such as iron would develop through various stages and ultimately become gold. Again following the connection to technê, if metals did indeed develop naturally in the earth, then alchemists could develop an art that simply accelerated the process of nature. The alchemist's crucible was seen as a surrogate womb for Mother Earth. In the Middle Ages, alchemy and other "mystical sciences" were centered in the Islamic world, where a key connection was made: "Islamic alchemists believed that the transmutation of base metals into gold should be similar to the perfection of the person" (Channell 50). This connection led not only to ethical, moral and religious connotations but also to a focus on chemical substances that have medicinal value and more intense interest in traditional herbal medicine.

The Renaissance became a key moment in the transformation of vitalist ideas because it criticized both medieval texts and the authority of Aristotle while at the same time being dominated by a mystical or animistic worldview. Channell argues that although most historians see the Renaissance in terms of Neo-Platonism, current research sees at the core of the period a Hermetic tradition, which stems from a body of works on astrology, alchemy, and magic called *Corpus Hermeticum* (51). These writings, thought at the time to have been produced by an Egyptian priest from the time of Moses, give a different account of creation. In that story, humans are a direct spiritual link between earth and heaven and they thus have divine magic powers over the world. Ficino, a scholar in the court of Cosimo de Medici, developed a theory of magic based on an animistic worldview derived from Hermeticism, Neo-Platonism, and Pythagorean music theory. Following the Stoics, he saw the universe as alive and believed that humans could absorb its breath. This breath or spirit, he believed, provided a link between the heavens and individual bodies. The goal of the magician, as with the alchemist, was to "purify and nourish the spirit of earthly things by attracting and absorbing the world spirit" through "certain plants, foods, metals, or even music" (51–52).

Though these theories and practices were often based on more mystical interpretations of Aristotle, they actually laid the groundwork for astronomy, chemistry, medicine, and even modern physics. Renaissance-era astrology and alchemy were based on a somewhat more mystical notion of vitalism as either a vital substance such as gas or a mystical element such as spirit, but they became connected to a desire to learn more about the Creator and consequently "placed great emphasis on direct observation and experience" (49). Alchemists, for example, believed so strongly in the macro-micro connection, which assumes that experiments on small aspects of the universe amount to experiments on the universe as a whole, that they strove to create a direct connection to the Creator. This assumed relationship between the macro and micro persists today in the experiments of modern science. The animistic worldview also played an important role in Renaissance science. According to Channell, "Even scientists and philosophers who appeared to be 'modern' and 'rational' in their scientific discoveries were influenced by Hermetic ideas. For example, many of those who supported the sun-centered universe of Copernicus did so for reasons associated with solar magic as much as for reasons of empirical evidence" (52).[2] The new interest in magnetism circa 1600 was also associated with the action of magical forces. It was held up as an example of an animistic force in the universe. William Gilbert, for instance, saw the Earth as a giant magnet, using the animistic association to support the theory that the earth rotated around its axis. Gilbert's theory later influenced Kepler, who argued that the planets are kept in their orbits by an animistic force like magnetism that emanates from the sun.

Despite the fact that many read astrology, alchemy, and animism as forms of mysticism in opposition to science (or more specifically mechanism), the link between the organic and the technological set up in Aristotle continued through these theories of life. And though Aristotle's theory of entelechy is greatly transformed over time into forms of mysticism, the potential within his thought set into motion an entelechy that did lead to more scientific theories in the modern period. Essentially, both magicians and scientists look to define the laws of the universe in order to effect change in the world. What is critical for thinking about the movement of vitalism toward complexity is the evolution of theories of substance, such as a vital fluid or spirit, into theories of force. As modern science began to develop theories of magnetism, gravity, and electricity, the old mystical conceptions fell away and more contemporary models for the relationships among elements of the world developed.

Movement into Modernism

The concept of life took a new series of turns as science and philosophy moved into the modern episteme and away from the mystical theories of the Renaissance episteme. In *The Order of Things,* Foucault recounts the standard linear narrative that traditional historians use to describe the discovery of the sciences of life in the seventeenth and eighteenth centuries and juxtaposes it with his own position. Traditional historians tend to see the rise of a scientific approach to nature as the result of the new powers of observation: on the theoretical side they point to Bacon's work and, on the technical side, to the development of the microscope. These advancements extend the rationality of the already existing physical sciences to the realm of living beings. Looking for direct causes, historians note three new interests that support the investigation of living beings: the economic attitude toward agriculture (supported by the Physiocrats and the first efforts to create an agronomy), a new curiosity about exotic plants and animals (e.g., the voyages of Tournefort to the Middle East and Adanson to Senegal), and the ethical valorization of nature (Rousseau, in the eighteenth century, was also a botanist). The linear histories then posit the various forms the new sciences of life take based on these causes, one of which is the reaction against mechanism. Interest in living beings began under Cartesian mechanism, which eventually became problematic but led to an interest in experiments on living beings and a new form of rational science. By the end of the seventeenth century, the initial efforts of chemistry called mechanism into question. Consequently, throughout the eighteenth century, "vitalist themes are thought to have attained or returned to their privileged status, finally coalescing to form a unitary doctrine—that 'vitalism' which in slightly differing forms was professed by Bordeu and Barthez in Montpellier, by Blumenbach in Germany, and by Diderot then Bichat in Paris" (126). Despite this perceived reemergence and dominance of more vitalist work in the eighteenth century, linear histories see the science of life as being fulfilled through a positive and rational science: nineteenth-century biology.

In contrast to this account, Foucault establishes his historiography by positing different epistemes—or regimes of thought—in which theories of labor, life, and language share a mode of thought and are thus dissimilar to their counterpart theories in other epistemes and more similar to each other. He sees the Renaissance episteme as founded on resemblances or associative linkings, which support a mystical form of vitalism. The Classical episteme, his term for the dominant mode of thought in the seventeenth and eighteenth centuries, relies more strictly on exterior, visible characteristics than on an ethereal pneuma and consequently privileges a more mechanistic view. But rather than form oppositions between vitalist and mechanistic views, Foucault sees the different Classical perspectives as providing different answers to the same fundamental problem: "the possibility of classifying living beings" (126). Linnaeus feels that nature can be organized into a taxonomy. Buffon argues that nature is too heterogeneous for a taxonomy. Others focus on the generative process and range from those who espouse mechanistic preformation to those who focus on the specific development of germs. Still others look to analyze and organize functions: circulation (after William Harvey), sensation, motivity, and later respiration. But at root they all emphasize the classification of living beings. The focus on classifying in the Classical episteme, for Foucault, sets up the emergence of natural history as a completely new phenomenon. Classical thinkers see structure as purely external and visible, which prompted them to write "natural histories" that set out to describe the visible characteristics of the natural world. These descriptions then allow them to construct classical tables that ordered living beings.

Since Foucault sees both mechanists and vitalists writing these histories within the context of the same episteme, he finds oppositional histories of ideas problematic. He notes that it is easy enough for historians to "reconstruct the great controversies" of the day from a linear-causal history: (1) a theology positing God as the mystery beneath life and its movement versus a science trying to define the autonomy of nature, (2) a science still attached to the old mechanistic physics versus a science that is attempting to deal with the specific contents of life, and (3) the opposition between those who believe in the immobility of nature (Tournefort and Linnaeus) versus those who have a presentiment for life's creative powers (Bonnet, Benoît de Maillet, and Diderot). Foucault writes, "Long before Darwin and long before Lamarck, the great debate on evolution would *appear* to have been opened. . . . Mechanism and theology, supporting one another or ceaselessly conflicting with one another tended to keep the Classical age as close as possible to its origins—on the side of Descartes and Malebranche; whereas, opposite them, irreligion and a whole confused intuition of life . . . *are said* to be drawing [the study of life] towards its immanent future—toward the nineteenth century" (127; emphasis added). Foucault is, of course, arguing against this causal, linear, oppositional history that sees the triumph of mechanism in the nineteenth century as a fulfillment and logical conclusion of the eighteenth century. Following an epistemic logic, Foucault concludes, "Historians want to write histories of biology in the eighteenth century; but they do not realize that biology did not exist then, and that the pattern of knowledge that has been familiar to us for a hundred and fifty years is not valid for a previous period. And that, if biology was unknown, there was a very simple reason for it: that life itself did not exist. All that existed was living beings, which were viewed through a grid of knowledge constituted by *natural history*" (127–28).

For Foucault, there are archaeological, epistemic breaks between the Renaissance, the Classical, and the Modern epistemes. Therefore, it is problematic to read the vitalisms of the Classical episteme as a return to Renaissance vitalisms. Likewise, it is problematic to see the natural history of the Classical episteme and the biology of the Modern episteme as seamlessly connected. For Foucault, they are fundamentally different. The Classical episteme views the world in terms of natural history and places various living beings in a taxon-omy based on external characteristics, whereas the Modern episteme of the nineteenth century sees the emergence of the concept of life viewed biologically through internal organic structures: life is "a principle alien to the domain of the visible—an internal principle not reducible to the reciprocal interactions of representations" (227). In the late eighteenth century, from 1775 to 1795, sci-entists and philosophers recognized that the external characteristics are related to internal functions, which are a part of the larger, complex functioning of the organized being. Some theorists such as Jussieu, Lamarck, and d'Azyr re-alized that what is most important for classification is not necessarily the most visible characteristics. They began to see the need to look at the coherent to-tality of organic structures. For Foucault, this shift from an external to internal basis for classification is a mutation in natural history, but its epistemic basis is still taxonomy. Its major consequence, however, is the organic/inorganic dis-tinction, which became a primary basis for classification and did away with the old system of four kingdoms—making the old system "impossible" (232). The living "produces, grows, and reproduces" and the nonliving are deprived of these possibilities. Nevertheless, both forms intermingle: the inorganic is that which kills, undoes life, turns the organic back into the inorganic. This leads to a philosophy of "two powerful forces" at play in nature: "each perpet-ually destroys the efforts that the other succeeds in producing" (232).

This opposition fragments natural history and taxonomy at a level of ar-chaeological depth and makes biology in the nineteenth century possible. In Foucault's history, "What was to take place was not the more or less precar-ious triumph of a vitalism over a mechanism; vitalism and its attempt to define the specificity of life are merely the surface effects of those archeological events" (232). The shift during the late eighteenth and early nineteenth centuries was not simply the resurgence of an older form of "mystical" vitalism (which was grounded in the Renaissance episteme). Those who read the situation in this manner miss the fact that an archaeological shift is under way that signals the emergence of a new mode of thinking, not a return to an old one.

This new mode of thinking turns from surfaces and tables to depth and hidden forces. The shift in the early nineteenth century was not the transformation of natural history into biology: these are two different forms of knowledge with different objects, concepts, and methods. The concept of life rather than living beings requires new perspectives. Foucault looks at Georges Cuvier as his primary example of this shift. In (late) Classical analysis, an organ is defined by structure and function, producing a type of double-entry notebook model for classification. This arrangement is what Cuvier overthrows. He values function over organ and rejects the independence of the organ as something that can be extracted from its operating system and classified individually. Function needs to be separated from organs because the same function (respiration) can operate through different organs in different species (e.g., lungs versus gills); for Foucault, this makes function "invisible"—not a set external characteristic or organ but an abstract form. Foucault explicitly characterizes this as a return to Aristotle: function is defined by a "non-perceptible form as an effect to be attained" (265). The key to life's movement is its internal form, a functional homogeneity that operates as a hidden foundation. Foucault notes, "When the Same and Other both belong to a single space, there is natural history; something like biology becomes possible when this unity of level begins to break up, and when differences stand out against a background of an identity that is deeper and, as it were, more serious than that unity" (265). This creates new kinds of relations: coexistence, internal hierarchy, and dependence. Organisms are no longer independent but parts of a system of other organs as well as external ecology—the form of an animal's teeth is related to the type of available prey, for example. Organs are seen not as elements on a table but hierarchically in terms of which ones are more important for the being's survival, for life. Internal organs become primary over external appendages and appearances. Organisms, therefore, are dependent on a formal "plan" or structure that controls and protects the vital functions.

For Foucault this internal, formal unity of a living being is often still seen as mysterious, but it is fundamentally different than vitalist theories during the Renaissance. Life is now seen as the functional homogeneity that provides the abstract, hidden foundation of all living beings. It withdraws from living beings "into the enigma of a force inaccessible in its essence" (273). This concept of life is no longer something that can be placed in opposition to the mechanical. It is the force that moves living beings, gives inorganic matter organic motion. Scientists and philosophers are attempting to grapple with a fundamental co-productive relationship that produces a new epistemic constellation. In short, Foucault writes, "[i]t is the transition from the taxonomic to the synthetic notion of life which is indicated, in the chronology of ideas and sciences, by the recrudescence, in the early nineteenth century, of vitalist themes. From the archaeological point of view, what is being established at this particular moment is the conditions of possibility of a *biology*" (269).

Three Vitalisms

It is this shift in the nineteenth century and the formation of biology that requires a multiplicity of views on vitalism. Seeing vitalism only from the perspective of the Renaissance or even the Classical episteme closes off the recognition that new modes of thought emerge in the Modern episteme and continue to coalesce today. Both Channell and Foucault argue against the vitalism/mechanism opposition. As a historian of science, Channell charts a more linear narrative that shows how both influence each other in various periods and ultimately synthesize in the twentieth century. He shows very clearly that throughout the history of vitalism and mechanism, the perceived opposition is never a clearcut antagonism. Foucault also argues that the vitalism/mechanism opposition is never simply an opposition, but for different reasons. Laying out his version of history in terms of breaks, it becomes clear that most of the proponents on both sides operate on the same archaeological base or regime of thought. When that base is stable, both theories are working on similar problems in similar conditions. When that base changes, new theories and practices emerge in all fields to address the new conditions. For me there is something correct in both Channell's and Foucault's accounts. In each view, the crucial period of development is the nineteenth century, or what Foucault calls the Modern episteme. Consequently, I want to look more closely at these transformations with an eye on vitalism. It is the romantic period in the early nineteenth century that rhetoric and composition scholars see as a resurgence of old vitalist philosophies. But a closer look reveals early, middle, and late versions of vitalism specific to the Modern episteme—or what I am calling oppositional, investigative, and complex vitalisms.

These three vitalisms are not epistemic breaks but developments in the Modern episteme. To analyze these movements I follow Frederick Burwick and Paul Douglass in *The Crisis in Modernism: Bergson and the Vitalist Controversy.* They make the distinction between a "naive vitalism" and a "critical vitalism"— a distinction also made between animism and vitalism by Hans Driesch in the scientific literature. For Burwick and Douglass, naive vitalism arises during the Enlightenment as a contemporary reformulation of animism in reaction to the overly mechanistic theories of the time. This vitalism is adopted to allow a space for religious faith along with a scientific worldview.[3] Critical vitalism, like that of Hans Driesch and Henri Bergson, "emerged in the nineteenth-century transition from a matter-based physics to an energy-based physics. . . . Whereas naïve vitalism had posited a substance (*archeus,* vital fluid) in order to fit the evidence of a materialist ontology, critical vitalism focused on process and dynamic impulse in the context of an ontology of energy and idea" (Burwick and Douglass 1). While one may debate the notion that vitalism in the Enlightenment period is only a resurgence of animism, as Foucault shows, the articulation of a critical vitalism is important. I break Burwick and Douglass's critical vitalism into three parts or stages to focus more specifically on its development, which, following Foucault's concept of the episteme, happens both in the sciences and in philosophy.

Oppositional vitalisms of the late eighteenth and early nineteenth centuries look to notions of electromagnetic force. As far back as the mid-seventeenth century, Newton introduced the concept of force, in addition to matter and motion, in mechanical philosophies, which cannot account for magnetic or gravitational forces. Mechanical philosophies tried to posit some substance or gas as the cause, but Newton showed mathematically that a force can act at a distance across an empty space. In the eighteenth century, chemical philosophy followed suit and made the move from substance to force. The German chemist Georg Ernst Stahl argued that chemicals alone could not explain growth, development, and resistance to decomposition, so he viewed organic life as a force that preserves matter. By mid-century life was seen as analogous to magnetic and gravitational force by figures such as Georges-Louis Leclerc, Comte de Buffon, and John Turberville Needham, who "proposed a universal vegetative force consisting of an expansive force and a resistive force in equilibrium. The continual *tensions* and *interactions* between these *two forces* were responsible for all vital activity including embryological development" (Channell 55–56; emphasis added). By the late eighteenth and early nineteenth centuries, it had become more common to conceptualize this balance of oppositional forces in terms of electricity. In addition to doing experiments that sent electricity through dead bodies to generate movement, scientists such as Hans Christian Oersted and Michael Faraday began to experiment with the connection between magnetism and electricity, ultimately associating both with lines of force that can act at a distance and engender action. It is clear that a theory of energy based on a relational force that exercises influence over organic processes was not a look back to animism nor was it reducible to mysticism or even idealism. Reducing vitalism to a mysterious cause, whether it is an external substance, Platonic ideal, or god, ignores the historical moment of oppositional vitalism that sees life as the outcome of productive tension.

Investigative vitalisms of the mid-nineteenth to early twentieth centuries examined evolution and cell theory. Even before Darwin, Lamarck proposed a theory of biological change based on two causes: an inner life force that compels the movement toward perfection, and a changing environment that creates a specific need for new levels of complexity. Lamarck's theory brought back Aristotle's vitalism—teleology directed by some goal—and tried to connect the inner form to the outer world. Darwin then problematized the inner, goal-directed teleology in favor of the environment as the primary factor in change, but it still did not account for the source of inner change, leaving it up to random variation. By the 1830s and 1840s microscopes were strong enough to see into the inner movements of cell division and the formation of cells from other cells. This close-up view allowed cell theory to become associated with vitalism, self-replication being analogous with self-motivation. The German biologist Matthias Jakob Schleiden was the first to argue that all plants are composed of cells and that cells operate both independently from and as a part of larger systems. Similarly, French physiologist Claude Bernard argued that the body's cells are interconnected through an internal environment of fluid in plants and blood in animals that allows it to be a unified system but also responsive to external changes. For many of these thinkers, the physical and chemical processes of cells at micro levels are connected to external stimuli and their interrelationship manifests itself as vital phenomena at a macro level.

Hans Driesch, one of the last scientists of the nineteenth century to investigate vitalism critically, also tried to reconcile micro and macro levels of organization. He conducted experiments on blastomeres—cells produced during cleavage of an egg—and found that certain types of embryos can generate a whole from different parts. From these experiments, he put forward three empirical proofs of vitalism. His first proof was that only an organism, not a mechanical machine, could develop into a whole from various parts as well as repair and regenerate the life form. Driesch called these organisms "harmonious equipotential systems"—wholes whose parts cooperate in the formation of an organic unity. The entire organism is available in every cell, each cell playing a particular role because of its position in the system. The second proof was the existence of "complex equipotential systems." Not only will the blastomere, half of an egg, form a full larva, but that larva will go on to develop a whole animal. More complex organisms, he argued, develop from replication and division of a cell or egg—an internal unfolding of form and function that cannot be reduced to mechanism. Driesch's third proof was the existence of human agency. Even though this is commonly seen as conscious choice with the human as the primary efficient cause, Driesch argued that human agency is the same type of agency that functions in other vital processes like embryological development—the same process that operates at the micro level also operates at the macro level of organization. Driesch was essentially using contemporary science to reread Aristotle's concept of entelechy. Humans as an efficient cause cannot be isolated from the context created by the other four causes, in particular nature as a formal cause. Natural laws place constraints on the possible activities of a system, just as gravity places constraints on human actions. But laws cannot mechanically predetermine all of these activities in terms of simple cause and effect. Life operates in the open possibilities created by the multiple forces of natural laws. It is the agency that arranges cells, organs, and environments into complex equipotential systems.

Complex vitalisms of the twentieth century ultimately turned the opposition of mechanical and vital theories into a complex cooperative system, completing the shift from substance-based theories to event-based theories. Einstein's theory of relativity challenged a mechanical conception of the universe by modifying its concepts of length, time, and mass, making them relative quotients rather than unchanging material absolutes. The discovery of electrons and radiation in the late nineteenth century combined with Einstein's work in the early twentieth led Ernest Rutherford and Niels Bohr to propose a new model for the atom with a positively charged nucleus and negatively charged electrons orbiting the nucleus. This new model for matter based on force and polarity rather than substance led Werner Heisenberg and Erwin Schrödinger to deal the final blow to the mechanistic model when they showed that electrons, while carrying small weights like particles, acted instead as waves, leading to the development of quantum mechanics. Similarly, the discovery of DNA made it possible to see life in terms of information rather than substance. In *What Is Life?* (1944), Schrödinger proposes that seeing genes as crystals with small units that arrange atoms in a script similar to Morse code shows how DNA can self-replicate. Sounding much like Aristotle, Schrödinger argues that the miniature code is "a highly complicated and specific plan of development and should somehow contain the means to put it into operation" (quoted in Channell 130). Life in the first part of the twentieth century could no longer be seen as a thing: it was clear that complex forces ground matter and that micro levels of information affect development and organization. In all of these theories, events are a series of developing relations that provide the complex, constitutive ground of substance and life.

These developments at the micro level were eventually connected to larger environments. Paul Weiss's influential book *Morphodynamik* (1926) proposed the concept of field theory: the field as a whole organizes undifferentiated cells into a pattern. By the 1940s and 1950s, this basic idea had expanded into general systems theory. In 1950, Ludwig von Bertalanffy wrote "The Theory of Open Systems in Physics and Biology," putting forward a theory that sees atoms, organisms, machines, and human societies equally as kinds of systems. In 1954 he co-founded the interdisciplinary Society for General Systems Research, which established systems theory as a fully developed framework for contemporary thought. In *General System Theory: Foundations, Development, Applications* (1968), von Bertalanffy argues that general systems theory formulates scientific principles that are valid for any kind of system, "whatever the nature of their component elements and the relations or 'forces' between them. General systems theory, therefore, is a general science of 'wholeness' which up until now was considered a vague, hazy, and semi-metaphysical concept" (quoted in Mark Taylor, *The Moment of Complexity* 140). The "vague, hazy, and semi-metaphysical concept" of wholeness that von Bertalanffy refers to is the older notions of vitalism. Von Bertalanffy is trying to move the older notions of vitalism toward physical and biological systems and establish a logical, if not mathematical, discipline that can be applied to various empirical sciences. Even though von Bertalanffy wanted to develop principles for these complex organizations, systems are not simply abstract mental constructs but embodied realities. Any system is a complex living set of interacting components, each of which can be a subsystem of a larger organization or at times a separate system with its own interacting components, involving feedback loops within or among the systems. By the end of the twentieth century, the emphasis on events rather than substance was inflected outward from cells to ecological systems as whole organizations. Life had become an emergent property produced by the complex interactivity among cells, organs, bodies, and environments.

At the end of *The Order of Things,* Foucault hints at a final shift to what has since been characterized as postmodernism in the late twentieth century. But I read all three of these vitalisms—oppositional, investigative, and complex—as operating on the Modern episteme that sees function and internal relations as a founding principle rather than as external, visual characteristics. The convergence, or erasure, of vitalistic and mechanistic theories happening in physics, biology, and systems theory sees internal, abstract function as the key to life. What counts as internal—atoms, molecules, cells, organisms, environments—depends on how the circumference is drawn. Any body has inner systems and is also an inner part of larger systems. When Foucault proclaims the death of man at the end of *The Order of Things,* he is recognizing that the archaeological base of the Modern episteme will eventually reach the human sciences. Work in biology and physics had to come around to the humanities and anthropology

—the study of humans. Foucault knew that when it did, the notion of the subject would have to reach the epistemic shift that began early in the nineteenth century, resulting not in postmodernism but in posthumanism. The death of man is not anti-human but the collapse of an isolated, substantive image of the subject and the emergence of viewing humans in the complex context of nature, technology, and language. Foucault speculates that "perhaps one day, this century will be known as Deleuzian" because Deleuze articulates most completely the extension of the contemporary sciences into philosophy and the humanities ("Theatrum Philosophicum" 165). Looking at the situation from this perspective allows a much more specific and complex image of vitalism in philosophy and rhetoric to emerge.

Oppositional Vitalism

The oppositional vitalism of early-nineteenth-century science set the stage for Coleridge's philosophical vitalism based on the concept of polarity—opposite forces that drive power. While France, Great Britain, and Holland were generally dominated by mechanical philosophy, organic philosophy continued to be dominant in Germany. The *Naturphilosophie* that Coleridge followed was influenced predominantly by Leibniz and Kant. Though Leibniz is often associated with mechanical philosophy, he saw his notion of monads not as simple mechanistic units or substances but as "centers of vital force that combined the passivity of matter with the activity of mind. Unlike mechanical atoms that underwent change because of external causes, a world composed of monads underwent change through its own inner growth" (Channell 57). Kant similarly tried to overcome the mechanistic duality of matter and vital force. He argued that the concept of substance is the result of the mind's perception of forces rather than physical bodies. In *Metaphysical Foundations of Natural Science* (1786), Kant argues that nature could be explained as a conflict between the forces of attraction and repulsion. Some forces appear to us as material bodies, some as magnetism, gravity, or electricity. Though Kant's notion of forces would seem quite reasonable today in the context of quantum physics, in his day it was read with lesser or greater emphases on idealist notions of mind. Though he was trying to replace mechanistic philosophy with dynamic and organic concepts, Kant retained the notions of subject and object, mind and nature. Schelling, and other German *Naturphilosophers,* attempted to find a common ground for subjects and objects that would resolve the opposition. Schelling saw matter and mind as phases of the same ground and argued that both science and philosophy should work to show how matter starts as force and through dynamic processes becomes mind. This makes nature a purposive system with a *telos*—the world becomes a dynamic process of movement from object to subject caused by the tension between two polar forces of the same power.

This backdrop of polarity and force in German philosophy clearly influenced Coleridge, who is the most notable interpreter of German philosophy in the English romantic movement. In "Theory of Life," Coleridge enters the materialist-vitalist debate of the early nineteenth century.[4] Drawing upon concepts in *Naturphilosophie,* he attempts to distance himself both from earlier vitalist thought and from mechanistic science, both of which were grounded on the concept of substance. He makes it very clear that his position is not a return to alchemy or a naive vitalism based on a vital substance—he "distinctly disclaim[s] all intention of explaining life into an occult quality" (500). He also makes it clear that even though he believes humans have souls, unlike animals, his discussion in "Theory of Life" is specifically limited to physical reality. Consequently, he rejects two opposing views: that life is derived from the unconscious actions of the rational soul (à la Georg Ernst Stahl) and that life is the effect of organization, that the organization of *previously existing substances* causes life (à la William Lawrence) (501). Such a position presupposes the concept of substance, thus providing an "account" of life rather than an "explanation" of it. Coleridge was attempting to explain life theoretically, not just give an empirical account of it. To say that matter comes from other matter is like saying the material cause of a house is its efficient cause. For Coleridge, it simply does not make logical sense to explain matter in terms of matter. To say that the organization of pre-existing substances causes life begs the question of what caused the material substances in the first place, not to mention what caused them to organize.

Consequently, Coleridge rejects fluids, ethers, magnetism, electricity, and chemicals as singular causes of life: for him they are effects of life (502). In the shift from external classification to internal functions, many in Coleridge's day took a single function of life, such as nutrition, to be central and thus the basis of life. For Coleridge, this view excludes other functions and ignores the systematic relations among functions and their overall context. Any emphasis on one element or substance ignores the agency of the whole system (494). What Coleridge was after is definitely not animism or naive vitalism based on vital substance or mechanical philosophy based on material substance. He was trying to find a general law that can explain a dynamic world, a law that does not give a description of the world but explicates its self-regulating, internal power. Knowingly or not, he was clearly grappling with Aristotle's causes, trying to figure out what theoretical principle would explain efficient cause within nature.

The issue is Kantian: because of the limits of the body's sense perception, humans cannot perceive a power or force that is immaterial. If material substance is a product or effect of the perception of forces operating in the whole system, then perception cannot get beyond substance to a direct perception of forces. Consequently, any explanation of life force has to operate through analogy. In the debates of Coleridge's day, mechanical philosophers were troubled by arguments from analogy because theorists could say life is "like" anything they wished, producing a connection that may or may not correspond to reality. Lawrence, for example, argues that magnetism, gravity, and electricity are not like each other much less like life (529). But for Coleridge, physics and physiology were not randomly alike. There is a difference between resemblance and analogy: resemblance implies a similarity in kind, analogy a difference in kind (531). Coleridge was operating on the epistemic shift from Classical to Modern, from visible external form to abstract internal function, and he was making it clear that he was not going back to the Renaissance resemblance that produced alchemy. He was using argumentative analogy in relation to function. Gills and lungs are different in kind but similar in function. The analogy underlying Coleridge's argument is that magnetism, gravity, and electricity are different in kind but similar in function. Force is like an abstract function. And because the nature of magnetism, gravity, and electricity is similar, understanding one can help us understand the others. An important analogy for Coleridge is that we know the forces of magnetism, gravity, and electricity only by their effects. Similarly, we can only know life force through its effects (529n3). The importance of magnetism, gravity, and electricity is not that they *are* life or *cause* life but that they provide a way of understanding vital power: for example, electromagnetic force can help us understand life force (508–9). Coleridge is addressing the charge that he is a naive, substance-based vitalist. Rather than a material substance, fluid, gas, or chemical reaction, life is the product of relations among forces (530), and he is attempting to find a way to theorize an immaterial force.

For Coleridge, life is a "self-renewing power," and he is interested in determining a "law or principle of action" for this power (495). Following *Naturphilosophie*—primarily Schelling and Henrik Steffens—he sees nature not as a great chain of being or as a tableau of living beings but as a ladder that moves in concentric circles, expanding outward as it rises upward (509): life is not linear or static but a continuous process that folds over on itself and produces increased complexity and individuation. This centripetal force is a fundamental law of life that Steffens calls the principle of individuation—the internal force of attraction that holds many things together in a single whole and is presupposed by all of its parts. Steffens sees this principle of individuation as both means and end (efficient and final cause): "Through her whole organization, Nature aims at nothing but the most individual creations" (quoted in Coleridge, "Theory of Life" 510n4). As nature moves forward, upward, and around on itself it creates a force of attraction or organization. For Coleridge, this unifying power is in everything, but it is more *intense* in more complex individual beings—in other words, nature's most intense composition is a human individual (512). This increased complexity and intensity creates greater interdependence among parts and wholes and "expresses an intellectual act" as its highest point of complexity (513). Coleridge's use of the term "expresses" is important here. He is not talking about the expression of an isolated, individual, subjective mind but the expression of forces and relations in the world that at a certain level of intensity and complexity is manifested as thought.

Coleridge's vitalism ultimately rests on the oppositional forces of attachment and repulsion or the productive tension of polarity, which is the highest law or most general form of nature: it appears and reappears in different configurations in higher and higher levels of reality. This law of polarity operates on a basic analogy to magnetism, which has two poles that both attract and repel—the poles create individuation as well as connection (517). Coleridge is operating on a paradox inherent in magnetism: opposite poles are derived from a single source. One power (magnetism) is the foundation of both opposite forces. This unity of force can attract other forces and produce a new composition or unity. But it can also repel opposite forces and create differentiation even in its tendency toward balance or stability. This constant strife of force and balance drives both differentiation and individual unities. As this play of forces increases in degree and complexity, it exposes itself to human perception as a tendency toward individualization, even as these unities are further connected to and dependent on the whole process. This is the basic law or function behind life as a dynamic process rather than a thing or substance. For Coleridge it is "essential to all actual existence, [and] expands, or produces itself" (520). From this perspective, "[n]ature is the scheme of ever-varying relations" (520) driven by polarity, which, again following German *Naturphilosophie,* he expands from two poles to four poles—attraction, repulsion, contraction, expansion (524).

It is important to recognize that in Coleridge's scheme chemical, magnetic, and electrical forces are not the life force, but all are manifestations of the vital power of polarity at different stages of development or intensity (524–26). What we experience as life is the combination, composition, or unity of all of these forces and levels of intensity. In other words, life is manifested through these forces—all of which obey the same general law of polarity. Coleridge writes that "[t]he chemical process acts in depth, and first, therefore, realizes and integrates the fluxional power of magnetism and electricity, [which] is involved in the *term* composition; and this will become still more convincing when we have learnt to regard *decomposition* as a mere correlative, i.e., as decomposition relatively to the body decomposed, but composition *actually* and in respect of the substances, *into* which it was decomposed" (555). This notion of the world as one set of ever-varying relations of composition and decomposition is essentially Spinozist. Spinoza's equating of God with nature is clearly an influence on German *Naturphilosophie.*[5] At the level of human perception, we can see differentiation as a body (or unity) being decomposed. But at the level of underlying unity, power is simply shifting from one composition to another. The tension of the forces of composition and decomposition are ultimately one and the same power—life.

In this context I tend to read Coleridge's image of concentric circles on the ladder of increasing intensity as a way of articulating an initial theory of ecology with an ever-widening circumference of interdependence. More forces in the ecological mix increase intensity and ultimately both individuation and interdependence. It seems clear that at this point in his thinking Coleridge is working on a return to Aristotle's entelechy in the context of the shift from a Classical to a Modern episteme. Any attempt to read Coleridge's vitalism in terms of a mystical or animistic paradigm or to read this emerging, oppositional vitalism in terms of substance and not forces and relations takes Coleridge out of his epistemic context. Coleridge's vitalism is oppositional not only in his opposition to philosophies of substance (both vital and mechanical) but also in his sense of polarity and oppositional force. To say that Coleridge's vitalism is a mystical, idealist, or religious position is simply mistaken.[6] Coleridge heralds the integration of the sciences with the humanities, but because of his epistemic position his notion of the subject is affected the least. As Foucault recognizes, it takes until the last half of the twentieth century for what begins with Coleridge and German philosophy to fully hit the humanities and the concept of subjectivity.

Investigative Vitalism

In the context of the mid-nineteenth to early twentieth centuries, the two most prominent vitalist philosophers were Nietzsche and Bergson, who investigated more deeply into becoming and movement. Nietzsche examines the force of will in the process of becoming and deploys it critically against the naive idealisms and reified positivisms of the day. Nietzsche rejects the substantial materialism and atomism of his time as well as Platonic idealism, seeing life and creativity in terms of power. The will to power is not a substance that causes the flow of the material world but a becoming with its own source of fertility. Being anti-Platonic, Nietzsche contrasts this fertility with any absolute or abstracted form. Any abstract notion such as volition, cause, or substance is simply the perceivable effect of a set of forces that are beyond human awareness. Nietzsche is rejecting the atomistic and mechanistic philosophies of his time by emphasizing force as a dynamic tension of impulses and willings, themselves products of forces the whole of which is the will to power. This will to power expresses immanent change. The fixed rules of Being, idealism, and mechanism violate the reality of life as flux. Power is not a hierarchical social power, which Nietzsche calls the will-to-oppress, but a creative impetus that vitalizes all social power, both domineering as well as resistant (terms that in Nietzsche's model are abstractions akin to volition, cause, substance, and God). In this world of flux, art becomes one of the primary remedies for nihilism. The productive creativity of the will to power is the only thing that can give meaning to life.

Bergson is generally considered a prominent vitalist figure, but his relationship to that history depends on how it is drawn.[7] One thing is clear: Bergson is not a naive vitalist who reduces life or movement to a pre-existing material or even final cause. In *Creative Evolution,* he clarifies his position in relation to both mechanism and vitalism. A mechanistic view of matter posits a preexisting cause, either in another material body or material circumstances, that pushes matter and produces motion. Likewise, vitalism, or finalism as he initially calls it, posits a pre-existing plan or final cause that matter strives to complete or achieve. Even though Bergson accepts certain aspects of each model, the problem is that both are too narrow: "That life is a kind of mechanism I cordially agree. But is it the mechanism of parts artificially isolated from the whole of the universe, or is it the mechanism of the real whole? The real whole might well be, we conceive, an indivisible continuity. The systems we cut within it would, properly speaking, not then be parts at all; they would be partial views of the whole" (*Creative Evolution* 31). Both mechanism and vitalism essentially make artificial interventions into the overall movement of the universe in order to explain it. Mechanism uses matter to explain motion, which is partially true, but it narrows movement to one particular instance and closes off the possibility of any other explanation beyond mechanistic cause. Initially vitalism posits a predetermined plan for the whole universe that it plays out. But because such a position can never be empirically proven, vitalists begin to draw the circumference smaller to the internal plans of individual bodies or cells. But "internal finality" simply cuts a partial view of the whole just like mechanism (41). The notion of a final cause does not fully explain the vital principle of the whole, but at least it opens the door to the question rather than closing it off as mechanism does, and it is this approach to the whole that Bergson wants to investigate.

Bergson articulates the whole by positing two different kinds of order, mathematical and vital. Mathematical or geometric order does not address nature itself. Even though its calculations can produce predictions about material reality, which are important to human action in the world, it is only a representation of this reality at a certain level of generalization. If it did correspond exactly to materiality, science would not be contingent and everything would easily correspond to geometry. The problem with this model of order is that it generates the idea of disorder, which for Bergson has no positive content. As an abstract negation, disorder does not represent anything material or real. Assuming that it does creates the false problem of having to impose order on disorder. Consequently, older versions of vitalism imagine a vital principle that stands outside chaos, repairs its divergent lines of development, and keeps them on the single path to the final cause. Vital order, on the other hand, is the material development of evolution. It also repeats itself, which allows humans to generalize phenomena into genera and species. But in vital order this is not an exact repetition based on the same cause, as in mathematical or mechanistic order. Even though species may look the same at our level of experience, they are created by "infinitely complex elementary causes" that are different in each case (225). From this perspective there is no such thing as complete chaos or exact mathematical repetition. Life operates in the middle of these extremes as one complex, evolving order of "infinitesimal causes" that engender living beings (225). The vital principle or impetus for Bergson, then, is not an external force, substance, or god. It is the unceasing, immanent transformation of life that passes through individual living beings. Accident, chance, disorder, and mystery are simply ways of talking about the fact that vital order opens causes to infinity, and our level of human perception does not have complete access to that complexity.

This model of the whole is bound up with a particular conception of time. Mathematical order divides time into spatialized units; mechanism order thus sees the moment right before the present as its singular cause. But vital order embraces the notion that all time is one continuous movement of interlocking organizations. In Bergson's concept of duration, present moments arise and perish in the context of their entire past and potential future, which are given continuity via memory. It is important to realize that this memory is both material and mental. Each material body has its own history. Through the one vital order, each organism is connected with its most distant ancestor and all of the descendants of that ancestor in all directions. The whole of this past from cell to environment survives in the present organization, which in turn structures possible future developments of life. In animals and especially humans, this bodily memory rises to the level of mental memory. In animals, instinct connects the bodily knowledge to a present situation, bringing recollections momentarily into the present to serve some urgent need and "complete [the] present situation" (167). In humans, memory is more extensive and can be recalled into consciousness and held there without an immediate need, which gives "the organism greater choice of possible actions" (180). For Bergson, humans think at a conscious level with relatively few past memories, but we desire, will, and act with the whole of the past. In each moment, "all that we have felt, thought and willed from our earliest infancy is there, leaning over the present which it is about to join, pressing against the portals of consciousness" (5). Without this building up of the past in the mind there is no memory and no will. Intuition taps into the conditions of possibility created by vital organization and turns that toward conscious, intellectual understandings. Memory similarly taps into our past experience and allows the imagination to extend our past into a potential future. Intuition and memory, then, create the will or impetus to strive for a possible future from our particular line of decent. And once the mind receives the impulsion, it "continues its course" (202).

Bergson's vital impetus is ultimately not a push from the past or a pull from the future. It is the radical renewal of external material and efficient cause and internal final and formal cause in every moment of vital organization. The vital impulse produced in this organization is difficult to discuss analytically since the intellectual mind does not have direct or complete access to it. Science can represent material reality and living beings mathematically, but once that is exhausted it becomes necessary to turn to philosophy to represent life. Therefore, somewhat like Coleridge, Bergson has to use a number of analogies to discuss it: the vital impulse is like consciousness, will, a current, a wave, gravity, or energy. Even the use of the term impulse is an analogy (257). In many ways,

Bergson's more material analogies ground his more philosophical ones. Impulsion is like gravity, a force that makes an object fall continuously or move until arrested. But this analogy alone is too deterministic. More like solar energy, the vital impulse moves through all material life and energizes it. At its most fundamental level, life is the gradual storing up of energy and the channeling of this energy into unpredictable directions via bursts of movement that ultimately result in "free acts" (255). Plants, for example, store energy from the sun and animals feed on plants (or other animals that feed on plants) and process this energy to use for action. These actions are bursts of energy, like a spark igniting gunpowder, that move in diverging and unpredictable directions. Ultimately, this movement of energy through matter manifests itself as consciousness. This is not an individual consciousness but a consciousness that permeates the whole of life and becomes both a cause and an effect of the system. Consciousness of the environment further initiates will, desire, and movement; it drives organisms to find food for energy and desire mates for reproduction, all to further produce consciousness or life (111). Consciousness and materiality, then, are two interconnected movements of the same process: life.

While Bergson's discussions of consciousness would result in his being labeled a vitalist, with its negative connotation, his position is quite different than the older models of vitalism he set aside.[8] Rather than a harmonious whole that develops from an initial plan, the whole is made of discord. In this model, evolution does not build or progress: it divides and reconnects. The movement from energy is turned, divided, and opposed, and the unfolding of this conflict is life. For Bergson, there are no things, only actions. Never fully stable or motionless, actions continually decompose the organization they are in and recompose new organizations. The consuming of energy is one organization with matter, and the use of this energy decomposes that relation in order to create a new organization. Vital activity is the continual combination of "the automatic and strictly determined evolution of this well-knit whole [that] is action unmaking itself, and . . . the unforeseen forms which life cuts out in it, forms capable of being themselves prolonged into unforeseen movements [that is action] making itself" (248). These two movements of matter and life are counter-currents that create new forms of organization. This duality, which I characterized with Coleridge as "two forces, one power," is a function of the continually moving whole that is so expansive, so open, that no closed, deductive theory can be drawn to predict it. Thus Bergson's vitality has no plan, no predetermined teleology (265). There is no life in general marching to some goal that was predetermined in a past form, only the continual creation of new forms of organization in each moment. Such a self-organizing system is essentially creative. A reduction to mechanism or finalism leaves no room for invention, for the development of new organizations of matter.

Bergson's philosophical investigations into movement and time build a philosophy commensurate with the sciences of his day. Coming out of developments in evolution and biology, he charts a course between idealism and materialism that shows vitalism cannot be flatly equated with mysticism or an ahistorical romanticism. Rather, he is operating in his epistemic position at the tipping point between oppositional vitalism and the full complexity embraced later in the twentieth century. He plays out Foucault's shift from looking at living beings to investigating life as "perpetual growth, a creation pursued without end" (239).[9] If entelechy can still be seen in his model, it would have to be an entelechy that is radically renewed. Bergson writes explicitly about Aristotle's attempt to get beyond the forms of Plato. His attempt to put forms into the world leads to the idea of a prime mover that pours ideas out into matter. In a sense, science as a whole is given all at once and the human intellect is left to put it back together piecemeal. The initial cause as push is then coupled with the desire to "[follow] to the end the natural movement of the intellect" (323). Bergson sees in Aristotle both the push from the motionless mover and the aspiration toward divine perfection to regain the original unity. But both the divine cause and the aspiration to return to it necessitate a third option. The two causes essentially affirm the degrees of intermediate reality between them just as the numbers zero and ten presuppose one through nine. And following Zeno's paradox, mathematically there is an infinite number of points between the beginning and end. In Bergson's reading, therefore, Aristotle affirms not the necessity of a motionless mover, but that "this movement could not have begun and can never come to an end" (325). Vitality, action, and movement come from life's continual reorganization. The system generates its own striving. Entelechy becomes the renewed conditions of possibility in every situation, a radically situated set of forces. In short, entelechy becomes vital impulse.

Complex Vitalism in the Sciences

My discussions of vitalism in this book are not an attempt to resurrect any model of vitalism from the past. I am interested in what these philosophies have become, both in the sciences and in philosophy. If vitalism writ large was an attempt to study and theorize self-organizing or self-motivating systems, then the majority of this work in the mid- to late twentieth century was done in systems theory and complexity theory, which, along with Bergson, set the stage for Deleuze's philosophical vitalism. Ironically, perhaps, the most important element in the study of complex biological systems was the development of computers. Computer models allow researchers to perform complex calculations and to model systems for establishing principles of their functionality. This means that many of the investigations into life turned toward artificial intelligence and its development into the field of artificial life. Artificial intelligence tries to model cognitive and psychological processes: it builds computers to do things minds can do, such as playing chess or making a diagnosis. This approach presupposes a general purpose computer and an external designer to write the code that determines the structure of the task. Artificial life, on the other hand, seeks to define simple reflex-like rules that allow more complex actions to emerge. Rather than operate from the top down, artificial life looks to work from the bottom up to generate order at a higher level. Instead of pre-programming the task, artificial life develops systems with their own principles of organization by taking input from the system to determine its operation and movement.

The study of these principles of organization began with the Macy conferences on cybernetics in the late 1940s and early 1950s.[10] The cybernetics group, whose key figures were Norbert Wiener, Julian Bigelow, Warren McCulloch, Walter Pitts, and John von Neumann, began focusing on the general problem of circularity. In Norbert Wiener's book *Cybernetics: Or Control and Communication in the Animal and the Machine* (1948), Wiener and his partner Julian Bigelow realize the importance of feedback, where the performance of a machine folds back in as input. They theorize that the human nervous system might function in the same way, as a circular process moving from the nervous system to the muscles and back to the nervous system. Wiener reads this as a form of communication in both living and inorganic systems rather than a form of mechanical engineering and thus turns the issue toward information theory. Cybernetics, from the Greek word for steersman, is the theory that information steers systems. Information as both positive and negative feedback influences maintenance, adaptation, and direction of a system. For example, a room thermostat operates on a negative feedback loop in which the information gathered by the system maintains homeostasis. In the thermostat/room/ furnace system, "the incoming information from the room (variations from a set baseline in temperature) is processed in such a way (engaging the compensatory mechanism of the furnace) as to maintain the homeostasis of the system (the desired room temperature)" (Rasch and Wolfe 11). Since the thermostat sets what counts as difference in the system, information is not a static, atomistic element in the world outside the system but an element specific to that system. If the system is said to have a cause, it would come from feedback in the system itself.

The theoretical seeds of artificial life, however, were developed by von Neumann, who was one of the first to theorize cellular automata as self-reproducing systems. Von Neumann was interested in the logic of reproduction and in how systems spontaneously generate order. Before the discovery of DNA and the development of genetics, von Neumann "realized that part of the self-replicating system must function both as instructions and as data" (Boden 6). In 1945 von Neumann developed a machine that could store a set of instructions and distinguish between those original instructions and incoming data. While this machine removed the primary physical relation between humans and machines (in early computers humans changed the circuits in order to reprogram the computer for different tasks), it led to a more metaphorical similarity. Like Wiener, von Neumann argued that the computer is analogous to the associative networks of the human nervous system. In "General and Logical Theory of Automata," a lecture delivered in 1948, von Neumann drew on the notion of neural networks to argue that computer and biological systems process data in a similar manner. With Stanislaw Ulam, von Neumann developed the concept of cellular automata, which is "a computer program or piece of hardware consisting of a regular lattice or array of cells. Each cell is assigned a set of instructions by means of an algorithm that tells it how to respond to the behavior of adjacent cells as the automaton advances from one discrete step to the next" (von Neumann, quoted in Mark Taylor 143). Without overarching design or pre-programmed direction, each cell evolves from simple rules that respond to changes in surrounding cells. As cells interact, complex forms emerge and produce lifelike movements.

Von Neumann produces cellular automata only in theory, but once more powerful computers became available researchers started going back to his model. In 1968, John Conway created a simplified version of von Neumann's cellular automata called the "Game of Life." Von Neumann's mathematical proof, which contained 200,000 cells in any one of twenty-nine states, showed that cellular automata could in principle reproduce. Conway simplified this model and found that fairly simple rules create complex dynamic, global changes that emerge, evolve, settle into patterns, and disappear, all in a lifelike manner. (The "Game of Life" looks like swarms of bees or flocks of birds.) A simple rule, such as "if a cell is surrounded by at least three cells with the same color, then the cell will take on that color," results in some patterns that are simple, some that are complex, some that stay stable for long periods, and some that evolve and then die away quickly (Channell 134). As Mark Taylor notes, "[L]ife appears to be informational, and . . . information seems to be lifelike" (145). It is not just that life *is* information but that life and information both *function* as complex systems.

In the early 1970s, Christopher Langton saw in cellular automata and the "Game of Life" the possibility of creating a computer specifically for generating the properties of life. In a 1987 conference paper entitled "Artificial Life," Langton delivered a manifesto that names the field, outlines its assumptions, gives a historical overview of research, and sets its future aims. Langton sees life as "a set of vital functions implementable in various material bases" (Boden 8). Functions can be described in terms of information but the goal of artificial life (AL) is to determine how life comes about through material systems. The reason biology moves toward information and away from chemistry proper is because the same chemical can function differently in different systems, species, or stages: "In slime moulds, for instance, one and the same chemical substance (cAMP) has different biological functions, or meanings, in three phases of the organism's life history. In the first phase, cAMP causes separated amoebic cells to aggregate into a mass, or slug. In the next, it acts as the pacemaker for the contractions by which the slug moves along the ground. Finally, it causes the homogenous cells of the slug to differentiate into three distinct types, forming a base, stalk, and spore-containing head" (8–9). The three different developmental contexts create different meanings or different interpretations of the chemical information. Many of these processes cannot be studied directly, so Langton uses computers to model ecological environments and study how life emerges and evolves from an initial context or set of parameters into something new. Programs can map out specie evolution in response to predators or different landscapes, follow the effects of mutation rates, establish degrees of interaction among species, and chart the gradual accumulation of genetic changes that occur before an "evolutionary leap" (12). The development of more powerful computers provides a way to study these material processes that are extremely complex or that extend over vast amounts of time and cannot be studied directly in an embodied situation.

These models initiate a move from systems theory to complexity theory. In 1984, Langton and Stephen Wolfram, working under John Holland, a student of von Neumann, found that cellular automata have four typical behaviors: a rigid structure that does not change, oscillating patterns that change periodically, chaotic activity with no stability, and patterns that are not too structured or chaotic that divide, recombine, and develop in multiple complex ways. Langton was most interested in this complex behavior. It exhibits the same type of transition as a solid to a fluid, or a fluid to a gas: the changing patterns move in a typical sequence—order-complexity-chaos-complexity-order. Complexity is the moment of transition from order to chaos and back to order. Mark Taylor points out four key characteristics of this transitional complexity: (1) states of order and chaos emerge from interaction of parts not outside agents, (2) the complex events have effects disproportionate to their causes, (3) the dynamic interactions create global events that require holistic analysis and cannot be reduced to the individual parts, and (4) at the "tipping point"—the moment of transition between states—the effects of the individual events are unpredictable (*The Moment of Complexity* 146–49). This emergent logic can help explain both informational and biological systems: the same rules that apply to cellular automata also apply to natural phenomena. In a paper delivered in 1992 at the third Workshop on Artificial Life, Mark Millonas wrote, "The notion that complex behavior, from the molecular to the ecological, can be the result of parallel local interactions of many simpler elements is one of the fundamental themes of artificial life. The swarm, which is a collection of simple locally interacting organisms with global adaptive behavior, is a quite appealing subject for the investigation of this theme" (quoted in Mark Taylor 153). The complex probability distributions of evolution and the complex behavior of swarms of bees, flocks of birds, schools of fish, and colonies of ants all emerge from the interactions of multiple organisms in relation to the complex conditions of an ecological environment. None of the individual organisms of the group has access to or knowledge of the system as a whole. The local interactions and communications among parts generate the emergence of global behavior.

Even with the emergence of complexity theory, there is still at this point no agreed upon definition of life. At best, it is an assemblage of properties: self-organization, emergence, autonomy, growth, development, reproduction, evolution, adaptation, responsiveness, and metabolism (Boden 1). The central concept in artificial life is self-organization—the emergence and maintenance of order via complexity and the development of spontaneous or autonomous change generated from the internal working of a system in relation to its environment. In contrast to artificial intelligence's focus on Cartesian models of mind and disembodied conscious mental tasks, artificial life assumes that intelligence is grounded in life, in specific embodied situations, and focuses on more unconscious, embodied tasks. Situated robotics, for example, looks to construct robots that operate on bottom-up environmental cues, using the robot's own body movements to generate perpetual feedback that directs future actions. It focuses on the robot's brain as a sensory motor nervous system, rather than abstract notions of mind. As Margaret Boden puts it, "Classical AI depends on general-purpose models, but there are no general-purpose animals: each species behaves appropriately only within its own ecological niche" (15). In this model, all of the basic properties of life can be reproduced artificially except metabolism. Metabolism—the chemical changes in living cells that provide energy for vital processes and activities—requires biological as well as physical embodiment. While artificial life does involve forms of energy exchange (electrical, for example), only biologically embodied life can break down chemicals and synthesize them (i.e., digest food). But in both physical and biological embodied life, there is a feedback loop that generates energy from the system to drive the system's self-organization.

Essentially the study of life through artificial means extends the shift from examining characteristics of living beings to examining functions of living systems. The emergence of the concept of life in the Modern episteme is the result of more complex investigations of all the functional moments that drive organization from simple to complex systems. From this perspective, life is far from mysterious or miraculous, or even accidental—it is to be expected that systems will generate life from basic sets of conditions. Ultimately, life is an inherent property of embodied organization. What this means is that genetics and natural selection are not the only principles of evolution. Boden writes, "Granted, the genes specify the internal conditions (at various stages) of development . . . [and] so crucially affect the resulting organism. And natural selection determines which of the slightly differing variants of developed forms will thrive. But . . . these two factors alone cannot explain the form of living things. That an ordered organism develops at all, out of relatively homogenous, unstructured beginnings, is due to the inherent self-organizing properties of complex systems" (13). Evolution is not random, but it is still difficult to determine functional traits from mutations that are recessive, not to mention determining the fitness of functions. Mark Bedau argues that artificial life can help answer these problems by providing models that allow criteria for selection to change as the system evolves, and he offers a measure of "vitality"—the rate new adaptations arise and persist in a given system, which would indicate whether or not a system involves life (cited in Boden 24). Vitalism in this context has become something very different than mystery. Vitality is an emergent aspect of complex systems and their primary function, self-organization. In the late twentieth century, vitalism as a theory of both energizing force and holistic scope emerged in a new form.

Complex Vitalism in the Humanities

It is only in the context of this larger development of complexity theory that contemporary philosophers such as Martin Heidegger, Michel Foucault, and Gilles Deleuze can be fully understood. While Heidegger teeters on the cusp between the phenomenological perspective of investigative vitalisms and later complex vitalisms, all three thinkers look to examine our complex situatedness within the world, language, technology, and institutions. Deleuze more than the others operates out of complexity theory, explicitly taking scientific concepts and remaking them through compositions with the history of philosophy. Through his readings of Bergson, Nietzsche, and Spinoza, Deleuze formulates an expressionism (the expression of complex relations), not an expressivism (the expression of an individual subject). In rhetoric and composition, anything postmodern or poststructuralist is read through the terministic screen of expressivism or social-epistemic rhetoric, both of which are founded on theories of substance rather than events—expressivism is centered on the individual body and social-epistemic rhetoric is centered on a dialectic among distinct, pre-existing elements in the world. This perspective obscures the possibility of seeing something like Deleuze's expressionism from the epistemic ground of the late Modern period, or what I am calling complex vitalism. The problem with many theories of human action is that they operate from an opposition between human intention as active and material context as static and passive, thus privileging human action. In contrast to this humanist model, human action is actually a part of the feedback loop of complex systems. It not only is a product of these systems but also feeds information and movement back into the system. This posthumanist model sees humans as functioning parts of life, and any theory of action or change must take this larger, more complex situatedness into account. Deleuze pushes this position further by seeing any body, organic or inorganic, not as a whole but as a constellation of parts that participate in multiple systems. Expression from this perspective can be only the expression of a world, of an entire system, of life, not just one element or function within it.

In *Anti-Oedipus* Deleuze and Guattari lay out this posthumanist model and its connections to vitalism. For Deleuze and Guattari, the mechanism/organism binary is insufficient. They are not simply looking to examine the machine/human interface but also to examine their interrelationship as desiring-machines —assemblages of parts that produce desire, which generates movement and production. These machines are not objects to be used by a subject, nor are they objects that suppress the subject. They do not operate at the level of a human organism or technological machine. Rather, parts of the human body connect to different parts of other bodies: the breast-machine that produces milk and is connected with the mouth-machine of a baby, for example. Desiring-machines are not at the level of mother and child but breast and mouth, parts that connect, transfer energy, and then break away. This mouth-machine can break away and participate in multiple machines: connected with food it is an eating-machine, with language it is a talking-machine, with oxygen it is a breathing-machine. It has not one function but multiple functions within multiple machines. Importantly, these machines are not simply organic. For Deleuze and Guattari, "There is no such thing as either man or nature now, only a process that produces the one within the other and couples machines together. . . . [O]utside and inside no longer have any meaning whatsoever" (2), and "there is no such thing as relatively independent spheres or circuits" (4). Parts of organisms, technologies, nature, or language combine and recombine to create a desiring-machine and break apart to form new ones. In each case, there is always a flow-producing machine and a machine that connects to it, breaking or redirecting that flow, and the first machine is always connected to a machine whose flow it interrupts and draws energy from—energy is always consumed and action produced. This process of production is not a goal or end in itself or an infinite perpetuation of itself. It arises in order to play out its process to completion and then breaks away into a series that is "linear in every direction" (5).

Deleuze and Guattari call their method of studying desiring-machines schizoanalysis not simply because *Anti-Oedipus* is a critique of Freudian psychoanalysis but because *schize* is a French word coined from the Greek verb *schizein*, which means to split, to cleave, or to divide (39; translators' note).[11] Accordingly, Deleuze and Guattari define a machine as "a system of interruptions or breaks" (36) and posit three key types of breaks. The first type of break is in the domain of continuous flux and partial objects: a part that cuts into the continuous material flow. Rather than being the opposite of continuity, breaks constitute the flow they cut into. A cut breaks the flow of another machine that is breaking a flow of another machine in infinite regress: anus-machine, intestine-machine, stomach-machine, mouth-machine, flow-of-milk-from-herd-machine, et al. This is a basic logic of ecology: "[E]very machine functions as a break in the flow in relation to the machine to which it is connected, but at the same time is also a flow itself, or the production of a flow, in relation to the machine connected to it. This is the law of the production of production. . . . [T]he partial object and continuous flux, the interruption and connection, fuse into one: everywhere there are break-flows out of which desire swells up, thereby constituting its productivity and continually grafting the process of production onto the product" (36–37). The second kind of break is in the domain of "the code of the unconscious": this code is created by a chain of signs that do not signify in the traditional sense and do not follow an overarching plan or model. Deleuze and Guattari are following Lacan and clearly differing from the Freudian Oedipal model in that a chain is a series of characters collected from "different alphabets": a picture, an ideogram, an image of an elephant, a rising sun, a phoneme, a morpheme, a father's mustache, a mother's hand, a girl, a cap, a shoe with its string pulled out. "Each chain," they write, "captures fragments of other chains from which it 'extracts' surplus value, just as the orchid code 'attracts' the figure of the wasp: both phenomena demonstrate the surplus value of the code" (39). These partial-images collect in a set and produce their own code—an entire system of cuts and selections that bring aleatory fragments together in a chain of signs. These chains do not signify, do not refer to a mommy or daddy, but they do produce effects, desires, fetishes. The third type of break is the residual break that produces a subject as a by-product of the first two breaks. The subject is not a person, a whole, but a part of the whole that is made up of parts: it is part of the machine and also itself divided into cuts from the continuous material flow and parts of the detached signifying chain. As with cellular automata and complexity theory, the subject is a global effect of local parts and a part itself that is continually emerging with every break and reconnection. Again contra Freud, this subjective break is not produced from a lack but from an excess of desiring-production. As with Bergson, the subject is the result of the basic process of life that draws on an excess of energy: (1) a connection is made to the continuous flow to draw off energy and signs; (2) a break is made from the flow and the energy is stored up, signs are connected in a chain; (3) the residual energy and desire is then mobilized for action and reconnection.

It is important to understand that the subject is not at a higher level of organization, or whole above all the parts below it; rather, it exists in addition to, and alongside, desiring-machines as what Deleuze and Guattari call a body without organs. This is a body but not a whole unity like a human body with internal organs. The subject, or any global effect of desiring-machines, has no connections to any original unity or to a future totality. There is no harmonious whole, just parts connecting, reconnecting, and producing. Any totality is peripheral, is "added to [the parts] as a new part fabricated separately" (42). The whole is a product produced alongside parts; it does not unify but can produce feedback and affect the system. It establishes paths of communication among the parts, drawing them together and connecting the fragments. As both whole and connective tissue of the parts, the body without organs has two faces or sides, molar and molecular: "the molar direction that goes toward the large numbers and the mass phenomena, and the molecular direction . . . [that] penetrates into singularities, their interactions, and connections" (280). The molar level deals with statistical formations of large, organized crowds— human, nature, society, industry, capital—which can be divided and juxtaposed. Human-nature and human-machine are opposites only at a molar level. At the molecular level they each have parts and fragments with the potential for connecting to each other and producing desiring-machines. The molecular level is on the scale of parts and no longer obeys statistical laws: "waves and corpuscles, flows and partial objects . . . are no longer dependent on large numbers" (280). Deleuze and Guattari point out that this distinction is *not* collective and individual. Both molar and molecular are collectivities or populations. The molar is aggregates and persons; the molecular is partial objects and flows. Molar and molecular are both the same body without organs, just at different levels or views. Deleuze and Guattari argue that this notion of whole as body without organs—not an organic whole but a system that is part of a desiring-machine—continues to be misunderstood in terms of both mechanism and vitalism, both of which see the whole as (1) a totality derived from parts, (2) an original totality from which parts emanate, and (3) a dialectical totalization. Contra mechanism, vitalism, and dialectics, nothing causes a body without organs to progress from an integrated whole, progress in the direction of an integrated whole, or dialectically synthesize into an integrated whole.

In articulating the concepts of desiring-machines and the body without organs, Deleuze and Guattari are collapsing mechanical philosophy and older vitalist models in order to articulate a philosophy and psychology commensurate with contemporary complexity theory. Both desiring-machines and the body without organs operate on unconscious levels, but for them "the unconscious belongs to the realm of physics; the body without organs and its intensities are not metaphors, but matter itself" (283). Or as they say earlier, "The desiring-machine is not a metaphor. . . . To withdraw a part from the whole, to detach, to 'have something left over,' is to produce, and to carry out real operations of desire in the material world" (41). The unconscious is not predicated on literary metaphors, as with Freud, but on literal, physical forces. In order to articulate this position, they make the distinction between the functioning of a machine and the autoproduction or formation of a machine: "A machine works according to the previous intercommunications of its structure and the positioning of its parts, but does not set itself into place any more than it forms or reproduces itself" (283). This, they point out, is the typical distinction between mechanism and vitalism. Mechanism sees machines in terms of structural unity and thus accounts for workings of organizations but not their formation. Vitalism sees machines in terms of an individual unity that every machine presupposes (every machine is subordinate to organic life and its continuance) and thus accounts for the formation of machines from organic life. For Deleuze and Guattari, "the machine and desire thus remain in an extrinsic relationship" (284). Mechanism sees desire as effects; vitalism sees desire as cause. The link between cause and effect here is indirect. Similarly, mechanism sees organisms as machines; vitalism sees machines as extensions of organisms.

Deleuze and Guattari invoke Samuel Butler to outline a third position: "Butler is not content to say that machines extend organisms, but asserts that they are really limbs and organs lying on the body without organs of a society. . . . [And] he is not content to say that organs are machines, but asserts that they contain such an abundance of parts that they must be compared to very different parts of distinct machines, each relating to the others, engineered in combination with others" (284). Deleuze and Guattari read Butler as pushing both arguments to their limits. He breaks vitalism's argument by problematizing personal, individual unity and mechanism's argument "even more decisively" by problematizing the structural unity of the machine (284). Just as the bumblebee is part of the reproductive system of the clover, humans are part of the reproductive system of machines.[12] This is all one system, one continuous material flow of life. In arguing that machines *do* have their own reproductive systems of which humans are a part, Deleuze and Guattari are taking the concept of self-organization and reproduction and showing how it exists in the entire physical world, not just the biological world. Seeing a single machine as a unity or totality for them is "unscientific": to assume that reproduction arises only from a single center ignores the scientific reality that it takes the whole ecology to engender reproduction. As Burke noted, it does not take just the seed but the ground of the process as a whole. Any body, organic or otherwise, is created by various parts that produce other parts. By putting parts of machines and humans together as desiring-machines, Deleuze and Guattari are combining the vital flow of metabolism with artificial life. They are complex systems that are interconnected; there is no distinction. Deleuze and Guattari thus collapse vitalism/desire and mechanism/machine into desiring-machines. This is complex vitalism.[13]

THE TRAITS that Aristotle attributed to life—self-nutrition, growth, decay, reproduction, appetite, sensation or perception, self-motion, even thinking—have in some ways come full circle in the context of the twentieth century. The development of contemporary theories of complexity brings a new perspective to his theory of causes and entelechy. From the perspective of complexity theory, each individual cause has resulted in a narrow philosophy—material cause in mechanism, efficient cause in humanism, formal cause in idealism, and final cause in naive vitalism. But if all four causes work simultaneously to produce entelechy (motion or actuality), then the material and efficient causes do not stand behind or outside the system and push it but rather exert force within the system. Likewise the formal and final causes do not stand outside the system and pull it to a teleological end but form a continually renewed potentiality within each moment. Material cause becomes the entire ecology, including language and technology; efficient cause becomes the self-organization and reproduction of complex systems from a multiplicity of converging causes; formal cause becomes the structure of the entire situation at a macro level all the way down to the micro level; final cause becomes the tension among all of these forces that propels the system toward a potential but undetermined future. Entelechy becomes not the striving for a single, predetermined goal but the striving itself that generates multiple lines of divergence as a residual effect. What is entelechy in Aristotle becomes vital impulse in Bergson and desire in Deleuze and Guattari. Just as Einstein recognized that matter generates energy, Deleuze and Guattari recognize that material forces generate desire. The coming together of forces in a desiring-machine channels energy into multiple directions or lines of flight, whose enaction is fundamentally creative.[14]

 Deleuze and Guattari also bring together the attributes of Foucault's Modern episteme: the shift from external form to internal function and the culmination of this view in theories of the subject. Classical physics addresses molar phenomenon that are generally formal. Twentieth-century physics is molecular and addresses functions within a system. The machine as a structural unity and the organism as a personal unity are molar phenomena that tend to follow classical physics, which points to an extrinsic existence between machine and organism. But at the molecular, intrinsic level, there is interpenetration and communication between them: "there are as many living beings in the machine as there are machines in the living" (*Anti-Oedipus* 286). The difference for Deleuze and Guattari is not mechanical and vital but molar machines—social, technical, or organic—and molecular desiring-machines. Desiring-machines intermix function and formation. They are productive machines in which function is indiscernible from formation: machines whose functions are engaged in their own assembly. This is the level of desire, motion, force, energy, production, complexity. Deleuze and Guattari write, "It is only at the sub-microscopic level of desiring-machines that there exists a functionalism—machinic arrangements, and engineering of desire: for it is only there that functioning and formation, use and assembly, product and production merge. All molar functionalism is false, since the organic or social machines are not formed in the same way they function" (288). For Deleuze and Guattari, there is desire and materiality. The molar level separates these domains while the molecular integrates them. Meaning, purpose, and intention are all molar and separate subject and object, but the desire and force behind them are molecular and collapse subject and object.

In other words, desire does not come from the subject. The subject is a molar residual, off to the side, a side effect of desiring-machines, not a single center from which desire is born. If the subject is just a residual effect of the process of life, then any action produced by this subject, whether material or linguistic, is an expression of the whole process as a series of events, not the subject as an individual, unitary substance. Like the subject, expression is an effect we see at the molar level but is a product of desiring-production at the molecular level. To posit the subject as the center of expression is to cut out and isolate or freeze one moment of the overall movement, which separates subject and object and then requires a molar theory, such as dialectics, for their inter-action. But there is no absolute stasis or division. Even inanimate objects have the potential to become hot or cold (e.g., wood burning, water evaporating) and thus contain the potential for change, for movement, in the right circum-stances. Expression is an internal function of this ecological potential, a prod-uct of a desire that sets a line of flight in motion from potentiality to actuality.[15] And just as the subject and expression cannot be seen as separate from their larger material ecology, rhetoric, technê, and heuristics have to be seen in the complexity of their ecological grounds. Complex vitalism recognizes this vir-tual potential. The "mysterious" element so many of the late-eighteenth- and early-nineteenth-century thinkers were looking for becomes the "tipping point" of complexity—that point at which the interaction of a multitude of in-dividual parts begins to act with coherence as if it had a molar purpose or in-tention driving it or pulling it but is in fact a moment of emergence. It is this moment of complexity, which has been mistakenly dismissed as mystical, that haunts rhetoric and composition.

5

TECHNOLOGY-

COMPLEXITY-

METHODOLOGY

A KEY DEVELOPMENT IN THE 1990s changed the way rhetoric and compositionists look at the concepts of technê, rhetoric, and heuristics. Neither Richard
Young nor James Berlin could have anticipated the emergence of digital technologies in the mid-nineties and their cultural dominance in the first decade
of the twenty-first century. Young's understanding of technê operates on a
more strict definition that ultimately nudges technê toward rigid, formalist
practices. And Berlin's heuristic opens pedagogical practices to the dialectical
procedures that Young aspires to achieve but cannot attain because his definitions of rhetoric and technê hold him back. But even so, Berlin's historical moment and narrow disciplinary focus keep him from seeing that technology is
beginning to reshape the larger rhetorical landscape. Network culture puts the
importance of ecology and immersion in sharp relief, making Berlin's mind-

centered heuristics much less relevant and Paul Kameen's phenomenological approach much more timely. Kameen's initial attempts to deal with this kind of immersion not only rest on Coleridge but also, and perhaps more importantly, with Heidegger.[1] Heidegger's view of technology shows how seeing technê in the context of complexity can provide a new basis for methods and practices. Reconfiguring technê from the perspective of embodiment and complexity explores what Victor Vitanza might mean by "nontechnological thinking" and "nonsystematic heuristics" ("Three Countertheses" 171n14). Vitanza is typically seen as someone who views technê as purely mechanical and to be avoided, which simply places him in the generic "vitalist" category. But Vitanza is not against technê or technology. He questions the instrumentalist underpinnings in approaches to technê and technology that work to exclude the body, all of its possible combinations with the world, and the use of these relations for invention. Seen from the perspective of complex vitalism, his position opens up invention and rhetoric to multiple methods, techniques, and practices.

Both Hal Rivers Weidner and Young base their readings of technê largely on Aristotle. For Weidner, art is the knowledge of making, of bringing into being: "Art . . . is the power to make something intelligently" (Aristotle quoted in Weidner 66). Both science and art are essentially inductive: a scientist will look at the world and extrapolate its mathematical, natural laws; an artist will look at a cultural practice and generalize it into a method. But the artist is involved in making something with this generalized method. Science discovers or tests conditions; art brings about conditions. The Greeks did not make the distinction between artists and artisans, fine arts and crafts. The fact that "the art of politics creates the social conditions for man's fullest self-realization" through the art of speeches (Aristotle quoted in Weidner 66) is no more or less an art than the creation of a poem or the raising of a building. The key is that they all have conscious methods and can repeat their productions. Artists who *know* their art can produce the desired result, unless they make some sort of miscalculation. For Weidner, "If one wants a theory of rhetoric to be useful to a practitioner, then it must be formulated at the level of *awareness* at which he perceives the fundamental relationships of rhetoric, i.e., at the level of social interaction and opinion" (72; emphasis added). The key issue is what it means to know, or to be aware. For Young, art or technê means "the knowledge necessary for producing preconceived results by conscious, directed action" ("Arts, Crafts, Gifts, and Knacks" 56). It means to control outcomes by knowing them consciously and rationally beforehand. In short, the technician is the efficient cause that holds the formal cause clearly in mind as he or she moves toward the predicted final cause. This particular linear, and instrumental, model of entelechy is what allows Young to divide composition pedagogies between those who follow rational heuristics and those who are "designers of occasions" that leave pedagogical outcomes up to pure chance (55). The result is the exclusionary binary new rhetoric (art as technê)/romanticism and current-traditionalism (art as genius).

The concept of technê, however, has undergone a surge of interest in the past two decades, partly because technology has come to encompass a large (and growing) part of our daily lives. Many today argue for revisionary concepts of technê that run counter to conceptions that reduce it to an instrumental understanding of technology.[2] Such a reduction leads to a humanist reading of the ancient concept. Joseph Petraglia, for example, continues to see technê as acontextual, overly formal procedures and argues that reducing rhetorical education to technê is problematic. For him, "the *technê*-centric classroom" has won out over philosophical rhetoric because of anxiety over the lack of communication and writing skills in students, but rhetoric cannot be reduced to the technical because it is more than that—as an art, it is not reducible to simple, objective skills ("Shaping Sophisticates" 90–91). While I agree with his basic position on education and the retrieval of art from instrumentalist approaches, I do not agree with the reduction of technê to "technical rhetoric." The concept of technê deserves to be rescued from instrumentalism as well. From the perspective of complex vitalism, technê cannot be read solely in the narrow reading of Aristotle's concept of knowledge, one that divorces it from a fuller vision of his vitalism. Extending that vitalism into a contemporary context links technê to its related concept of technology, but the move from industrial to information technology means that it is more difficult to see technology as an object to be controlled by a subject. Technology, as with any technical process or technique, is only one element in a larger, more complex set of relations that problematizes simple notions of cause and effect. This shift to a larger ecology means that technê is both a rational, conscious capacity to produce and an intuitive, unconscious ability to make.[3] All of the contextual elements that affect a technique, pedagogy, or method can never be fully accounted for. The bodily knowledges and contextual constraints also produce art along with conscious knowledges and move technê away from an instrumental conception of the technical toward a more complex model.

This notion of technê pushes the discussion away from a humanist conception of the subject that is caught in a subject/object dilemma—do humans control technology or does technology control humans? The human and the technological are no longer seen in opposition but as operating in complex ecologies. As Mark C. Taylor notes in *The Moment of Complexity,* "ecologies, immune systems, the development of multicellular organisms, and the processes of evolutionary genetics" all operate as self-organizing systems called "complex adaptive systems" (165). For Taylor, cultural as well as biological complex systems remain open to their environments and adapt accordingly, situating agency and change as a product of complex contexts that include technology. The humanist subject/object dichotomy operates on presence/absence—a stable, coherent presence prefigures effects and uses technology to produce them. Technê, in this instrumental model, is under the control and will of the subject, which forecloses open-ended invention that emerges out of complex adaptive systems. As N. Katherine Hayles argues, posthumanism operates not on presence/absence but on pattern/randomness. Pattern is grounded in randomness, not a coherent subject. As she puts it, "In this dialectic [pattern/randomness], meaning is not front-loaded into the system, and the origin does not act to ground signification. . . . Rather than proceeding along a trajectory toward a known end, . . . [complex] systems evolve toward an open future marked by contingency and unpredictability" (*How We Became Posthuman* 285). Randomness is not coded as absence but as "plenitude": "the creative ground from which pattern can emerge" (286). The humanist model simply does not apply to a contemporary situation that is not grounded in presence/absence.[4] The assumption of autonomy, presence, and control ignores the ambient, unconscious, habitual elements of invention that emerge out of the complex technological systems that human bodies inhabit today. Importantly, "the posthuman does not really mean the end of humanity" (286). As Hayles notes, "we have always been posthuman," but the ubiquity of technology is only now allowing us to recognize our relational complexity (291).

It is in such a vitalist, complex ecology or network that I wish to situate technê, rhetoric, and heuristics. In this context, entelechy does not follow the instrumental model exhibited in Weidner and Young. If technê is seen as grounded in complex systems, then any heuristic or method will have to combine with unforeseen elements to produce divergent lines of flight. This creates a space for moving away from a view of technê such as Petraglia's toward a view of technê that is more commensurate with a pedagogy based on invention. Coleridge's method, for example, is open-ended and cannot completely predict the outcome of its application, which allows Weidner and Young to read Coleridge's method as unknowable and thus unteachable. They ignore, however, the fact that the method itself is teachable and can be used for learning and ultimately for generating new methods. Remaking technê from such a posthuman perspective moves our conceptions of pedagogy from Petraglia's "technê-centric" classroom toward techniques for integrating humans into technological environments with the goal of invention.

Technology and Ecology

To get the most out of the concept of technê, the shift in historical context from classical Greece to the technological present should be taken into account. In his book on the history of rhetoric, Renato Barilli notes that the suffix -ic in the word rhetoric implies technê, or the combination of art and technique, in the Greek language. So, in one sense, rhetoricians are also technicians, whose "task is to intervene in 'political' occasions" (x). Rhetorical technique in this context embraces all human concerns and thus can never be as specialized or as technical as analytics (or modern science), as Young and Petraglia imagine. Barilli concludes, "In the context of rhetoric, the technical will always be *side by side* with the non-technical" (x; emphasis added). Rhetoric, then, puts abstract, technical knowledge and lived, habitual knowledge on equal footing— a combination that is thoroughly occasional. Reading R. L. Rutsky's *High*

Techné makes it clear that the complex, ecological contexts that exist today no longer reproduce the classical civic space in which the subject intervenes via rhetoric as technique. Recognizing that this new context is emerging, Rutsky theorizes techné's role as technology through Martin Heidegger. A humanist reading of classical rhetorical theory tends to uphold the concept of the human subject in control of the technological object. Heidegger's view of techné, on the other hand, rethinks the human relationship with technology as one that can no longer be reduced to preconceived human intervention, to a narrow view of human control over the contextual situation, especially human control via technology or technique. For Rutsky, the reality of high tech is that the alliance of technology-nature-culture has become its own ecological process, or complex adaptive system, much of which functions outside human control.

In his famous tool analysis in *Being and Time*, Heidegger is looking at particular technologies in particular configurations or constellations, which is more appropriate for examining the kinds of technological environments that students will be living and writing in for the foreseeable future. With the shift from industrial to digital technologies, it is becoming more and more difficult to see technology as producing a particular set of effects or even as an all-encompassing media environment like the large-scale television culture that Marshall McLuhan theorizes. More contemporary complex ecologies are increasingly specific configurations of immediate relations among a number of technologies, bodies, and texts. Heidegger's more phenomenological method is significant because it is after the conditions of possibility that a particular technology in a particular environment establishes. Heidegger's premise is that specific modes of Being come alive or show up in certain ecological constellations. Any technology is always experienced in terms of its belonging to other equipment: "ink-stand, pen, ink, paper, blotting pad, table, lamps, furniture, windows, doors, room" (*Being and Time* 97). Technologies are never distinct objects: they are only experienced in relation to other entities arranged in complex constellations to form particular environments. What human bodies encounter is the room in its totality, and the room is not simply a geometric space but is experienced ecologically "as equipment for residing" (98). The overall constellation sets the conditions of possibility or virtual potentiality for particular acts, processes, or products. The totality of equipment in the room

Heidegger describes, for example, establishes the conditions in which something could be written.

Heidegger's method looks to examine two things: that these ecological arrangements can be drawn narrowly to determine a tool's "specific manipulability" or that they can be drawn more broadly to discern their "manifold assignments" (98). What shows up in the use of a technology is its specific manipulability, a specific mode of Being and future structural possibility integral to it. When picked up and used, a hammer comes with a specific manipulability that allows it to hammer a nail into a board in a way that a drinking glass does not. But a hammer (or any material entity) can carry out its full potential only within a larger ecological structure. Within larger arrangements there is what Heidegger calls a manifold assignment. These assignments are the potential paths of future action and development that the whole ecology makes possible. A hammer's specific manipulability may allow it to push a nail into wood, but a hammer by itself does not carry the possibility, or assignment, for a house in the way a hammer, saw, nails, wood, a plane, a blueprint, a human body, and a sturdy, level plot of earth carry the conditions of possibility for a house. The multiple ways that a hammer can be connected to all of the other elements establish a constellation or field of relations that can play out a particular path of potentiality toward a house. It is only through a constellation's relations that the tool, its specific manipulability, its ecologies, and its manifold assignments can be discovered or known. Though Heidegger's tool analysis seems to center on the tool, or in many readings even on human purposes, the tool is really just a methodological starting point for mapping out the "purposes" of the ecological relations as a whole. Rather than technology causing effects or humans determining purposes, technology and humans combine with many other elements in the environment to create conditions of possibility that suggest potential futures.

For Heidegger, then, the essence of technology is nothing technological. As he argues in "The Question Concerning Technology," its essence is that it reveals—it brings certain ways of being and seeing to light. After a polemic on the destructiveness of an instrumental perspective on and use of technology (enframing), Heidegger performs a *dissoi logoi*. Reflecting on enframing, he recognizes that the instrumental conception and implementation of technology is also a way of revealing that allows us to see one truth about the world: by pushing us to see the world's limits, instrumentalism forces us to see ourselves in an ecological relationship with technology, nature, and language. This ecological reading of Heidegger is echoed by Graham Harman, who in *Tool-Being* argues against both human- and language-centered readings of Heidegger in favor of reading him as fundamentally concerned with bodies in the world.[5] Heidegger conceives the world not simply in terms of subject/object (presence-at-hand) but through ecological relationships in the world (readiness-to-hand). Readiness-to-hand is not just about the relations between subjects and objects but between *all* bodies. Just as dasein (Heidegger's nonsubjectivist word for human being) understands things only as they show up in certain ecological constellations, all bodies understand each other and dasein only through such relationships. For Harman, understanding is nothing subjective. In ecological terms, as Mark Taylor argues, animals and plants understand and adjust to their environments much as humans do. Harman pushes this even further, to inanimate objects: even rocks colliding in space engage (know, understand) each other only through that point of contact—all things show up only as something specific to a particular constellation or encounter. Readiness-to-hand, then, is not about technology's usefulness for dasein but the immediate relation of one thing to another thing. It does not subsume the world under dasein but puts dasein on an equal plane as a body in relation to all other bodies.

For Heidegger, any material body, its structure and qualities, establishes certain conditions of possibility both for its connectivity and for any future outcomes of the larger tool-contexts it connects to. But this brings up the issue of what counts as a material body, as a unified object. As Harman sees it in *Guerrilla Metaphysics*, "any relation must count as a substance" (85). At an internal level, all beings are nothing more than densely interwoven sets of relations among electrons, protons, atoms, molecules, and cells, and these sets exert material force in the world. But this also must mean that the larger external constellations among these material bodies are equally sets of relations and can carry the same force as traditionally conceived substances. This opens up "nonmaterial" elements such as techniques and language to equal participation in the force of a constellation and problematizes any instrumental approach to technê. Heidegger argues that technology as tool and technê as art reveal conditions of possibility. Revealing is also the essence of art, but "only if reflection on art, for its part, does not shut its eyes to the constellation of truth" ("Question" 35)—the truth that any object, body, word, or technique individually and collectively exerts force in any action. At the end of "The Question Concerning Technology," Heidegger makes it clear that he is not talking about art as subjective aesthetics. He hopes that "in our sheer aesthetic-mindedness" we will not lose sight of "the coming to presence of art" (35). Heidegger does not fall into a modern opposition of technological instrumentality versus a transcendent aesthetic.[6] Art, rather than aesthetics, is "the saying of the world and earth" (*Poetry* 74); it is expressions of material relations, not internal subjectivities. Both technology and aesthetics are connected and viewed as art, as technê, which produces ways of seeing and ways of being in the world.

Rutsky attempts to articulate this realization in the context of the late twentieth century. His notion of high technê combines both aesthetics and technology into a larger, evolving system. In addition to providing a utilitarian function through an assembly line that produces products, technology is also a vital part of an aesthetic process through which culture is continuously reproduced. The key shift from conceptualizing technology as tool to technology as culture happens in the shift from industrial capitalism to consumer capitalism—from production to consumption. As Rutsky puts it, the Fordist slogan "form follows function" gives way to the consumer slogan "styling follows sales" (100). Marketing and product design acknowledge that nonutilitarian aspects of style cannot be subordinated to mechanical function: almost all shoes are functional, but which ones sell well depends on style and its dissemination via technology. Utility becomes an accessory to consumption, and any purely functional conception of technology is subordinated to mass *cultural* reproduction. Our contemporary conception of technology is intimately linked to a complex notion of culture and ecology, one in which (productive) technology and a (consumptive) "high-tech" style go hand-in-hand. In this constellation of aesthetics, technology, and culture, high technê is the art of bringing forth elements in the world, unsecuring them, and bringing them into cultural representation. Reconceiving technê in this way unsecures technology from use value and art from aesthetic value: a utilitarian or instrumentalist conception of technology seeks to secure, fix, or regulate objects in terms of their potential use to humans; a humanist or subjectivist aesthetics tries to fix eternal aesthetic value; but high technê is an artistic practice that emerges from a constellation of humans, technology, culture, and the world that "continually breaks things free of a stable context or fixed representation, representing them instead as part of an ongoing process or movement" (105). Rutsky's key point is that the human being in the contemporary digital world is not reduced to exerting human will through technology; it is not about intervening through technology but about dwelling with/in technology, with/in a culture that is intimately intertwined with technology in multiple, complex ways.

Toward the Posthuman

Just as the development of industrial technology ultimately revealed an ecological model of the world, the development of digital information technology creates the conditions of possibility for a posthumanist conception of the subject. Tamise Van Pelt characterizes Heidegger's position as anti-humanist and positions more recent theorists such as N. Katherine Hayles and Espen Aarseth as posthumanists ("Question Concerning Theory"). But at root, Heidegger presents a proto-posthumanist perspective.[7] An anti-humanist stance would privilege technology as object over the human as subject. But Heidegger shows quite often that he is critical of technological dominance. In *Poetry, Language, Thought,* he argues that it is the building up of technology as an object that makes humans a function of technology, which is a fundamental problem because it shuts down human possibility and understanding. But even technological domination is essentially the imposition of human domination through technology. It is the "technological exercise of his will" (116). Such an extension of human will can come to accept only an instrumental view of technology. Overemphasizing either side of the subject/object divide comes down to privileging domination over contextual possibility. This puts Heidegger outside the humanist/anti-humanist opposition, which he would see as congruence, and moves him toward something more like posthumanism.

In "The Question Concerning Technology," Heidegger draws on Aristotle's theory of four causes to argue that a contemporary focus on instrumentality makes efficient cause primary and misattributes it to autonomous human will, veiling causality "in darkness with respect to what it is" (6). For Heidegger, Greek thought is not compatible with instrumental notions of cause and effect.[8] Rather, the four causes are "co-responsible": they are "ways, all belonging at once to each other, of being responsible for something else" (7). This co-responsibility should not be read from humanistic morality but from the tool-analysis and conditions of possibility: "The four ways of being responsible bring something into appearance. They let it come forth into presencing. They set it free to that place.... The principal characteristic of being responsible is this starting something on its way to arrival" (9). This is the basic logic of emergence. Each cause is responsible for setting some aspect of the occasion into movement from potentiality to possibility. Their forces in relation to each other generate an inducing to go forward. Heidegger notes that the *telos* of final cause is often read from a humanist frame and is misinterpreted as aim or purpose. In ancient Greek, however, *telos* means that aspects of matter circumscribe what something will become; they give it "direction" rather than a human purpose (*Being and Time* 100). Similarly, efficient cause is misinterpreted as the lone human cause for an effect. But humans gather together the other causes and with them are co-responsible. This reading of the four causes decenters human technê: "Not only handicraft manufacture, not only artistic and poetical bringing into appearance and concrete imagery, is bringing-forth, *poiesis*. *Physis* also, the arising of something from itself, is a bringing-forth, *poiesis*. *Physis* is indeed *poiesis* in the highest sense" ("Question Concerning Technology" 10). Technê as handicraft or as rhetoric and poetics is set in the context of *physis*: nature, the ecology as a whole, including humans, is the ground and thus highest form of technê, which is simply one aspect of co-responsibility. This recognition is a key to moving beyond instrumentality and humanism. Heidegger asks, "Does this revealing happen somewhere beyond all human doing? No. But neither does it happen exclusively *in* man or decisively *through* man" (24). A human body does not create by itself. It enters into a situation, and the new form taken by that constellation plays out its own potentiality.

By neither dismissing the human nor elevating the human, Heidegger is clearly becoming posthuman, especially in the context of information technology. Hayles characterizes posthumanism as locating thought and action in the complexity of distributed cognitive environments. The navigation of a ship, for example, requires the distribution of decision-making across a complex interrelationship of technology, humans, and nature. Technologies assess the natural conditions, humans interact with instruments in response to that information, and the ship correspondingly changes its relationship to the natural conditions. Each is co-responsible for the movement. For Hayles, "modern humans are capable of more sophisticated cognition than cavemen not because moderns are smarter, . . . but because they have constructed smarter environments in which to work" (*How We Became Posthuman* 289). Posthumanism does not usurp the human, then, but situates it in the development of distributed cognitive environments. Hayles writes, "No longer is human will seen as the source from which emanates mastery necessary to dominate and control the environment. Rather, the distributed cognition of the emergent human subject correlates with—in Bateson's phrase, becomes a metaphor for—the distributed cognitive system as a whole, in which 'thinking' is done by both human and nonhuman actors" (290). In the move from an industrial model of technology that Heidegger critiques to the complex environments created by informational technology, a new model of thinking and acting is revealed. As Rutsky puts it, when human environments become so overwhelming, and human interactions with them are so complex that "they are no longer subject to rational prediction and control" (106), our conception of technology is forced to change its instrumentalist view. Rather than do away with human agency, human subjects are now defined by the "ability to exert a sense of productive agency that is not based on autonomy and mastery but on relationality" (148).

Thomas Rickert offers a conception of the posthuman subject based on relationality in terms of complexity theory and emergence and links it to the concept of ambience. In "In the House of Doing: Ambience, Rhetoric, *Kairos*," he writes that "ambience connotes distribution, co-adaptation, and emergence, but it adds an emphasis to the constitutive role of the overall environment. . . .

The ambient is immersive in that it is *post-conscious* and auratic, being keyed to various levels of attention that are nevertheless always in play at a given moment" (904). This notion of post-consciousness, as I read it, is related to Michael Polanyi's bodily consciousness, but in post-consciousness the body is distributed in its environment. One of Rickert's primary examples is the effort at MIT to create an ambient room.[9] The researchers are concerned with processing large amounts of information and take as their point of departure the fact that humans have a high capacity for processing background information—people know the weather from ambient cues such as light, temperature, sound, or air flow, none of which is necessarily processed consciously. Most interface designers, they argue, do not take this level of information processing into account. The goal of this research is to construct a room "as a personal interface *environment*" in which "common appliances like lamps or air conditioners could be networked and re-engineered to supply various kinds of information" (910). This takes cognition, thinking, and invention beyond the autonomous, conscious, willing subject. A text or action is the product not simply of foregrounded thought but of complex developments in the ambient background. Likewise, a human body is not merely in a situation but is a part of it, constituted with it. The key, as Harman notes, is not that there are different things that operate differently in different contexts but that bodies, technologies, texts, et al. *are* their context (*Tool-Being* 23). From the perspective of ambience, there is no separation. There is only relationality.[10]

Rickert is looking to integrate the network logic of complexity with the ambient logic of Heidegger, which signals a move from distributed cognition to distributed vitality. Any object or substance in the world is at one and the same time an element in a network and a unified, ambient environment. This means that human thought is both a conscious, individual element in the world and a tacit post-consciousness that is dispersed through the environment as a whole. But it also means that human action is both the product of an individual body and a fundamental property of life as a whole. The individual human still exerts force in the world but no longer has a sovereign inside. It garners vitality through multiple relations. Rather than having life, bodies encounter life in the ambient environment and draw on its energy. Vitality is a becoming that emerges between nodes on a network but produces life as a whole. Richard

Doyle calls this postvitalism and distributed vitality, which he relates to Deleuze's notion of the superfold (*Wetwares* 121, 124).

In his book on Foucault, Deleuze notes that when language gets treated as an object in the nineteenth-century discipline of linguistics, language regroups, and by the end of the century literature takes on a completely new function beyond what it designates and signifies (131)—just as Heidegger sees the objectification of technology as revealing the importance of ecology. The same thing happens in the study of life when molecular biology jumps to the investigation of the genetic code and releases life from living beings into all kinds of systems. This shift to a new form of life is also the condition of possibility for a new form of humanity. Deleuze traces the genealogy from infinity, to finitude, to unlimited finitude. But in the terms being developed over the last two chapters of my book, the distinctions might be characterized this way: God-infinity-fold–final cause—an infinite future folds back on the present to pull it forward; man-finite-unfold–efficient cause—finite being unfolds from the past to push it to its future; posthuman–unlimited finitude–superfold–co-responsibility — unlimited connections among finite beings drive life and let it continually emerge. Deleuze builds the idea of the superfold out of Nietzsche's superman, Foucault's death of man, and his own work with Guattari. But essentially it is a posthuman model of subjectivity based in complex vitalism. Deleuze explicitly calls this power of life a vital power. He asks, "[I]s not the force that comes from the outside a certain idea of Life, a certain vitalism, in which Foucault's thought culminates?" (92–93).

This new configuration of complex vitalism provides an ecological basis for humans, technê, and rhetoric. For Heidegger, the person is caught up in distributed vitality along with all of the other equipment: "The work produced refers not only to the 'towards-which' of its usability [final cause] and the 'whereof' of which it consists [material cause]: under simple craft conditions it also has an assignment to the person who is to use it or wear it. The work is cut to his figure; he 'is' there along with it as the work emerges" (*Being and Time* 100). This complexity that frames human beings makes *physis* an additional if not primary source of agency for technê. Diane Davis argues that technology, technê, and technique cannot escape *kairos;* they are caught up in emerging contexts: "*technê* is always situated within the wild excesses of a nonrational *physis*. . . . [*T*]*echnê* is simply one of the phases of *physis*. *Technê*, that is, turns out to be a 'little game' *physis* plays" (*Breaking Up* 121). Despite the image of wild excess, at root Davis's nonrational is not irrational. It is not pure chaos but complexity, which has its own kind of system that is different than mechanism and instrumentality but not reducible to an old vitalist model of mystery. Likewise, Vitanza is skeptical of technê conceived in a humanist/instrumentalist frame. A "nonsystematic heuristic" would not be an irrational informal procedure, in Young's sense, but a technique that operates co-responsibly in a complex system. Method can operate from a posthuman frame, but it would have to be about situating bodies in contexts rather than directly producing texts or knowledges as if from a Fordist production line. What complex vitalism does is provide a new philosophical frame for thinking about rhetoric and method.

Rhetorical Situation and Complexity

Examining rhetorical principles in the context of complexity theory can establish a point of departure for what rhetoric is becoming in a contemporary technological context.[11] Coleridge's concept of polarity, for example, is related to the ancient doctrine of *dissoi logoi* but points the way toward a distributed model. The exercise of *dissoi logoi*, or reversing the obvious argument to make an argument that is culturally or situationally counter-intuitive, is meant to unfreeze rigid, accepted concepts or positions. John Poulakos sees the basis of *dissoi logoi* in the Protagorean position that on every issue there are (at least) two opposing arguments. At any point on any issue a contrary argument can be found and put forth. But in order to act, people must be persuaded to one side or the other, even if temporarily. Poulakos gives an example from Prodicus: in the story of Heracles at the crossroads both Vice and Virtue argue for their means to happiness. Both make arguments for their positions and against the other's, but in the end Heracles still makes no decision. Poulakos reads this as leaving the choice up to the reader, who in similar circumstances will have to choose: "since the imperative to action demands that an impasse be overcome and that a choice be made, the human subject must in some way disturb the balance of perfectly opposed alternatives. This means that in the final analysis *one must prefer one option over all others*" (*Sophistical Rhetoric* 59; emphasis added). Such a position on *dissoi logoi* sets aside the possibility that action can occur even without such a choice by the traditional subject—that such a polarity can have its own force or power to generate action.

In *The Moment of Complexity,* one of Mark Taylor's recurring positions is that such oppositions are not really competing oppositions—each side exists because of its relationship with its "opposition." Rather than competing oppositions that produce a winner or synthesis via human choice, they are polarities, or nodes caught up in co-producing systems. Jean Baudrillard, according to Taylor, argues that the oppositions implode—one pole, such as simulacra, engulfs its opposite, the real. But for Taylor, these polarities are caught up in "strange loops": "Strange loops are self-reflexive circuits, which, though appearing to be circular, remain paradoxically open" (75). Oppositions, then, are polarities caught in these complex relationships in which each side is evolving and changing in relation to the other. One pole does not overtake the other: it changes and thereby changes its opposition. In the end, polarities do not function alone but in complex, co-adaptive relations with other polarities, creating a larger whole. Any rhetorical system that uses opposition or dialectics to privilege one pole or the other should recognize the ecological, co-productive nature of the "weaker" argument that can easily turn around to become the stronger. If an alternate position is always on the horizon, why not work toward another, and yet another? In "Kairotic Encounters," Debra Hawhee notes that in "Encomium on Helen" by Gorgias his approach to *dissoi logoi* does not simply put forth two possible arguments but several possible reasons Helen might not be responsible for her own actions: "Gorgias does not settle on one definitive explanation, but enumerates several viable ones" (26). Helen acted not because she chose between two options but because multiple forces moved her. Following Deleuze and Guattari, Hawhee concludes that "[t]he movement of Gorgias' speech, then, occurs in the middle, in the realm of the between. . . . Gorgias' betweenness, not necessarily Gorgias himself, seeks not to replace the previously accepted 'truth' about Helen with another truth, but rather to undermine the very notion that one truth . . . exists" (27). This logic of the "*and*" of an always expanding *dissoi logoi* situates the subject in a network of multiple forces where polarities open into multiplicities rather than oppositions.

This model of multiplicity ultimately affects the way a rhetorical situation needs to be conceptualized. Its early development as a concept participated in a generative polarity: Lloyd Bitzer argues that the situation causes discourse as a direct response, and Richard Vatz counters that discourse is always already a part of the situation and can thus create or determine situations. These positions have been the mainstay in the field at large, but Barbara Biesecker attempts to get beyond this initial polarity to a larger complexity in her contribution to the debates. She questions Bitzer's and Vatz's assumptions about the autonomous elements of the rhetorical situation and the causal logic that establishes the relationships among them through Derrida's notion of *différance*. Bitzer presupposes a causal chain from reality to speaker to text to audience to reality, positing the initial exigence as the origin of the causal chain. Vatz, she argues, simply starts the chain with the speaker, who through interpretation of an exigence puts his or her intention into the situation via discourse. The "Bay of Pigs," for example, was created as an event because of the decision to create a particular type of discourse about it, which turned an "event" into a "crisis." In other words, the causal relationship is reversed: rhetoric becomes a cause, not simply an effect.

The problem for Biesecker, of course, is the dialectical simplicity of this model. She initially problematizes the notion that an origin stems from an autonomous situation or speaker. For her the originary moment is not in the situation or speaker but in their difference, in the absent space between them created by their relation. Rather than an event or speaker initiating a relation, their emergent relation co-produces each one through an ongoing development. Her example is Derrida's *Glas*, which enacts *différance* by placing two columns of text side by side in the same book. The meaning of the text is not in the left side on Hegel or the right side on Genet. It is in the absent space between them, in all the possible relations and connections between them that can arise during a reading of the text. Such a perspective displaces subject and substance and "refuses to think of 'influence' or 'interrelationship' as *simple historical phenomena*" (Spivak quoted in Biesecker 121). If a speaker's subjectivity is formed through such a moment of *différance*, the same can be said of audience, not to mention language and the world.

Biesecker's basic position can be productively extended via the concept of complex adaptive systems. The dialectic of context-text actually operates as a polarity that generates strange loops, and Taylor calls the combination of multiple strange loops a "complex adaptive system." Both biological and cultural complex adaptive systems remain open to their environments and adapt accordingly. Never static, they produce larger scale behavior, texts, or structures from the movement and interactions of smaller parts. Individual ants, an example Taylor frequently uses, form the larger entity of the colony, even though the ants are unaware of this larger whole. The ant colony can react to environmental conditions and adapt/evolve accordingly, even though the colony has no equivalent of a "mind" at the level of the whole. Similar to the concept of cellular automata discussed in chapter 4, each ant reacts only to its immediate neighboring ants and circumstances, but the larger flow of the colony nevertheless has a coherent, complex movement. Such complex adaptive systems produce strange loops among their individual parts that create "effects disproportionate to causes" (*The Moment of Complexity* 165)—the interaction of the individual parts will at some point reach a "tipping point" or a "moment of complexity" where their interaction and feedback loops produce a qualitative change at the level of the whole.

In order to do this, these self-organizing systems have to process information in a way that goes beyond simple reaction. They also adapt. A complex adaptive system has to: (1) identify regularities in its environment, (2) generate schemata (or models, theories) that enable it to recognize these regularities, (3) have schemata that adapt to the changing circumstances as well as in relation to other schemata (different schemata in a complex adaptive system form a subnetwork or complex adaptive system within a complex adaptive system), (4) have schemata that can predict environmental activity (as with evolution, reliable schemata continue to function, while unreliable ones change or disappear), and (5) tie into its environment through feedback or strange loops (166–68). All the elements of a rhetorical situation are effects of their place in an economy of differences—they each form polarities with the others and evolve co-adaptively at higher and lower levels of materiality.

Seeing rhetorical situations as complex co-adaptive systems essentially updates the traditional concept of *kairos*—both the situation's ability to seize a rhetor at an opportune moment and the rhetor's ability to recognize the right timing and discourse for a given situation. Carolyn Miller notes that there are "two different, and not fully compatible, understandings of *kairos*" (foreword to *Rhetoric and Kairos* xii). One places the importance on the rhetor, choice, and decorum (adapting to what is already culturally established as appropriate for the situation); the other places importance on "the uniquely timely, the spontaneous, the radically particular" (xiii). This position asks the rhetor to be creative in the face of human life's "lack of order" (xiii). E. C. White takes up the latter in his seminal work *Kaironomia*. Noting that *kairos* traditionally meant the right moment or opportune time, White argues that we can never manage present opportunity, even provisionally. Success depends on "adaptation to an always mutating situation. . . . Such an activity of invention would renew itself and be transformed from moment to moment as it evolves and adapts itself to newly emergent contexts" (13). White uses the concepts of *dissoi logoi*, or polarities, and a Heraclitean worldview of flux and becoming to theorize the emergent space between polarities, ending up with a polarity of rhetor and context. A rhetorical choice in the moment only solves the "tension between contraries" by a force of will in the hope that chance produces an utterance that has meaning within a situation (16).

Rather than pure chance or chaos, *kairos* is complex and requires the rhetor's ability to participate in the co-adaptive development of a situation by infusing discourse into it. Taylor regularly makes the distinction between chaos and complexity. Chaos theory was developed in opposition to Newton's mechanical physics and examines situations that cannot be conceptualized due to lack of information. Complexity theory examines situations that emerge between the polarity of chance and order where "self-organizing systems emerge to create new patterns of coherence and structures of relation" (24). Polarity is essentially a balancing act between too much order and too little order, but it is this dynamic that fuels emergence. Emergence is that moment of complexity when the interaction of parts or system components generates unexpected global properties not present in any of the local parts. Microscopic and macroscopic systems operate in loops that have both negative and positive feedback. Negative feedback turns the balance toward equilibrium, which shuts down the movement of the system. Positive feedback interrupts equilibrium by increasing both speed and heterogeneity. Speed increases the interaction among parts and increased interaction creates more diverse components—more diverse components move the system from linearity and stability to recursiveness and complexity. These two properties can give rise to effects disproportionate to the immediate causes, thus producing emergence (143). The polarity of order and chaos also tends to follow a particular sequence from order to complexity to chaos to complexity to order (146). The transitions in this sequence are generally unpredictable but can be seen in retrospect. As they are happening it appears as if chance is a predominant cause that accounts for "effects disproportionate to their causes," but in retrospect it becomes clear that many of the patterns of complex activity and interrelatedness of the systems emerge from their parts. It is this point of emergence that signifies *kairos*.

Again I think complexity theory can give us a language that articulates the two apparently incompatible conceptions of *kairos*—one that favors the rhetor and one the situation—within a rhetorical situation. Seizing the moment means being able to anticipate it, unconsciously as well as consciously, not just reacting to it but adapting to it, with it, and often quickly. Humans may never be able to completely predict or control complex behavior, only recognizing elements of it in retrospect, but being able to recognize more of it as it is developing and to understand how we might co-adapt along with it will become a vital rhetorical skill. As Carolyn Miller notes, "[T]he most complex and interesting rhetorics, both ancient and contemporary, include both dimensions of *kairos* in some way, keeping them in *productive tension*" (xiii; emphasis added). It is just such a polarity that can be fruitfully theorized via complexity theory and thus shed more light on contemporary technological contexts.

Arguing in Ecologies

Even the traditional Aristotelian proofs get a new gloss when examined from the perspective of complex vitalism. In traditional rhetorical terms, the concept of logos ranges from a narrow notion of logic that generally follows the enthymeme, a fairly simple system, to a larger conception of language and the power of the word, a fairly abstract or chaotic system. G. B. Kerferd notes that the term carries at least three levels of meaning that refer to three different applications or uses: language—speech, discourse, argument, description, statement; thought—mental processes, thinking, reasoning, accounting for, explanation; world—structural principles, formula, natural laws, which "are regarded as actually present in and exhibited in the world-process" (*The Sophistic Movement* 83). In other words, the term implies the larger complex in which bodies, texts, and thought are always connected. Kerferd warns that whenever we see the term in the pre-Socratics, Aristotle, or the sophists, it always carries elements of all three meanings. Thinking in terms of this larger, ecological connotation, it is easy to see why someone like Vitanza would place emphasis on the power of logos. In *Negation, Subjectivity, and the History of Rhetoric* he sees logos both as a system whose power excludes as well as a force that continually resists systematization: logos as hegemony and logos as *dynamis* (127). These two elements form a polarity that is never static. Following Heraclitus, Vitanza equates logos with strife, the ongoing movement of logos as law, discourse, custom against but alongside logos as world, force, movement. No one side wins this battle. It is the ongoing movement that produces complexity or heterogeneity, or what Vitanza calls *dissoi paralogoi* (111).

The energy produced by the force of tension in such a polarity breaks out into multiplicity, which operates on a network logic. As Mark Taylor notes, network is not a static, frozen logic. It is in motion, it adapts, it never stands still. For Taylor, of course, the two poles of logos, simplicity and complexity, are not oppositions but "are braided 'like hair intricately tressed and knotted.' Such knots create binds and double binds that transform seemingly simple questions into exceedingly complex puzzles . . . [and] we [have] become ever more deeply enmeshed in the logic of networks" (*The Moment of Complexity* 199). Logic is not just the imposition of simplicity, linearity, and system onto the world or the chaotic power of language but also the knowledge that emerges from networks of relations, complexity, and noise. The simple sequence of emergence outlined above is not really a sequence—it functions through a network logic, which has three basic characteristics: its basic structure is a set of nodes (or knots) and the relations among those nodes; its basic dynamics are determined by the strength of the connections or relations; it "learns" or evolves via the changing strengths of the relations that adapt to the nodes around it (154). Network logic operates through nodes that communicate with one another like switches or routers that send, receive, and transmit information. As Taylor puts it, "The ways in which connections intersect create the distinctive traits and functions that differentiate nodes. While the connections of each node ramify throughout the network, the relations that are most decisive are relatively localized. . . . [I]f there are too few connections the network freezes, and if there are too many it becomes chaotic. Since the interrelations of nodes are both reciprocal and many-to-many, feedback loops can be both positive and negative" (154). Networks, then, are decentered and do not have to operate on ordered sequences but run in parallel and recursive sequences. Such a logic means that networks become complex adaptive systems because there are multiple networks co-adapting to one another (171).[12] The seemingly simple, static logic of the enthymeme and the abstract power of language over us need to give way to a more complex middle ground.

As I have argued in this chapter and the two preceding it, the concept of subjectivity or ethos necessarily changes when confronted with such a network logic. Ethos is the classical concept of character or the identity of a person as exhibited to an audience or social group. It is generally linked to the modern notion of the self or subject, but ethos implies no such inner morality. Rather, it signifies an ethics that is relative to the rhetorical situation. James Baumlin, in his introduction to *Ethos: New Essays in Rhetorical and Critical Theory*, notes that "the etymology of the term *ethos* invites such an opposition [between a central self and a social self]. Translated as 'character,' *ethos* would seem to describe a singular stable, 'central' self. Translated as 'custom' or 'habit,' *ethos* would describe a 'social' self, a set of verbal habits or behaviors, a playing out of customary roles" (xviii). He links these two positions to Plato and Aristotle, respectively. Plato's emphasis on truth and the individual predisposes this position toward a concept of morality. Aristotle, on the other hand, is interested in "an active construction of character" (xv) based on ethics. For Aristotle, the rhetorical situation makes the speaker an element of discourse, not its origin— ethos becomes a product of delivery within a specific situation (xvi). In *The Use of Pleasure* Foucault takes up this distinction between a central self and a social self, arguing that the Greeks generally followed Aristotle's social self. If people want to have credibility within a community, they are expected to act with moderation, no matter what type of relations they establish. The Greeks are not interested in specific acts, as the Christians are with their notion of the flesh, or in an inherent sexuality per modernity. Rather than follow an abstract morality based on a central self and specific acts, people are expected to operate under self-mastery with regard to their desires and the ethical relationships they establish based on their desires. Though this approach to ethos sets up the further historical development of the subject, our contemporary period, as Foucault notes in *The Order of Things,* highlights the subject's situational complexity.[13]

Taylor extends this situational model of ethos from internal subject to environmental screen: for him, "[i]n a network culture, *subjects are screens* and *knowing is screening*" (200; emphasis in original). A screen is something that divides an individual from its environment; it protects or conceals or screens out material while at the same time allowing certain outside elements through. It divides and links. Screening or filtering the noise of the world and developing screens to negotiate the surrounding environment generate knowledge. This allows the particular body or node in question to link or connect to its local situation. In our digital economy, the excess of information creates an excess of noise and the increased demand for screens. A set of screens comprises a node, a point of connection in a network. As Taylor notes, "The self—if, indeed, this term any long[er] makes sense—is a node in a complex network of relations. In emerging network culture, subjectivity is nodular. Nodes . . . are knots formed when different strands, fibers, or threads are woven together. As with the shifting site of multiple interfaces, nodular subjectivity not only screens the sea of information in which it is immersed, but is itself a screen *displaying what one is and what one is not*" (231; emphasis added). Taylor's pun on the term screen, from partition to sieve to computer monitor, elaborates on the social aspects of ethos. No longer linked to an inner subjectivity (and abstract morality), who we are is a function of how we are linked and presented to the surrounding ecological situation. This "self" as node emerges from the screening process "without any centralized agency or directing agent" (205). Therefore, any account of the subject in a contemporary rhetorical theory for technological culture cannot presuppose an interiority (at the very least one that pre-exists its situatedness), linking the concept of ethos to an ethics that is based on a relational network logic and complex adaptive systems.

The image of a single, central, stable subject gives way to a multiplicity of selves that emerge through complex relations, which goes beyond Aristotle's custom, or dramatis personae. The subject is not simply the political position or identity someone chooses but the relationships established through those identities and the effects of those relationships on bodies. Deleuze turns to Spinoza to find an ethics for this ethos. Such an ethics does not look to a subject but to a body and how that body sets itself into relations or compositions with other bodies. The body's ethical goal is not only "to actualize its potential to increasingly higher degrees" (Massumi, *A User's Guide* 82) but also to actualize and increase the potential of the other bodies within that relation. Such an ethics/ethos of networked relations will be a key to future understandings of rhetoric in networked cultures.[14]

Perhaps the biggest change in basic argument theory would need to come with the concept of pathos. Pathos is one of the key elements of classical rhetoric that distinguishes rhetoric from logic. Human minds do not just judge information logically, they respond to information emotionally. Traditional rhetorical theories put most of the emphasis on psychological approaches to emotion, character types, or ideology.[15] Pathos is about using the values and assumptions of an audience to ground persuasion or turn feelings toward an argumentative position. But as many contemporary cultural theorists have recognized, bodies *also* respond, not just minds. Affect moves toward relations among bodies, which is critical to understanding rhetoric in network culture. Charles Taylor, recognizing affect's importance to theories of language, notes that Herder is one of the first to see that the acquisition of language created a new reality, not language as the representation of objects but language as the production of affect and consciousness. Language produces "not just anger but indignation; not just desire but love and admiration" ("Heidegger" 105). This new affective dimension to life makes possible new sets of relations—"intimacy and distance, hierarchy and equality" (106). This concept of affect is based on using language to create affective relations among singularities or nodes. The body is essentially a node with multiple screens: language produces new screens and schemata that affect the body's links with the environment and other bodies, allowing us to adapt, to form new relations, connections, and networks.

Charles Taylor's notion of affect still operates through language, though he recognizes the key element of opening new potential relations. But for Brian Massumi, language and emotion still operate at the level of the conscious mind rather than the tacit body. For Massumi, "[a]n emotion is a subjective content, the socio-linguistic fixing of the quality of an experience which is from that point onward defined as personal" (*Parables* 28). Affect, on the other hand, operates at an asubjective, pre-linguistic level. Massumi's affect is a bodily experience that "lies midway between stimulus and response": it is that point at which the body is enacting multiple relations below its cognitive ability to perceive them; the body is "bathing [in] relationality" but not consciously accounting for every molecule of water (61). Massumi recognizes the key connection to complexity theory: "It is all a question of *emergence*, which is precisely the focus of the various science-derived theories that converge around the notion of self-organization. . . . Affect or intensity . . . is akin to what is called a critical point, or bifurcation point, or a singular point in chaos theory and the theory of dissipative structures. This is the turning point at which a physical system paradoxically embodies multiple and normally mutually exclusive potentials" (32). Affect, then, is "an ability to affect and a susceptibility to be affected": it is a body's capacity for relations within a network—the potential for linking to and being linked to. Emotion is simply consciously, linguistically "recognized affect" (61). Operating outside of a consciously recognized personal or subjective mode, affect functions at the level of distributed vitality, node, and screen. The body may screen out some potential relations while filtering in others, keeping it open to relations. A node is not unified or self-contained but multiple and fragmented, connected to the world through various affective relations. Because media operate as additional screens for a node, any understanding of rhetoric in the contemporary world needs to understand rhetoric at the level of affect. Like language, new media make new affections and new relations possible.[16]

Invention as Evolution

The previous discussion has been but a sketch of how rhetorical theory might map onto complex vitalism or distributed vitality, especially with regard to rhetorical situatedness and how argument might be rethought for such situatedness. Much more work would need to be done to flesh out these connections. For the remainder of this book, I focus in a little more detail on how complexity might affect the way we think about invention and pedagogy. Heuristics—sets of questions, a mental grid, or a generic process that aids its user in inventing and articulating ideas—have traditionally been the cornerstone of invention. The writer sets this grid between himself or herself and the world in order to impose order on its complexity. In "The Meaning of *Heuristic* in Aristotle's *Rhetoric* and Its Implications for Contemporary Rhetorical Theory," Richard Enos and Janice Lauer attempt to interpret heuresis as more than techniques used "to find out or discover." They argue that the term also means to create meaning through language, not just to discover what already exists. Heuristics under this reading enable the rhetor to create probable judgments— to assess a situation and co-create meaning with the audience. Though Enos and Lauer hint at the possibility of producing "entirely new proofs" beyond "existing *topoi*" (82), they are firmly situated in the autonomous subject who makes such a rhetorical choice. Their level of complexity does not really move beyond a rhetor/audience dialectic for producing socially constructed meaning. They step back from a purely epistemic approach by noting that Aristotle "considers empirical investigation and syllogistic reasoning as processes of thinking that are not necessarily discursive" (83). But even this nod to reality does not move them beyond the simplicity of the communications triangle, the linear movement of solving social problems, and the return to culture (and language) as the primary medium.

Though most who discuss heuristics tout their open-endedness—each enaction will generally produce unpredictable results—in practice they inevitably function as grids—the heuristics themselves remain unchanged. Mark Taylor's use of "schemata" revises this gridlock. The grid maintains both stability and simplicity (*The Moment of Complexity* 23)—the heuristic questions remain the same or the tagmemic grid remains the same. But schemata actually move such mental grids from a synchronic position into an evolving process. Schemata change in response to input: "Emerging schemata identify, compress, and store the regularities of experience in a way that makes it possible for the system to adapt by responding quickly and effectively" (206). In other words, we start with experience, generalize a pattern or schema from that experience, turn that pattern on future experience, and then adapt the pattern to devise a new schema. Taylor turns this process onto the instrumentalist notion of grids, revising it for a contemporary context. Using the paintings of Chuck Close as an example, he shows how a grid can actually produce work with greater complexity. Each cell in the grids that comprise Close's paintings contains its own abstract painting. Each individual cell-painting combines to create the effect of a larger work, thereby emulating a network logic in which the whole extends beyond the sum of the parts. As the example of grids shows, a schema (like the notion of a grid itself) is caught up in complex networks that evolve and adapt to new circumstances. This basic process has implications for rhetorical heuristics. One implication is that students need to develop their own schemata to fit their particular topics and situations. Another is that if teachers give the students schemata first, their goal should be to revise those schemata as a part of the invention process rather than to follow them prescriptively.

This model for heuristics needs a conception of the writing process that goes beyond typical linear models. The writing process (prewriting, writing, rewriting) is credited for bringing rhetoric and especially invention back to the forefront of composition. In many ways it has performed this function well, linking the frozen product of writing to the immediate history that produces it. But while starting out as an attempt to bring movement and recursivity to writing studies, the writing process has been reified into a rigid, linear pedagogical practice. This notion of process has been regularly questioned. In the 1980s, for example, Kameen argued against notions of process based on cognitive, problem-solution models, arguing that once the problem is articulated, the solution is already contained in it. Invention, then, is only finding the solution that is already predetermined, often by the teacher or the structure established via heuristics. More recently, Thomas Kent's edited collection, *Post-Process Theory: Beyond the Writing-Process Paradigm,* takes a social-constructivist view against what has become a fairly simple, generalizable notion of process. In the introduction Kent argues that "writing constitutes a specific communicative interaction occurring among individuals at specific historical moments and in specific relations with others and with the world and that because these moments and relations change, no process can capture what writers do during these changing moments and within these changing relations" (1–2). While recognizing the importance of change and relations, most of the work in the collection seems to focus (explicitly or implicitly) on dialectics and the communications triangle, missing much of the complexity involved in the movements of a distributed vitality.

Most process theorists have never fully considered the connections among evolutionary processes, writing, and thinking. Taylor explicitly makes these connections, arguing that the writer as screen operates in a polarity with the situation and in an ecology of personal experience, texts that are read, and words that are written. In this context, the writer reaches evolutionary roadblocks (schemata no longer fit the circumstances, forms are no longer relevant). These evolutionary dead ends change schemata, which change possible relationships, and thereby affect the larger evolutionary development. The writer becomes a circuit relay in this larger ecology: "Words, thoughts, ideas are never precisely [our] own; they are always borrowed rather than possessed" (*The Moment of Complexity* 196). Just as bodies are the vehicles for genes that live on after bodies pass away, writers perform a host function for ideas in our cultural ecologies. Writing, though, has another layer of complexity: "Rewriting does not merely repeat but also transforms in a way that complicates the host/parasite relationship" (196). The text is at one point in the process a parasite on other texts, but during the process it reaches a "tipping point" and is transformed into a host with which others will enter into a parasitic relationship and ultimately transform. This parasitic complexity problematizes any simple relationship to time. Writing has "rhythms of its own," and so it is also "impossible to know just how much time is required for thought to gel because [the writer is] not in control of this process" (197). And although evolutionary time appears linear, "[t]he time of writing does not follow the popular figure of the line because present, past, and future are caught in strange loops governed by nonlinear dynamics" (198). Like ants, writers are a "colony of writers" caught up in the larger evolutionary flows of other networks. In short, "[t]he moment of writing is a moment of complexity" (198). And in Taylor's view, we write to produce and embody these moments in order to contribute to the evolution of thought-schemata and thus the whole (cultural) ecology. Our writing should disturb, create more noise, push equilibrium into new relations and assemblages (198).

This evolutionary model creates a new context for invention, in which Kameen's reading of Coleridge shows up as a precursor. In methodical thinking, "the specific route that inquiry will follow cannot be mapped *a priori*; it reveals its pattern as exploration proceeds, each step preparing the ground for its (often unanticipated) successor; and because methodical thinking is spontaneously self-questioning, it is more nearly subversive than recursive in its capacity to adjust to the unexpected" ("Coleridge"). Such a model opens itself to evolutionary thinking and subverts linear processes. Conducting a journey through the history of rhetoric, Roland Barthes provides a clear example of what it might be like to invent in a networked context. In *The Semiotic Challenge*, he collects fragments of rhetorical discourse to produce a network that folds and refolds to invent more discourse (15–16). Movement through networks creates new links and new networks to be traveled through and re-linked. Likewise, rhetoric becomes a system that moves and evolves.[17] Consequently, rhetoric, technê, and heuristics must not be read as instrumental but as co-responsible and co-evolutionary. If the entire ambient constellation of equipment establishes a continuously emerging world, rhetoric cannot be read as theory-application, which is simply an instrumental operation. A theoretical idea or a particular technique is only one element within a larger constellation that produces an idea or action. They should be seen as equal parts of any complex situation that are co-responsible with a multiplicity of other parts and causes for invention. Rhetoric as theory is not different, better, or worse than rhetoric as practice—all elements contribute to distributed vitality, to life, to the movement forward of any becoming.

If invention emerges out of these complex networks that are amplified by technological contexts, then the basis of invention must be the mapping of these networks. This is one of the key recognitions made by James Berlin in his attempt to develop a heuristic for composition pedagogy. In *Rhetorics, Poetics, and Cultures,* Berlin constructs a heuristic that identifies key terms, sets up an opposite term, and then prompts the students to value one term over the other (117–19). Berlin uses the technique to place his students dialectically in relation to the discourses that map out the world for them. Following David Harvey, Berlin finds the "aestheticization of politics" or "the insertion of myth between the realm of truth and the realm of ethical action" problematic (54). These myths are oversimplified narratives or clichés that nonetheless provide ground for action. The clichés provide coherent pictures but they cover over the complexity and contradiction in historical events by creating incorrect or manipulative links between local and global realities (Hitler's fascist ideological aesthetics, for example). For Berlin, this use of aesthetics prevents adequate cognitive mapping. Contra Harvey, however, Berlin sees this aestheticization as a "normal feature of our response to political events" (55), citing Roland Barthes's *Mythologies* as a case in point. Because "such narratives are inevitable in responding to the complex conditions of experience," Berlin concludes that English studies must respond and address them by providing possible counternarratives for "consciousness formation" (56). It is on this basis that Berlin places both rhetorics and poetics as mediators between the true and the historical: both a poetic genre such as film and a rhetorical genre such as speeches function as public discourse about the world. In order to offset general theories about the world that propose to account for its totality, Berlin follows Martin Jay and Hannah Arendt in emphasizing "paradigmatic examples rather than general concepts" (92), which do not subsume all particulars under a general principle but can still provide a more complex and acceptable aesthetic experience to serve as a basis for community through public discourse.

Berlin's heuristic attempts to combine the nineteenth-century poetics of Coleridge and rhetoric of Marx into a contemporary dialectical method, but ultimately keeps him from (re)considering complex vitalism. I read Berlin as not going as far as Fredric Jameson does with the concept of cognitive mapping. In "Cognitive Mapping," Jameson is looking for an "aesthetic of cognitive mapping" that links art and pedagogy—the combination of which constitutes the cognitive. He posits three stages of capital to outline the development of the problem of representation, or figuration. Classical or market capitalism functioned through the logic of the Cartesian grid as the primary map of the social totality. This level of capital is more local and is analogous with the city—spaces that at this point in history people are still able to map or represent. In the imperial stage, a local or phenomenological experience no longer corresponds to the colonial state. A more complex map is needed because the local is no longer "true" in the global sense. A "play of figuration" arises because fundamental realities are now unrepresentable. In order to characterize this absent cause people find aesthetic figures that become reified and ultimately function as primary contents in their own right, even though they do not accurately map historical or political realities. Monopoly capitalism moves even further beyond this problematic that developed with the nation-state. It extends the local/global disjunction, locking us into local, individual experience—people are fixed into immediate space and the other layers of space are removed. This contemporary situation creates the problem of mapping one's relationship among local places and global spaces.[18]

Jameson derives the concept of cognitive mapping from Kevin Lynch, who did a study in which people were asked to draw their city context from memory. It "suggests that urban alienation is directly proportional to the mental unmappability of local cityscapes" (353). Though Jameson argues that Lynch is limited by phenomenology, he sees his notion of cognitive mapping as a spatial analogue to Althusser's formation of ideology—"the Imaginary representation of the subject's relationship to his or her Real conditions of existence" (353). Ideology, like Berlin's aesthetic, attempts to map the gap between the local and the global space. By extending Lynch into politics, the inability to map the social becomes a difficult yet central political problem. For Jameson, critics and theorists have not found an appropriate figuration for this contemporary problematic—in his reading, the death of man, schizophrenia, and the decentered subject offer no map of the larger space. He recognizes that "postmodernism gives us hints and examples of such cognitive mapping on the level of content" (356)—such as postmodern art that plays with film, tapes, video, computers, and conspiracy theories. Each provides content for something that is formless, that cannot be mapped, but this play of figuration still provides no direct form of the totality. Therefore, for Jameson, an aesthetics of cognitive mapping is essential, though he cannot give it a generic form. He recognizes that we can have politics without a total map but, like Berlin, claims we cannot have a socialist politics without a total map (355). For him, the emphasis on micro-politics, rather than socialist politics, is a symptom of trying to imagine and map a sense of place beyond the local. The problem is the "unsolved dilemma" of imagining the social—a community or collective. Contemporary society either needs the transcendent logic of capital or religious beliefs to live cooperatively—the only other option is some form of "oriental despotism." The problem with socialism is that it wants none of these. Thus, its major crisis is to confront this utopian problem of creating an all-encompassing map that can function in the place of the logic of capitalism, religion, or totalitarianism.

This project, however, is doomed to fail. As an example of this aesthetic problematic, Jameson cites the book *Detroit, I Do Mind Dying*, which discusses a workers' movement that grew out of a successful local effort. The leaders of the movement thought their local tactics would be generalizable. But when they tried to move from grassroots, neighborhood politics in the city to the national and international levels, the tactics proved ineffectual and the leaders lost their ties to the local base of supporters. Their attachment to reality evaporated, as Debord and Baudrillard argued it would. Jameson, however, thinks there can be success from this kind of failure: "successful spatial representation today need not be some uplifting socialist-realist drama of revolutionary triumph but may be equally inscribed in a narrative of defeat" (352). Even this narrative of defeat is an important aesthetic attempt at cognitive mapping. For Jameson, even though this totality cannot be mapped, positive political moments can come from our failed attempts to map it. The key is that the aesthetic failure itself is pedagogical. Jameson recognizes that the local failure forms the political landscape, whereas Berlin wants the political map to determine the aesthetic pedagogy. And this is Berlin's major problem. The dangers for him are overly simplistic narratives. The problem is that the narratives his pre-directive pedagogy provides are overly simplistic—they are based on binaries and the generic categories of race, class, and gender. He merely provides simplistic counter-myths, not more complex cognitive maps. Unless we can get people to link from their local situations to the global networked spaces, it will always remain a case of your myth versus my myth, which is precisely where Berlin's pedagogy is still situated. Berlin has to step back from complexity because his ideology and his pedagogical heuristic lean too heavily on a dialectic that stems from and leads to a predetermined politics. But predetermination does not work neatly in practice: the dialectic of local and global that Berlin calls for fell apart in Jameson's Detroit example.

Berlin's dialectical sensibility allows him to see the problematic elements of the aesthetic as well as potential positive ones, but he reads the positive elements in people such as Paul de Man and Jean-François Lyotard only in terms of negative deconstruction. For Berlin they are able to critique only mythic aesthetic production, not pose counter-myths (93). Since they have no positive politics, according to Berlin, total theories are still needed even if they are tentative. But that is not the only way to read the situation. Theorists such as Deleuze and Guattari *do* provide an affirmative approach. For Harvey, local (and even national) is simple and global is complex. But for me, following Deleuze and Guattari, the local is eminently complex, so the local complexity becomes an entry point into the global complexity. It is important to note that in the Detroit example the move is from local to global, not a predetermined map. Teachers cannot impose a general form on the local because the general form cannot be (pre)mapped. The pedagogical value comes from the attempted mapping, not the implementation of a given method. This is what Berlin misses in his pedagogy and in his map of rhetoric and composition. Even though Jameson still maintains that the local needs to be generalized into a form, for him the map of a socialist utopia is always deferred. The failed attempts leave us with many strategies for our own mappings, but it leaves us no total map. In the end, Berlin devalues the complexity of this aesthetics. Because Berlin accepts a stricter version of socialist politics, he cannot see, and perhaps Jameson cannot see, complex vitalism and the mirco-politics of Deleuze and Guattari's theories as the important beginnings of mapping the local toward the global. It is out of the failures of micro-politics that any socialist politics is grounded. Micro-mapping is more detailed than general theories and dialectics, leading to more complex groundings that serve as a basis for new attempts at cognitive mapping.

Diagrammatics and Expression

The key to mapping out these networks so they can be traversed for invention is that they need to be mapped as they are being traversed, not beforehand. Reading from this perspective allows us to move from cognitive mapping to distributed cognition to distributed vitality. It changes the way Deleuze and Guattari's concepts of the book as a literary machine and expression as a material process can be approached. Deleuze and Guattari see the book as an assemblage (desiring-machine or machinic phylum). As part of an assemblage, a book has no subject or object. A book is a multiplicity that on the one side faces a totality (a whole or organism), while on the other side it faces a body without organs (an open-ended desiring-machine that has no set functions within a given system) that continually decomposes the totality—breaks it off from one desiring-machine and makes it function within another assemblage. Because a book faces a totality it can be attributed to a subject, but this is just a name for traces of complexity and connection to and through the book rather than a distinct body. There is also no distinction between what the book is about and how it is connected. In other words, a book has no separate object; it has only itself in connection with other assemblages. Deleuze and Guattari write, "We will never ask what a book means, as signified or signifier; we will not look for anything to understand in it. We will ask what it functions with, in connection with what other things it does or does not transmit intensities, in which other multiplicities its own are inserted and metamorphosed, and with what body without organs it makes its own converge" (*A Thousand Plateaus* 4). For Deleuze and Guattari, the book is a literary machine that operates in relation to a war machine or a love machine or a revolutionary machine. Likewise, "Writing has nothing to do with signifying. It has to do with surveying, mapping, even realms yet to come" (4–5). The book is not an image of the world but forms a connection with the world and establishes potential conditions for future connections. Writer-book-world is one "self," one assemblage in which any point can be connected to any other. Semiotic chains of every kind are connected to "diverse modes of coding (biological, political, economic) that bring into play not only different regimes of signs but also states of things of differing status" (7). Literary machines use language to connect to semantic and pragmatic collective assemblages, to a micro-politics of a social field.

In this micro-politics, expression is not of a subjective mind but of a whole social, textual, and material field. Berlin reduces expressivism to an isolated self. In Deleuze and Guattari, it is not simply humans that express; it is the world that expresses. For them, matter is unformed, unorganized bodies and flows—subatomic, submolecular particles and forces; content is formed matter; expressions are functional structures. For example, nucleic acids express compounds, organs, and functions or organisms. Plants, animals, rocks, rivers all have forms of expression—a river's banks are an expression of its functional operations; even fish that live in it are expressions of the river's evolving ecology. In a poetics in which functional, material relations express, the point is not to interpret or decode the expressions but to do something with them, to map them and create new relations with and through them, to invent.

This problematizes the type of language/world distinction of representation. In addition to material expressions, linguistic expressions do not represent the world but function with it. Since content and expression have their own separate forms, expression cannot represent content (*A Thousand Plateaus* 86), but the two can enter into a relation (an assemblage or desiring-machine). Linguistic statements do not represent machines; they are parts of machines: "expressions or expressedes are inserted into or intervene in contents, not to represent them but to anticipate them, or move them back, slow them down or speed them up, separate or combine them, delimit them in a different way" (86). Linguistic statements such as incorporeal transformations are speech acts that do not speak of things but speak on the same level as things and contents —they function in contexts as affectively as physical bodies do. A judge's sentence, for example, transforms an accused person into a convict. Corporeally, materially, what takes place before (the crime), after (the penalty) are actions-passions that affect bodies (the property, victim, convict, prison): "but the transformation of the accused into a convict is a pure instantaneous act or in-corporeal attribute that is the expressed of the judge's sentence" (80–81). The body is still the same material body, but incorporeally it is changed in a par-ticular way that affects it materially. And the sentence does not spring from the judge as a subject but from a whole network of functional, material rela-tions expressed through the body of the judge. Expression does not uncover or represent content, then: expression and content communicate, work in concert, and function in connection with each other.

For a post-dialectical method, then, the point is not to determine an origin or even a meaning but to map points of intervention, insertion, or connection. This is why mapping the local to global is problematic for Jameson and Berlin. It is not an issue of representation but an issue of assemblage. Deleuze and Guattari give the example of the feudal assemblage. A map would have to con-sider all of the interminglings of bodies, both material and textual, that define feudalism: "[T]he body of the earth and the social body; the body of the over-lord, vassal, and serf; the body of the knight and the horse and their new rela-tionship to the stirrup; the weapons and tolls assuring the symbiosis of bodies —a whole machinic assemblage. [A map] would also have to consider state-ments, expressions, the juridical regime of heraldry, all of the incorporeal transformations, in particular with oaths and their variables . . . [and] consider how all this combines in the Crusades" (89). In trying to map such a situation, it cannot be looked at in terms of causal connection where expression reflected or reacted to content. This approach, which subordinates expression to pri-mary economic content, runs into all of the problems of dialectics. A dialectics that sees nodes or connections at the molar level "appeals to an ongoing dialec-tical miracle of the transformation of matter into meaning, content into ex-pression, the social process into a signifying system" (90). For Deleuze and Guattari this situation is not just about production of expressions from con-tents but about the intermingling of the two in the process of emergence. They seek to move to another level of complexity that involves attractions, repul-sions, sympathies, antipathies, amalgamations, permutations, and expansions, not just causes or dialectical turnings. This is why Jameson and Berlin have difficulty mapping the local onto the global dialectically: it is not as simple as turning (troping) from one to the other.

Deleuze and Guattari's post-dialectical method is more complex because it goes into the molecular (local) to find multiple links to the molar (global). Any method, then, would be diagrammatic rather than dialectical. A diagram looks at an assemblage in its entirety: it is a superlinear or rhizomatic mapping of networks of relation. They see two aspects or states of the diagram. In one, content and expression are examined in the heterogeneous and reciprocal flows. In the other, content and expression are unable to be mapped as separate fields; they prevail over any duality (91). But Deleuze and Guattari's method, which they call schizoanalysis in *Anti-Oedipus* and pragmatics in *A Thousand Plateaus,* even goes beyond these two levels. A machinic assemblage (the new term for *Anti-Oedipus's* desiring-machines) assembles three machines: literary machines (expressions, language, texts), concrete machines (contents, bodies, formed matter), and abstract machines (unformed, unconnected functions). They write that "[a]n abstract machine in itself is not physical or corporeal, any more than it is semiotic; it is diagrammatic (it knows nothing of the distinction between the artificial and the natural either). It operates by matter, not by substance; by function, not by form. Substances and forms are of expression 'or' content. But functions are not yet 'semiotically' formed and matters are not yet 'physically' formed. The abstract machine is pure Matter-Function—a diagram independent of the forms and substances, expressions and contents it will distribute" (141). These functions do not have forms, only traits—degrees of intensity, resistance, conductivity, heating, stretching, speed, slowness—that they use to produce connections. A diagram is a set of an abstract machine's functions and connections to materiality, which are key elements in setting the conditions of possibility (or potentiality) for expression and content.

Adding this third element to pragmatics—whether poetic, political, or rhetorical—produces four components for studying a regime of signs. The first component is the generative, the study of mixed semiotics, their mixtures and variations, which shows how a form of expression is linked to multiple regimes of signs or mixed with other regimes. The second is transformational, the study of pure semiotics and the creation of new semiotics, which shows how one regime can be translated or transformed into another: if all regimes are mixed, then they carry the potential to function for the creation of new regimes. The third is diagrammatic, the study of abstract machines from the perspective of unformed traits in both semiotic and material systems, which extracts traits from regimes of signs or forms of expression. These are the abstract functions within machinic assemblages that produce the material effects of expressions and contents: the creations and transformations operate through these traits. The fourth is the machinic component, the study of assemblages that affect abstract machines, which shows how abstract machines operate in concrete assemblages. Concrete assemblages give form to traits of expression and content, showing that a semiotics cannot function separate from material relations. A pragmatics, then, would consist of making *traces* of mixed semiotics, making *maps* of transformations and their potential translations, making *diagrams* of abstract machines as potentialities or effective emergences, and outlining *programs* of the assemblages that distribute and circulate within the system (145–46). Any approach even approximating this method would increase the complexity of our understanding of both the texts under investigation and the lives affected by these texts.

Mapping as Methodology

Such an embracing of complexity goes far beyond Berlin and maybe even further than Jameson would want to go, though this complexity is apparent in the logic of his essay "Cognitive Mapping." When Berlin returns to poetics in *Rhetorics, Poetics, and Cultures*, he sees it as literature or interpretation or in terms of the history of the English department, which makes it almost impossible for him to consider the connections between poetics, rhetoric, and materiality put in play by Deleuze and Guattari. Such a complex vitalism simply does not show up. Berlin's notion of romanticism as literature based on Raymond Williams's model of class taste will not let him see something like Deleuze and Guattari's expressionism or the epistemology that operates within it at the level of distributed vitality and tacit knowledge. The politics that operates in this context is not the conscious ideology of a dominant class, or the state's power, or an "oriental despot," or even a religious structure. This is why Jameson recognizes that a socialist politics cannot be mapped, which is what Berlin tries to do with his heuristic. Ira Livingston notes, "The problem . . . is that storming the Bastille or cutting off the head of a king can no longer address the working of the invisible hands of a headless despotism that has already reduced its 'original' to a straw man or figurehead. Finally only a *molecular* or *viral* politics can be effective in such a regime" (*Arrow of Chaos* 124). Our attempts to map global space necessarily spring from local, embodied space, by mapping out the bodily relations through which humans come to know their world. If socialism depends on a map of the global, but the global cannot be mapped, then the resulting politics has to be postsocialist (Livingston xiii). It is here that complex vitalism might point the way to enacting these kinds of political contacts in and through more inventive pedagogical methods.

In *Connected: Or What It Means to Live in the Network Society*, Steven Shaviro provides another way to think about making these local connections materially. For Shaviro, and I think Jameson too, postmodern space, hyperspace, or cyberspace is different from place: distance and speed are no longer determined by geography alone and face-to-face meeting. Networking or being connected has a whole new set of connotations and practices. Local places such as gyms, parties, reading groups, workshops, or tour groups give way to global nonplaces such as hotels, airports, global chain stores, strip malls, and gated communities, in mega-cities such as Mexico City, São Paulo, or Guangzhou (131–32). Such nonplaces are constellations of spatial fragments and social engagements that are detached from local surroundings and roughly equivalent no matter their geographic location—they are connected globally but locally disconnected. These new physical and social arrangements are precisely what make mapping totalities a difficult proposition. For Shaviro, though, what is needed is not a nostalgic form of community or totality but new forms of contact—"serendipitous encounters between strangers" (132)—that these spaces make available.[19]

Berlin follows Martin Jay and Hannah Arendt in emphasizing "paradigmatic examples" as a basis for community. But this notion of community is essentially nostalgic. The contemporary context will not allow us to go back to the agora of ancient Greece or the salon of nineteenth-century Europe.[20] By clinging to older notions of totality and community, Berlin is essentially locking himself into reading micro-politics as negative deconstruction only. Shaviro, on the other hand, wants to think about these practices affirmatively.[21] He writes that "one of the big questions today facing artists, thinkers, and activists alike is how to find a twenty-first century equivalent, within the space of flows, for Benjaminian *flanuerie* and Delanyesque contact" (*Connected* 133). Such a method would provide connections between local place and global space that follow from three key material supports for the kinds of networked spaces that make connection possible today: (1) the hardware and software of new media technologies; (2) the geographic nodes and hubs for the technology (to access technological, global spaces people still need physical places); and (3) the spaces, or nonplaces, in which global financial and political elites live, work, and travel. Teachers, students, artists, critics, and workers need methods for inventing new forms of contact as they are navigating these spaces. As Shaviro notes, Jameson sees this space as unrepresentable but not necessarily unknowable (189). Teachers and theorists cannot get caught up in equating conscious representation with knowledge—new methodologies are needed to correspond with such an epistemology.

As I argue in this book, Berlin's maps of the epistemologies behind composition pedagogies have no place for such methodologies. Berlin's social-epistemic rhetoric is still caught in a rationalist epistemology and a dialectical methodology. If rhetoric and composition is to move forward and go beyond the dialectics of social-epistemic rhetoric's model of the communications triangle, it can no longer settle, much less strive for, the production of overly simple heuristics and process models to account for the complexity of invention and writing.[22] In *A Thousand Plateaus* Deleuze and Guattari explicitly reject the communications triangle upon which Berlin's mappings are based: "An assemblage, in its multiplicity, necessarily acts on semiotic flows, material flows, and social flows simultaneously. . . . There is no longer a tripartite division between a field of reality (the world) and a field of representation (the book) and a field of subjectivity (the author). Rather, an assemblage establishes connections between certain multiplicities drawn from each of these orders, so that a book has no sequel nor the world as its object nor one or several authors as its subject" (22–23). Margaret Syverson is one of the few who have taken up complexity theory to counter the simplicity of the communications triangle, replacing the static poles of writer, text, audience, and world with distribution, embodiment, emergence, and enaction (*The Wealth of Reality* 23). She situates cognition in social and material development. Sounding somewhat like Mark Taylor, she notes that "a theory of composing as an ecological system is particularly vexing because it challenges our present investment in and assumptions about ownership of intellectual work, such as creative ideas and textual productions" (202). If everything co-evolves, drawing such distinctions as ownership becomes moot, an abstraction unrelated to an idea's, text's, or political act's emergence.

In a similar vein, Louise Wetherbee Phelps is one of the few to turn complexity theory toward inventing. Working out of complexity theory, as Taylor and Hayles do, she argues that invention is "an attribute of a system" that emerges from complex self-organization ("Institutional Invention" 70, 77). Viewing institutional structures in this way means that those who work within them must become radically inventive and continually adaptive. Phelps is specifically interested in academic institutions and the leadership roles of WPAs and administrators in the process of creating a new program or department. These leaders should make invention show up as a possibility in these contexts and create environments that afford invention within institutional structures. In the context of these thinkers, a technê, technique, or method for invention must start with the structure of particular constellations and the invention of techniques for and out of those specific occasions; it is thus more attuned to co-responsibility, *kairos,* emergence, and ambience. Composition theorists should be striving to develop methods for situating bodies within ecological contexts in ways that reveal the potential for invention, especially the invention of new techniques, that in turn reveal new models for action within those specific rhetorical ecologies. Method in this context is happening at two levels when approached pedagogically: the techniques or heuristics that teachers use to situate students in learning contexts, and the techniques the students produce in and through those specific contexts—some of which are conscious, some of which remain bodily and intuitive. The remainder of this book looks at some of these possibilities.

6

TOWARD INVENTIVE

COMPOSITION

PEDAGOGIES

MOST PEDAGOGICAL DISCOURSE IN THE 1990s revolved around critical pedagogies that generally mirror James Berlin's image of social-epistemic rhetoric.
While much other work was done in the period, it inevitably evoked the social-
epistemic question: does this pedagogy seek to produce the proper political
subject and corresponding critical text? The emergence of technological contexts in the middle and later 1990s changed the landscape in which this question would arise. The Internet opened the way for completely new social and
pedagogical contexts. Much critical pedagogy began to focus on media literacy
as decoding the dominant political assumptions and values in films and adver-
tisements. This strategy is based on mind-centered heuristics and a predetermined ideological viewpoint, which ultimately limit rhetorical invention, and

it continues to produce print-based texts. A whole new technological apparatus means that teachers cannot assume students are simply walking into classes as passive consumers of dominant texts. More students produce their own media texts and create their own online contexts and communities. Pedagogical methods should be found that address these contexts and build from them as opposed to breaking them down. This revaluation of student context serves a basis for more open-ended invention. Paul Kameen's and Gregory Ulmer's pedagogical methods attempt to map the complexity of students' local contexts onto larger spaces in ways that offset predetermined conclusions and products. As a part of an emerging complex vitalist paradigm that is neither expressive nor social-epistemic, their pedagogical methods situate student bodies in complex ecological environments as an epistemological basis for invention. In this newer model of method and technê, particular heuristics are seen as parts of larger constellations rather than as abstracted general procedures. This more open method fits our current electronic context and the complex ecologies in which students write and think.

Whether the heuristic is Young's tagmemics or Berlin's critical heuristic, the application of a pre-set strategy inevitably becomes law when implemented in the first-year course. The writing process movement, for example, began in the 1970s largely as a reaction to the reified practices of current-traditional rhetoric. The overemphasis on form and grammar began to overshadow content and exclude other possible forms. The process paradigm recognizes that in order to teach writing, pedagogues need to examine the stages a writer goes through during the production of a text so that they can intervene and suggest better strategies at each stage and promote the conscious direction of the recursive movement in and among the stages. While this project was originally meant to counter the law of current-tradition rhetoric, the process paradigm went through its own process of reification. One of the main tenets of the process movement is that the writing process is generalizable. This belief leads to the examination of "expert" writers and the production of a general model that is meant to be applied to new writing situations. Once this reification process becomes a staple of student handbooks, the general model begins to function as its own law. Teachers begin to demand drafts, demand that invention be explicitly exhibited in writing, and continue to focus on the end product of the process and the implementation of many of the features emphasized by current-traditional rhetoric.

Berlin began to notice problems with process pedagogy fairly early on. In "Contemporary Composition: The Major Pedagogical Theories," he argues that process pedagogies are no better than product pedagogies. What is crucial for Berlin is that teachers are not teaching the same process pedagogy (777). Rather than counter its reification into a single, generalized process, Berlin argues that different processes are being taught and that they correspond to the categorical distinctions he has been developing.[1] He argues that the real issue is being able to argue for and justify the process being taught. In *Rhetoric and Reality*, Berlin traces the beginning of the process movement back to the 1920s, rather than the 1970s, to show why it cannot be justified. He cites Raymond Weaver's work in the twenties, which argues against product-centered pedagogy in favor of examining process from a psychological viewpoint (75). This emphasis on the self allows Berlin to see the seeds of process pedagogy in the expressivism of this early work in the twenties. Berlin then concludes that process is no better than product in that they are both grounded in individualism and separate writing from the social. For him, the concept of writing as process is for individual ends, not social ends, which promotes a politically problematic subjectivity. Therefore, he reformulates the question posed by Young, "Can writing be taught?" For Berlin, the question is, "Can pedagogy produce a proper political subject?" His answer is yes, but only if it follows his outline for social-epistemic rhetoric.[2] However, it remains to be seen whether or not Berlin's social-epistemic pedagogy can be justified, whether it can avoid its own reification into law.

This issue of reification and generalization goes all the way back to Paulo Freire, who lays the groundwork for much American critical pedagogy. His groundbreaking book *Pedagogy of the Oppressed* makes the now famous distinction between the banking model and the problem-posing model of education. In contrast to seeing students as passive receptacles in which knowledge is deposited, Freire utilized a method that sees the student as an active participant in the production of knowledge through dialogic exchange—the teacher poses a problem and the students proceed to work through possible solutions. This practice not only respects the students as a site of agency and knowledge but also engages critically with dominant discourses that are imposed as law. This of course is a clear precursor to Berlin and all contemporary critical pedagogies. However, as Henry Giroux notes in his introduction to Freire's *The Politics of Education,* Freire specifically argues against those who universalize his pedagogy. His approach is generated out of the specific political situation of South America. Freire recognizes the problems created by transferring a pedagogical practice into a universal model, which makes it a general process imposed as law.

Nevertheless, many critical pedagogues do just that—they follow in the footsteps of the current-traditional and process models that they initially problematize. As C. H. Knoblauch, writing in "Some Observations on Freire's *Pedagogy of the Oppressed,*" also recognizes, this universalizing tendency has dominated American compositionists' appropriations of Freire. Freire and Ira Shor provide an example of this in *A Pedagogy for Liberation.* As coauthors, they attempt to put their pedagogical practice into book form by engaging in a literal dialogue about critical pedagogy. The most interesting thing about the transcription of their dialogue is the difference between Shor and his mentor. It seems clear that Shor is universalizing his own experience of the 1960s into a pedagogical method. He waxes nostalgic about the sixties and early seventies as a time of resistance and change and attempts to relive that moment in all of his pedagogical contexts. After a particularly optimistic monologue about the potential resistance that teachers can give to their students, Freire responds with, "Yes, that's a very important point," and moves right on to talk about the importance of institutional forces that impinge on pedagogical practices. In other words, Freire understands that teachers should not turn his pedagogy into law but rather should look to their specific contexts to invent and develop pedagogical practices, processes, and methods. Establishing a pedagogical method as a universal law simply produces its own resistance.

Shor provides a clear example of this tendency in *When Students Have Power,* in which he discusses teaching Utopian discourse in a particular class. Ironically, the discussion spawned a student uprising. Since he lets students have a say in the syllabus, readings, and evaluation process by constructing the course with their initial input and having them sign the syllabus, Shor attributes the uprising to the students' constant state of previous oppression. He believes that allowing the students to have a say in their own education released a surge of democratic desire. Even though he quells the rebellion democratically and ends his book on an optimistic note, one cannot ignore the implications: teachers are a part of institutional structures, a manifestation of law. In his review of Shor's book, Joe Marshall Hardin notes that Shor's critical theorizing "occasionally causes Shor to assume that certain methods will lead to specific results, and he is sometimes caught off guard by the students' unexpected reactions to his pedagogy" (527). Hardin recognizes that the problem lies in differing expectations of law. The students expect a traditional academic level of authority; instead, they get a "critical" law. Shor expects that a linear, instrumentalist method will lead to a particular political subjectivity; instead, they take that agency and attempt to change the course's form—they want to drop all tests. Hardin concludes, "What occurs to me is that Shor, like the students, is held under the rule of an authoritarian system that undermines his best attempts to empower students and decenter the teacher, and that the students, at least in this situation, *intuitively* understand this more than he does" (528; emphasis added). Both the academy and the students thwart critical attempts to undo law via law. One thing liberatory pedagogy tends to sidestep is the fact that students can and do see teachers as embodying the power of law, no matter how much the teacher may genuinely want to help them. Help can be patronizing when distributed downward from a point of authority.[3]

James Berlin's Heuristic

Berlin's critical pedagogy falls into these same problematics. Rather than focus on process in the writing process tradition, Berlin attempts to construct a heuristic that is structured around emphasizing, if not imposing, his politics. In order to have a process pedagogy that he can argue for per his own criteria in "Contemporary Composition," he has to delineate a social-epistemic process.

The issue, for me, becomes whether or not his pedagogical practice lives up to its "methodical" Coleridgean heritage. I have argued that even though Berlin's program is commendable, and understandable, the fatal turn came when he chose to set Coleridge's notion of method in relation to a more progressive Marxist-Hegelian version of dialectics. This issue is an important one because it carries over into his writing instruction and the heuristic he develops. Back in "The Rhetoric of Romanticism" (1980), Berlin establishes the basis for his future work in invention: "The process is more important than any one product [written or social]. Coleridge thus combines the view that rhetoric is epistemological with an absolute value structure: in other words, truth exists independent of the discoverer, even though it cannot be communicated and so must be discovered by each individual. This view of rhetoric even provides for a kind of inventional system within rhetoric since *the dialectical process itself becomes a heuristic device*" (71; emphasis added). Though Berlin would go on to problematize the individuality put forth in expressive pedagogies, the individual here functions as the dialectical fulcrum of interpretation and invention. This individual process, for Coleridge, is foundational to his open-ended method. But Berlin takes this as a cue to develop his own heuristic, and he makes his version of dialectics the basis of his pedagogical heuristic.

In *Rhetorics, Poetics, and Cultures*, Berlin's cultural studies approach to composition pedagogy receives its fullest account. Berlin describes two courses (one lower level, the other upper level) that he presents as possibilities: "their purpose is finally illustrative rather than prescriptive" (115). But his description of the lower level course called "Codes and Critiques," which lays the foundation for TA training and the first-year course at Purdue (116), presents a fairly prescriptive process. The goal is to make students aware of cultural codes and encourage them to learn to negotiate and resist these codes, ultimately moving the students from awareness to resistance.

Berlin wants his pedagogy to produce "citizen-rhetors" who are "empowered" with an "agency" and a "democratic consciousness." As Berlin says, "We thus guide students to locate in their experience the points at which they are now engaging in negotiation and resistance with the cultural codes they daily encounter. These are then used as avenues of departure for dialogue" (116). Though this dialogue sounds open-ended, Berlin's three-step semiotic heuristic is in many ways as instrumental as Young's or Shor's. After having the students locate their personal experience in the contexts surrounding a film or text, Berlin has them follow a set heuristic process through three stages: locating the key terms in a text, looking for their marginalized opposite, and then having the students "explore their own complicity and resistance in responding to this role" established by the key oppositions in the narrative (118). The heuristic is meant to place the student in a particular type of dialectic among the codes, the world, and the other participants in the course and to result in a particular form of critical consciousness.

I read this process as an attempt to combine Coleridge's dialectic with Jameson's mapping strategy (or rather, Berlin's interpretation of Jameson's strategy).[4] Like Coleridge, Berlin wants the students to identify themselves as the locus of interpretation in a dialectic with the world and language (or cultural codes). Like Jameson, Berlin begins with the local and attempts to get the students to map this locality onto global ideologies—capitalism, racism, gender inequality, and so forth. By starting with personal experience in relation to the texts at hand, Berlin is beginning locally, and the first stage of the heuristic poses few problems for the students. Difficulties arise in the students' attempts to take this local mapping and extend it into global space. The second stage of the heuristic expects the students to see abstract oppositions that do not always exist in the text itself—either they are implied or they are a function of the symbolic or economic economy in the context of the text. Berlin acknowledges that this is not an "exact operation" and results in debate (117). For students who do not already operate on definitive binaries, these global abstractions do not always correspond to their local space. Nevertheless, for Berlin, this phase functions to set the students up for the final phase. In it, the students are expected to place these terms and their oppositions "within the narrative structural forms suggested by the text, the culturally coded stories about patterns of behavior appropriate for people within certain situations. These codes deal with such social designations as race, class, gender, sexual orientation, ethnicity, and the like" (118). Berlin notes that the students have little trouble recognizing the stereotypes associated with male-female binaries, for example. But this phase does not stop there. Students would be expected to see "themselves as metaphorically enacting the masculine narrative," as being called to occupy that subject position. As Berlin notes, "students discover that the essay attempts to position the reader in the role of a certain kind of masculine subject. They can then explore their own complicity and resistance in responding to this role" (118).

The problem is that students cannot simply make the dialectical turn that maps them onto global space. In "Writing in a Post-Berlinian Landscape: Cultural Composition in the Classroom," Michelle Sidler and Richard Morris, two of Berlin's former graduate students who were trained in his methodology, discuss the problems with his heuristic and posit their own revised version. As Sidler and Morris note, identifying the key terms does not pose a problem, but the students have a very difficult time decoding oppositions. Often the opposing terms are not that clear, and when Berlin points out his interpretation of these opposing terms, the students point out that the terms did not actually form an opposition. Even more problematic is the attempt to get the students to see their own complicity in domination. Despite the fact that Berlin sees his pedagogy as geared toward creating "citizen-rhetors" who are "empowered with agency," a "democratic consciousness," and an ideology of "the possible," the students resist being coded as marginalized or complicit in the marginalization of themselves or others. In addition to the fact that race, class, and gender are reductive inventional topoi—which may or may not connect to students' local lived lives in the way Berlin anticipates—nothing may be more disempowering than students seeing themselves as complicit in their domination by law. Recognition of their complicity breeds guilt, and guilt often breeds cynicism and passivity, rather than agency.

Perhaps it is the invocation to accept a subjectivity of complicity that breeds resistance. As Sidler and Morris note, "[T]eachers lead and prod students to find the prejudices set up in the privileging of certain roles and the devaluing and denigration of others" (279). And the prodding is one of the things that students tend to resist. Thus, such an oppositional pedagogy typically leads to an opposition between the teachers and students. Again, Sidler and Morris note, "As Berlin records and we have found in our classes, students resisted this type of 'in-your-face' confrontation. Opposition and confrontation only breed stiffer opposition and resistance. The teacher became polarizer, not enlightener" (280). By stating their ideology up front, teachers invite confrontation, and confrontation tends to lead to resistance, not democracy—as evidenced in Shor's attempt at student democracy. In "*Rhetorics, Poetics, and Cultures* as an Articulation Project," Patricia Harkin discusses this problem, noting that "Jim [Berlin] himself somewhat ruefully admitted [that] these procedures were not entirely successful" (496).[5] The students would either resist outright or simply comply in order to overcome an obstacle to the grade they needed to move on in the university and into their place in the capitalist economy. Harkin notes that teachers at Purdue gave the school's rural and conservative students the moniker of "postmodern Hoosier rhetors" (496). Even if they could manage a map of these global structures, it would be difficult for them to recognize themselves in these "contingent metanarratives." Harkin writes, "When the postmodern Hoosier rhetor has a contradiction pointed out to her, then, she is less likely to contemplate the cognitive dissonance as a spur to invention and more likely to say 'whatever.' And since Jim's method calls for students to arrive at genre as a function of their invention process, the pomo Hoosier rhetor reinvents the 'whatever' genre—the essay that concludes by asserting that 'everyone is entitled to their own opinion'—the very kind of writing that we hoped cultural studies would eliminate" (496–97). Ultimately, Berlin is trying to perform the same kind of ideological maneuver that he is critiquing. His heuristic is meant to relocate the "pomo-whatever" subjectivities into a global narrative of resistance rather than individualism or capitalism. His narrative is a different ideology, but the process is the same.[6]

For me, the issue comes down to process versus method. Despite Berlin's constant proclamations that his heuristic is open, his dialectic is a general process not a method.[7] As Paul Kameen notes, a process is linear and pre-directed. Method, as employed by Coleridge, follows an open, circuitous path, resulting in unpredictable outcomes.[8] If Berlin's pedagogy is unsuccessful and leads to unforeseen conclusions, then perhaps it is implemented in a methodical way. But if it is successful and produces the subjectivity he desires, then it is process. Should the student perform an interpretation that Berlin agrees with, the student has properly followed the heuristic to arrive at the accurate interpretation of the cultural codes and to recognize his or her place in the global schemata. And consequently, such a student has stepped into a subject position toward which Berlin's heuristic "guided" him or her. The creation of a specific subjectivity, via the link to the global narrative that stems from Berlin's politics, makes it a process toward a particular product rather than a method that is open to contextual possibility.

Pedagogical Desire

What emerge from Berlin and critical pedagogy are competing desires—the teacher's desire for a universal, conscious subject, a citizen rhetor, and an embodied student whose desire emerges from a particular context and cannot be predicted. In his introduction to *Between Borders,* Lawrence Grossberg posits four pedagogical categories to provide a place for these desires: in addition to a hierarchical banking model and a dialogic problem-posing approach, he includes praxis pedagogy and a pedagogy of articulation and risk. Praxis pedagogy is full of a teacher's hope that their pedagogy would enable students "to understand and intervene into their own history" (16). This approach, however, assumes that teachers already understand how to intervene and that their pedagogies can transfer that knowledge. The goal of a pedagogy of articulation, on the other hand, is not to "save the world" but to get the students to invent and link, to make connections and map articulations. But there will always be an element of risk involved. Sometimes the students will not adopt the politics the teacher desires. But accepting this situation is the only way to avoid pedagogy as law. "Such a pedagogy . . . must leave the field of articulation as open as possible" (19). A good example comes from Geoffrey Sirc's "Never Mind the Sex Pistols, Where's 2Pac?" which responds to Seth Kahn-Egan's article, "Pedagogy of the Pissed," which is a response to Sirc's "Never Mind the Tagmemics." Kahn-Egan makes the dual mistake of reading Sirc's open-ended approach as a "cultural studies" work on punk subculture and then turning it into a dominant/resistant binary. Sirc counters with an anecdote from one of his courses. A student e-mailed him, telling the story of his attempt to discuss 2Pac with his dad. When prompted by the question "What do you think of 2Pac?" the student noted his father's recitation of all the basic commonplaces he had heard from mainstream media. The student gave his father some of the essays they had been reading in Sirc's class and noted how his father's facial expression changed as he read the material—he began to see 2Pac differently. Sirc closes his counter-response by saying that this is precisely the kind of change he is interested in, but there is no way to codify it. It is a throw of the dice. As Sirc designates it in "Godless Composition," it would be a "pedagogy of heterogeneity," which lies beyond articulation" (557). Sirc's pedagogy is not a critical pedagogy that focuses on resistance but a pedagogy of articulation that accepts risk. He could not have predicted this kind of result from the student's complex situatedness.

A teacher's pedagogical desires typically have nothing to do with a student's emergent desires—whether our desires take the form of programs, courses, or subjects. Early in *Composition in the University*, Sharon Crowley writes, "Ostensibly, academics in all disciplines want the first-year course to teach students how to write. Here writing seems to mean that students are supposed to master principles of arrangement and sentence construction; they are also to learn correct grammar and usage. This desire that students master grammar, usage, and formal fluency has remained constant throughout the history of the course" (7). This institutional desire for a disciplined subject of instrumentality would be shared by some teachers and certainly by many administrators. But for Crowley, "[t]he problem is that this desire simply cannot be enacted within a universal requirement that is not intellectually connected to any other feature of the curriculum. . . . The requirement provides first-year composition with an instrumental motivation [as its object of desire] rather than a rhetorical one" (8). What is needed to enact this other rhetorical subjectivity is a composition curriculum that extends into upper-division courses in rhetorical study.[9] But the ancient "good man speaking well" and the nineteenth-century liberal humanist subject do not really connect to our present conditions any more than the disciplined subject of instrumentality. Crowley concludes, "I have serious doubts about whether a universal student subjectivity is any longer possible or desirable to attain" (10). What is needed is a model of the subject that responds to rhetorical exigency.

In contradistinction to philosophers, and instrumentalists, rhetoricians desire embodiment rather than abstraction: "In its desire to abstract, philosophical reading differs from rhetoric, which inhabits time and space and which is manifestly interested in people and events—a sculptor's visit to Croton in the fourth century BCE, a city's desire to foster civic pride—as well as the politics and ethics they provoke and entail" (*Composition in the University* 31). For Crowley the universal, philosophical desire is an "antidesire: The bourgeois desire is to avoid seduction by art or nature, to avoid noticing the body's immediate responses to experience and particularly to pleasure" (44). Thus, an appropriate rhetorical subject would embrace desire, seduction, and embodiment —the particularities of situatedness. A critical pedagogue like Berlin would support a subjectivity of anti-desire: a position that conflates the good man speaking well and the universal liberal humanist subject of anti-desire. Crowley states, "It is my desire to resist equations like these that in part drives my resistance to the universal requirement, which tends towards standardization and away from the recognition of students' diverse abilities and desires" (257). Crowley recognizes that teachers have to acknowledge student desires in particular embodied contexts. If the universal requirement adheres to institutional desires, then an extended rhetorical curriculum would be awash in competing desires—desires structured by capitalism, the desire to be serviced, the desire for a job, the desire for no tests, the desire for theoretical sophistication, the desire to learn, the desire to work as little as possible, ad infinitum.

What emerges out of Crowley's discussions are an institution's desires, a teacher's desires, and a student's desires, all competing for their fifteen minutes of fame. In the penultimate chapter of *Composition in the University,* "Composition's Ethic of Service, the Universal Requirement, and the Discourse of Student Need," Crowley comes full circle to the question of desire. She lists the standard reasons given for why students *need* composition. But these reasons are all predicated on our institutional or academic desires for them. Teachers can no longer look to these reasons without examining them in terms of power relations—without acknowledging that the institutions and teachers desire on behalf of students. So desire, power, and situatedness would be necessary sites for exploration in a full undergraduate curriculum of rhetoric as embodiment. Rather than promising our students some instrumental value in taking our curriculum, which may or may not actually turn out to have that value for them, it may be better to seduce them into studying rhetoric even if they do not know why it is seductive. It may be better to let them follow that desire to create whatever composition or constellation that they desire, let them determine what use-value the curriculum may ultimately have for them in their particular contexts. It may be better to create a pedagogical context in which they can build their own desiring-machines. In a simple sense, we would be avoiding the banking model for something akin to Freire's problem-posing pedagogy minus the problem-solution logic. Here is a set of texts, theories, arguments, ideas, technologies, contexts, desires, forces, subjectivities: what can the student make with them? What can the body do?

This open-ended model would be the rhetorical subjectivity of Crowley's desire but one that teachers cannot specifically create or predetermine. If the university does drop composition as a requirement, as Crowley desires, the new rhetorical curriculum would have to be seductive in order to bring in students. Perhaps seduction would be the ethical thing to do. Now, this is not a seduction that has a seducer. It may be that the presentation, the language, of a curriculum could be seductive. Perhaps the very fact that it does not try to sell itself as instrumental will project some seductive power. But this of course does not mean that our curriculum would be necessarily or inherently useless. Rather, the students will be encouraged to develop their sense of use-value out of their desires for composition, using the curriculum as a set of common-places for invention, linking, and connection. The students would need to, and be encouraged to, work out their own constellations that would mix our curriculum with their context, our theories and methods with their own political interests—should they have them. Teachers cannot determine their students' desires; we cannot make them need what we think they need. Berlin misses this element of desire in the power-desire-subject matrix. There will always be those who want to instrumentalize—who proceed to tell the student the value of taking their curriculum. But in a world of the reversability of all signs and values, perhaps seduction is the ethical thing to do—let the potential in 2Pac create a desiring-machine with a student and his father.

From Post-Process to Ecology

The conflicting desires within composition practice generate the need to revisit conceptions of process and push them beyond instrumentalist, linear readings of entelechy toward functional ecologies and lines of flight. This complexity beyond the generic writing process provides the exigence for attempts to articulate post-process pedagogies. In *Grading in the Post-Process Classroom* (1997), Libby Allison, Lizbeth Bryant, and Maureen Hourigan define post-process in terms of the critical pedagogies that have come after the writing process movement. For them, "[t]he collection is titled 'Post-Process' because the contributors move beyond the process writing movement's focus on a scientific, cognitivistic, and universalistic approach to writing expertise toward a focus on such social factors as race, class, ethnicity, and gender in constructing which writing is considered 'expert' and who is authorized to produce it" (9). Their entry way into post-process, perhaps ironically, originates at the end opposite from student invention—the institutional necessity of grading some product. For them, it is the external, institutional push for evaluation as much as the internal, disciplinary emergence of new social theories that creates the need to re-evaluate process pedagogy. The backlash to external pressure for evaluation leads many to call for the abolition of grades altogether. Some opt for a pass/fail system, some for grading curves, some for contracts with students, some for narrative grading. But everyone in their edited collection is "caught between the NCTE's call for alternative grading schemes and administrators who demand even more finely tuned ones, caught between liberatory approaches that seek to teach students to become resistant, critical thinkers and the consumer approach some students bring to education" (6–7). This cross-section of desires among student invention, institutional assessment, and disciplinary theories drives the need to rethink process pedagogies.

As Victor Villanueva states in the afterword to *Grading in the Post-Process Classroom,* it is the desire for liberatory and critical pedagogy that grounds the book. Villanueva lays out the assumptions that point to the social constructionist tenor of their conception of post-process: the emphasis on language as epistemological and ontological, on rhetoric and dialectic as being at the root of education, and on writing as a process of discovery. The emphasis on dialectic as a way to mediate the problematic oppositions teachers find themselves in, on a dialectic between reading and writing, between conventions and the students' own processes of discovery, between writing and product, between grading and the students' writing processes, displays "a careful coupling of several sources that come under the umbrellas of hermeneutics, cultural studies, and critical pedagogy" (Villanueva 178). Under this social dialectic, assessment in the post-process classroom inevitably becomes a political activity, which, if one substitutes writing for assessment, is perhaps one of the most common recognitions of the social construction movement in the 1980s. In short, the volume contributors' desire for something post-process is still caught in dialectics and social-epistemic rhetoric.

Likewise, Thomas Kent, in his edited volume *Post-Process Theory* (1999), sees the concept of social-construction as a basis for moving beyond the process paradigm. He notes that all of the contributors to that volume share three main assumptions: writing is public, writing is interpretive, and writing is situated. Though Kent focuses on interpretation (hermeneutics), these three basic assumptions formulate a social-constructionist position, broadly defined, with an emphasis on the local factors that influence writing processes. Perhaps Kent opts for such general assumptions in order to cover the wide range of viewpoints in the collection, but his attempt to roughly outline "post-process theory" does depict his own position. By public, Kent means that writing happens in the dialectical interaction among the elements of the communications triangle—reader, writer, language, and text. From such a social view of writing, "the possibility for a 'private' writing evaporates" (1). For him, writing occurs in specific interactions among people in specific situations. Since writers or theorists cannot predetermine these situations, interpretation becomes central. Writers must interpret each moment as it arises in an "attempt to align our utterances with others" (3). This process of interpretation, for Kent, ultimately rests on the "hermeneutic guesswork": "When we write, we elaborate passing theories during our acts of writing that represent our best guesses about how other people will understand what we are trying to convey, and this best guess, in turn, will be met by our reader's passing theories that may or may not coincide with ours" (4–5). Convention is not a requirement for communication, but the interpretation of dialogic interaction is. Thus, Kent's notion of post-process theory relies on the dialectical "give and take" of hermeneutic guesses rather than a structuralist notion of *langue* or a socially constructed discourse community.[10]

Kent attempts to make a move away from law with his notion of post-process. However, his dialectical approach to the social is still within Berlin's social-epistemic rhetoric. Positing a deterministic notion of social construction allows him to overestimate the uniqueness of his hermeneutic model. Kent appears to be post-structuralist, but in his essay "Paralogic Hermeneutics and the Possibilities of Rhetoric" he proves to be a more traditional hermeneut.[11] Rather than going into detail about Lyotard's notion of paralogy, he reads it as dialogics: "'dialogic' means an open-ended, non-systematic, paralogic interaction between hermeneutic strategies" (31). The dialogic guessing game between one person's strategies and another person's strategies may in fact be never-ending—a person can never come to a complete alignment with another's prior knowledge—but his conception of it is not necessarily paralogic. He even equates the two terms with a slash: "dialogic/paralogic" (36). Rather than linking paralogy to dialogics, Victor Vitanza disperses the binary model altogether. Paralogy is not a give-and-take with the goal of communication and interpretation. It is an ever-new invention that breaks out of dialectic and into multiplicity. But Kent comes to espouse collaboration and dialogue, which is more traditionally hermeneutic rather than paralogic; he sees this social life in terms of Hans-Georg Gadamer's concept of horizon, not Lyotard's notion of the pagus, "the border zone where genres of discourse enter into conflict over the mode of linking" (quoted in Vitanza, *Negation* 43). As Stephen Yarbrough argues, Kent's notion of hermeneutic strategies promotes a reified notion of language use. He sees Kent as positing "the strategies we always use to get everything done" (*After Rhetoric* 222). For Yarbrough, "As Kent's theory stands, all the advice it could offer . . . is a set of formal 'strategies' used by others" (222). If his guessing game is the primary mode of language use, then teachers are left discussing our guesses that have worked in past situations and proposing those as possible strategies for others to employ in similar situations—ultimately a generalized heuristic, not a paralogic dispersal via ever-new linkages and inventions.[12]

Following these roadblocks to thinking post-process, Sidney Dobrin and Christian Weisser have put forward the concept of ecocomposition in an attempt to push post-process further toward the concept of ecology than the critical categories of race, class, and gender. In "Breaking Ground in Ecocomposition: Exploring Relationships between Discourse and Environment" (2002), they argue that to be truly post-process requires the inclusion of natural and physical environments and issues in ecology, place, location, and habitat in discussions of the social, language, and interpretation. They cite Marilyn Cooper's essay "The Ecology of Writing" as a foundational text. Cooper suggests that the static and simplistic categories of contextual models, such as the communications triangle, need to be replaced by ecological models that postulate "dynamic interlocking systems that structure the social activity of writing" (quoted in Dobrin and Weisser 568). Writers are to be viewed as organisms that are intimately linked to their dynamic and complex environments. Though I do not follow their distinction between context and ecology throughout this book, generally meaning ecology when I use the word context, Dobrin and Weisser follow Cooper to argue that "context suggests that potential effects of all local systems can be identified through heuristics in order to provide writers with accurate and complete information prior to writing" (568). The use of the concept of ecology moves discussions of writing, rhetoric, and invention beyond the standard inventional heuristics and social categories toward models that integrate environments into writing and invention processes. Dobrin and Weisser explicitly link this movement to pedagogical uses of hypertext (584–85), which can help map out the complex relations among environments, texts, and bodies at the local levels of students' material ecologies.

While Dobrin and Weisser's work is clearly on the right track, they do seem to be held back from pushing the concept of ecology to its limits by continuing to rely on forms of social-epistemic rhetoric and social construction—largely, I would argue, because there is no other completely articulated and accepted paradigm beyond expressivism and social-epistemic rhetoric in which to place their work. Consequently, their pedagogy still leans heavily on public action through discourse, on discourse determining and changing material contexts, and on ecocomposition's "links to Paulo Freire's dialogical methodology" (582). This emphasis on discourse and dialectics is a blinder to ecological complexity, which is post-dialectical. Dialectics still appear in their work because rhetoric and composition is a field that privileges language and the social and molar levels of explanation and operation. Each of these has its affective place in the overall economy, but ecopedagogues may continue to run into the same trouble as those espousing older forms of critical pedagogy, which Dobrin and Weisser critique in their articles. In the end, when they overprivilege language or social construction they can actually oversimplify the ecology rather than account for its complexity.[13]

As Marilyn Cooper notes in her foreword to Dobrin and Weisser's edited collection *Ecocomposition: Theoretical and Pedagogical Approaches,* the paradigm shift in the twentieth century toward ecological models that are based on complex relationships and systems theory has been happening in many other fields in both the sciences and humanities, but the shift, "at least in composition studies, is still struggling to happen" (xii). Her articulation of this shift is clearly in line with the complex vitalist paradigm I have been discussing in this book: a focus on systems, dynamic change, complexity in both physics and the life sciences, an emphasis on situatedness, and an acceptance of the unconscious or tacit elements of lived experience. As she puts it, the field is still struggling to see relationships as primary rather than continuing to think in terms of a static subject operating on a static object (as dialectics and the communications triangle is often used and theorized) because it is "harder to see writing as a part of a whole, interrelated, ceaselessly changing environment rather than as a social system through which humans act on and make conscious choices about the nonsocial other system, the natural environment" (xiv). In order to enact the "post-cognitive, post-process, post-expressivist" shift that ecocomposition hopes to usher in (Dobrin and Weisser, "Breaking Ground" 572), pedagogues will need to put more emphasis on the material and affective ecologies that exist in and link to their classrooms and start inventing methods and heuristics out of these complex ecologies.[14]

Paul Kameen's Method

In *Writing/Teaching: Essays Toward a Rhetoric of Pedagogy* (2000), Paul Kameen provides a good example of using the ecology of the classroom to foreground invention and imagine a more open pedagogy beyond social-epistemic and post-process:

It is the position of the teacher when he knows enough to listen to something "other" than his own voice. This space between question and answer is filled with possibility. It is where my hopefulness about teaching begins, and where I try to return when I've lost it. That space is very much like the position of the writer, just before he starts to write, except here there are many authors present. From the "text" that is about to issue from this collaboration, changes of consequence may be effected, for all the involved parties. Here writing and teaching might be said to (e)merge. (252)

Kameen invites academics to see classroom ecologies as open spaces that produce knowledge. All knowledge, not simply knowledge about teaching or writing, emerges from ecologies, in which ideas surface through the possibilities that the rhetorical situation opens up. For Kameen, the issue is not the knowledge in the teacher (researched information, ideology, or even intention) or the meaning that the students produce (in their writing or subjectivity). Rather, both the teacher's knowledge and the student's texts evolve in the emerging moments between the two. This rhetorical activity, modeled on Coleridge's method, operates from no set starting point and progresses to no predetermined end point other than inquiry and invention. The starting points, for Kameen, are different with each teacher, student, and classroom, which means that the production of knowledge is contextually specific and emergent, unlike the deductive transmission of research in teaching or the inductive development of research out of the classroom. As a series of reflections on this basic premise, Kameen's book is genuinely hopeful, not necessarily about what teachers can help students do or even become, as in Grossberg's characterization of praxis pedagogy, but about that moment of emergence in the classroom. Possibilities lie in that moment between the placing of a question in the air and the occurrence of some muddled and/or insightful response. This is the moment of teaching and the moment of invention. Though Kameen's focus on the personal may be misread as expressivist, his focus on method is rhetorical and his approach becomes much clearer when read from the perspective of a complex vitalist paradigm: he is working to find a pedagogical method that enters into the ecology of the classroom and utilizes its complexity for rhetorical production.

The first half of *Writing/Teaching* consists of a group of essays written during and after a graduate seminar on twentieth-century poetry that Kameen and Toi Derricote team-taught. In the seminar both the professors and the students write essays Kameen characterizes as "ideological autobiography"—the essays highlight key ideological issues as they relate to the seminar participants' experiences. Everyone responds in writing to the week's readings or to previous class discussions and has the option of choosing the genre (autobiography, argument, poetry, journal entry, or story) in which to write. At the beginning of each class, everyone reads his or her paper. While some material is only read aloud, other material is also distributed to the seminar participants. After each presentation, there is no response or commentary, only silence, until it is broken by the next speaker. Class discussion follows these readings and focuses on selected texts from the syllabus. The texts and course emphasize race, class, and gender as they are deployed and thematized through twentieth-century poetry, so the read-arounds highlight these issues in the local contexts of the participants. The ideological autobiographies have a pedagogical purpose beyond the articulation of a life story: they provide an ecological context for the discussion of the poetry that relates directly to the participants, which keeps the issues from being discussed as abstract concepts. Such localizing establishes a rhetorical situation for both the students' and the teacher's knowledge production: it provides a background from which the participants in a class can interpret the poetry and criticism and produce knowledges specific to them individually as well as to the class.[15]

Kameen's primary interest in such a pedagogy is change, particularly the effect of pedagogies on both the students and the teachers. This change, however, is different from many cultural-studies or critical-pedagogy notions of change. Berlin, for example, states his ideology up front, confronts the students' ideology, and attempts to change his students' minds rationally and consciously. Kameen is not interested in that kind of change. Because he approaches the classroom texts and the literature from the position of someone who is developing knowledge rather than already in possession of it, Kameen does not change his students as much as comment on the texts, think through them, and use them to do something that is not simply disciplinary or academic: "What I want to do is present the ways in which *my* knowledge about these kinds of texts—my past, the poems—was brought to bear, and was then *changed,* by the activity of teaching" (7; emphasis added). Kameen puts himself on the line and shows his students that he will also be changed by the course. Academics tend to avoid discussing this kind of change in any systematic way by focusing on theories, pedagogies, and curricula that preconstruct the classroom and students. In other words, academics emphasize pedagogical matters as they exist outside the classroom context and deemphasize any potential aftereffect (or complexity) produced by the pedagogies' contextual enaction. The read-arounds as a pedagogical practice function in the place of preconstructed theories and curricula and allow the course to take on a development specific to it that no one could anticipate or preconstruct. The practice highlights (and uses) the fact that the effect will differ for each participant and each course. Beginning each class with the reading of auto-ethnographic material by both teachers and students puts them on a more equal footing. Since all the participants expose a part of themselves by bringing unexpected positions to the table, all of them put themselves at risk in a way that forestalls preconstruction and opens each party to the possibility of change.

Kameen is after a change in knowledge, in a person's way of thinking. He recognizes that the contemporary emphasis on race, class, and gender actually keeps this type of change from happening because of its "ideological intensity" (4). Therefore he wants to reground politics in the specific histories of the participants rather than in "abstractions" and "imperatives" (4). If these kinds of issues are raised and discussed only in the abstract (i.e., in a preconstructed way), it is much easier to dismiss their importance and their relevance to people's lives. Such dismissal means that no one has changed—no one has produced new knowledge for themselves or others. Kameen praises Derricote for creating a context for the possibility of such change through her range of emotion, her rigorous and precise use of language, and her ability to bring her experience to bear on the lives of others. The personal, as a rhetorical and pedagogical concept, should be read not as private or self-expressive but as "the modifying effects of prior reflection, collegial engagement, and public presentation" (9). In this rhetorical approach, the audience (the student and/or the reader) is not a passive receiver of knowledge via research and lecture but is fully engaged in the ecological context the teacher creates and is a key element in the emergence of knowledge. As Kameen puts it, "My work emerged out of what I experienced, during the process of its composition, as an essentially collective, rather than individual, enterprise. My essays are merely small parts of a very *complex*, multivocal, and densely textured set of interchanges" (11; emphasis added). By including some of his material in the first part of the book along with written material submitted by other seminar participants, Kameen models how his thinking changes through the complex, interdependent development of the seminar as a whole. In other words, he lays out the rhetorical situation of the class that led to the invention, the emergence, of his book.

Kameen provides no explicit theory or mechanism for his model of change qua invention. But I read him as expanding Heidegger's concept of forestructure to a collective pedagogical activity. Articulating the importance of this concept for rhetoric and composition, James Kinneavy argues against conceiving of invention rigidly as the moment pen is put to paper: "Professional writers don't just sit down and begin an exercise in freewriting." Writing processes and invention begin well before the act of writing, and Kinneavy theorizes this open space by means of forestructure, "the mental structure which the interpreter brings to the object being interpreted" ("The Process of Writing" 3). This mental structure has three subprocesses: forehaving (developing an intention or purpose), foresight (imagining something as a unified whole), and foreconception (grasping the structure of the object in question). The key point is that these subprocesses are never static. As new ideas and experiences are integrated into the person's prior knowledge, the forestructure is changed and thus changes the basis for interpretation. When Kameen uses personal experience, he is using forestructure as "the entire history of the author [the reader or the student], including complex cultural conventions which have been assimilated" in order to enact a particular kind of change (6). It is not a change that can be predicted or prescribed, but it is the most significant kind of change from a pedagogical perspective. It allows all the participants slowly to build a new well of knowledge (a new sense of structure, or a revised concept of the whole, or a remedied sense of purpose) that will inevitably change the way they see the world.

Kameen's pedagogy enacts this change in the collective social and material ecology created in the classroom. It is a set of interchanges accomplished not simply through the personal prior knowledge of each participant but through the collective prior knowledges created by the read-arounds that forestructure the course. For Kameen, "[t]his mode of the personal is an intellectual and not a therapeutic act. In that respect it strives toward the scholarly" (9). The scholarly, as a written end product, is not the goal—it does not simply conclude with a final exam or an article. Instead, it is the continual, communal striving for knowledge. Kameen is enacting a form of complex vitalism that sees drive, power, and striving in the context of the whole. The ecological conditions of the classroom construct a desiring-machine that produces multiple lines of flight; the collective elements produce their own movement beyond any of its individual components. Reading Kameen from Berlin's articulation of the expressivist paradigm covers over the ways in which his pedagogical method is attentive to material and ecological matters and thus reduces what teachers can learn from such approaches.

Listening over Dialogue

Having another paradigm from which to read rhetoric and compositionists such as Kameen is important for developing pedagogies that acknowledge ecological contexts. In "Rewording the Rhetoric of Composition," Kameen uses an emphasis on dwelling to posit an alternative to formalist, expressivist, and audience-based pedagogies. Working out of Heidegger, he looks to build a more integrated and complex conception of the embodied nature of writing and invention.[16] Heidegger's position is that "[d]welling and building are related as end and means. However[,] as long as this is all we have in mind, we take dwelling and building as two separate activities, an idea that has something correct in it. Yet at the same time by the means-end schema we block our view of the essential relations. For building is not merely a means and a way toward a dwelling—to build is in itself already to dwell" (Heidegger quoted in Kameen, "Rewording" 82). To move out of theories of composition that separate self, world, audience, and language as just so many means to a text, it is important to realize that to write/teach is in itself already to dwell. Heidegger calls this primary space in which we dwell the clearing, or the open. To dwell in building a text is not to master self, world, audience, or language but to live in them, listen to them, and emerge with them. Just as the concept of forestructure grounds interpretation, the concept of dwelling grounds forestructure. Any mental operation of interpretation is grounded in a world in which it participates co-responsibly. Though Kameen does not name the ulterior position he is attempting to articulate, he is subverting the very categories used to describe and conceptualize pedagogy: his method is not formalist, expressivist, or audience-based but an early image of complex vitalism.

Though Kameen is not as explicitly post-dialectical as he could be, he subverts dialectics by emphasizing listening over dialogue. Kameen puts theory in the context of collective personal positions, for example, to de-emphasize terministic screens in an attempt to listen to the other. It is impossible to fully step outside one's own position and avoid doing violence to the other, but one must make the attempt nonetheless because listening, not dialogue, adheres more fully to the ecology of the situation. The silence after the read-arounds in Kameen's pedagogy turns out to be a key ecological element of his method. It is a productive silence that both sets the ecological context and also avoids prescription from the teacher as well as other students. But as Kameen finds out in his seminar, refraining from prescriptiveness can also create difficulties. Kameen remarks that the students begin to see the silence after each reading as silencing; it keeps them from initially articulating a position vis-à-vis the other student texts (*Writing/Teaching* 115). Nevertheless, the silence is necessary to keep the personal readings from becoming the content of the course, from becoming the main focus of the conversations and taking up all the class time. For student readings to function as ecological context rather than content, the participants in a class need to remain silent until everyone has read. For reflexive thinking to occur, the students (and teachers) need to focus on listening to others rather than jumping self-centeredly to their own positions. Silence creates the conditions of possibility for listening, which allows a larger context and forestructure to develop from all the personal readings and the assigned texts. This kind of active knowledge production often happens before speech and before writing, and reading becomes knowledge production only if the reader forgoes criticism and listens to the text. The teacher, author, student, or reader is always in that liminal phase of dwelling among the multiple positions in a classroom or a text.

Kameen's use of the personal, then, is not expressivist but vitalist: it establishes an ecological context through the act of listening rather than a social context through dialogue. Personal writing, in his pedagogy, is meant not to express an individual life, opinion, or thought but to do something particular rhetorically and collectively. Personal texts function "not as memoir but as syllabus; their purpose [in Kameen's classroom] was to model a learning process for others and [to enable Kameen himself] to engage in a learning process" (7). Part of this process is learning to listen. Kameen models for his students how prior knowledge functions rhetorically in interpretation and knowledge production through dwelling in the classroom ecology produced by listening to the read-arounds. Any one person might affect this larger environment, even in silence. Toby Fulwiler, in his review of *Writing/Teaching*, notes that "when certain participants who seldom spoke out loud were absent from the seminar, discussion did not go so well" (308). Silent persons, including the teacher, could affect the ecology of the classroom individually just by listening, by "paying close attention, nodding heads, raising eyebrows, smiling, looking puzzled" (Kameen, *Writing/Teaching* 130). Consequently, it is vital that the teacher be one of those who model how to listen and to link. Once the read-arounds are done and the students have thought carefully about each other's responses, the silence is over and the class moves into deliberation. The teacher's role then is to bring up connections among the assigned texts in the syllabus and the student read-around responses. The teacher is one of the key people who demonstrates this process of linking and building a constellation. Students tacitly and explicitly pick up on the thinking processes that operate in such situations, but the connections can be made only if both the teacher and the students listen attentively. This pedagogical method uses both silence and dialogue—both personal and academic texts—for invention. But importantly, everyone learns to hear the other *before* engaging in discussion. The teacher or the students may then refer back to other responses if they wish; in my experience with this method, heated, thoughtful academic discussions regularly arise.

Kameen's interest in the changes that emerge when we listen to the silent spaces created by our immersion in these classroom ecologies echoes Heidegger, who asks his readers to focus on the phenomenological reality of language as a part of larger material constellations. In Heidegger's view, people hear language in their minds in those few seconds before they speak or write. It emerges in our minds through the ecological conditions of possibility and becomes part of the forestructure of human understanding. In "Heidegger, Language, and Ecology," Charles Taylor asserts that "expression is not self-expression; creative language is a response to a call" (119). The call that we hear in our minds is an intuitive response to a given situation and is the basic phenomenological reality of language. It is produced by the rhetorical situation via language, so we must be attentive to both language and the larger ecological situation in order to hear, see, or understand the inventive response it calls for. Taylor emphasizes that Heidegger, "an uncompromising realist" (120), always looks to the larger ecology of things and humans to produce understanding. So listening to the call is also being attentive to others, because "the thing about a 'thing' is that in being disclosed it co-discloses its place in the clearing" (122).[17] As Heidegger knew, humans co-emerge with things in the world and with other people, and language participates in the construction of the situation in which this co-emergence occurs.

Listening to the other, the rhetorical situation, and the language is not an arbitrary, mystical endeavor or a matter of disclosing personal feelings; it is a basic rhetorical and ecological reality. It is a material response to an embodied situation. In a discussion of Plato and Shakespeare, Coleridge notes that "they were not visionaries or mystics; but dwelt in 'the sober certainty' of waking knowledge" ("Treatise on Method" 660). Reading them as expressivists covers over the ways they were attentive to the situations at hand and responded accordingly, and overvaluing dialogue covers over the fact that one effective rhetorical response is silence. "The question," Cheryl Glenn observes, "is not whether speech or silence is more productive, more effective, more appropriate; rather, it is one of a rhetoricity of purposeful silence when it [silence] is self-selected or when it is imposed. When silence is our rhetorical choice, we can use it purposefully and productively" ("Silence" 263–64). Silence operates intuitively and purposively. Intensive listening opens a space or a path for our own speaking and invention to emerge. Listening to the ecology means intuitively linking ourselves to the lines of flight that are emerging and being a good rhetor or teacher means letting this movement inform our decision to stay silent or speak. Teachers have to let whatever "arises out of the moment" emerge, let *kairos* take over and work "to perfect what the student has to offer," and put his or her "considerable resources somehow in the service of [the students]" (Kameen, *Writing/Teaching* 251). The academic knowledge that teachers have is not irrelevant—theory should not be scorned—but it must inform their listening as much as if not more than their speaking.[18]

I read *Writing/Teaching* as offering a new dwelling for pedagogy that begins to fulfill the promise of "Rewording the Rhetoric of Composition." Neither "Rewording," Coleridge, nor Heidegger appear prominently in the book, but they function silently, sub/versively, as the theoretical forestructure to *Writing/ Teaching*. Teachers always dwell in certain theorists, writers, and knowledge, and teachers tacitly carry these into the classroom. In "Rewording," Kameen tries to develop a methodical framework for understanding how dwelling influences writing, teaching, and learning. In *Writing/Teaching,* he tries to enact that framework sub/versively, silently. Berlin wants people to talk. He wants to state his politics up front and engage in dialogue. His use of theory and academic knowledge goes into developing that position and formulating his heuristic in order to persuade students to adopt that position. Kameen, on the other hand, is opting for silence, listening, letting the students' and his own thoughts tacitly develop out of the local ecology rather than a conscious, predetermined political position. Such a position is distinct from expressivism. Kameen is trying to enact Coleridge's open-ended method collectively in the classroom. Or put another way, he is enacting Deleuze's expressionism by fostering an ecology in the classroom that will express itself. Kameen, his students, their experiences, the texts they read, the theories they presuppose, the methods they develop, and the texts they write all dwell in this local ecology and play important roles in its development. Kameen's insistence on classroom ecology, on not predetermining his relations with his students, and on being open to change himself highlights this open-endedness. Kameen uses the collective desires of everyone in and around the classroom to build a desiring-machine that sends the students toward multiple lines of flight. This process encompasses "what a professor should be, to have no stable, durable, version of [his or her] 'subject.' . . . We are never who we are when we teach. Nor should we try to be. We are something always verging on the more" (256). Such a method listens to the ecologies that forestructure "the writing process" and the scene of teaching. Consequently, Kameen's book does not *tell* the reader how to teach. It does, however, open a space for us to begin to listen to the ecologies in our classrooms and to invent pedagogies that are attentive to our own specificities.

Mapping Constellations

A complex vitalist paradigm needs new methods, such as Kameen's, that utilize rhetorical ecologies. This perspective is especially needed in the context of contemporary technologies. Technology makes the fact that the body is immersed in networks of complexity much more immediate and harder to ignore. As Jameson argues, the key for contemporary theories as well as composition pedagogies is how to map and write these ecologies. Gregory Ulmer takes up this challenge explicitly and extensively: "Cultural critic Fredric Jameson proposed that what is needed in these conditions of fundamental alienation is a new method, a new aesthetic even, capable of composing a 'cognitive map': one may never be able to 'experience' directly the reality of one's world, but one may be able to 'write' it. Mystory is a textual method that responds to this challenge" (*Text Book* 244). Ulmer looks specifically to develop methods and heuristics that map the complex constellations of nature, institutions, technologies, and language in which students live and write, initially developing the genre mystory that evolves into a project he calls the widesite.[19] In his first major book, *Applied Grammatology* (1985), Ulmer emphasizes language as part of the environmental equipment that sets conditions of possibility. If a word is used in a particular rhetorical ecology, all of its meanings are co-responsible elements that contribute to potential lines of flight. In *Glas,* for example, Derrida decomposes proper names into their common meanings to open up their potential connectivity. For Derrida,

> [d]ecomposition . . . functions at the level of writing as the break up of words: . . . The first stage consists of the desublimation of the proper into the common noun—the common noun is the remains of the proper name. . . . Hegel decomposes into aigle (eagle), Genet into genet (a flower). . . . The decomposition of the name begins, then, as antonomasia (the rhetorical figure of this passage from proper to common), reversing the Aufhebung that cancels the literal and lifts it into the figurative. The second stage of decomposition enacts another usage of "signature," meaning the "key" of a musical composition. Glas, in this sense, is written in the key of GL, "as music composed 'in,' a book written in— such and such letters" (*Glas* 94). (Ulmer, *Applied Grammatology* 63–64)

These two aspects of decomposition are central to Ulmer's pedagogy. The first works with both proper and common names as a heuristic device to discover connections between the individual student and the world via common nouns. The second turns decomposition toward arrangement by creating a new "key" as a potential focal point for form. For example, Derrida uses the terms eagle and flower as a conceptual starting place for characterizing each writer's philosophy, and he consequently arranges *Glas* into two columns, one for each author, which produces two texts that appear side by side in the same book— two modes of the same key.

Rather than follow the *Aufhebung* of a dialectical method that would synthesize the two, decomposition is a post-dialectical method that opens possible connections through the multiple meanings of words and the sets of meaning that can be collected into a puncept—rather than concept—and then networked into a text. For example, one puncept that could be built out of my name is

- Hawk—eagle (American ideology)
- Hawk—to sell one's wares (a economic practice)
- HA—laughter (Diane Davis's *Breaking Up [at] Totality: A Rhetoric of Laughter*)
- Whak—WAC (an aspect of my teaching)

Extending this method of invention to the issue of arrangement, these four conceptual starting places could be four sections in a text that links me to cultural ideologies, economic practices, disciplinary theory, and workplace practices, all of which relate specifically to me and my local circumstances. This montage technique of selection and combination follows the model of decomposition—"deconstruction extended from a mode of criticism to a mode of composition" (*Applied Grammatology* 59). Rather than function as composition, a school rhetoric built on linearity, clarity, and coherence, the merging of deconstruction and composition into decomposition looks to map an individual's local space and connect it to these larger discourses, practices, and institutions.

In his next book, *Teletheory* (1989), Ulmer takes this understanding of grammatology in relation to pedagogy and turns it toward media culture. *Teletheory* was published in a pre-computer boom moment when television was the technology many critics juxtaposed with the book. In a classic high/low polemic, many critics lamented the decline of literacy in the face of television culture. Rather than criticize the current age of "videocy," as Ulmer calls it, he tries to map out a practice for electronic cognition. He wants to "invent or discover a genre for academic discourse that could function across all our media—voice, print, and video" (1). Toward this end, Ulmer proposes mystory as a genre that integrates three levels of discourse—personal (autobiography, memory), popular (community stories, oral history, or popular culture), and expert (disciplinary or scientific knowledge). Ulmer says explicitly that the genre is meant to account for the "new discursive and conceptual ecology interrelating orality, literacy, and videocy" (vii). Just as decompositional pedagogy sought to create a set of connections and meanings as a basis for invention and arrangement, mystoriography "assumes that one's thinking begins not from generalized classifications of subject formation, but from the specific experiences historically situated, and that one always thinks by means of and through these specifics, even if that thinking is directed against the institutions of one's own formation" (vii–viii). Such a genre is advantageous pedagogically because it does not ask the student to reject his or her culture before starting to enter academic culture. Instead, it uses each person's background as a way of situating him or her in cultural and disciplinary discourses.

To make the shift from word to image as the link between these three levels of discourse, Ulmer shifts from Derrida's decomposition to Barthes's notion of the punctum. Barthes's method for engaging photographs in *Camera Lucida* lends itself as a model for operating in an image-based media culture. The punctum is the detail in a photograph that jumps out at the viewer as odd and triggers a thought, feeling, memory, or connection. Typically, the punctum is seen as opposed to the studium, the aesthetic or social meaning of the overall image. But it is precisely because of the studium that the punctum shows up. It is the cultural ecology as a whole that situates the out-of-placeness of the punctum and allows Barthes to recognize the oddity of a shirt collar or "the hand at the right degree of openness" (*Camera Lucida* 58). The complex intersection between all the particular details in a photo and all of its cultural connotations and practices allows the punctum to emerge as "something not quite in harmony, a problem or an impasse, always pointing to other routes and destinations ... [that] provoke[s] something like, but not identical to, involuntary memories" (Saper, *Artificial Mythologies* 16). Ulmer's method in *Teletheory* is to collect these images, memories, and practices into a set, juxtapose them, and write a text out of the associative connections among them. The typical associative relation is assumed to be one of analogy—the standard Freudian approach. But the punctum is much different than analogy. The punctum may not trigger what is analogous. A shirt collar might stir a feeling or memory that has no figurative link to a shirt or a collar. Once these connections are collected into a set, the fact that the other discourses, images, and histories appear to be connected to the writer creates pleasure—a Bliss-sense (*jouissance*): "Bliss-sense, as distinct from sense or common sense, concerns the pleasure of the text, the love of learning, the subject's desire for knowledge, which is grounded not in a specialized discipline but in the family story and everyday life" (*Teletheory* 96). It is this affective dimension that drives the student's desire to learn and to further research the connections that emerge out of the collected set.

In Ulmer's example of the mystory genre in *Teletheory*, "Derrida at Little Big Horn," he draws on the three storehouses of memory: mental (personal), oral (cultural), and textual (disciplinary). For a private biography, he relies on his personal memories of being a truck driver for his father's company in Miles

City, Custer County, Montana. Though his public/mythic story, Custer's Last Stand, has been spread via texts, its primary location is in our oral, cultural mythology. And his disciplinary story, his participation in and experience with Derrida's grammatology and its dissemination through American academia, is primarily a textual dispersal, even though it too has its element of orality within the discipline. Ulmer argues that even though "Derrida at Little Big Horn" appears in book form, the logic of its rhetoric, written in fragments and scenes arranged around Ulmer's academic vita and contextualized with accompanying images that provoked his narrative, could easily be reproduced in video form. The emphasis on orality, narrative, and images remakes what it might mean to do academic discourse in the context of media culture. He notes that mystoriography, the method generated out of the genre mystory, is a response to Hayden White's call for a new historiography (method of writing history). Ulmer writes, "An experiment in mystoriography derives its guidelines from the sciences and arts of our time, just as 'history' was invented based on the naturalistic tenets of nineteenth-century science and art" (44). As a remake of historiography, mystoriography looks to "recognize the peculiar configuration of possibility in one's own moment" by "designating the nexus of history, politics, language, thought, and technology in the last decade of the millennium" (82). Such an approach to history is grounded in our particular, local experiences of time and place and looks to map them to larger, global histories through a new form of writing.

Gregory Ulmer's Heuretic

The beginning of the Internet in the early 1990s provided Ulmer with a new medium in which the "peculiar configuration of possibility" could be mapped. In *Heuretics* (1994), he turns the genre mystory toward hypertext rather than video and develops a heuristic for producing juxtapositions that generate invention. Ulmer gives an exemplar: Derrida is asked to collaborate with American architect Peter Eisenman on an exposition in Paris. Derrida responds to the invitation by sending the architect a reading of Plato's *Timaeus* entitled *Chora*

(61). Derrida later meets with the architect's team to discuss the project. The point is not to get the architects to understand Plato but to engage an alternative discourse to move thinking in new directions. Discussing the philosophical concepts gave the architects ideas for buildings even though the eventual structures had no necessary connection to philosophy. The *chora* or space between the two different discourses is a virtual space, in Brian Massumi's sense (see chapter 3), which sparks a punctum and sets invention in motion. The distinct discourses of the popcycle—family, entertainment, school, and academic discipline—work the same way: their juxtaposition creates potential affects that open new possibilities. The method behind mystoriography is to negotiate and write these virtual spaces among the texts, logics, and practices of the popcycle's institutions. Though the personal and local provide starting points, autobiography is not the genre to follow; it quickly dissolves in the context of the multiple genres and forms of the popcycle and the openness of hypertext as an emerging genre. Coming out as a more radical version of Kameen's ideological autobiography, mystory is just a pretext for inventing new architectures, new genres, and new methods.

This emphasis on open spaces moves mystoriography into chorography. Generated out of the term *chora*, chorography becomes Ulmer's characterization of the practice of memory—"a rhetoric of invention concerned with the history of 'place' in relation to memory" (*Heuretics* 39). This is not altogether new. In *Teletheory,* memory as place is already in use: Miles City, Little Big Horn. A personal place that resides physically on the earth and in the person's memory is used as the scene for invention. In *Heuretics,* however, Ulmer notes the difference: "The strategy of chorography . . . is to consider the 'place' and its 'genre' in rhetorical terms—as a *topos.* The project is then to replace *topos* itself (not just one particular setting but *place* as such) with *chora* wherever the former is found in the *trivium.* In order to foreground the foundational function of location in thought, choral writing organizes any manner of information by means of the writer's specific position in the time and space of a culture" (33). What makes this notion of place distinct in the context of *Heuretics* is the relationship between *topos* and *chora.* Following Derrida's characterization of *chora* as "the spacing which is the condition for everything to take place"

(Derrida quoted in Ulmer 71), Ulmer wants to conflate the binary of *chora* as space and *topos* as place. From a Platonic viewpoint, the *chora* is the space where the philosopher's eternal truths are stored, a metaphysical memory bank, and the *topos* is the situated, literal place the sophists use as a memory aid. The combination Ulmer is looking for is the literal but empty space between philosophy and architecture in his work with Eisenman. Metaphysical and material combine to produce the virtual as the locus of emergence—the conditions for everything to take place.

For Ulmer, hypertext provides a technological means for producing such choral spaces, and he invents a corresponding heuristic or heuretic (heretical heuristic) to facilitate their production. The heuretic CATTt—Contrast (opposition, inversion, differentiation), Analogy (figuration, displacement), Theory (repetition, literalization), Target (application, purpose), and tale (secondary elaboration, representability)—juxtaposes disparate situational elements to make these choral spaces show up. As he proceeds through *Heuretics,* Ulmer connects these topoi to specifics and links them together to produce a mystory. He notes, however, that his heuretic is an experiment, not a direct scientific or dialectical method to follow. For those who choose to do their own such experiment, he offers three possibilities. The first is to fill in the heuristic slots of the CATTt with your own choices—what are you contrasting your work with, what is it similar to, what is the goal of the project, what theories will you use, what personal or cultural story will you use? These choices might be random, motivated by curiosity, or initiated by a connection to a particular theory, discourse, genre, purpose, or place. A second possibility is to accept the CATTt Ulmer uses in *Heuretics* (C = argumentative writing; A = method acting; T = Derrida; T = hypermedia; t = cinema remake) but to use your own particulars for some or all of the materials—"a different popular work for the remake, different emotional memories for the rehearsal, a different aspect of Derrida's writings, and so on" (39). A third possibility is to do chorography—to use the function of location to map your specific position in time, place, and culture and invent a heuretic in the process. Ulmer notes that chorography is close to choreography, but he is specifically thinking about geography. In the discipline of geography, "chorological analysis" tries to capture a more specific experience of space than a generic, scientific one. Such an analysis attempts to "capture the particular connections between people and places" (40). In short, doing chorography means inventing your own method for mapping your particular conditions of possibility. Sounding like Jameson, Ulmer notes that even if this attempt fails to create a successful hypertext, "the history of science shows [that] experiment teaches as much or more by failure as by success" (39).

This spirit of experimentation in relation to mapping and digital technologies is extended in Ulmer's next book, *Internet Invention* (2003). In Ulmer's view, researchers should not think of technology as a machine but as an apparatus—the combination of a technology, an identity, a genre, a practice, and an institution to support them (*Internet Invention* 141, 155–56, 213). Print literacy as a technology has generated the unified self, multiple genres from Plato's dialogue to the academic essay and user documentation, a set of scientific and rhetorical methods to practice, and the institution of school to teach and support all of the above. Much work in rhetoric and related fields such as technical communication and composition has already addressed the change in technology from the book to the Internet, issues of online identity, the emergence of digital genres, and pedagogical practices. The institutional question, however, has been largely left unasked. In *Internet Invention*, Ulmer takes the associative linking he has been developing in the genre of mystory, the emphasis on the image and the punctum as an affective rhetorical practice, and the popcycle's process of identity formation and extends these local mappings to the global level through the Internet in order to imagine what new institutional structure might fill this void in the emerging apparatus. He calls the experimental institution the EmerAgency—a global, networked, consulting agency for problem solving.

At the beginning of *Internet Invention*, Ulmer outlines the two primary initiatives for the experimental institution. In the first initiative, the agency would help anyone around the globe to establish an online identity that articulates his or her affective relationship to a particular discipline or profession. For Ulmer, this practice takes the form of a Web site he calls the widesite. The model of hypertext that informs *Heuretics* is largely the stand-alone hypertexts of the early 1990s. The widesite seeks to expand this local mapping by helping writers use the Internet as a database for invention. The shift in technology means that the new apparatus is breaking down the old discursive boundaries both within university disciplines and mainstream culture. Traditional institutions no longer provide a stable or unitary basis for problem solving, so people have to compile, articulate, and map their own conceptual starting places.[20] With the proliferation of information on the Web and of tools for developing, publishing, and finding it, the potential for producing choral spaces is limitless. Through juxtaposition, any information can potentially provide the insight for a solution to any given problem. The EmerAgency consults on using this model of invention to develop and articulate new grounding values and identities rather than simply accept the default values of the popcycle and corporate culture. Ulmer states explicitly that this process is not about an individual critiquing dominant identities but a "collective entity" inventing new identities (*Internet Invention* 315). For Ulmer, it takes a collective body like the EmerAgency to equal the corporate power to invent and disseminate default values. The widesite, then, becomes a new place to begin the search for solutions, and it is a place grounded in a local constellation rather than a dominant ideology.

The widesite also taps into the affective nature of images in the production of these grounding connections. The Internet makes it possible to manipulate and circulate images in a manner that is unprecedented in human history. For Ulmer, this manipulation and juxtaposition have "located the existence of a new unit of meaning, in the way that the Greeks noticed the abstract idea (*dike*) once the story could be scanned visually" (167–68). The shift from orality to literacy allowed the Greeks to see common traits among characters that they had never noticed during oral performances. Plato capitalizes on this potential by inventing categories and definitions—shifting from the actions of the characters to the abstract concepts they exhibited such as justice or virtue. Ulmer argues that our shift in apparatus from literacy to electracy is doing the same with images. Rather than recognize the concept, we are able to recognize what Ulmer calls the "syntagm"—the personal, affective meanings that create our own identifications with images and the mood or atmosphere that they create. For example, the name connection between Lucille (my grandmother) and Lucille Ball cuts across the family and entertainment quadrants of the popcycle.

The juxtaposition of their images in the widesite produces an uncanny feeling that creates a new relationship between the popular figure and me. Rather than critique the given meaning of Lucille Ball, a goofy female who always screws things up, I connect her to my grandmother, who owned her own businesses. With further research, I find out that Ball was the first female executive of a Hollywood studio. This personal connection opens up the possibility, establishes the personal grounds for me to see Ball as a strong, independent female rather than a ditzy redhead. Lucy is still a public icon, but now my affective connection to that icon creates a particular relationship between the larger culture and me.[21] Again, Ulmer notes explicitly that this is not critique as an element of my individual consciousness but the production of a counter-image through affective connections of the body (318). And with the widesite, this new image is put back out into the collective culture and disseminated through the Internet.

In the second initiative, the EmerAgency would use digital networking to match these new affective grounds "with problems confronting both specialized disciplinary and public policy arenas" (18). *Internet Invention* is primarily devoted to the first initiative, and Ulmer promises a follow-up book that details the connection of this affective identity to collective problem solving. It seems clear, however, that the EmerAgency is to be modeled on social-networking sites such as Wikipedia and MySpace.[22] A much more affective relationship to work that is more commensurate with one's specific histories, desires, and abilities would create a stronger motive for solving problems. Through the development of a widesite, a person in California might decide to go to school and specialize in crop irrigation and work hard to develop better irrigation methods because his father struggled to keep the family farm in business. Through its social-networking technologies, the EmerAgency would then connect this person to a community in Africa that is struggling with similar problems. The affective connections to the person's life work would generate a particular desire to help solve these kinds of problems, which generates a much different problem-solution model than the early work of Richard Young and Janice Lauer. Ulmer writes, "Making a mystory tends to produce uncanny connections, which is just one variety of the larger experience of 'recognition' that is central to the practices of creativity. . . . My basic point is to locate the uncanny moments when I experienced that sense of destiny I understand not as 'proof' but more in the style of intuition or even an omen, signaling that the path or way is open in a certain direction" (99). Through the EmerAgency, the conditions of possibility for these lines of flight are mapped, and the knowledge, expertise, and intelligence that emerge from them will be more widely distributed to promote ethical social action and problem solving. Ulmer's ultimate goal is to map the larger constellations that produce affective connections and drive student desire, bring these lines of flight from tacit potential to conscious possibility, and extend these connections from the local to the global.

Linking over Law

It should be clear at this point how Ulmer's model of invention addresses my concerns with schemes such as Berlin's. In general I would say that Berlin's heuristic pre-maps students' textual productions, whereas Ulmer's heuretic is more open to students' local cultures and invents ways to map them to larger contexts particular to the students. This difference contains a number of key elements with regard to the overall argument in this book. First, the binary of privileged/marginalized does not play a role in Ulmer's heuretic. Placing the binary of privileged/marginalized as a central element in Berlin's heuristic closes off a number of possible directions for invention and generally reinstates privilege. At the close of their essay, Sidler and Morris claim that "only citizen-rhetors, consciously equipped with critical-composing skills, will be prepared to face the complex challenges of the next century" ("Writing in a Post-Berlinian Landscape" 290). This position contains the implicit desire to overthrow the Other and institute one's own position in the privileged space; only those who follow the proper reading protocols are of value. In his later work, Berlin discusses student resistance to his heuristic procedure because he fails to move on to question his privileging of the privileged/marginalized binary. Students will resist accepting marginalized positions in their own consciousness, in part because it actually reduces their sense of agency. In some cases, affirmative forgetting of one's marginalized position may be precisely what individuals need to spur them to further action (see the afterword). Rather than change consciousness, Ulmer's method taps into local student embodiment first. Whether they ultimately argue against the institutions that construct them or not, this ground puts them in the position to do so. Where that ground leads is up to the student and the lines of flight that emerge out of the particular constellation or desiring-machine they enact.

Second, Ulmer's approach actively seeks to map out the students' local interconnectedness. Berlin's emphasis on coding and placing students in global narratives actually represses their immediate historical circumstances. In "What Is Cultural Studies Anyway?" Robert Johnson maps cultural studies methodologies into four types—those based on production, texts, reading, and lived cultures. Berlin's cultural studies–based composition pedagogy focuses almost solely on reading. Little emphasis is placed on lived cultures as something distinct from dominant cultural codes. Learning to decode an advertisement has little to do with agency and more to do with ideological interpellation. Berlin is more interested in having students decode privilege and then seeing how they do not match up than he is in fostering the realization that they are historically constructed but also have the potential for inventiveness, for new compositions. Decomposition initially carries a textual focus, but Ulmer's work as a whole explicitly connects it to the larger material constellations around student experience and the institutions that frame that experience. This material connection links Ulmer's textual de/composition to Deleuze's material de/composition. Deleuze and Guattari write, "The first positive task [of schizoanalysis] consists of discovering in a subject the nature, the formation, or the functioning of his desiring-machines, independently of any interpretation. What are your desiring-machines, what do you put into these machines, what is the output, how does it work . . . ?" (*Anti-Oedipus* 322). This task is the basic goal of Ulmer's method: to locate the subject as an effect of its compositions/assemblages/desiring-machines with a whole set of partial objects, fragments. Essentially, mystory is a form of diagramming. In his book on Foucault, Deleuze discusses diagramming at the molar level (the level of culture, the level of the "subject"). A molar level of diagramming produces interpretation. A molecular level maps the fragments that constitute or (un)ground the subject. Ulmer's method can be turned in either of these directions, but Berlin's heuristic is almost exclusively molar. Ulmer's pedagogy can function as a heuristic not only for textual invention but also for the invention of new compositions within life. Such a position would worry less about large-scale (dialectical) binaries and more about possible future relationships. It would not ignore student desire or foreclose on potential compositions, potential lines of flight, or potential actions.

Third, Ulmer's pedagogy provides a more open heuristic for writing than reading. Berlin's heuristic emphasizes reading and interpretation over writing and invention no matter how much Berlin wants to conflate the two. For Berlin, interpretation always comes first rather than being co-emergent with invention. In "Contemporary Composition," Berlin cites Richard Young, Alton Becker, and Kenneth Pike: "The writer must first understand the nature of his own interpretations and how it differs from the interpretations of others . . ." (775). Though the quote is in the context of understanding the social as audience, it highlights Berlin's desire for the foundational necessity of interpretation and its role in a dialectic of individual and social. To the extent that he teaches invention at all, race, class, and gender are his primary topoi for reading the world. This is a limited lens for invention, not to mention for students thinking about their own lived culture and modes of production. Many cultural-studies approaches, such as Grossberg's, focus on the individual/personal as the site of articulation. To promote social-epistemic rhetoric, Berlin needs the personal to be expressive and to function as a marginalized term. This closed system does not allow students to explore the multiple ways their personal experiences are related to the social, not in opposition to it, and thus beyond the oppositional topoi of race, class, and gender. Ulmer's choral topoi give the students the opportunity to examine their own lived cultures beyond these political commonplaces and actually encourage students to invent their own topoi specific to their situations and compositions. Rather than a heuristic that directs student to see their own marginalization, a decompositional pedagogy allows the student a wider field of possibility—a "liberatory pedagogy" that allows students to be liberated from a predetermined way of viewing and linking up to the world: he allows the students the agency to invent and articulate their own compositions or desiring-machines.

Fourth, Ulmer's approach acknowledges and makes use of contemporary electronic spaces for writing and mapping. Berlin does not address this emerging context at all, and most scholarship on hypertext and pedagogy has drifted toward a focus on product—either the problem of identifying and teaching structural differences between hypertexts and print texts or on the ultimate form or genre of new media compositions. Kevin Brooks, for example, writes on the relationship between hypertext and genre, arguing that using familiar genres such as autobiography or soap opera or the detective story can provide a strong pedagogical basis for the production of creative media texts. Brooks is interested in hypertext composition: in producing texts that will (or can) be read. But such approaches have lost sight of Michael Joyce's distinction between exploratory hypertexts, which are to be read, and constructive hypertexts, which are to be written. For Joyce, constructive hypertexts should be used to "develop a body of information that [the authors] map according to their needs, their interests, and the transformations they discover as they invent, gather, and act upon that information." Such encounters with hypertext are about inventing "a structure for what does not yet exist" (*Of Two Minds* 42). Structure/form does not come first. It only comes after or through invention. This distinction is key to understanding the pedagogical role Ulmer wants a project like the widesite to play. Operating from the concepts of *chora* and the virtual, his pedagogy enacts potential through mapping and invention. In "The 1963 Hop-Hop Machine" for example, Jeff Rice notes that multiple juxtapositions produce "whatever" genre is particular to its own movement, which is analogous to Massumi's notion of systematic openness. For Massumi, the goal of writing in the humanities is to take already established concepts from various disciplines but to make sure they are not "applied." Taking an established concept and applying it is to operate in the realm of the possible. To engage potential he suggests taking concepts out of context, disconnecting them, juxtaposing them. Find one example or detail from a discourse and then start reconnecting it. "Then, take another example. See what happens. Follow that growth. You end up with many buds. Incipient systems. Leave them that way. You have made a systemlike composition prolonging the active power of the example," the parable, the potential, the virtual

(*Parables* 19). The Internet is a medium for writing a map that is open, connectable, and inventive.[23]

Lastly, Ulmer directly addresses the nature of method in the context of a complex vitalist paradigm. As he notes, the difference between "Derrida at Little Big Horn" and his mystory in *Heuretics* is that chorography shows how to use the mystory to produce a method. Ulmer's sense of method, like Coleridge's and Kameen's, is fundamentally different from dialectics or science. Like law, which looks to desire things as exactly as possible, scientific and dialectical methods seek to control things in advance. Ulmer, on the other hand, says that the key to "working heuretically is to use the method that [one is] inventing while [one is] inventing it" (*Heuretics* 17). Historically, methods have always been invented out of a specific sense of place and inscribed in a tale— for example, Plato's use of myth to form a symbolic network for the practice of dialectics, Descartes's use of autobiography to ground his rationalist method, or Freud's use of his own dreams to develop psychoanalysis. Method always emerges out of a specific contextualization, and a story serves "as a 'place' within which the theory may be displayed" (42). Ulmer is asking students to participate in the production, rather than application, of method, and he articulates a corresponding form of logic to replace the binary of induction/ deduction—conduction. Ulmer puns on the term: conduction as it links to electricity forms the ground, the circuitry, for connecting "disparate fields of information; it is also implicated in conduct, behavior, how one follows one's desire"; and the term also brings to mind the conductor, leader of the group, someone who "guides the flow of significance from one semantic field to another" (65). The paradox of the conductor is that he or she is both initiator of action and invention as well as the empty space of the *chora* that allows discourses to pass through and reconnect to other circuits. Rather than be concerned with replicating Ulmer's experiment, the goal should be to learn about one's place in the circuitry and to invent a method particular to these circuits. This is especially important in the case of our emerging electronic contexts. All the new structures, forms, and genres of electronic writing, the new social spaces on the Web, and the new economic practices surrounding technology make the nature of contemporary place that much more dynamic and complex. The Web becomes a space for not only experiencing these complex realities but also writing ourselves into them.

Creating Contexts, not Subjects

In "Arts, Crafts, Gifts, and Knacks," Richard Young characterizes "designers of occasions" as reducing context to vitalist mystery, and he argues in favor of direct, conscious, heuristic approaches. Setting up the opposition of new romantic mystery, habit, and context and new classical science, technê, and texts allows Young to disregard context as the ground of heuristics and to overlook the importance of designing occasions as a predominant aspect of composition pedagogy and inventional heuristics. A complex vitalist paradigm, on the other hand, seeks to enact Hayles's recognition: "Modern humans are capable of more sophisticated cognition than cavemen not because moderns are smarter, ... but because they have constructed smarter environments in which to work" (*How We Became Posthuman* 289). In the context of composition pedagogy, teachers need to build smarter environments in which their students work. Just as researchers are working on making rooms into interfaces, teachers in rhetoric and composition need to start thinking about classrooms as ambient interfaces. These environments are constellations of architectures, technologies, texts, bodies, histories, heuristics, enactments, and desires that produce the conditions of possibility for emergence, for invention. Heuristics, then, cannot be reduced to generic, mental strategies that function unproblematically in any given classroom situation. They are enacted in particular contexts and through particular methods that reveal or conceal elements of a situation and enable or limit the way students interact with and live in that distributed environment. Attending to this level of specificity in our classrooms is ultimately a fundamentally ethical act that should no longer haunt our pedagogical practice.

There are multiple ways beyond "mystery" to design occasions from happenings to heuristics. Geoffrey Sirc, in *English Composition as a Happening,* posits the most recent and fully articulated account of the connections among Jackson Pollock, Marcel Duchamp, the situationists, participants of the happenings movement, and compositionists from the 1960s such as Charles Deemer, William Lutz, and William Coles. Just as Duchamp's urinal is effective only in a particular art scene and even gallery space, particular pedagogies are effective only in certain historical and rhetorical spaces. Sirc writes, "[D]esigning spaces, I think, is what it's all about. It's a matter of basic architecture: . . . simplified compositional programs, programs that ignore the complexity and contradiction of everyday life, result in bland architecture; and . . . bland architecture evokes simplistic programs. The spaces of our classrooms should offer compelling environments in which to inhabit situations of writing instruction" (1–2). In this context, Sirc discusses Coles much differently than Young, who cites Coles as a prime example of reducing occasions to mystery. But happenings are not simply about doing something outrageous in the classroom and hoping it sparks the students to write something interesting. Sirc tries to get at Coles's method rather than brush it off as mystery: "Coles strip[s] his material down to a sequence of text-events: conceptual problems or questions to work through" (145). Then he weaves in a range of readings, creating a context, but then abruptly reverses it, questioning commonplace responses to the first context by creating a counter-context. Coles wants a space for students to dwell that produces new experiences, new positions from which to see and think. Sirc reads Coles's method as a semester-long happening that rests on "the ongoing situational aggregate that develops" through the enaction of his method (147). Such an aggregate links local events to the global movements and overall rhythm of the course. Once such a context is put into motion via method, a heuristic can then be connected to or even invented out of the "energy, intensity, and vitality" of our classrooms (181).

Many have proposed heuristics that explicitly try to operate in concert with occasions. Janet Atwill, for example, proposes a heuristic for acting situationally: discern a point of indeterminacy in the situation, overreach a boundary that the situation places on you, and intervene in the systems of classification and standards of value set up within or by the situation (*Rhetoric Reclaimed* 45). This heuristic situates a body within an occasion and operates on the grounds of that encounter. Sounding somewhat like Hayles, she uses the example of a navigator to illustrate the point that context can be seen as the very ground of heuristics. Atwill writes, "[T]he art of the helmsman can only be exercised within the framework of the uncertainty and instability of the sea" (95). The navigator does not have mastery over nature but is carried along with it, works in a relationship with it, against but alongside it. The navigator's intervention does not necessarily change the sea but allows her to operate co-responsibly with it. Similarly, but perhaps even more openly, Cynthia Haynes posits a pedagogical technique that involves co-responsibility with contextual ecologies:

> Give your students (or yourselves) this assignment: Write something offshore, i.e., put a message in a bottle, in response to this statement: WE ARE ALL BOAT PEOPLE. Now take your paper and make a paper boat. Leave it in a prominent place such as a doorstep, a computer terminal, the university administration building, or wear it on your clothes, whatever. Then imagine its trajectory, where it will go, who will see it, what they will think (what you would LIKE them to think). And then, put that in writing; trace the trajectories, and give it ballast—so that the main question you should ask yourself as you write is this: WILL IT FLOAT? ("Writing Offshore")

What Haynes proposes is a technique for mapping complexity. The goal for Haynes is not intervention as much as invention through the human body's situatedness in a context that draws on the potentiality of that particular movement. Like Hayles, Haynes utilizes human co-development with its distributed ambient environment.

Especially in the emerging field of professional writing it is becoming vital to work from contextual ecologies rather than abstract heuristics or genre. In *Writing Workplace Cultures: An Archaeology of Professional Writing,* Jim Henry creates a method for mapping out contexts and linking workplace writing to academic knowledges in a way that would transform discourse practices in each. Though Henry does not explicitly articulate his method as such, the heuristic he uses in his course "Cultures of Professional Writing" can be abstracted from the book: (1) map the institutional dig, (2) uncover discursive shards, (3) link to other shards and sites, and (4) intervene in and reform discursive formations. First, Henry asks his students, who are typically researching and writing in their own workplaces, to situate themselves among the forces that produce the emergence of their subjectivities. This mapping is done both in terms of the academic institutional discourse and the workplace institutional discourse. The students look at the theories and values of each and how those discourses situate them. Second, they create an inventory of these sites, especially from their workplaces. They approach their work site as if they were doing ethnographic fieldwork and look to uncover as many of their organizations' writing practices and writing positions—such as reporter, indexer, editor, or Web designer—as they can. Third, they look to link these sites and shards in the inventory to larger complexities. All of these sites and shards imply ecological connections to larger institutional, economic, and social complexities. Academic theories, like Heidegger's technologies, come in to make these linkages show up and to make connections to the workplace writing practices show up. Henry asks students to link these across affect and desire, which often do not show up in either institutional discourse. Fourth, he asks his students to get involved in the construction of the sites and subjectivities in their workplaces. The student-workers need to work from below to bring these shards and links into their writing practices, their discussions and meetings with bosses and colleagues, and their collaborative writing projects in order to situate themselves within those institutions and their narratives. The goal is not to undo the institutions but to remake and rearticulate the discourses, subjectivities, and lines of flight that emerge from them.

In a certain sense, Atwill, Haynes, and Henry are all designing methods to situate student bodies in pre-existing situations and co-produce with those situations. But it becomes equally important, as Sirc attempts to show, to design the occasions of our classrooms to foster the potential for emergent, inventive moments rather than uncritically apply generic heuristics or processes. In "The Meaning of *Heuristic* in Aristotle's *Rhetoric*," Richard Enos and Janice Lauer argue, "Aristotle used the term *heuristic* to capture the way meaning is cocreated between rhetor and audience and how, through this process of interaction, participatory meaning is shared" (79). Though their argument is based on the concept of co-creation, it focuses on the dialectical relationship of rhetor and audience as unproblematic elements. Heuristics are to facilitate communication between these pre-existing entities. For Enos and Lauer, "Aristotle himself gives us insight into heuristic as creating meaning within the rhetor and cocreating meaning within the audience" (80). But in the context of a post-dialectical, complex vitalist paradigm, the "between" is the space of invention rather than communication. The issue is not meaning in the teacher (his or her ideology or intention) nor meaning in the students (their writing ability or subjectivity) but the actions and inventions co-produced alongside any possible meanings through the emerging moments between teacher and student, technology and text, or architecture and culture in a particular classroom. This model is the key to thinking about designing occasions not in opposition to heuristics but in conjunction with them.

As Graham Harman notes in *Tool-Being*, all of Heidegger's work comes down to the fact that ecological constellations allow certain possibilities to emerge and limit other potentialities. A tool's being, its structure and qualities, establishes certain conditions of possibility both for its connectivity and for any future outcomes of the larger tool-contexts it becomes a part of. But the "problem of *specific* constellations of revealing and concealing is precisely what Heidegger needed to solve, and never managed to solve" (189; emphasis added). The implication of this insight for composition scholars and teachers is clear: take Heidegger's general point about Being and put it into Time—take this understanding of constellations and bring it to the particular occasions created in the classroom. An overly simple example: Adobe Photoshop creates a greater possibility for producing an image than Microsoft Word. But more specifically, Photoshop plus a detailed and insightful assignment plus a theoretical grounding in visual rhetoric plus the historical development of the Internet plus open copyright laws establishes a constellation that creates a greater possibility for producing an image. This simple example should not detract from the fact that the same holds true for finer and finer levels of detail that extend from the multiplicity of traits and qualities for each of these elements to every aspect of its larger constellations. What this means for pedagogies of invention is that any heuristic exists in many potential sets of relations with particular writing assignments, theoretical or conceptual ideas, selected readings, individual user histories, and institutional constraints. All of these and more need to be taken into account when developing heuristics, implementing digital tools, designing assignments, choosing readings, and grouping students collaboratively. The spaces between all of these molar elements are ripe with molecular complexity, and it is these moments that are truly generative.

The point is not to just copy Kameen's method, Ulmer's heuretic, Atwill's heuristic, Haynes's tactic, or Henry's pedagogy but to design your own occasions, build your own constellations, and invent your own heuristics specifically for those contexts. Heuristics are the specific, explicit processes or strategies that a teacher might provide for the students. But method is the way a teacher designs the constellations in which these heuristics are deployed. As techniques that situate student bodies within ecological contexts to enact bodily knowledge and open up the potential for invention, method is something that the students rarely see explicitly. They experience its enactment only in the classroom ecologies. This approach to method is clearly different than a banking or lecture model, but it is also different from traditional collaborative group work and even problem-posing pedagogies. Rather than set the context or problem and then let students work out solutions on their own, a complex vitalist method makes the teacher a crucial part of the ecology (as with Kameen) and theory a particularly crucial element (as with Ulmer). Theory is not something separate from practice that is applied to a situation: it is linked to a pedagogical-machine and becomes an integral element in the mix. Every element contributes to the situation being what it is and contributes to the learning, thinking, and understanding that emerges in that context. Paying attention to classroom contexts and injecting an alternate theory, a key text, or a new heuristic at the right time can yield a major shift in the ecology, and this is the primary role of the teacher—to operate kairotically in the context of complexity. In this context teaching composition would no longer be a matter of practitioners applying heuristics developed by researchers or scholars. All teachers of rhetoric and composition would become theorist-practitioners—theorists of their own situations, constellations, and methodologies. Giving teachers a few heuristics or general process models and sending them into the classroom does not give them a basis for creating and negotiating the complexities of the classroom environment and inventing methods out of it that can fold back into their pedagogical-machines. When theorist-practitioners develop and deploy heuristics in these complex contexts, the heuristics become nonsystematic—they no longer operate on a linear, instrumental model of entelechy but open the complex system to multiple lines of flight.

Such an openness to context, ecology, assemblage, and emergence means that teachers cannot have a pre-set desire for student subjectivity. Diane Davis writes, "We teachers of composition, of course, launch our own torpedoes of desire, aimed directly into our students and designed to make something happen, something that will affect their structural formation and, therefore, their productions/excretions" (*Breaking Up* 228). Davis, on the other hand, wants to disrupt attempts to create a composition pedagogy that imposes these pedagogical desires as law. Rather than put pedagogy in the service of a particular politics or definitive subject, teachers can avoid such "humanist hope" by launching their torpedoes into classroom ecologies and leaving the affects open (230). A posthuman pedagogy in the service of invention leaves much of the linking up to the students and focuses on structural formation rather than subjectivity. The subject, then, becomes a side effect of the pedagogical-machine that cannot be completely determined. In *In Defense of the Accidental*, Odo Marquard argues that people are their accidents. Accidents that emerge from contexts are the individual parts of us that are not socially constructed and cannot be predicted. Pedagogy in a complex vitalist paradigm accepts this reality and tries to work it into a system without eradicating it, accounting for it, or predetermining it. If everything emerges from a moment of complexity, then subjectivity would be closer to Ulmer's notion of the conductor. As conductors we are active initiators of movement and organization, passive conduits that allow discourses and forces to pass through and reconnect to other circuits and function in new machines, and participants in constellations that are co-responsible for our conduct. We are our accidents and our connections as much as our choices.

The issue of linking and connectedness eventually becomes an ethical concern. For Spinoza, ethics is centered on creating compositions—productive relationships among bodies and forces. In Deleuze's reading of Spinoza, "every time a body encounters another body there are relations that combine and relations that decompose, sometimes to the advantage of one of the two bodies, sometimes to the advantage of the other body" ("Deleuze – Session on Spinoza").

When a body consumes food, for example, it decomposes the food's prior relations but composes a new relation with it that allows the body to produce new actions. In nature, these two processes always accompany each other as equivalent processes. There are only compositions. There is no particular point of view from which an ethical value judgment could be made about what would constitute a decomposition. Only from the viewpoint of human understanding can a relation be designated decompositional. Deleuze writes, "I would say that there is composition when my relation is conserved and combined with another, external relation, but I would say that there is decomposition when the external body acts on me in such a manner that one of my relations . . . is destroyed . . . [or] ceases to be carried out by the current parts" ("Deleuze – Session on Spinoza"). An ethical goal for pedagogy, then, would be to design occasions in which students are more likely to create compositions rather than decompositions. A pedagogical act would be evaluated based upon the relationships it fosters and the relationships it severs—on its ability to increase rather than decrease a student's agency, power, or capacity to produce new productive relations.

The ethico-pedagogical problem, of course, is that a particular pedagogy does not create a particular ethical outcome any more than a particular subjectivity does—it contributes to the desiring-machine or constellation that produces capacities, affects, and subjects as side effects of its movement and evolution, but it does not generate a definitive outcome. This is what gets many critical pedagogies into difficulties. A heuristic such as Berlin's, which promotes a predetermined ideology and subjectivity, is actually more likely to generate decompositions than compositions with students. If a particular outcome is imposed as law, it can actually reduce an individual's agency. Oftentimes people who attempt to obey a moral imperative do not feel empowered; they can feel guilty or become cynical. Such affects promote becoming-passive rather than becoming-active. Perhaps, if we follow Jameson, we may recognize that Berlin's pedagogy will inevitably fail (create a decomposition), and we can hope that some success (composition) may arise from it. But reducing possible relationships to a privileged/exploited binary forecloses all the other possible compositions that students may produce and thus makes creating decompositions more likely. It excludes all other ethico-political possibilities and promotes a violence to other political compositions. Perhaps if we recognize the fact that all linking is potentially violent, more attention would be paid to an ethics of composition and decomposition rather than our own political desires for our students. To desire an outcome for them is to commit a certain violence to them. Instead, perhaps teachers should ask the students to map out the various territories that they intersect, investigate the multiple potential relationships the situation could enact, and determine which ones might be compositional or decompositional in relation to their particular contexts. These examinations would surely come to include issues related to race, class, and gender, or larger economic realities, but they would also leave the field open to the multitude of other possibilities by addressing the students' specific local situations more directly. For me, this is a preferable methodology that encourages students to begin thinking about their relationships to lived experience in both an ethical and political way without imposing a reductive or deductive heuristic on them.

In a complex vitalist paradigm, being attentive to the ways we design our constellations and to the ethical effects they produce becomes the central pedagogical concern. A decade into his career Kameen realized that "the teacherly personae and pedagogical techniques that had worked so predictably for [him] . . . were not working with the same efficacy any longer, or were producing entirely different, and often quite troubling, effects" (*Writing/Teaching* 247). This problem was disturbing not only for his students but also for Kameen, who wondered why he was still teaching, what he was accomplishing, and what he had to offer his students. He challenges his readers not to answer these questions with the easy clichés that so often function as alibis: "If you are looking for a place to start thinking about teaching, ask yourself ['What am I doing here?'] while you're standing in front of a class, just before it starts" (249). Such a Heideggerian question opens a space specific to that classroom and that moment. Kameen urges us to pause and actually listen to the variety of answers produced by such questions, moments, and contexts, since typically "we don't bother to wait for, and then listen to, the responses [these questions] elicit, even when they are our own" (249). Especially in the classroom, teachers do almost anything but listen. We plan the next question, fill in the students' answers, think about where we want to make the answers go, look for the chalk. Kameen asks us instead "to focus . . . on this very small and specific kind of 'between' . . . that silent space between the question's having been posed and the answer it is about to elicit" (250). The few seconds after the question is posed is a moment of complexity that affects the compositions that emerge out of it. In asking all teachers to be attentive to this level of situatedness, *Writing/ Teaching* is genuinely one of the most hopeful books I can recall about the act of teaching. It is not hopeful about what we can tell students to do or make them become. It is hopeful about that moment of emergence in the classroom—the potentiality that lies in that moment between the placing of a question in the air and when some muddled and/or insightful response occurs.

A pedagogy of invention such as Kameen's or Ulmer's seen from a Deleuzian ethics of composition and decomposition would place the student in the midst of mapping and investigating these problematics. From this perspective, Kameen's hope is clearly posthumanist—though I doubt he would use such language. An expressivist hope would take a passive role in pedagogy and hope that the students' desire can produce good writing. A social-epistemic hope would take an active role in determining the pedagogical goals and hope the students adopt the teacher's desires. A complex vitalist hope would take an active role in designing pedagogical contexts and hope the students come to understand their situatedness and learn to develop ethical connections that will lead to productive acts and texts. Since no pedagogy can be purely mathematical, there will always be hope, there will always be desire involved. But a posthumanist hope does not let desire reside only in the student or teacher. It recognizes that desire also exists within the complex ecologies we actively develop but can never fully control. This posthuman model of subjectivity emerges from the between spaces in the classroom that our students conduct. We have to hope that we will design occasions that increase their potential for compositions rather than decompositions. Or, at least, our primary desire is that our pedagogies can promote more compositions than decompositions. Increasing the potential for productive compositions is my hope every day when I reach for the door of the classroom.

AFTERWORD

Toward a Counter-Historiography

We want to serve history only to the extent that history serves life.

Nietzsche, "On the Uses and Disadvantages of History for Life"

... the problem with classification systems is not that they are bad but that different people—and the same person at different times—require different ones.

George Landow, *Hypertext 2.0*

BREAKING VITALISM FROM ITS CURRENT categorization in romanticism and placing it in a new category with complexity theory requires the production of a counter-history. Consequently, I would situate this book in the line of revisionist histories from Albert Kitzhaber to James Berlin and from Sharon Crowley to Robert Connors. I am building on the examination of what gets excluded from other (more dominant) histories in order to rethink received concepts and categories that at this point are more of an impediment to the growth of the field than a useful conceptual starting place or map. However, it is important to engage in revisionary history not only as a self-corrective for exclusion but also to employ "sub/versive" historiography to open the way for other possible categorizations.[1] As Diane Davis notes in *Breaking Up [at] Totality*, the

point is not "to offer an objective and/or *corrective* History" (4). For her, "[p]ro-
ponents of expressionist, feminist, and social epistemic rhetorics of composing
typically deal with this problem by turning the pedagogical task toward myth
re-vision/re-production. But, while re-inscriptions are certainly not nothing
(they are necessary), they will also not have been enough to effect a rigorous
hesitation in the machinations of exclusion" (13). In other words, revisionary
historians tend to allow their opposition to exclusionary or reductive traditional histories to transform into new dogmas and therefore reinscribe exclusions. Sub/versive historiography, on the other hand, emphasizes the openness
of history to human redescriptions. It moves beyond the binary designations
and teleology of revisionary history to produce multiple counter-histories. A
counter-history for my project in this book not only requires a revisionary history that brings the excluded practices and figures into the dominant history
but also requires a different form of historiography to produce a new kind of
history. In order to write one such counter-history, I follow these conceptual
starting places for counter-historiography.

**Acknowledging that writing history is fundamentally rhetorical and re-
sponds to rhetorical situations.** Nietzsche argues that histories should address
their present-day situations and employ different rhetorical strategies for dealing with historical material and for re-imagining the way that material is *used.*
In "On the Uses and Disadvantages of History for Life," he proposes three
rhetorical tactics, or attitudes, as the cure for the positivistic history and culture
of the nineteenth century: monumental, antiquarian, and critical.[2] A monumental approach to history is needed when there are no models for action in
the present culture. Historians would write biographies of great figures and
typologies of archetypal individuals who through rare and bold deeds influenced history. Such a suprahistorical stance employs a mythic, poetic perspective in order to persuade contemporaries to act and strive, and it requires a
forgetting of historical details that may hinder present actions in life. The greatest disadvantage of such an approach is that it can inspire foolish acts, or create
a false sense of culture in a people (à la Nazi Germany's uncritical application
of this attitude). It is precisely because of such potential disadvantages that
one may need to employ an antiquarian attitude.

The antiquarian historian's job is to preserve, to go back in history and bring up forgotten details, to *remember* those people and events that were pushed aside by historical forces. Antiquarian history can be used in the service of life by giving a people who have had their culture stripped away a sense of community, which can positively influence their present actions. But the clear problem with this approach is that it can easily fall back into positivist history, which assumes objectivity and valorizes the past, and its rhetorical effect can paralyze a people if they begin to believe that their present and future are determined by the past. In an effort to bring forth the attitude that the past does not determine life, Nietzsche posits a third approach. His critical stance *remembers only to forget.* It remembers the past in order to judge it, condemn it as life negating, and subsequently to forget it. Both monumental and antiquarian histories operate as poetic and narrative accounts. Critical history is argumentative. Nietzsche says, "[I]f he is to live, man must possess and from time to time employ the strength to break up and dissolve a part of the past: he does this by bringing it before the tribunal scrupulously examining it and finally condemning it" (75–76). While this critical stance may seem negative, it affirms the present by saying no to histories that negate the present and by arguing for new historical frameworks.

These attitudes toward history are fundamentally rhetorical. Nietzsche's method requires the writer or historian to assess the current situation and use the attitude appropriate to that context. As John Poulakos notes in "Nietzsche and Histories of Rhetoric," Nietzsche employed all these attitudes throughout his career (91–93). Though he is best known for his genealogical work, which takes a great deal from so-called critical history, Nietzsche also used monumental history in *Philosophy in the Tragic Age of the Greeks* and *Thus Spake Zarathustra*, where past figures are elevated to suprahistorical heights, and antiquarian history in *Twilight of the Idols* and in his lecture notes on rhetoric. They each open up possibilities that the others exclude, and only the particular rhetorical situation can set the conditions of possibility for which method is to be employed. Such an approach affirms the present through rhetorical invention. Monumental history invents an archetypal past. Antiquarian history invents a narrative of the past. Critical history invents an origin in the past. As

Nietzsche notes, critical history is "an attempt to give oneself, as it were *a posteriori,* a past in which one would like to originate in opposition to that in which one did originate" ("On the Uses" 76). These inventions can be used in an "untimely" manner to argue against the life-negating forces in the present, as Nietzsche did when he argued against contemporaries who were positivist historians and philologists, but even critical history can go too far and start critiquing for its own sake, rather than for life.[3] Consequently, there will always be a need for new counter-histories.

Following Nietzsche, I envision this book as one such a counter-history out of a set of multiple possibilities. I read Weidner's approach as monumental; therefore, I use antiquarian and critical perspectives to open new possibilities. It is not that Weidner and Young are simply wrong in some objective sense. Their particular rhetorical situation called for monumental history. In the 1970s, there were few models for action in rhetoric and composition, so Weidner wrote a typology of suprahistorical categories that forgot key historical details. His typology, explicitly or implicitly, enables Young and those who came after him to strive for the production of rhetoric and composition as a discipline. However, the situation has changed. The old categorical maps no longer fit institutional and technological contexts in which teachers and theorists of writing and rhetoric operate. Therefore, I want to remember the past differently than Weidner and Young in order to affirmatively forget their categorizations, and I do so in the hope of positively affecting the field in the present. It is part of my project to invent an origin from which I would like to have emerged as a counter to current exclusionary histories of rhetoric and composition.

Examining the change in meaning of key terms as they shift from various periods and categories. Like Nietzsche, Arthur Lovejoy develops a fundamentally rhetorical approach to the history of ideas. Though Lovejoy's methods are always being revised in the light of his practice, two primary tactics can be derived from his writings on historiography: identifying key terms and their elementary ideas and tracing the shifting meaning of those terms and ideas across various periods, disciplines, thinkers, and texts. In his introduction to *The Great Chain of Being,* Lovejoy notes that the total doctrine of any philosopher or school is almost always a "complex and heterogeneous aggregate" (3) and rarely corresponds to larger key terms: God, for example, is not an elementary idea but a term for a complex composition of more specific ideas, values, and assumptions. Likewise, terms ending in -ism or -ity are not elementary ideas but larger compounds that need to be broken down: idealism and Christianity, for example, do not stand for one doctrine but for several distinct and competing ideas. Consequently, -isms are generally thought-obscuring terms, classifications that are almost always misleading. To begin clearing away these confusions, Lovejoy attempts to identify the more specific rhetorical elements in a given period, text, or work of a particular thinker that ground those key terms. He looks for value assumptions, key rhetorical or logical moves, appeals to pathos, assumed associations of ideas, and fundamental propositions or principles.[4]

While he is concerned with each of these rhetorical elements in various texts and contexts, especially the shifting associations of ideas surrounding the terms nature and romanticism, Lovejoy is most concerned with propositions or principles in *The Great Chain of Being*. Principles are foundational ideas that have a natural or logical capacity for connecting with other rhetorical elements in disparate philosophies or periods to produce a more general idea or term. In *The Great Chain of Being*, for example, Lovejoy examines how the philosophical principles of plenitude, continuity, and gradation were first articulated in Plato and Aristotle, brought together as a unit in Plotinus to produce the idea of the great chain of being, and then disseminated in various aggregates, disciplines, and genres from the medieval through the romantic periods. For Lovejoy, these ideas seek to "answer a philosophical question which it was natural for man to ask—which reflective thought could hardly have failed to ask, sooner or later" (14). The great chain of being answers the question "How is the universe ordered?" While all people and all periods have probably attempted to answer this question in many ways, the history Lovejoy lays out is one particular series of answers that, while clearly divergent in historical articulation, is connected through the conception of the universe as a chain of beings arranged hierarchically from the most meager to the most perfect. The great chain of being, as a unit-idea composed of the principles of plenitude, continuity, and gradation, can be connected to different and often competing rhetorical elements, assumptions, ideas, and conclusions while still maintaining its particular core identity and historical trajectory.

Since these unit-ideas naturally form different aggregates in differing periods and contexts, Lovejoy seeks to observe their fusion with other ideas, their influence across diverse fields, how later generations develop them in divergent ways, and their appearance in the arts and culture (21). As Lovejoy argues in "The Historiography of Ideas," this method requires interdisciplinary movement. A passage in Milton, for example, can cross over into science (astronomy) and philosophy (Aristotle). Looking at it only from a background in literature creates a certain historical blindness that overlooks much of the passage's importance (3–6). For Lovejoy, the need to investigate this interdisciplinary dissemination of ideas poses a number of difficulties, not the least of which is the limited breadth of a disciplinary scholar and the limited depth of the generalist. In addition to the obvious need for collaboration across disciplines, Lovejoy recommends a basis in philosophy. Since he argues that most ideas begin in the history of philosophy and are then disseminated through science and the arts into the wider culture, philosophy can serve as a common conceptual starting place and help alleviate disciplinary blindness. Studying philosophy gives a historian of ideas the grounding in its history but also practice in its analytical method of taking apart "idea-complexes" (8). With this background, critics can individually and collaboratively examine the life history of a unit-idea across historical and disciplinary lines.

For Lovejoy, this interdisciplinary practice is grounded in three primary assumptions. The first is that even in diverse constellations or groupings, ideas retain a core identity that remains and cuts across the various discourses and periods. Unit-ideas such as the great chain of being retain their basic principles. Second, despite a core identity, key terms are multivocal and can shift in meaning due to historical context and taste. Nature, for example, can mean many things even in the context of the romantic period. The third assumption is that, while historians and critics typically confuse the usage of these terms, even primary writers from a period can waver in a term's ambiguity, which makes the historian's job that much more difficult. On the one hand, many authors typically try to minimize the difficulties or discrepancies in terms to present a more coherent book or unified argument. On the other, according to Lovejoy, the best thinkers accept diversity and attempt to use it or work through it. These multiple possibilities can offer fruitful territory for the historian of ideas but cause trouble for critics who try to impose unity on such thinkers (preface to *Essays*).

Lovejoy's basic rhetorical approach has many implications for an examination of vitalism. I begin with an initial term or -ism that is generally misleading and break it down to elementary ideas. The most important fundamental question that cuts across all vitalisms is "What is life?" It is almost certainly a philosophical question that reflective thought would inevitably ask. And I see in a wide variety of answers a core identity built on two key assumptions: that life is fundamentally complex (and that complexity must be accounted for or addressed), and that life is fundamentally generative (force, energy, will, power, or desire is central to this complexity). But because this core identity finds a diversity of expression in each period, discipline, thinker, or text, it is clear that histories of rhetoric and composition should not be separated from histories of the humanities in general and of philosophy in particular. Following Lovejoy, I take an interdisciplinary approach to counter the disciplinary blindness of those who accept a general characterization of vitalism. My issue with Weidner, Young et al. is that one answer to the question cannot stand for all vitalisms: a critic cannot make generalizations based on one meaning. Lovejoy lists Coleridge as one of the thinkers who accepts complexity and diversity and attempts to work through it (preface to *Essays* xvii). In order to simplify this complexity, too many compositionists reduce Coleridge's work and give it the generic label vitalism instead of using his complexity to interrogate vitalism.

Describing relations among these terms and the discourses, institutions, and practices surrounding their emergence to produce new groupings. Just as Nietzsche enacts a critical and inventive historiography in response to the positivist historians of his day, Foucault sets his historiographic method in distinction to the history of ideas that preceded him. In *The Archaeology of Knowledge*, he questions the traditional notions of continuity, unity, and the search for origins. Traditional historians look to establish historical continuity through the notion of influence, which reduces difference to identity and assumes a linear cause-and-effect logic. The simple identification of an associative resemblance and the successive occurrence of its repetition is often enough to assume a direct influence. And if an idea is repeated enough in a loosely associated time or place, a general "spirit of the age" can be identified and classified under a single, unifying name. Similarly, the boundaries of the material book, the oeuvre, and the author assume a unity and coherence that establish a stable basis for analysis and classification. All of these unities imply an origin that traditional historiographies are set up to search for, whether the origin is in the hidden intentions of an author or the obscurity of past texts. But even though Lovejoy's approach to the history of ideas accepts the notion of influence, a unified core identity, and the search for origins, it also accepts the necessity of boundary crossing, the multiple meanings that can exist in an author or book, and the problematic nature of categorization that Foucault makes even more prominent.

Rather than assume the linear, cause-and-effect logic of influence and origins, Foucault's archaeology is a method for describing emergence. Instead of looking for past origins or influences in books, authors, or oeuvres, Foucault examines specific discursive objects and the statements and practices that make them possible in the present. Madness, for example, is not an inherent, isolated object but is brought into being, or revealed, through a specific rhetorical and material situation via statements that "named it, divided it up, described it, explained it, traced its developments, indicated its various correlations, judged it, and possibly gave it speech by articulating, in its name, discourses that were to be taken as its own" (32). The archaeologist looks to map the connections from these statements to the institutional fields, sets of events, practices, political decisions, economic processes, manpower needs, and demographics that surround them and make them possible. Consequently, no simple or linear cause-and-effect logic is adequate for describing the complexity of such discursive events. No common origin as an easily identifiable cause can be named that cuts across time periods, disciplines, or ideas. Every articulation of an idea, such as madness, can be described only by mapping out the specific set of real-world relations that gave rise to it in that moment.

Foucault's emphasis on conditions of possibility and the process of emergence means that any classification is not a grand unity but one possible grouping of statements and events. Foucault's epistemes in *The Order of Things*—Renaissance, Classical, Modern—are not the great unified periods of traditional histories. They are particular descriptions of statements and their "positivities." Thinkers and writers do not communicate via isolated texts across great time spans. For Foucault, they communicate through the immediate form of positivity that "defines a field in which formal identities, thematic continuities, translations of concepts, and polemical interchanges may be deployed" (127). Any archaeological description is one snapshot cut out of this complex mass of texts and material relations that set the *a priori* conditions for communication. Because these discursive formations do not simply belong to one field but enter "simultaneously into several fields of relations" and form "a tangle of interpositivities whose limits and points of intersection cannot be fixed in a single operation" (159), any classification is not the last word on the period. The historical conditions are so complex that one writer cannot describe everything. Consequently, other writers can examine those same time frames, select different texts, examine overlapping practices, and produce different groupings. These various groupings are not simply true or false but are equally valid as archaeological descriptions. As Foucault makes clear, his books "aren't treatises in philosophy or studies of history" but "anticipatory strings of dots, . . . philosophical fragments put to work in a historical field of problems" ("Questions of Method" 74).[5]

For this project, I am most interested in Foucault's emphasis on the emergence of discursive objects through specific statements and practices and the development of new groupings or assemblages. Looking to map the emergence of vitalism within a particular discursive formation rather than establish disciplinary origins or foundations, as Young and others do, allows me to examine vitalism and its relation to rhetoric and composition as a field—a cluster of related issues, texts, theorists, and practitioners on a flat, nonhierarchical surface—rather than as a discipline and to develop new subgroups or assemblages. In an attempt to problematize the rigid categories that ground the discipline, I describe the relations surrounding vitalism in the discourse of rhetoric and composition, reassemble vitalism into the subgroups of oppositional, investigative, and complex, and examine pedagogical practices in relation to these new groupings. Approaching the traditional categories of classical rhetoric, current-traditionalism, cognitive rhetoric, expressivism, and social-epistemic rhetoric as open rather than closed categories allows me to show that vitalism actually draws upon ideas and practices from many of these categories while also working out of positions that do not fall into any of them. Such a specific constellation is a unique formation and will ultimately reveal ulterior functions for key terms and concepts. So what I am doing in this book is describing an ulterior constellation of conditions that reveals vitalism as a different discursive object, ultimately exposing the disciplinary memory as a forgetting.[6]

Using names and dates as key points in the shifting of terms and the diagramming of their relations. Deleuze and Guattari follow a historiographic method of assemblage similar to Foucault's but have a particular take on the traditional usage of names and dates. Their book, *A Thousand Plateaus*, is "a network of 'plateaus' that are precisely dated, but can be read in any order" (Massumi, translator's foreword to *A Thousand Plateaus* ix). Rather than signify the unities and progressions of traditional histories, the book is a series of events and the larger assemblages of texts, bodies, and practices that the events make possible. Deleuze and Guattari write, "We will never ask what a book means, as signified or signifier; we will not look for anything to understand it. We will ask what it functions with, in connection with what other things it does or does not transmit intensities, in which other multiplicities its own [intensities] are inserted and metamorphosed, and with what bodies without organs it makes its own [intensities] converge" (4). A book is not an isolated or unified object but is an assemblage, or body without organs, in connection with other assemblages. Likewise, a name and a date are not simply facts to be listed but terms that signify a collection of statements, practices, and their affects and effects in the larger constellations to which they are connected.

The name is simply a function of this larger network. Throughout Deleuze's work, he creates an orphan line of philosophy by taking names that are known in traditional philosophy but inhabit its outer fringes—Lucretius, Hume, Spinoza, Nietzsche, Bergson—and giving them new functions within new assemblages. As names on and in books they too are to be broken into and reconnected to other constellations of signs, bodies, texts, events, forces, enunciations. As part of these larger bodies, names "designate not persons or subjects but matters and functions" (142). For example, a name designates a mode, mood, or method in the same way that a painter's name designates a color, nuance, tone or intensity. Wagner's name designates a certain type of voice or instrumentation, the mathematician's name Galios designates a particular theorem and mathematical operation (142). Deleuze and Guattari's basic method is to take a name from one context, link it to a similar mode, mood, or method from another context, and then mobilize it in a third context. Similar to Nietzsche, they are not so concerned with what these names represent in the world but in the intensities, affects, or actions the name's mode, mood, or method can deploy once in the new assemblage.

Dates function in a similar way to designate the affects of statements and the constellations to which they are connected. In *A Thousand Plateaus* dates are linked to what Deleuze and Guattari call "incorporeal transformations," which are enacted by "order-words," decrees, or commands. For example, a judge's sentence transforms an accused person into a convict. Corporeally, materially, what takes place before (the crime) and after (the penalty) are actions-passions that affect bodies (the property, victim, convict, and prison), "but the transformation of the accused into a convict is a pure instantaneous act or incorporeal attribute that is the expressed of the judge's sentence" (80–81). The body is still the same material body, but incorporeally it is changed in a way that affects it materially. Similarly, all bodies mature and grow old, but the movement from one category to another, graduation or retirement, is an incorporeal transformation that takes an order-word or command to enact it. Oftentimes these transformations generate immaterial changes as well. Love is an intermingling of material bodies, but the phrase "I love you" produces a transformation of those bodies from one conceptual category to another and produces greater intensity in the relationship. Eating bread and drinking wine during communion are an intermingling of bodies, but the statement of a priest transforms them into the body and blood of Christ, which heightens the affective, religious experience.

For Deleuze and Guattari, what is interesting about incorporeal transformation is its "immediacy, . . . the simultaneity of the statement expressing the transformation and the effect the transformation produces; that is why order-words are precisely dated, to the hour, minute, and second, and take effect the moment they are dated" (81). A hijacker, for example, can by decree instantaneously transform the plane-body into a prison-body, turn passengers into hostages, and enact an event that changes both affective and material relations thereafter: a constellation marked with the date Tuesday, September 11, 2001, 8:46:30 A.M. ("9/11"). It may seem that this immediacy can only occur through human decree, but Deleuze and Guattari suggest that "the sum of the 'circumstances' [can] suddenly [make] possible a semiotic transformation that, although indexed to the body of the earth and material assets, [is] still a pure act or incorporeal transformation" (82). A stock market crash, for example, has no single human actor or origin but signals an incorporeal transformation nonetheless, one that can have extensive effects on the whole body of the economy: a constellation marked with the date Monday, October 19, 1987, 4:00 P.M. ("Black Monday"). Consequently, names and dates will always be a function of history, and Deleuze and Guattari turn this reality into a very particular method. Each chapter in A Thousand Plateaus is a "plateau"—a description of texts and events that they raise out of the complexity of history and title with a name and a date. Throughout the chapter, they then proceed to unpack and diagram the extensive assemblages of texts, bodies, affects, and intensities of that plateau.

This book is full of names and dates, which often look like traditional historiography. However, I do not see my usage as traditional. Key names and dates designate particular functions or decrees within the history of the discipline. I use the names Weidner or Young insofar as they are linked to a particular method—the conflation of vitalism, romanticism, and mysticism that without delay or debate transforms vitalism into a scapegoat category within the field. I use the date 1980 to mark the critical moment when Young, Berlin, and Kameen all wrote articles responding to this discursive practice in ways that connect it to divergent trajectories or assemblages within the field's history. And I see the publication of Berlin's categories, for example, as functioning like decrees that instantaneously change the way compositionists view the field. These events are plateaus in my book that begin certain chapters, through which I attempt to work out the assemblages of ideas and effects that follow from them.

Writing affirmatively by using categories to open up possibilities rather than exclude them. Victor Vitanza's sub/versive historiography, to which Diane

Davis appeals, emerges from a similar assemblage of historiographic practices, especially with regard to classification. In *Negation, Subjectivity, and the History of Rhetoric,* he develops an affirmative historiography in response to a strict use of historical categories. Edward Schiappa, for example, argues against the general category of "sophistic rhetoric." For him, definitive historical evidence of a school of thinkers with common theories and agendas is unavailable; since an ahistorical definition is "misleading, unhelpful, or superfluous," sophistic rhetoric is "expendable" ("Sophistic Rhetoric" 15). Schiappa employs a strict species/genus analytics in which definition functions as a dividing practice that excludes.[7] Vitanza provides a detailed, and one might argue book-length, response to Schiappa in *Negation, Subjectivity, and the History of Rhetoric.* For Vitanza, "[t]he issue is not Schiappa, but the methods he, and we, associate ourselves with; and yet, the issue *is* Schiappa, for he is the method that he consumes and asks us, in turn, to consume so as *to forget* the Sophists, so as to make the Sophists the Forgotten" (29). The very methods historians use, and the methods that their names designate and deploy, can have important, real-world consequences. Vitanza makes the analogy to revisionary readings of the Holocaust that, given the rules of evidence in the courtroom, deny the testimony of survivors. Such a method excludes the reality of the Holocaust just as Schiappa's method excludes sophistic rhetoric (45). Rather than exclude what cannot be defined as a genus, Vitanza argues that in a situation with less than exact evidence it becomes even more important to keep the question open, to avoid doing violence to the past (as well as the present and future).

Consequently, Vitanza seeks another method. He sees sub/versive historiography as the continual positing of "some more"—the displacement of a fixed, negating program through the infinite search for new conceptual starting places. Rather than simply asserting a political position and bringing forgotten figures into the linear history (the standard procedures of revisionary historiography), sub/versive historiography uses categorization openly. Vitanza, for example, applies one of Kenneth Burke's historical attitudes, casuistic stretching, to the history of rhetoric. He sets up the categories First, Second, and Third Sophistic, and casuistically stretches Gorgias from the First to the Third category, linking him to contemporary thinkers such as Baudrillard, Foucault, and Barthes. When sub/versive historiography uses categories, they are fluid, porous, and open to new assemblages.[8] Categories such as first, second, and third so-phistic have no fixed content, which allows theories and theorists to be casu-istically stretched from one category or time period to another.

The fact that categories are used affirmatively to create multiple, renewed compositions is precisely what keeps them from excluding. A sub/versive his-toriography uses categories to open a line of thought, open the bounds of an argument, as a beginning (or perpetual rebeginning) rather than as a conclu-sion to an argumentative position. As Vitanza says explicitly, "This third ele-ment, it should be obvious by now, is nonsynthesizing; it is, instead, a voiding of all categories . . . a means of voiding categories such as 'traditional' and 're-visionary'" ("An After/word" 240). Following Lyotard, Vitanza makes it clear that he is not operating on a revisionist notion of critique—for him there is no neutral ground from which to judge the past. In place of critique Vitanza opts for Nietzschean critical extension—taking a text, a category, or argument and using the process of deconstructing it to build something new out of it that can be deployed in a contemporary context in the attempt to affect the present affirmatively. His use of the First and Second Sophistic allows him to invent a Third Sophistic to address contemporary practice in the history of rhetoric.[9]

This open and affirmative approach to the use of categories is precisely the attitude I take in addressing the issue of vitalism. In one sense, I agree with Schiappa; ahistorical categories are misleading and problematic. The ahistor-ical approach to categorizing vitalism is precisely what I argue against in this book. However, the answer is not to exclude vitalism, as Schiappa excludes so-phistic rhetoric. The answer to the problem is to produce counter-categoriza-tions that incorporate the initial category in order to both move beyond it and to address a present-day historical problem or practice. Such an approach is based on affirmation rather than exclusion. Vitanza, for example, is not simply disproving Schiappa. He sees Schiappa as the conditions of possibility for something new and uses him to turn thinking toward new directions. In this sense he is using traditional historiography by using Schiappa. Schiappa sees definition as important and argues that we can determine good definitions from bad ones and thus exclude the bad ones. Vitanza would affirmatively in-clude them all, definition 1 plus definition 2 plus definition 3 ad infinitum (in-cluding Schiappa's).

Vitanza employs the same tactic in *Negation, Subjectivity, and the History of Rhetoric* with Susan Jarratt. He argues with Jarratt's position but does so in a way that extends it rather than negates it. Vitanza writes, "I would, therefore, say Yes to Jarratt's text. YES. And then, continue to give (gift) my own foolish redescriptions" (222). These redescriptions through names such as Schiappa and Jarratt are used to create assemblages or new groupings. Traditional, revisionary, and sub/versive are not exclusive. Sub/versive methods draw on the others to create assemblages of concepts, open up possibilities for new thoughts, new practices, new inventions. My use of categories should be read only in this manner. This book is not possible without Weidner, Young, Berlin and their categories, and for that I am forever in their debt, which I try to pay back in excess with the gift of redescriptions in this book.

MY USE of categories as a means of critiquing categorization must appear paradoxical. But in fact it does not operate with the same "zeal for classification" that John Schilb calls "taxonomania" ("Future Historiographies" 129). The categories Schilb critiques "attempt to map a whole field of study by dividing it into neat, distinct parts, often assigning them varying degrees of worth." He finds these general categories problematic because "emphasizing the difference *between* the items so classified can lead us to ignore the differences *within* them" (129). My use of categories does not fall into these traps. I am not trying to map an entire field. My categories of oppositional, investigative, and complex vitalisms are subgenres. As a movement toward specificity rather than generality, my categories are trying to articulate differences rather than wash over them. They are specifically trying to get at the differences *within* a particular category—or at least to make an initial move toward that end. Since complex vitalism is not a general categorization of rhetoric and composition, it is less likely to be reified in the way Berlin's current-traditional, cognitive, expressivist, and social-epistemic categories have been. In addition, rather than operate at an abstract level of species/genus analytics, as Richard Young does, the designations serve primarily to denote movement over time. This movement, however, should not imply a linear development from simple to complex—no vitalist assumes life is simple. Therefore, none of the answers or thinkers should be automatically excluded or surpassed. I make no elaborate attempt, as Berlin

does in his mapping of rhetoric and composition, to set up an order that necessitates valuing one category over another. Even though I think complex
vitalism best fits our current context, I have no interest in devaluing the importance of oppositional or investigative vitalisms in their contexts. Schilb also
notes the problem of having to limit categories to a small number to make
them manageable, often to the "mystical number three": traditional, revisionary, sub/versive (Vitanza); cognitive, expressivist, social-epistemic (Berlin);
scholars, researchers, practitioners (North); play, game, purpose (Lanham) (129).
I too evoke a triptych but in the tradition of Vitanza, who importantly uses
his third category to extend the three into a multiplicity in order to dispense
with a rigid notion of categorization.[10]

It should be clear that I am not deductively employing Nietzsche, Lovejoy,
Foucault, Deleuze, or Vitanza but using their approaches as conceptual starting
places for responding to the particular rhetorical situation in rhetoric and composition that surrounds vitalism.[11] The historiographical method I employ in
this book is rhetorical, it looks at terms and their multiple meanings, it describes sets of relations or assemblages, it sees names and dates and central
points for diagramming these assemblages, and it uses categories openly and
affirmatively. There are no impenetrable/impassable lines dividing the categories, names, or practices. Every category, person, or method functions as a
composition of species, a multiplicity that can be connected to other species
in an endless variety of combinations to form new assemblages. Authors, texts,
and ideas can be stretched from category to category, historical period to historical period. Just as Vitanza's First, Second, and Third Sophistic can stretch
Gorgias from the pre-socratics to poststructuralism, Aristotle's vitalism can be
stretched into the scientific vitalisms of the nineteenth century. Or I can create
an assemblage with Coleridge, Bergson, and Deleuze, or Hamann, Nietzsche,
and Foucault, and deploy them in different situations but then link Heidegger,
Foucault, and Deleuze in another context. As the primary principle underlying
vitalism, the question of life similarly cuts across categories, paradigms, authors,
and texts, opening them to various combinations—all of which are potentially
valuable if the conditions of possibility set the rules for their emergence.

NOTES

Chapter 1: Mapping Rhetoric and Composition

1. This book focuses specifically on the discipline of rhetoric and composition and the rhetoric behind its emergence, and I generally make a distinction between discipline and field. A discipline is an administrative category based on departments and institutional hierarchies. Rhetoric and composition is generally not a discipline in this respect, though writing departments are beginning to break away from English departments. I use the term discipline when referring to early desires to make rhetoric and composition a discipline as a way of asserting rhetorical power or authority and placing it onto the work of rhetoricians and compositionists. A field is a cluster of related issues, texts, theorists, and practitioners on a plane of immanence—on a flat nonhierarchical surface (i.e., a field). In most cases rhetoric and composition is not a distinct discipline but a (sub)field of the discipline English that also has links to (sub)fields in other disciplines. The term discipline has to do with categorization— English as a category. Rhetoric and composition is an assemblage. For more on these distinctions see the afterword.

2. Today, we give credit to Kitzhaber's *Rhetoric in American Colleges, 1850–1900* (1953) for delineating the institutional structure of first-year composition and the basic characteristics of composition textbooks in the late nineteenth century, but the term/category current-traditional rhetoric comes from Fogarty. Young notes in "Paradigms and Problems" that Kitzhaber surveys a wide variety of texts that do not readily create the picture of a paradigm. It is Fogarty who recognizes that these practices had stabilized in the twentieth century, forming an identifiable paradigm (*Roots for a New Rhetoric* 30). It was Young who added the hyphen to current-traditional rhetoric and popularized its use as a paradigm.

3. Fogarty's call for a new rhetoric is looking for "a synthesis suited to the times" (*Roots* 126). His fundamental assumption is that social, political, economic, and cultural changes will affect the type of rhetoric needed at various points in history. This wholesale change in cultural context necessitates a change in teaching: "[Y]oung people [must] be trained in critical abilities that will make them aware of and responsible for the means of controlling mass media" (128–29). Such abilities require a new philosophy of communication, and Fogarty assigns the dissemination of this philosophy to the first-year course (129). Fogarty imagines building his new rhetoric out of a synthesis of Richards, Burke, and the General Semanticists, and it would need to consider its own assumptions, move beyond persuasion to every kind of symbol-using, draw upon the psychology and sociology of communication, and make an adjustment for a new kind of speaker-listener situation that revolves around discussion. Fogarty proposes a new course for this new art of symbol-using, which would include Aristotelian persuasion, Richards's emphasis on interpretation, and Burke's conception of identification and notions of scope and circumference, along with newer theories of signs. In my mind, this is a clear articulation of Berlin's entire program. And essentially I am following the same logic— articulating a philosophical grounding for rhetoric in our contemporary period. Berlin is really working off of this model from 1959. The decade from roughly 1995 to 2005 has seen an extension and reformation of these changes through digital technologies.

4. The philosophy Fogarty comes to espouse through Burke, Richards, and the Semanticists has elements that I characterize as vitalistic: a recognition of the importance of language ("functional as opposed to decorative importance of metaphor"); a gestaltist notion of wholeness

applied to psychological context, social and economic motivation, or "organism-as-a-whole" attitudes; movements from beyond Aristotle's genus-species classifications to attempts to define and identify things as specifically situational (singular not individual); an emphasis on interdisciplinarity; and a focus on "abstraction theory," a primary element of Bergson's philosophy (*Roots* 122–23).

5. This information comes directly from Vitanza's James Berlin Web site: http:// www.uta .edu/english/V/berlin/neh.html; see also http://www.uta.edu/english/V/berlin /week1.html. For published discussions of the seminar, see Vitanza, "A Retrospective," and Berlin, "A Prospective," both in Vitanza, *Pre/Text: The First Decade;* Almagno, "An NEH Fellowship Examined."

6. Lovejoy notes that he has identified more than sixty different senses of the term nature ("On the Discrimination" 239n35).

7. D'Angelo gives a good description of tagmemics in "The Evolution of the Analytic Topoi" (65–66).

8. While some of the contributors to *Perspectives on Rhetorical Invention* do attempt to situate invention relative to postmodernism, Gregory Ulmer—one of the most prominent theorist-practitioners of the intersections among postmodernism, invention, and pedagogy —is notably absent from the discussions. It seems a particularly odd exclusion since his work has been at the forefront of producing heuristics in this context, precisely what the contributors claim is lacking (Atwill, "Introduction" xi). The implicit value of a particular notion of research in relation to a particular notion of rhetoric could account for this unnoticed (or possibly noticed) exclusion.

Chapter 2: Cartography and Forgetting

1. Ironically, in his later work Berlin falls into this very same problematic ("to learn to criticize is to learn to compose") in terms of cultural criticism rather than literary criticism when he extends Fogarty's call and introduces it into his own cultural studies work with social-epistemic rhetoric, as I discuss later.

2. While Berlin uses both the terms expressivism and expressionism across his various essays and books, for simplicity's sake I use expressivism throughout even though some quotes from Berlin use expressionism. There are perhaps some historical distinctions between these two terms, but each one represents the same epistemology or philosophy in Berlin's terminology and the discipline more generally uses to the term expressivism to denote this model. I also use this distinction in the next three chapters to mark the difference between Berlin's expressivism and Deleuze's expressionism.

3. Berlin notes explicitly that he is following Paul Kameen's "Rewording the Rhetoric of Composition" (1980) in the move to deal with "the metarhetorical realm of epistemology and linguistics" ("Contemporary Composition" 766).

4. This link, probably unknown to Berlin, supports my argument that the only vitalism that can be equated with current-traditional rhetoric is an earlier vitalism based on animus, spirit, and some forms of idealism as distinct from the further developments of oppositional and investigative vitalisms—both scientific and philosophical—made in the nineteenth century (see chapter 4). Berlin's maps exclude the possibility of this recognition that vitalism has a history beyond spiritualism. Berlin misses the possibility that the basis of other forms of vitalism might lie in Coleridge's and Emerson's romanticisms when he recognizes that their Platonisms go beyond Plato—a beyond that is extended by both Nietzsche and Bergson, the two most prominent vitalist philosophers of the period, both of whom were trying to move beyond mechanism and idealism. Berlin sees the use of language/metaphor as primary for both rhetoric and poetics but misses the obvious link to Nietzsche and Bergson as anti-Platonic.

5. Romanticism's synthesis of ideal/material provides a step toward Bergson—oratory-voice-body-intellect all function through a dialectic of subject and object. Romanticism sees

current-traditional positivism as inhuman, missing the central place of the individual in any truth-seeking endeavor—a point that arises in Berlin's "Contemporary Composition" (777) and in Berlin's later cultural studies phase. Marx's humanism is one of the links Berlin sees between romanticism and Marxism, a point that fuels his debate/dialectic between the two. What is ultimately forgotten in this dialectic is complex vitalism—a post-humanism—as I argue in chapter 5.

6. Although Fogarty sees the General Semanticists as a possible basis for new rhetoric, Berlin sees the communications course—the pedagogical application of the semanticist's movement—as functioning from a positivistic epistemology, and he thus places it in objective theories. The course's practices are similar to epistemic rhetoric, but they assume a world or reality separate from the linguistic propaganda the semanticists hope to dispel. For selected citations on "rhetoric as epistemic" as developed in speech communications, see http://www.uta.edu/english/V/berlin/epistemic.html.

7. In the emerging expressive, nondirective pedagogies, teachers did not want to force a subjectivity onto students; students were encouraged to find their "own genius" based on life experiences (76). Consequently, the subject of writing textbooks of the period is not writing but students (Berlin, *Rhetoric and Reality* 77). This is why examining writing in terms of epistemology is so important. For Berlin, all writing creates a particular kind of student/subject, so as writing instructors we have to take that into account. Even though expressivists emphasize nondirective pedagogies, they still create a particular kind of aristocratic subject.

8. For other histories of expressivism see Kinneavy, *A Theory of Discourse*, and Abrams, *The Mirror and the Lamp*. For social readings of expressivism see Gradin, *Romancing Rhetorics*, and Harris, *Expressive Discourse*. The latter argues that the expressive category as it is generally imagined is inaccurate and misleading and would be better characterized as four separate writing practices.

9. In "Changing the Subject of Postmodernist Theory," Marshall Alcorn critiques Berlin for ignoring the irrational, libidinal element of consciousness. By brushing off psychoanalytic theory as individualistic and hence bad, Berlin cannot account for it in his theory of false consciousness and his pedagogy based on this theory. In *Acts of Enjoyment*, Thomas Rickert extends Alcorn's critiques with the psychoanalytic theories of Slavoj Žižek and Jacques Lacan and shows the positive impact psychoanalysis can have on rhetoric and composition.

10. In "Rhetoric and Ideology," Berlin acknowledges Marx's notion that we cannot make histories as we wish (489), and he concludes his essay claiming that "behavior is always open-ended . . . and the outcome is always unpredictable" (492). It is very difficult, however, to see how this theoretical admonition corresponds to his utopian pedagogy. I address this point in more detail in chapter 6.

11. Berlin derives his notion of the subject from Paul Smith's *Discerning the Subject* (1988). Smith, according to Berlin, sees this as an overreaction: for Smith, there are possibilities for agency in postmodern subjectivity. Smith sees the subject as multiple, being hailed into a variety of contradictory subject positions. Our agency, as distinct from subjectivity, is in the rifts between these various positions. We can resist by choosing one subject position over another in a given rhetorical/historical situation. Our agency resides in the dialectic between subject and agent. The agent negotiates among different positions and creates a dialectic among them, which provides for the possibility of political action and creates the possibility for a type of individuality since "each agent enjoys a unique set of interacting formations, each of us has a 'specific history'" ("Postmodernism" 174).

12. In *Madness and Civilization* and *Birth of the Clinic*, Foucault examines the development of hospitals as sites of institutional power. No false consciousness is needed on the part of the patients. They are placed in a matrix of power/knowledge that disciplines their bodies, not necessarily their minds, hence Berlin's deterministic reading of Foucault. But this reading ignores Foucault's later work, from *The History of Sexuality* onward, which discusses the body

as a site of its own bio-power. Berlin's emphasis on consciousness and the forgetting of vitalism keeps him from seeing this as a model for engaging institutional constraints.

13. For example, Berlin's epistemological and ideological mappings do not allow him to read Foucault's definition of power in terms of complex vitalism. He can read it only in terms of Marxism and therefore cannot see the potential for resistance in Foucault's complex vitalist notion of power, seeing it only as historical determinism. (See, for example, Keating, "Foucault, Vitalism, Resistance"). Berlin's view that Foucault is placing discourse at the center is also somewhat misleading. Nondiscursive practices that work on the body are equally important. Berlin cannot see bio-power in vitalist terms. It is precisely at the level of the body and bio-power that some form of resistance is possible (but no liberation). Berlin's ties to the nineteenth century do not allow him to see complex vitalism in the ideas of Foucault and Deleuze.

Chapter 3: Remapping Method

1. "Rewording the Rhetoric of Composition" was originally published in one of the first issues of *Pre/Text*, the journal that Victor Vitanza and others started on the heels of the seminar. While the journal went on to develop a fair amount of credibility in the field, it was initially seen with some suspicion for its unorthodox approach and more theoretical focus. Another of Kameen's essays, "Coleridge: On Method," was published in a small newsletter, *Correspondences*, put out by Ann Berthoff. Another full chapter on Coleridge and Heidegger was never published because editors were not sure how it fit into the discourse of the discipline.

2. Stephen Fishman calls for viewing romanticism in the context of its relationship to the Enlightenment and industrialization. Romantic poets were reacting against the alienation of Enlightenment thought, the view that the social contract, as the basis of human interaction, alienated people from each other. It was this notion of the social contract, not romantic poets, that assumed people were individuals in a state of nature and came under the purview of the social contract only out of necessity. According to Fishman, the romantics sought "not isolation for the creative artist, but reunification" (650). The disconnection of the artist from his or her work was seen in the context of the anonymity of industrial workers who were alienated from their work (a clear link between the humanism of the romantics and the humanism of Marx): "With the treatment of writing as a commodity, writers became increasingly isolated in the demands of mass production" (653).

3. For more on Herder see Luanne Frank's "Herder, Jauss, and the New Historicism," in which she argues that Herder is a precursor to New Historicism—anything but a precursor of the isolated writer.

4. Two other notable examples of reclaiming romanticism and expressivism by linking them to the social are O'Brien, "Romanticism and Rhetoric," and Paley, "Writing and Rewriting Racism."

5. While Gradin critiques Berlin's dismissal of expressive theories in *Rhetoric and Reality*, her approach is actually similar to Berlin's reading of nineteenth-century romanticism—recoup expressivism or romanticism by linking it to the social. In her reading of Berlin, she sees him as favoring romanticism in *Writing Instruction* but by *Rhetoric and Reality*, "Berlin no longer favors expressivism and finds much to fault in romantic rhetorics" (3). She does not put forward the distinction between the nineteenth-century romanticisms of Emerson and Coleridge and twentieth-century expressive rhetorics. She does recognize Berlin's distinction between the two readings of Emerson—one Platonic and the other social-democratic (Gradin 111–12)—but reads Berlin as positing this as a strict binary rather than linking this to Berlin's reading of Coleridge and his notion of dialectics.

6. North is following the distinction he had made earlier in *The Making of Knowledge in Composition* between researchers, scholars, and practitioners, which argues against valuing scientific knowledge over historical, theoretical, or practical knowledge.

7. Kameen, in "Afterthoughts," his postscript to "Rewording the Rhetoric of Composition" when it was published in Vitanza's edited collection *Pre/Text: The First Decade*, notes that his article originally "was turned down by the other major disciplinary journals" (29). He leaves the reader to speculate as to the reasons, but it is not much of a stretch to assume that one possible reason could have been the general misunderstanding of Coleridge's contributions to rhetoric.

8. Perry's essay is in the on-line journal *Romanticism on the Net*, http://users. ox.ac.uk/~ scato385/antirom.html; therefore, no page numbers follow my citations.

9. Perry's argument is actually an analysis of the rhetoric of anti-romanticism. Perry notes that critics do not need a categorical definition of romanticism to write about Coleridge or Wordsworth, but they do if they want to define themselves against romanticism. Perry recognizes that these arguments form a genre with a clear strategy similar to the one I outline in chapter 1 with regard to Young. Such a strategy first defines romanticism as a category based on idealism and then critiques it through an appeal to concreteness. Perry sees this strategy in many new historicists' and Marxists' arguments against romanticism. But the irony is that he traces this duality to Coleridge. When Marxists and historicists embrace anti-romanticism, they are participating in one line of development from the romantic tradition.

10. The kind of anti-romantic reading that Perry highlights still plays itself out in the field. In an exchange published in *JAC*, Tim Mayers calls Gary Olson on the use of anti-romanticism. Mayers objects to Olson's characterization of "unthinking expressivism" as a backlash against theoretical scholarship. Mayers asks, "When we summarize, characterize, and make generalizations about the work of others—as we must—what obligations do we have toward those whose scholarship we write about, whether in the spirit of praise or blame?" ("The Struggle over Composition" 448–49). As a contributor to the *CCC* issue that Olson characterizes as "unthinking expressivism," Mayers resists the use of such a general category to describe the work presented in the issue. Olson's response, "Struggling over Composition," is interesting. Though he is gracious, he (purposely or not) sidesteps the real force of Mayers's criticism. Olson apologizes for his characterization of the *entire* issue as representing "unthinking expressivism" but does not question his own use of the category as such—which is how I read Mayers's argument. Olson reads Mayers's critique as centered on the way Olson characterizes Mayers specifically, not as centered on Olson's use of anti-romanticism as a general rhetorical strategy. See also Mayers's more recent book, *(Re)Writing Craft*, which tackles the divisions in the English department that embody these larger categorical distinctions.

11. Nietzsche's view of language comes into play in Kameen's reading of Coleridge and Berlin's readings of Emerson and Coleridge. Nietzsche argues against positivism's reductive faith in the ability to represent the objective world, in favor of an acceptance of truth as extra-moral or metaphoric. Nietzsche calls for intuition as the guiding force of this enterprise: "There is no regular path which leads these intuitions into the land of holy schemata, the land of abstractions. There exists no word for these intuitions; when man sees them he grows dumb, or else he speaks only in forbidden metaphors and in unheard-of combinations of concepts. He does this by shattering and mocking the old conceptual barriers" ("Truth and Lies in a Nonmoral Sense" 895). This is, to a large extent, Coleridge's secondary imagination —a rhetoric of ever-new metaphors that mock the old dead ones. For another reading of Coleridge's use of metaphor and its relation to rhetoric, Freud, and de Mannian deconstruction see Hodgson, *Coleridge, Shelley, and Transcendental Inquiry*. For another examination of Coleridge's relationship with language see Goodson, *Verbal Imagination*.

12. Just as there are many readings of Coleridge's method, there are many different readings of Hegel's dialectic. Here I am working out of Derrida's characterization in *Glas* of *Aufhebung* as a massive negating process that thinks it is a positive/erecting process and forgets that it creates a suppressed remains as well as an erected remains. Hegel wants to raise mankind to perfection of the human mind, to absolute spirit, through the method of dialectics. Derrida,

however, argues that what Hegel forgets or represses in this elevation is sexuality, especially female sexuality. I argue, like Derrida, that what ultimately gets repressed is the body. Berlin's dialectics forgets bodily knowledge.

13. Reading primary imagination, secondary imagination, and fancy in terms of Coleridge's method makes other arguments over whether primary or secondary imagination is more important somewhat moot. Primary imagination, secondary imagination, and fancy are all necessary aspects of an ongoing dialectic. For more on these issues see Wordsworth, "The Infinite I AM"; McFarland, "The Origin and Significance of Coleridge's Theory of Secondary Imagination"; and Christensen, "The Marginal Method of the *Biographia Literaria*."

14. To examine static things would result in a method that strictly arranges the world into a tableau—a function of the Classical episteme as Foucault defines it in *The Order of Things*. The Classical (or Enlightenment) episteme employs a taxonomy that separates things from their relations with other things by placing them on a tableau based on species/genus thinking—thus privileging those relations of appearance over other types of material relations. From this perspective, Coleridge is clearly moving toward the Modern episteme.

15. Because Phelps is operating on such a dialectic, one that incorporates oppositional elements into an overarching system (or understanding), she is less critical of Young and tagmemics, eventually turning it on the discipline itself, adopting a dialectic grid reminiscent of tagmemics (*Composition as a Human Science* 236–37). She does go a long way to further a more complex or ecological approach to composition and literacy, but does so by dialectically adding critical thought onto the natural or tacit base, following a hermeneutic dialectical tradition. I work through the problem by pushing further into post-dialectical thought and extending a vitalist paradigm, rather than the hermeneutic one.

16. White connects this sense of method to the middle voice. Once a codified grammatical space floating in flux somewhere between subject and object, the moment of the middle voice is that moment where language, the body, culture, and the environment come together to spark, invent, and constitute language, an utterance: "the middle voice would unfold as a dynamic of repetition and difference in which the genuinely novel and unprecedented is continually converted into reassuring familiarity" (E. C. White, *Kaironomia* 61).

17. For Feyerabend the historical context of discovery and the disciplinary context of justification and evaluation are one and the same. In other words, nonscientific procedures cannot be ignored. A large part of scientific operation is actually irrational (or at least nonrational). Galileo, for example, gave no explicit reasons for why the telescope gave a more accurate observation of the sky. There was no rational reason to believe that it did. Nevertheless, scientific advancement has to operate on such intuitive beliefs in relation to historical context. Later the justification may come, so such a position cannot be excluded for all time.

18. For studies on affect and bodily knowledge in rhetoric and composition see T. R. Johnson, "Discipline and Pleasure," in which the author critiques traditional composition taxonomies for closing off affect; Hawhee, "Bodily Pedagogies," in which she argues that for the Greeks rhetoric was a bodily art, a recognition that contemporary pedagogy has forgotten; Fishman et al., "Performing Writing, Performing Literacy," in which they lay out the importance of enacting performance as a stage of the learning and writing process; and Edbauer, "Executive Overspill," in which she shows the importance of a Deleuzian model of affect for rhetorical studies.

Chapter 4: A Short Counter-History

1. See Dunne, *Back to the Rough Ground,* for an extensive reading of technê that situates it in the context of experience and embodiment.

2. As Paul Feyerabend notes in *Against Method,* "rational" science is often founded on

an "irrational" base, especially at certain points in history where the social, political, or theoretical circumstances make this inevitable if not necessary.

3. Naive vitalism is not a genus with a clear consensus definition or historical specificity. Even though epistemic bases shift, an episteme is a composition of various species, not a historical determinant. Therefore, naive vitalisms can still show up in various periods and forms, such as animism (spiritualism, God as ground of Being/life), idealism (Platonic forms, ideas, consciousness as ground of Being/life), and naive vitalism (in Burwick and Douglass's sense, which posits a fluid or substance as the vital force/ground of life). In the twentieth century there were still people who supported these kinds of naive vitalism. C. E. M. Joad, in *Unorthodox Dialogues on Education and Art* (1930), is an excellent example of someone who purports "genius" in the context of vitalism. And later in the century, Edmund Ware Sinnott, in *The Bridge of Life: From Matter to Spirit* (1966), seeks a philosophy of life that brings together materialism and spiritualism.

4. Coleridge wrote "Hints Towards the Foundation of a More Comprehensive Theory of Life," or "Theory of Life" as it is generally known, in 1817 for James Gillman as the philosophical introduction to a work of science that Gillman was supposed to write but never did. Coleridge's interest in "life" extended back to the 1790s when he attended lectures on philosophy and natural history in Germany, and much of "Theory of Life" is exposition of Schelling's and Steffen's works. "Theory of Life" was not published until 1848, after Coleridge's lifetime, not only because Gillman never wrote his part but also because Coleridge eventually became more critical of German *Naturphilosophie* as his idealism developed.

5. On many occasions Coleridge's theories, especially of life and nature, are Spinozist. In "Note on Spinoza" Coleridge defends Spinoza against his detractors, primarily because Coleridge values Spinoza for his method. Most of the arguments against Spinoza are on the grounds that "he saw God in the Ground" (609). But Coleridge agrees with Spinoza on this point, pointing out that the only problem with Spinoza is that "he saw God in the Ground *only*" (609). Coleridge, in order to remain a proper Christian, feels that he must retain an *a priori* position for God in addition to seeing God in nature—a position that keeps him from being labeled a vitalist proper. I would argue that it is this element of idealism that attracts the most attention when Coleridge is considered a mystical romantic—and it is precisely this idealism that cannot be read as vitalism. For another take on Coleridge's idealism see Aers, Cook, and Punter, "Coleridge: Individuals, Communities, and Social Agency."

6. "Theory of Life" is Coleridge's most explicit connection to the vitalist debates, but his vitalist conceptions become outweighed by his overall idealism and his tendency to foreground religious motives. As editors H. J. Jackson and J. R. Jackson note in their edition of "Theory of Life," the essay is a phase of Coleridge's thought on life. Later he became more critical of *Naturphilosophie* because it saw nature at the beginning and end of the process and Coleridge wanted to see God as ground. *Naturphilosophers* generally equated nature with god, and Coleridge wanted God to be more than the sum of nature's parts. His religious motives ultimately pushed him more toward idealism, mind, and consciousness: it is God as *a priori* force who objectifies himself in the individuations of the material world. This is not a critical vitalist position but an idealist or naive vitalist position. Jack H. Haeger argues in "Samuel Taylor Coleridge and the Romantic Background to Bergson" that Coleridge synthesizes elements from an idealist tradition that had a connection to the vitalist tradition, but he never became a vitalist, per se (98). Haeger makes the distinction this way: Coleridge had an idealist conception of consciousness and a vitalist conception of being that was manifested in act and will. In the final analysis, Coleridge's idealist conception of consciousness becomes more important to his overall thought than his vitalist conceptions of nature. He takes a vitalist notion of polarity and folds it into his notion of mental polarities—polarity works both in the subjective mind and the world of forces that we perceive as the objective world.

His vitalism, when pushed to its extreme, eventually comes to support his idealism. But it is the distinction between his vitalism and idealism that Weidner and Young fail to make.

7. For example, F. C. T. Moore, in *Bergson: Thinking Backwards*, claims Bergson is not a vitalist at all (121); John Mullarkey, in *Bergson and Philosophy*, claims Bergson is a vitalist only in a certain sense (62–63); Tom Quirk, in *Bergson and American Culture*, characterizes Bergson as a "maverick vitalist" (42); and Michael Weinstein, in *Structure of Human Life*, classifies Bergson as a "classical" vitalist (ix).

8. Even Bergson's definition of spirit is very particular and has little to do with mysticism: spirit is "that faculty of seeing which is immanent in the faculty of acting and which springs up, somehow, by the twisting of the will on itself, when action is turned into knowledge" (*Creative Evolution* 250). This, at its root, is not so different from Aristotle's definition of rhetoric as seeing the available means of persuasion in a given case. Spirit is the ability to intuitively see into the vital order of a rhetorical situation and derive conscious directions for rhetorical action from it.

9. Thomas Quirk, in *Bergson and American Culture*, gives an excellent summary of vitalism in the early nineteenth century through an account of the Fourth International Congress of Philosophy conference held in Bologna in 1911. He characterizes the period as a time when several philosophies of life were looking to replace philosophies of "closed system[s] and predictable certainty" (14).

10. For William Rasch and Cary Wolfe, who follow N. Katherine Hayles on this point, systems theory began at the Macy conferences, which signaled the reconsideration of basic Newtonian principles such as linear causality, determinism, and reductionism and a turn toward circular causality, self-organization, indeterminacy, and unpredictable emergence of order from disorder (*Observing Complexity* 9). Hayles, in *How We Became Posthuman*, follows a model broken into three stages: cybernetics from 1945 to 1950 focused on homeostasis, information, internal self-organizing, and circular causality (emphasizing the object); cybernetics from 1960 to 1980 focused on reflexivity, autopoiesis, and self-making (emphasizing the observer); cybernetics from 1980 to the present has focused on emergent behavior, openness to the body, and environment (emphasizing the combination of information and materiality). Quantum theory's recognition that observation brings the world into being in specific circumstances makes the position that the world is given problematic. But rather than closing in on the observer, third-wave cybernetics looks at how the world is brought into being in the dynamic dialectic of observer and observed, which bypasses the logic of inner and outer for, or in favor of, embodied action.

11. In the French edition of *Anti-Oedipus*, their method is called *schiz-analysis*, or the analyses of breaks. My thanks go to Chris Venner for pointing out this important quirk of translation.

12. Channell notes that the binaries between earth/universe (Copernicus), humans/nature (Darwin), and conscious/unconscious (Freud) have all been dispelled. For him, the next disparity to be eliminated is human/machine. According to Channell, all of the work that has already been done could still lead to further blurring of the organic and the machinic, as in the development of nanotechnology (*The Vital Machine* 133–36).

13. For more recent work on complex vitalism see Doyle, *Wetwares*, 38–40, 121–24, and Thacker, *Biomedia*, 133–36, 147–49.

14. Aristotle saw entelechy, at least in part, as the final form predetermined in the thing so that its movement is more predictable. Deleuze and Guattari, following Bergson, see desire and vital impulse as much more open to creative novelty where unpredictable breaks in the material flow produce new combinations, new machines, new forces, new desires. This distinction turns entelechy into multiple lines of flight, where an entelechy is broken into and redirected toward unforeseen paths.

15. I tend to use the terms potentiality and possibility synonymously because I see the two

concepts as part of the same system. The typical distinction is that possibility means the outcome is logical according to the form or structure of the situation; potentiality means the situation has potential for composition and production but that potential is not yet in motion toward actuality. Rather than see these as oppositions, I see them as a part of the same movement from potentiality to possibility to actuality. Potentiality is there first and then when it encounters the right circumstances, the right constellation of bodies and forces, it is put in motion and becomes possibility. In short, potentiality is the "condition" for possibility. So when I say conditions of possibility, that is potentiality.

Chapter 5: Technology-Complexity-Methodology

1. The other significant figure in "Rewording the Rhetoric of Composition" is Heidegger, who also figures prominently in Kameen's unpublished chapter from the 1980s, "Meditation and Method."

2. Given the *Technical Communications Quarterly*'s special issue on techné (spring 2002), it seems clear that many other writers and teachers are aligning themselves with an expanded understanding of the term beyond Young's more instrumental approach. See Hawk, "Toward a Post-*Techné*," my response essay to the special issue, from which much of the argument in this part of the chapter is derived.

3. All of the articles in the *Technical Communications Quarterly*'s special issue of spring 2002 try to recoup techné as a bodily art. James Dubinsky looks to combine art (techné) and knack to bring knack back into our notion of skill. Jay Gordon also looks at techné as something that gives us a certain amount of conscious control over chance while still recognizing the kairotic, "nontechnical," and intuitive elements of techné. Craft and craftiness both underlie more rational methods and make those methods applicable and even possible. Carlos Salinas attempts to link techné to both skill and savvy as well, setting these issues in the context of our contemporary image-based technologies. Ryan Moeller and Ken McAllister, perhaps even more than the others, work to move techné away from instrumental reason toward creativity, ingenuity, and unpredictability, giving a number of examples of techné as a combination of skill and habit.

4. For more on the problematic nature of the liberal humanist subject in relation to techné, in addition to the extended discussions in Hayles, see Janet Atwill's *Rhetoric Reclaimed*, in which she argues that humanism problematically takes a historically specific model of subjectivity from classical Greek culture and retroactively universalizes its common features (14–15, 23).

5. In *Embodying Technesis*, Mark Hansen argues that Heidegger is a linguistic determinist. While those elements can be read into Heidegger, Hansen's treatment is unfortunately overly polemical, ignoring all of the ecological elements in Heidegger's work. In his polemic against Heidegger, Freud, Derrida, Lacan, Foucault, and Deleuze and Guattari, he paints them all as linguistic determinists who ignore the body, which is a claim that runs counter to the way I characterize Heidegger, Foucault, and Deleuze and Guattari in relation to complex vitalism.

6. Robert Johnson and Frances Ranney make the distinction between instrumental "design" and fine art that I think Heidegger is after here. They see techné as "an inventively systematic knowledge that [is] aimed toward previously thought-out, but not pre-determined, ends" (239). Technique, in other words, can be at least partially thought out ahead of time, but its contextual enaction in a complex, ecological situation cannot be predetermined. Likewise, the locus of aesthetic production is not in a subject but in the contextual enaction, in the *doing*.

7. For more on Heidegger's link to posthumanism see Kroker, "Hyper-Heidegger." For a particularly clear articulation of posthumanism see Van Pelt, "The Question Concerning Theory." For more on Heidegger and ecology see Charles Taylor, "Heidegger, Language, and Ecology." Taylor emphasizes the importance of language to this larger ecological relationship,

and the importance of seeing Heidegger as a nonsubjectivist. For more on posthumanism and rhetoric see Brooke, "Forgetting to Be (Post)Human"; Muckelbaurer and Hawhee, "Posthuman Rhetorics"; and Rickert, "Engaging Modernisms, Emerging Posthumanisms, and the Rhetorics of Doing." For more on Heidegger, technê, and invention see Worsham, "The Question Concerning Invention."

8. For more on Heidegger's reading of Aristotle in relation to power and force see his *Aristotle's Metaphysics.*

9. Rickert's two key references are Ishii et al., "ambientROOM," and Wisneski et al., "Ambient Displays." For more on technology and ambient ecologies see Hawk and Rieder, "On Small Tech and Complex Ecologies," which is the introductory essay to Hawk, Rieder, and Oviedo, *Small Tech.*

10. At the end of *Tool-Being,* Harman comes to the opposite conclusion. If relations are equivalent to substance, then all that exists is substance. The main point of Harman's book is to build a new philosophy of substance and objects that is not based on old models of realism. This is an important move for his purposes, but for my purposes—the delineation of a new model of vitalism rather than objects—it makes more sense to say that relationality is all there is.

11. Much of this section is based on my article from *JAC,* "Toward a Rhetoric of Network (Media) Culture," used with permission.

12. For a discussion of this network logic in relation to writing and technology see Brooke, "Weblogs as Deictic Systems."

13. The concepts of *enkrateia,* or mastery, and *sophrosyne,* or moderation, form the beginnings of self-reflection. Foucault's insight is that these concerns over sexual activity "create the possibility of forming oneself as a subject" (*The Use of Pleasure* 138). It is this element in Greek thought that Christian thought follows and connects with Plato, setting the stage for an internal and eventually modern subject to emerge.

14. For more on the complexity of ethics see Mann, *Masocriticism.*

15. See Rorty, *Essays on Aristotle's Rhetoric,* for several views of Aristotle's theory of the emotions.

16. For more on the importance of affect to writing and rhetoric see Edbauer, "Meta/Physical Graffiti."

17. I stick to Mark Taylor's use of the term evolution here, even though Deleuze and Massumi have gone beyond evolution to movement. In *Bergsonism* Deleuze warns against two misconceptions in the use of the term evolution: seeing evolution as predetermined and seeing evolution as only occurring at the level of the actual, missing the level of the virtual, or affect (98–101). Massumi generally speaks of evolution positively, though he notes its connotation of progress, order, and predictability (*Parables* 218). The primary distinction for him is that evolution operates at the most global level (112); movement is what happens at particular nodes, its immediate relations that lead to larger scale change (evolutionary change at the level of the whole). Movement happens within particular bodies at the level of affective relations. Massumi chooses to emphasize the term movement because the terms process and evolution are so over-coded that movement has been largely excluded in cultural theory (3).

18. There is no doubt that these issues of space and place are becoming key elements for rhetorical study and pedagogy. For a recent study of place and mapping in relation to rhetoric and composition see Reynolds, *Geographies of Writing.* Nedra Reynolds's more feminist approach keeps her tied to race, class, and gender differences, but the movement is clearly toward seeing place and space as key points of intersection with these issues.

19. See Agamben, *The Coming Community,* for an analysis of community in the complex contexts of contemporary society.

20. The salon had perhaps its last heyday in 1920s Paris, with Gertrude Stein's salon and the Shakespeare and Company bookstore, which functioned as a gathering place for the multinational literati that flocked to post–World War I Paris because it was one of the most

inexpensive international cities of the period. It was this time and place that ushered in both literary and artistic modernism, and perhaps it is a signal of the shift from individual places to capital spaces—people now gather at Starbucks and Barnes & Noble.

21. Both Shaviro and Rutsky see science fiction as an important literary genre for providing figurative cognitive maps. Sci-fi and critical theory both engage with late capitalist society in attempts to map postmodern space, because this space is unrepresentable by traditional means. For Rutsky, figures such as William Gibson and his description of artificial intelligence in *Count Zero* are the only way to articulate a conception of such complex spaces (*High Technê* 21). Rutsky, however, reads Jameson much like I read Berlin, as still desiring totality. I, on the other hand, think Jameson goes beyond Berlin in thinking about pedagogy.

22. My attempt in this chapter to link terms from modern rhetorics to key terms in complexity theory is not simply an attempt to oppose the basic, dialectical notion of the communications triangle that has grounded rhetoric and composition from Kinneavy to Berlin. My attempt is to show what happens when terms are linked to a new paradigm, a new machine. It is not that dialectics or the communications triangle is wrong but that such simplicity can only take us so far—it can map only at the molar level. Linking dialectics to a new set of terms means that the local and the global become a polarity that is both local and global at the same time rather than an opposition. Starting with a finer level of local detail establishes connection at a more molecular level and therefore sets the conditions for more molar connections. Livingston characterizes this as an ironic movement that turns the polarity into a spiral, rather than a dialectic, that tends to "forget the continuity between points" and produces "an irreducible interpenetration of terms in the swamp of the Real, the tangle of texts and bodies in which we live" (*Arrow of Chaos* 96). As both Livingston and Brian Massumi note, polarity becomes the basis for a fractal, post-dialectical model, not a basis for dialectics. See Massumi's *A User's Guide*, 21–23, for a clear articulation of the way polarity operates on a fractal rather than dialectical logic.

Chapter 6: Toward Inventive Composition Pedagogies

1. See Faigley, "Competing Theories of Process." Faigley, following Berlin, breaks down the different processes into the expressive, cognitive, and social types.

2. The result of Berlin's categorization of process pedagogies is, of course, that any element associated with, or made to associate with, the expressive category is promptly excluded. Thus, something like intuition, which was a prominent part of pedagogical discussions in the 1970s, is removed from the discourse. William Irmscher in *Teaching Expository Writing* (1979) includes a chapter entitled "Acknowledging Intuition." But once something at the level of (bodily) intuition is coded as inherently ideological, these discussions are dropped from a majority of the texts of writing. Any unconscious process is deemed negative, an element of false consciousness to be demystified. There is no positive unconscious.

3. See Seitz, "Hard Lessons Learned since the First Generation of Critical Pedagogy," for a survey of these issues surrounding authority and critical pedagogy. Also see Xin Liu Gale's *Teachers, Discourses, and Authority in the Postmodern Composition Classroom*, in which she tries to get out of this rigid binary between a teacher's discourse (as law) and the students' discourse by creating a dialectic among academic discourse, teacher discourse, and student discourse. Also see the work of Ellen Cushman that attempts to overcome academic authority by getting students out into the community in nursing and retirement homes, halfway houses, shelters, or anywhere that volunteer work may be needed. Even though she explicitly warns readers to avoid the liberal "do-gooder" persona in her article "The Public Intellectual, Service Learning, and Activist Research," for example, Cushman's approach can be patronizing as well. People in a homeless shelter may resent having ostensibly upper-class teenagers forced to volunteer, and students may resent being required to volunteer.

4. See Berlin's *Rhetorics, Poetics, and Cultures* (107–108), in which he outlines the three-tiered method in Jameson's *The Political Unconscious* that attempts to map contextual complexity and is reminiscent of Berlin's heuristic version of mapping the local to these contexts.

5. Harkin's essay is a part of a group of responses to Berlin's final book that were delivered as a CCCC panel after his death. The entire group of essays was published together as "Jim Berlin's Last Work: Future Perfect, Tense," *JAC* 17.3 (fall 1997): 489–506.

6. Harkin notes that Berlin really did not have a theory of composing: invention or interpretation emerged from dissonance, but this never developed into a new approach to writing. For Berlin, the only way students can become "genuinely competent writers and readers" is through his notion of critical thinking exhibited in his heuristic (*Rhetorics, Poetics, and Cultures* 116). Susan Miller also argues that Berlin's heuristic is all reading, leaving writing only to record conscious analysis ("Technologies of Self?-Formation" 498). To write effectively is to have power, but because Berlin favors reading over writing he creates passive students. This is the problem Sidler and Morris set out to engage. They try to fit Berlin's heuristic into a standard process pedagogy to fill in the missing theory of composing. They pose a new heuristic that does away with the binary thinking (222–83) and then links it to arrangement ("Writing in a Post-Berlinian Landscape" 285).

7. Berlin says that his course descriptions are "illustrative rather than prescriptive" (*Rhetorics, Poetics, and Cultures* 115); that "the discussion that emerges from the use of these heuristics is itself conflicted and unpredictable" (119); and that "this hermeneutic process is open-ended, leading in diverse and unpredictable directions in the classroom" (119). "Finally," he writes, "I would again emphasize that the course described here is meant to be open-ended" (145).

8. The distinction between process and method plays into other distinctions like invention and imagination and Marx's and Coleridge's dialectics. Despite the fact that Young acknowledges the necessity for a balance between imagination and invention in "Arts, Crafts, Gifts, and Knacks," it seems to be left out of his tagmemic pedagogy. And even though Berlin recognizes the importance of Coleridge's dialectic, he seems to forget it in the desire for a progressive development that leads to enlightenment in his students.

9. In his article "Rhetoric as a Course of Study," David Fleming notes the disparity between first-year programs and graduate programs in rhetoric and composition. The obvious missing link is full undergraduate degrees. While Crowley agrees with his desire to fill in this missing space, she differs from Fleming on the type of subjectivity to be desired. He opts for Quintilian's "good man speaking well" as the goal of an undergraduate course of study. Crowley is looking beyond this.

10. Kent's dialogic view of communication is certainly predicated on the social, but he argues against social constructivism on certain grounds. In "Beyond System: The Rhetoric of Paralogy" (1989), Kent spends most of the essay spelling out Donald Davidson's arguments against "social semioticians" who base their position on the fact that language is founded on social conventions. The article sees social construction as a strict version of structuralism that separates signs from the world via the synchronic construction of a *langue*. For Kent, this systematic abstraction separates language from its action/effect in the world. As he notes in *Post-Process Theory*, "what really matters is how people employ their prior theories in action" (4).

11. Both "Beyond System: The Rhetoric of Paralogy" (1989) and "Paralogic Hermeneutics and the Possibilities of Rhetoric" (1989) provide the groundwork for Kent's book *Paralogic Rhetoric* (1993). For a critique of his edited volume, *Post-Process Theory*, see Kevin Porter's review in *JAC* 20.3 (summer 2000): 710–14.

12. Diane Davis, in a lecture entitled "Being-Written; Or, Notes Towards a Post-Post-Process Theory," also critiques Kent's view of communication. In his view, we communicate in order to get things done in the (social) world. But Davis recognizes that this assumes our hermeneutic guesses are always good enough, always understood well enough to get things

done in the world. For her, this ignores the excess of communication. According to Davis, Kent's position sounds like Heidegger's Being-with—people co-appear. But Kent ignores the fact that communication takes place at the expense of an Other, that understanding is a mutual appropriation. We have to assume that each is like the other, but we never actually understand the Other—we understand only our own understanding.

13. In Karen Burke LeFevre's well-known book *Invention as a Social Act* (1987), she acknowledges the importance of ecology with respect to writing and invention, but her characterization of what that entails is still completely tied up in language and the social (126–27). Her emphasis on groups, community, history, and the social does not push the concept of ecology toward the kinds of material and natural environments that Marilyn Cooper sees as central elements in the ecology of writing and invention.

14. Much of the next two sections are developed from Hawk, "A Rhetoric/Pedagogy of Silence," copyright © 2003, all rights reserved, used with permission from Duke UP.

15. In some senses Kameen is simply working out of a long tradition of writing-to-learn, group collaboration, and student-centered pedagogues such as Ken Macrorie, James Britton, and Anne Ruggles Gere. What distinguishes his approach is the way that it uses personal and academic texts. Rather than focus primarily on student texts or topics of the students' choosing or explicitly try to move students from the personal into an academic discourse community (see Bartholomae, "Inventing the University"), Kameen uses both the personal and the academic subversively. They are both used equally to open a space for the production of knowledge that can be personal or academic or some combination of both. The actual form of knowledge is not the point of emphasis. Invention is unprogrammatic and functions at a tacit, ecological level.

16. Even though Berlin spent much of his career examining these categorical distinctions, he never saw Heidegger as a possible alternative. Kameen's work thus goes beyond Berlin's. Berlin focuses on dialectics to offset expressive and current-traditional rhetorics/pedagogies; Kameen argues against audience-based and expressive pedagogies because they are not emergent—an implicitly Heideggerian concept that is much more complex than Berlin's use of dialectics. Marilyn Cooper makes an explicit connection between ecological approaches and Heidegger's work, seeing writing as more akin to breathing than conscious dialogue ("Foreword: The Truth Is Out There" xiv). All of this work at the very least suggests the need to articulate an alternative paradigm for which Berlin's categories do not account.

17. Language has within it its own path or way, but this path is not a clearing away of something that covers what is already there, like snow on a sidewalk: it means to bring the way along with it through the act of clearing. It is the way, the path, the *method* of rhetorical invention. In "The Question Concerning Invention," Lynn Worsham uses Heidegger to examine this context for invention in its relationship to the writing process and cites Kameen's "Rewording the Rhetoric of Composition" as "a treasure-house of possibilities for our thinking about language as 'a functionally creative element in acts of composition'" (215).

18. For an exchange on listening in the context of silencing, marginalization, deconstruction, and gaps or differends see Ballif, Davis, and Mountford, "Negotiating the Differend" and "Toward an Ethics of Listening"; Ratcliffe, "Eavesdropping on Others"; and Schell, "Tight Spaces in and out of the Parlor."

19. For more on Ulmer see Hawk, "Hyperrhetoric and the Inventive Spectator."

20. In *Empire*, Michael Hardt and Antonio Negri discuss the shift from disciplinary to control society with relation to identity. They write, "Today the social institutions that constitute disciplinary society (the school, the family, the hospital, the factory) . . . are everywhere in crisis. As the walls of these institutions break down, the logics of subjectification that previously operated within their limited spaces now spread out, generalized across the social field" (329). Modern disciplinary society fragmented our identities so that they correspond

to its institutions. With those borders breaking down, Internet technologies juxtapose those multiple identities together in one writing space, unifying what was once fragmented. Ulmer is simply trying to utilize the current conditions of possibility for articulating identities.

21. Ulmer provides the example of Dara Birnbaum's video analysis of *Wonder Woman,* which is a montage of Wonder Woman's spinning movement as she morphs into a superhero. The taped repetitions do not carry special meaning, like a concept, but locate an iconic signifier that carries a mood or atmosphere. The stereotypical mood of the depressive artist, for example, might connect me to the iconic images of Vincent van Gogh or Kurt Cobain. The juxtaposition of these images is then built into the widesite, and these images become conceptual starting places for thinking about my disciplinary approach to art, music, rhetoric—whatever. For more of these kinds of connections and an example of a widesite, see http://mason.gmu.edu/~bhawk/bystory.

22. Wikipedia and MySpace are probably the closest analogues for what Ulmer has in mind. Wikipedia, for example, has proposed the creation of Wikiversity, an "electronic institution of learning that will be used to test the limits of the wiki model both for developing electronic learning resources as well as for teaching and for conducting research and publishing results." Still in the initial start-up phase, Wikiversity could be an open repository for educational materials, serve as a host to online courses, and could even lead to degree-granting programs. This institutional model is not that far-fetched, and adding a public policy purpose to it stretches what education and work could mean or become in a more globally networked apparatus.

23. See Deleuze and Guattari, *A Thousand Plateaus,* in which the authors make the distinction between mapping and tracing: "A map has multiple entryways, as opposed to the tracing, which always comes back 'to the same'" (12). An important aspect of their method, however, is that "*the tracing should always be put back on the map*" (13; emphasis in original). Never settling for dialectical oppositions, the trace (pre-established heuristic) should always be linked back to the map (emerging heuretic).

Afterword

1. Vitanza, in "Notes toward Historiographies of Rhetorics," breaks down attitudes toward history into traditional (positivistic history: arhetorical histories of rhetoric), revisionary (histories that focus on promoting a political program and/or retrieving forgotten figures), and "sub/versive" (critical history that perpetually critiques current histories and practices in the process of inventing new ones). Vitanza recounts this topology in his entry "Historiographies of Rhetoric" in *The Encyclopedia of Rhetoric and Composition:* he writes that sub/versive historiography "hyperbolically extends the rhetoric of suspicion. . . . They do not believe that the errors of the past or present can simply be recoded, that is, fixed, but must be perpetually decoded, that is, perpetually revised or placed in dispersal" (324). For more on the historiography debates in rhetoric and composition see Connors, "Writing the History of Our Discipline," which provides a brief discussion of the debates starting with the CCCC's panel on "Historiographies of Rhetoric" in 1987.

2. Nietzsche's main complaint is that a positivist historiography actually separates people from their culture. By focusing on so many past details, by uncritically holding events as valuable simply because they are old, "historical culture" fills the mind of its people with the past, which creates a subjectivity that does not match up to the present-day "objective" culture. The educated people in a historical culture are presumed to have the greatest storehouse of facts. For Nietzsche, the Greeks would have scoffed at this idea. They lived in the mythic present; their culture was there for people to see and participate in. Hans Kellner, in "After the Fall," points out that for Nietzsche, "rhetoric arises among a people who still live in mythic images and who have not yet experienced the unqualified need of historical accuracy; they

would rather be persuaded than instructed" (Nietzsche quoted in Kellner 22). Nietzsche sees historical culture's fetish for collecting the old and storing it in museums as killing present culture—denying life. Historical culture is not simply dead; it is no culture at all.

3. In *Language and Historical Representation*, Hans Kellner notes that "[h]istorians do not 'find' the truths of past events; they create events from a seamless flow, and invent meanings that produce patterns within that flow. Whether these patterns are, as Nietzsche asked, useful for human life or not is a moral question" (24). Since history is always the development of rhetorical forms out of rhetorical situations, judgment from the perspective of rhetorical ethics has to be a part of the process.

4. While Lovejoy does not use the term rhetoric, it is clear from his historiographical writing and analyses that the breaking down of ideas is a rhetorical operation. He spends a good portion of the introduction to *The Great Chain of Being* elaborating on each of these types. Value assumptions are assumptions or unconscious mental habits that, for example, lend one to think in terms of categories or assume simplicity over complexity. Logical moves are dialectical motives, turns of reasoning, tricks of logic, or methodological assumptions such as the reduction of generalities to specifics (enlightenment nominalism) or assuming the essentiality of complex relations (romantic organicism). Appeals to pathos are underlying assumptions that persuade readers to identify with them at the level of affect, association, or mood, such as appeals to the sublime (Kant, Heidegger), the mysterious (Hegel, Schelling, Bergson), the universal (Plato, Shelley), or oneness (Spinoza, Fichte, James). Associations of ideas are key terms or phrases in a period or movement, such as nature in the romantic period, that have multiple or ambiguous meanings across various texts and thinkers that greatly influence the development or transformation of doctrines. Principles are key concepts in the history of philosophy, oftentimes in Plato and Aristotle, that can be combined and recombined in various historical contexts to produce particular ideas. Any rhetorician would recognize these as rhetorical elements.

5. At this point I have not made the typical distinction between archaeology and genealogy. Though counter-history is generally associated more with genealogy, I read genealogy as an extension of the method set up in archaeology. Archaeology places an emphasis on discourse while genealogy places an emphasis on the body, but each examines its object in a network of relations that establishes the conditions of possibility for it through a multiplicity of organisms, forces, energies, materials, desires, texts, and institutions. Archaeology points its critique to disciplinary formation while genealogy points its analysis to the formation of the subject. Both are political, but the latter engages a wider field. Since my project is pointed at the formation of rhetoric and composition, I invoke counter-history in the context of archaeology.

6. As Foucault notes in "Nietzsche, Genealogy, History" from *Language, Counter-memory, Practice*, counter-histories are histories not seen by or produced through traditional historiographies, and therefore they contest accepted disciplinary or discursive memory. A discipline writes a history of its origin not to remember it but to forget the truth of its origin, which is always founded on an exclusion, or a series of exclusions. This forgetting is a form of selective memory that enables a discipline to produce an idealized reading of its history, an object that is mistakenly seen as solely its own, and a practice whose origins and meaning are forgotten but still used in the present. Counter-histories show this disciplinary memory to also be a forgetting.

7. In *Negation*, Vitanza focuses on saying No to the ontological question "What is X?" (i.e., saying no to exclusion). In his most recent book, *Defining Reality* (2003), Schiappa revises this fact-based (strategic) essentialist question, making it "What should count as X in context Y?" Though the move is an even more explicit social constructionist/pragmatist one than his question in "Sophistic Rhetoric"—he explicitly changes the factual/definitional question into one of value/policy—it is still employed to evaluate the past and exclude (if a

negative evaluation is determined). In other words, his method is used for critique rather than invention and thus requires a counter-historical response.

8. Bruce McComiskey opens his book *Gorgias and the New Sophistic Rhetoric* with a discussion of Schiappa, who falls prey to his own form of categorization. In "Neo-Sophistic Rhetorical Criticism or the Historical Reconstruction of Sophistic Doctrines," Schiappa uses the categories historical reconstruction and rational reconstruction to define historiographic methods. Historical reconstruction attempts to place a writer's work in that writer's historical context and tries to recapture the past as much as possible. Rational reconstruction places the writer in a contemporary context and is freer to apply more creativity to the process of interpretation. McComiskey notes that these categories are not mutually exclusive—they "are fluid points on a continuum, not all or nothing categories" (*Gorgias* 8). Often historians are doing both at the same time. Even Schiappa brings his present-day pragmatist perspective to historical reconstruction.

9. Hans Kellner in "After the Fall" echoes Nietzsche in noting the potential downfalls of this "Evel Knievel" approach to histories of rhetoric. It can turn only on the ethos of the writer, and its No to No can inevitably turn into a dogma (if the rhetor/historiographer stops striving for ever-new readings or compositions). Nevertheless, this is the situation writers of history face. As Kellner notes, the alternative is to deny language's influence on history, and to do this would be a "fall" into traditional or positivist historiography. Historians must continue to invent and reconnect.

10. As Lyotard writes, "[T]he unity of genres is impossible, as is their degree zero. Prose can only be their multitude" (quoted in Vitanza, "An After/word" 247). Lynn Worsham sees this inevitability in Roland Barthes's taxonomic frenzy in his discussion of rhetoric in *The Semiotic Challenge*. Barthes's multiple, fragmented tableau of rhetorical principles shows that "an obsession with classification and taxonomy both creates the entity and its identity and then becomes a stake in its heart" ("Eating History" 146). Because language is multiple, categories can always be rewritten. Their construction ensures that they will be deconstructed. This is the situation I see this book addressing. The categories Young, Weidner, and Berlin created are beginning to break down, so I address them sub/versively.

11. Just as Lovejoy notes that his methods emerged from his practice, Foucault acknowledges that *The Archaeology of Knowledge* "is not an exact description" of his earlier books. *The Order of Things, Birth of the Clinic,* and *Madness and Civilization* were a process of developing these methods, not a clear application of them. *The Archaeology of Knowledge* "is different on a great many points [and] includes a number of corrections and internal criticisms" (16). As with each of these cases, my method is a product of emergence that is tied to particular situations and formations.

BIBLIOGRAPHY

Abercrombie, Nicholas, Stephen Hill, and Bryan Turner. "Determinacy and Indeterminacy in the Theory of Ideology." *Mapping Ideology.* Ed. Slavoj Žižek. London: Verso, 1994. 152–66.

Abrams, M. H. *The Mirror and the Lamp.* New York: Oxford UP, 1953.

Aers, D., J. Cook, and D. Punter. "Coleridge: Individuals, Communities, and Social Agency." *Romanticism and Ideology: Studies in English Writing, 1765–1830.* London: Routledge, 1981. 82–102.

Agamben, Giorgio. *The Coming Community.* Trans. Michael Hardt. Minneapolis: U of Minnesota P, 1993.

Alcorn, Marshall. "Changing the Subject of Postmodernist Theory: Discourse, Ideology, and Therapy in the Classroom." *Rhetoric Review* 13.2 (spring 1995): 331–49.

Allison, David B., ed. *The New Nietzsche: Contemporary Styles of Interpretation.* Cambridge, MA: MIT P, 1985.

Allison, Libby, Lizbeth Bryant, and Maureen Hourigan, eds. *Grading in the Post-Process Classroom.* Portsmouth, NH: Boynton/Cook, 1997.

Almagno, Stephanie. "An NEH Fellowship Examined: Social Networks and Composition Theory." Diss. U of Rhode Island, 1994.

Anderson, Virginia. "Property Rights: Exclusion as Moral Action in 'The Battle of Texas.'" *College English* 62.4 (Mar. 2000): 445–72.

Antliff, Mark. *Inventing Bergson: Cultural Politics and the Parisian Avant-Garde.* Princeton: Princeton UP, 1993.

Armstrong, Aurelia. "Some Reflections on Deleuze's Spinoza: Composition and Agency." *Deleuze and Philosophy: The Difference Engineer.* Ed. Keith Ansell Pearson. New York: Routledge, 1997. 44–57.

Atwill, Janet. "Introduction: Finding a Home or Making a Path." *Perspectives on Rhetorical Invention.* Ed. J. Atwill and J. Lauer. Knoxville: U of Tennessee P, 2002. xi–xxi.

———. *Rhetoric Reclaimed: Aristotle and the Liberal Arts Tradition.* Ithaca, NY: Cornell UP, 1998.

Ballif, Michelle, D. Diane Davis, and Roxanne Mountford. "Negotiating the Differend: A Feminist Trilogue." *JAC* 20 (2000): 583–625.

———. "Toward an Ethics of Listening." *JAC* 20 (2000): 931–42.

Barfield, Owen. *What Coleridge Thought.* Middletown, CT: Wesleyan UP, 1971.

Barilli, Renato. *Rhetoric.* Minneapolis: U of Minnesota P, 1989.

Barthes, Roland. *Camera Lucida.* New York: Hill and Wang, 1995.

———. *The Semiotic Challenge.* Trans. Richard Howard. Berkeley: U of California P, 1994.

Bartholomae, David. "Inventing the University." *When a Writer Can't Write: Studies in Writer's Block and Other Composing Problems.* Ed. Mike Rose. New York: Guilford, 1985. 134–65.

———. "Freshman English, Composition, and CCCC." *CCC* 40 (1989): 38–50.

Baudrillard, Jean. *Forget Foucault.* New York: Semiotext(e), 1987.

Baumlin, James. Introduction. *Ethos: New Essays in Rhetorical and Critical Theory.* Ed. J. Baumlin and T. Baumlin. Dallas: Southern Methodist UP, 1994. xi–xxxi.

Beckner, Morton. "Vitalism." *The Encyclopedia of Philosophy.* New York: Macmillan and Free Press, 1967. 253–56.

The Bedford Bibliography for Teachers of Writing. 5th ed. Ed. P. Bizzell, B. Herzberg, and N. Reynolds. New York: Bedford/St. Martin's, 2000.

Bergson, Henri. *Creative Evolution.* 1911. Mineola, NY: Dover Publications, 1998.

———. *Matter and Memory.* New York: Zone Books, 1994.

Berlin, Isaiah. *The Roots of Romanticism.* Princeton: Princeton UP, 1999.

Berlin, James A. "Contemporary Composition: The Major Pedagogical Theories." *College English* 44 (1982): 765–77.

———. "Freirean Pedagogy in the U.S.: A Response." *JAC* 12 (fall 1992): 414–21.

———. "Poststructuralism, Cultural Studies, and the Composition Classroom: Postmodern Theory in Practice." *Rhetoric Review* 11 (1992): 16–33.

———. "Revisionary History: The Dialectical Method." *Pre/Text* 8.1–2 (1987): 47–61.

———. "Rhetoric and Ideology in the Writing Class." *College English* 50.5 (Sept. 1988): 477–94.

———. *Rhetoric and Reality: Writing Instruction in American Colleges, 1900–1985.* Carbondale: Southern Illinois UP, 1987.

———. "The Rhetoric of Romanticism: The Case for Coleridge." *Rhetoric Society Quarterly* 10.2 (spring 1980): 62–74.

———. *Rhetorics, Poetics, and Cultures: Refiguring College English Studies.* Urbana, IL: NCTE, 1996.

———. "Richard Whately and Current Traditional Rhetoric." *College English* 42 (Sept. 1980): 10–17.

———. *Writing Instruction in Nineteenth-Century American Colleges.* Carbondale: Southern Illinois UP, 1984.

Berlin, James A., and Robert P. Inkster. "Current-Traditional Rhetoric: Paradigm and Practice." *Freshman English News* 8.3 (winter 1980): 1–4, 13–14.

Berlin, James A., and Michael Vivion. Introduction. *Cultural Studies in the English Classroom.* Ed. J. Berlin and M. Vivion. Portsmouth, NH: Boynton/Cook, 1992. vii–xvi.

Berndtson, Arthur. "Vitalism." *A History of Philosophical Systems.* Ed. Vergilius Ferm. New York: The Philosophical Library, 1950. 375–86.

Bertalanffy, Ludwig von. *General System Theory: Foundations, Development, Applications.* New York: George Braziller, 1968.

Berthoff, Ann E. "The Problem of Problem Solving." *CCC* 22 (1971): 237–42.

———. "Response to Janice Lauer, 'Counterstatement.'" *CCC* 23 (1972): 414–16.

Berthoff, Ann E., ed. *Richards on Rhetoric: I. A. Richards, Selected Essays (1929–1974).* New York: Oxford UP, 1991.

Biesecker, Barbara. "Rethinking the Rhetorical Situation from within the Thematic of *Différance.*" *Philosophy and Rhetoric* 22.2 (spring 1989): 110–30.

Bitzer, Lloyd. "The Rhetorical Situation." Rpt. in *Rhetoric: Concepts, Definitions, Boundaries.* Ed. W. Covino and D. Jolliffe. Boston: Allyn and Bacon, 1995. 300–310.

Bizzell, Patricia. "Cognition, Convention, and Certainty: What We Need to Know about Writing." *Pre/Text* 3.3 (1982): 213–45.

Bloom, Lynn. "Conclusion: Mapping Composition's New Geography." *Composition in the Twenty-first Century: Crisis and Change.* Ed. L. Bloom, D. Daiker, and E. White. Carbondale: Southern Illinois UP, 1996. 273–77.

Boden, Margaret A., ed. *The Philosophy of Artificial Life.* New York: Oxford UP, 1996.

Bolter, Jay David. *Writing Space: Computers, Hypertext, and the Remediation of Print.* 2nd ed. Mahwah, NJ: LEA, 2001.

Britton, James. "Shaping at the Point of Utterance." *Reinventing the Rhetorical Tradition.* Ed. Aviva Freedman and Ian Pringle. Ottawa: Canadian Council of Teachers of English, 1980. 61–65.

Brooke, Collin. "Forgetting to Be (Post)Human: Media and Memory in a Kairotic Age." *JAC* 20.4 (2000): 775–95.

———. "Weblogs as Deictic Systems: Centripetal, Centrifugal, and Small-World Blogging." *Computers and Composition Online* (fall 2005). http://www.bgsu.edu/cconline/brooke/brooke.htm.

Brooks, Kevin. "Reading, Writing, and Teaching Creative Hypertext: A Genre-Based Pedagogy." *Pedagogy* 2.3 (2002): 337–56.

Burke, Kenneth. *Dramatism and Development.* Vol. 6, 1971 Heinz Werner Lecture Series. Barre, MA: Clark UP, 1972.

———. *The Rhetoric of Religion: Studies in Logology.* Los Angeles: U of California P, 1961.

Burton, Gideon. "Rousseau." *Encyclopedia of Rhetoric and Composition: Communication from Ancient Times to the Information Age.* Ed. Theresa Enos. New York: Garland, 1996. 644–45.

Burwick, Frederick, ed. *Coleridge's Biographia Literaria.* Columbus: Ohio State UP, 1989.

Burwick, Frederick, and Paul Douglass, ed. *The Crisis in Modernism: Bergson and the Vitalist Controversy.* Cambridge: Cambridge UP, 1992.

Channell, David. *The Vital Machine: A Study of Technology and Organic Life.* Oxford: Oxford UP, 1991.

Christensen, Jerome. "The Marginal Method of the *Biographia Literaria.*" *Samuel Taylor Coleridge.* Ed. Harold Bloom. New York: Chelsea House, 1986. 139–48.

Coleridge, Samuel Taylor. *Biographia Literaria: Or, Biographical Sketches of My Literary Life and Opinions.* Ed. James Engell and W. Jackson Bate. Princeton: Princeton UP, 1983.

———. "Essays on the Principles of Method." *The Friend.* Ed. Barbara E. Rooke. Princeton: Princeton UP, 1969. 448–524.

———. "Genius, Talent, Sense, and Cleverness." *The Friend.* Ed. Barbara E. Rooke. Princeton: Princeton UP, 1969. 419–23.

———. "Note on Spinoza." *Shorter Works and Fragments.* Ed. H. J. Jackson and J. R. Jackson. Princeton: Princeton UP, 1995. 607–24.

———. "On the Origin and Progress of the Sect of the Sophists in Greece." *The Friend.* Ed. Barbara E. Rooke. Princeton: Princeton UP, 1969. 436–47.

———. "Theory of Life." 1848. *Shorter Works and Fragments.* Ed. H. J. Jackson and J. R. Jackson. Princeton: Princeton UP, 1995. 481–557.

———. "Treatise on Method." *Shorter Works and Fragments.* Ed. H. J. Jackson and J. R. Jackson. Princeton: Princeton UP, 1995. 625–87.

Coles, William. *The Plural I—and After.* Portsmouth, NH: Boynton/Cook, 1988.

Connors, Robert J. *Composition-Rhetoric: Backgrounds, Theory, and Pedagogy.* Pittsburgh, PA: U of Pittsburgh P, 1997.

———. "Writing the History of Our Discipline." *An Introduction to Composition Studies.* Ed. Erika Lindemann and Gary Tate. New York: Oxford UP, 1991.

———. Rev. of *Writing Instruction in Nineteenth-Century American Colleges,* by James Berlin. *CCC* 37.2 (1986): 247–49.

Cooper, Marilyn. "The Ecology of Writing." *College English* 48 (1986): 364–75.

———. "Foreword: The Truth Is Out There." *Ecocomposition: Theoretical and Pedagogical Approaches.* Ed. S. Dobrin and C. Weisser. Albany: State U of New York P, 2001. xi–xvii.

Corcoran, Amanda Inskip. "The Emergent Paradigm: Complexity Theory, Composition, and the Networked Writing Classroom." 1997. http://leahi.kcc.hawaii.edu/org/tcc_conf97/pres/corcoran.html.

Crowley, Sharon. *Composition in the University: Historical and Polemical Essays.* Pittsburgh, PA: U of Pittsburgh P, 1998.

———. "Composition's Ethic of Service, the Universal Requirement, and the Discourse of Student Need." *Composition in the University: Historical and Polemical Essays.* Pittsburgh, PA: U of Pittsburgh P, 1998. 250–65.

———. *The Methodical Memory: Invention in Current-Traditional Rhetoric.* Carbondale: Southern Illinois UP, 1990.

Cushman, Ellen. "The Public Intellectual, Service Learning, and Activist Research." *College English* 61.3 (Jan. 1999): 328–36.

D'Angelo, Frank J. *A Conceptual Theory of Rhetoric.* Cambridge, MA: Winthrop, 1975.

———. "The Evolution of the Analytic Topoi: A Speculative Inquiry." *Essays on Classical Rhetoric and Modern Discourse.* Ed. Robert J. Conners, Lisa S. Ede, and Andrea Lunsford. Carbondale: Southern Illinois UP, 1984. 50–68.

Davis, Diane. "Being-Written; or, Notes Towards a Post-Post-Process Theory." Lecture, University of Texas at Arlington. Feb. 4, 2000.

———. *Breaking Up [at] Totality: A Rhetoric of Laughter.* Carbondale: Southern Illinois UP, 2000.

Deleuze, Gilles. *Bergsonism.* New York: Zone Books, 1991.

———. "Deleuze – Session on Spinoza: 13/01/81." *Web Deleuze.* Trans. Timothy S. Murphy. http://www.imaginet.fr/deleuze/TXT/ENG/130181.html.

———. *Foucault.* Minneapolis: U of Minnesota P, 1988.

———. *Spinoza: Practical Philosophy.* San Francisco: City Lights Press, 1988.

Deleuze, Gilles, and Félix Guattari. *Anti-Oedipus: Capitalism and Schizophrenia.* Minneapolis: U of Minnesota P, 1983.

———. *A Thousand Plateaus: Capitalism and Schizophrenia.* Trans. Brian Massumi. Minneapolis: U of Minnesota P, 1987.

Derrida, Jacques. *Glas.* Lincoln: U of Nebraska P, 1986.

Desmond, William. *Beyond Hegel and Dialectic: Speculation, Cult, and Comedy.* Albany: State U of New York P, 1992.

Dobrin, Sidney, and Christian Weisser. "Breaking Ground in Ecocomposition: Exploring Relationships between Discourse and Environment." *College English* 64.5 (May 2002): 566–89.

Doyle, Richard. *Wetwares: Experiments in Postvital Living.* Minneapolis: U of Minnesota P, 2003.

Driesch, Hans A. *The History and Theory of Vitalism.* London: Macmillan/St. Martin's, 1914.

———. *The Science and Philosophy of the Organism.* London: n.p., 1908.

Dunne, Joseph. *Back to the Rough Ground: "Phronesis" and "Technē" in Modern Philosophy and in Aristotle.* Notre Dame, IN: U of Notre Dame P, 1993.

Edbauer, Jenny. "Executive Overspill: Affective Bodies, Intensity, and Bush-in-Relation." *Postmodern Culture* 15.1 (Oct. 2004). http://www3.iath.virginia.edu/pmc/text-only/issue.904/15.1edbauer.txt.

———. "Meta/Physical Graffiti: 'Getting Up' as Affective Writing Model." *JAC* 25.1 (2005): 131–59.

Elbow, Peter. "Closing My Eyes as I Speak: An Argument for Ignoring Audience." *College English* 49 (Jan. 1987): 50–69.

Elden, Stuart. *Mapping the Present: Heidegger, Foucault, and the Project of a Spatial History.* New York: Continuum, 2001.

Enos, Richard. Foreword. *Inventing a Discipline: Rhetoric and Scholarship in Honor of Richard E. Young.* Ed. Maureen Daly Goggin. Urbana, IL: NCTE, 2000. vii–x.

Enos, Richard, and Janice Lauer. "The Meaning of *Heuristic* in Aristotle's *Rhetoric* and Its Implications for Contemporary Rhetorical Theory." *A Rhetoric of Doing.* Ed. S. Witte, N. Nakadate, and R. Cherry. Carbondale: Southern Illinois UP, 1992. 79–87.

Faigley, Lester. "Competing Theories of Process: A Critique and a Proposal." *College English* 48.6 (Oct. 1986): 527–42.

Feyerabend, Paul. *Against Method.* 1975. 3rd ed. New York: Verso, 1993.

Fishman, Jenn, et al. "Performing Writing, Performing Literacy." *CCC* 57.2 (2005): 224–52.

Fishman, Stephen, and Lucille McCarthy. "Is Expressivism Dead? Reconsidering Its Romantic Roots and Its Relation to Social Constructionism." *College English* 54.6 (Oct. 1992): 647–61.

Fleming, David. "Rhetoric as a Course of Study." *College English* 61.2 (Nov. 1998): 169–91.

Florescu, Vasile. "Rhetoric and Its Rehabilitation in Contemporary Philosophy." *Philosophy and Rhetoric* 3 (1970): 193–224.

Fogarty, Daniel. *Roots for a New Rhetoric.* New York: Teachers College, Columbia U, 1959.

Foucault, Michel. *The Archaeology of Knowledge.* New York: Pantheon Books, 1972.

———. *Birth of the Clinic: An Archeology of Medical Perception.* New York: Random House, Vintage, 1994.

———. *The History of Sexuality: An Introduction.* New York: Random House, Vintage, 1978.

———. *Madness and Civilization: A History of Insanity in the Age of Reason.* New York: Random House, Vintage, 1988.

———. "Nietzsche, Genealogy, History." *Language, Counter-Memory, Practice.* Ithaca, NY: Cornell UP, 1977. 139–64.

———. *The Order of Things: An Archeology of the Human Sciences.* New York: Random House, 1970.

———. "Questions of Method." *The Foucault Effect: Studies in Governmentality.* Ed. G. Burchell, C. Gordon, and P. Miller. Chicago: U of Chicago P, 1991. 73–86.

———. "Theatrum Philosophicum." *Language, Counter-Memory, Practice.* Ithaca, NY: Cornell UP, 1977. 165–98.

———. *The Use of Pleasure.* New York: Random House, Vintage, 1985.

Frank, Luanne. "Herder, Jauss, and the New Historicism: A Retrospective Reading." *Johann Gottfried Herder: Language, History, and the Enlightenment.* Ed. Wulf Keopke. Columbia, SC: Camden House, 1990. 246–88.

Freire, Paulo. *Pedagogy of the Oppressed.* Trans. Myra Bergman Ramos. New York: Herder and Herder, 1970.

———. *The Politics of Education: Culture, Power, and Liberation.* Introduction by Henry Giroux. South Hadley, MA: Bergin and Garvey, 1985.

Freire, Paulo, and Ira Shor. *A Pedagogy for Liberation.* South Hadley, MA: Bergin and Garvey, 1987.

Freyhofer, Horst H. *The Vitalism of Hans Driesch: The Success & Decline of a Scientific Theory.* Frankfurt: P. Lang, 1982.

Fulkerson, Richard. "Four Philosophies of Composition." 1979. Rpt. in *The Writing Teacher's Sourcebook.* 3rd ed. Ed. G. Tate, E. Corbett, and N. Meyers. New York: Oxford UP, 1981. 3–8.

Fulwiler, Toby. Rev. of *Writing/Teaching: Essays toward a Rhetoric of Pedagogy,* by Paul Kameen. *CCC* 54 (2002): 307–10.

Gale, Xin Liu. *Teachers, Discourses, and Authority in the Postmodern Composition Classroom.* Albany: State U of New York P, 1996.

Glenn, Cheryl. "Silence: A Rhetorical Art for Resisting Discipline(s)." *JAC* 22 (2002): 261–91.

Goodson, A. C. *Verbal Imagination: Coleridge and the Language of Modern Criticism.* New York: Oxford UP, 1988.

Gradin, Sherrie. *Romancing Rhetorics: Social Expressivist Perspectives on the Teaching of Writing.* Portsmouth, NH: Boynton/Cook, 1995.

Grossberg, Lawrence. Introduction. *Between Borders: Pedagogy and the Politics of Cultural Studies.* Ed. Henry Giroux and Peter McLaren. New York: Routledge, 1994. 1–25.

Haeger, Jack H. "Samuel Taylor Coleridge and the Romantic Background to Bergson." *The Crisis in Modernism: Bergson and the Vitalist Controversy.* Cambridge: Cambridge UP, 1992. 98–108.

Hansen, Mark. *Embodying Technesis: Technology beyond Writing.* Ann Arbor: U of Michigan P, 2000.

Hardin, Joe Marshall. Rev. of *When Students Have Power,* by Ira Shor. *JAC* 17.3 (fall 1997): 525–29.

Hardt, Michael, and Antonio Negri. *Empire.* Cambridge, MA: Harvard UP, 2000.

Harkin, Patricia. "*Rhetorics, Poetics, and Cultures* as an Articulation Project." *JAC* 17.3 (fall 1997): 494–97.
Harman, Graham. *Guerrilla Metaphysics: Phenomenology and the Carpentry of Things.* Chicago: Open Court, 2005.
———. *Tool-Being: Heidegger and the Metaphysics of Objects.* Chicago: Open Court, 2002.
Harris, Jeanette. *Expressive Discourse.* Dallas: Southern Methodist UP, 1990.
Hawhee, Debra. "Bodily Pedagogies: Rhetoric, Athletics, and the Sophists' Three Rs." *College English* 65.2 (2002): 142–62.
———. "Kairotic Encounters." *Perspectives on Rhetorical Invention.* Ed. J. Atwill and J. Lauer. Knoxville: U of Tennessee P, 2002. 16–35.
Hawk, Byron. "Hyperrhetoric and the Inventive Spectator: Remotivating *The Fifth Element.*" *The Terministic Screen: Rhetorical Perspectives on Film.* Ed. David Blakesley. Carbondale: Southern Illinois UP, 2003. 70–91.
———. "A Rhetoric/Pedagogy of Silence: Sub-version in Paul Kameen's *Writing/Teaching.*" *Pedagogy: Critical Approaches to Teaching Literature, Language, Composition, and Culture* 3.3 (fall 2003): 377–97.
———. "Toward a Post-*Techne:* Or, Inventing Pedagogies for Professional Writing." *Technical Communications Quarterly* 13.4 (fall 2004): 371–92.
———. "Toward a Rhetoric of Network (Media) Culture: Notes on Polarities and Potentiality." *JAC Special Issue: Complexity Theory* 24.4 (2004): 831–50.
Hawk, Byron, and David Rieder. "Introduction: On Small Tech and Complex Ecologies." *Small Tech: The Culture of Digital Tools.* Ed. Byron Hawk, David Rieder, and Ollie Oviedo. Minneapolis: U of Minnesota P, 2008.
Hayles, N. Katherine. *How We Became Posthuman: Virtual Bodies in Cybernetics, Literature, and Informatics.* Chicago: U of Chicago P, 1999.
Haynes, Cynthia. "Writing Offshore: The Disappearing Coastline of Composition Theory." Conference on College Composition and Communication, Chicago, Mar. 22, 2002.
Heidegger, Martin. *Aristotle's Metaphysics: On the Essence of Actuality and Force.* Indianapolis: Indiana UP, 1995.
———. *Being and Time.* Trans. J. Macquarrie and E. Robinson. New York: Harper/Collins, 1962.
———. *Poetry, Language, Thought.* New York: Harper and Row, 1971.
———. "The Question Concerning Technology." *The Question Concerning Technology and Other Essays.* Trans. William Lovitt. New York: Harper Torchbooks, 1977. 3–35.
———. "The Way to Language." *On the Way to Language.* New York: Harper/Collins, 1982. 111–36.
Henry, Jim. *Writing Workplace Cultures: An Archaeology of Professional Writing.* Carbondale: Southern Illinois UP, 2000.
Hodgson, John. *Coleridge, Shelley, and Transcendental Inquiry.* Lincoln: U of Nebraska P, 1989.
Hughes, Richard. "The Contemporaneity of Classical Rhetoric." 1965. Rpt. in *Landmark Essays on Rhetorical Invention in Writing.* Ed. R. Young and Y. Liu. Davis, CA: Hermagoras Press, 1994. 37–40.
Innes, Shelley. *Hans Driesch and Vitalism: A Reinterpretation.* M.A. thesis. Simon Fraser University, 1987. Ottawa: National Library of Canada, 1989.
Irmscher, William. *Teaching Expository Writing.* New York: Holt, Rinehart, and Winston, 1979.
Ishii, Hiroshi, et al. "ambientROOM: Integrating Ambient Media with Architectural Space." *Conference Summary of CHI.* Los Angeles: Association for Computing Machinery, 1998. 1–2.
Jameson, Fredric. "Cognitive Mapping." *Marxism and the Interpretation of Culture.* Ed. Cary Nelson and Lawrence Grossberg. Urbana: U of Illinois P, 1988. 347–57.

Jenkinson, John Wilfrid. "Vitalism." *Studies in the History and Method of Science.* Ed. C. J. Singer. N.p.: n.p., 1917. 57–78.

Joad, C. E. M. *Unorthodox Dialogues on Education and Art.* London: Ernest Benn, 1930.

Johnson, Robert. "What Is Cultural Studies Anyway?" *Social Text* 16 (1986–87): 38–80.

Johnson, Robert, and Frances Ranney. Afterword (to the special issue on technê). "Recovering Technê." *TCQ* 11.2 (spring 2002): 237–39.

Johnson, T. R. "Discipline and Pleasure: 'Magic' and Sound." *JAC* 19 (1999): 431–52.

———. "School Sucks." *CCC* 52.4 (June 2001): 620–50.

Joyce, Michael. *Of Two Minds: Hypertext Pedagogy and Poetics.* Ann Arbor: U of Michigan P, 1995.

Kahn-Egan, Seth. "Pedagogy of the Pissed: Punk Pedagogy in the First-Year Writing Classroom." *CCC* 49.1 (Feb. 1998): 99–104.

Kameen, Paul. "Afterthoughts." *Pre/Text: The First Decade.* Ed. Victor J. Vitanza. Pittsburgh, PA: U of Pittsburgh P, 1993. 28–30.

———. "Coleridge: On Method." *Correspondences* 5 (summer 1986): n.p.

———. "Re-covering of the Self in Composition." *College English* 62.1 (Sept. 1999): 100–111.

———. "Rewording the Rhetoric of Composition." *Pre/Text* 1.1–2 (spring–fall 1980): 73–94.

———. *Writing/Teaching: Essays Toward a Rhetoric of Pedagogy.* Pittsburgh, PA: U of Pittsburgh P, 2000.

Keating, Craig Reynolds. "Foucault, Vitalism, Resistance: The Subject of Resistance in the Thought of Michel Foucault." Diss. McMaster U, 1995.

Kellner, Hans. "After the Fall: Reflections on Histories of Rhetoric." *Writing Histories of Rhetoric.* Ed. Victor J. Vitanza. Carbondale: Southern Illinois UP, 1994. 20–37.

———. *Language and Historical Representation: Getting the Story Crooked.* Madison: U of Wisconsin P, 1989.

Kennedy, George. "Some Reflections on Neomodernism." *Rhetoric Review* 6.2 (spring 1988): 230–33.

Kent, Thomas. "Beyond System: The Rhetoric of Paralogy." *College English* 51.5 (Sept. 1989): 492–507.

———. "Paralogic Hermeneutics and the Possibilities of Rhetoric." *Rhetoric Review* 8.1 (fall 1989): 24–42.

———. *Paralogic Rhetoric.* Lewisburg, PA: Bucknell UP, 1993.

Kent, Thomas, ed. *Post-Process Theory: Beyond the Writing-Process Paradigm.* Carbondale: Southern Illinois UP, 1999.

Kerferd, G. B. *The Sophistic Movement.* Cambridge: Cambridge UP, 1981.

Kinneavy, James L. "The Process of Writing: A Philosophical Base in Hermeneutics." *JAC* 7 (1987): 1–9.

———. *A Theory of Discourse: The Aims of Discourse.* New York: Norton, 1971.

Kitzhaber, Albert. *Rhetoric in American Colleges, 1850–1900.* 1953. Dallas: Southern Methodist UP, 1990.

Knoblauch, C. H. "Some Observations on Freire's *Pedagogy of the Oppressed.*" *JAC* 8 (1988): 50–54.

Kroker, Arthur. "Hyper-Heidegger." *CTheory* 25.3 (2002). http://www.ctheory.net.

Landow, George. *Hypertext 2.0: The Convergence of Contemporary Critical Theory and Technology.* Baltimore, MD: Johns Hopkins UP, 1997.

Lauer, Janice. "Response to Ann E. Berthoff, 'The Problem of Problem Solving.'" *CCC* 23 (1972): 208–10.

———. "Heuristics and Composition." *CCC* 21 (1970): 396–404.

LeFevre, Karen Burke. *Invention as a Social Act.* Carbondale: Southern Illinois UP, 1987.

Lindsay, Stan. *Implicit Rhetoric: Burke's Extension of Aristotle's Concept of Entelechy.* Lanham, MD: University Press of America, 1998.

Liu, Yameng. "Invention and Inventiveness." *Perspectives on Rhetorical Invention.* Ed. J. Atwill and J. Lauer. Knoxville: U of Tennessee P, 2002. 53–63.

Livingston, Ira. *Arrow of Chaos: Romanticism and Postmodernity.* Minneapolis: U of Minnesota P, 1997.

Lovejoy, Arthur. "The Historiography of Ideas." *Essays in the History of Ideas.* Baltimore, MD: Johns Hopkins UP, 1948. 1–13.

———. "Introduction: The Study of the History of Ideas." *The Great Chain of Being.* 1936. Cambridge, MA: Harvard UP, 1964. 3–23.

———. "On the Discrimination of Romanticisms." *Essays in the History of Ideas.* Baltimore, MD: Johns Hopkins UP, 1948. 228–53.

———. Preface. *Essays in the History of Ideas.* Baltimore, MD: Johns Hopkins UP, 1948. xiii–xvii.

Mann, Paul. *Masocriticism.* New York: State U of New York P, 1999.

Marks, John. *Gilles Deleuze: Vitalism and Multiplicity.* Sterling, VA: Pluto Press, 1998.

Marquard, Odo. *In Defense of the Accidental: Philosophical Studies.* New York: Oxford UP, 1991.

Massumi, Brian. *Parables for the Virtual: Movement, Affect, Sensation.* Durham, NC: Duke UP, 2002.

———. Translator's foreword. *A Thousand Plateaus: Capitalism and Schizophrenia*, by Gilles Deleuze and Félix Guattari. Minneapolis: U of Minnesota P, 1987.

———. *A User's Guide to Capitalism and Schizophrenia: Deviations from Deleuze and Guattari.* Cambridge, MA: MIT P, 1992.

Matthews, Eric. *Twentieth-Century French Philosophy.* New York: Oxford UP, 1996.

Mayers, Tim. *(Re)Writing Craft: Composition, Creative Writing, and the Future of English Studies.* Pittsburgh, PA: U Pittsburgh P, 2005.

———. "The Struggle over Composition and the Question of Might: A Response to Gary Olson." *JAC* 20.2 (spring 2000): 448–54.

McComiskey, Bruce. *Gorgias and the New Sophistic Rhetoric.* Carbondale: Southern Illinois UP, 2002.

McFarland, Thomas. "The Origin and Significance of Coleridge's Theory of Secondary Imagination." *Samuel Taylor Coleridge.* Ed. Harold Bloom. New York: Chelsea House, 1986. 117–37.

Miller, Carolyn. Foreword. *Rhetoric and Kairos: Essays in History, Theory, and Praxis.* Ed. P. Sipiora and J. Baumlin. Albany: State U of New York P, 2002. xi–xii.

Miller, Susan. "Technologies of Self?-Formation." *JAC* 17.3 (fall 1997): 497–500.

———. *Textual Carnivals: The Politics of Composition.* Carbondale: Southern Illinois UP, 1991.

Montag, W., and T. Stolze, eds. *The New Spinoza.* Minneapolis: U of Minnesota P, 1997.

Moore, F. C. T. *Bergson: Thinking Backwards.* Cambridge: Cambridge UP, 1996.

Moustakas, Clark. *Heuristic Research: Design, Methodology, and Applications.* London: Sage, 1990.

Muckelbaurer, John, and Debra Hawhee. "Posthuman Rhetorics: 'It's the Future Pikul.'" *JAC* 20.4 (2000): 764–74.

Mullarkey, John. *Bergson and Philosophy.* Notre Dame, IN: U of Notre Dame P, 2000.

Mullarkey, John, ed. *The New Bergson.* Manchester, Eng.: Manchester UP, 1999.

Negri, Antonio. *The Savage Anomaly: The Power of Spinoza's Metaphysics and Politics.* Minneapolis: U of Minnesota P, 1991.

Nietzsche, Friedrich. "On the Uses and Disadvantages of History for Life." *Untimely Meditations.* Cambridge: Cambridge UP, 1983. 57–123.

———. "Truth and Lies in a Nonmoral Sense." *The Rhetorical Tradition.* Ed. Patricia Bizzell and Bruce Herzberg. Boston: Bedford Books, 1990. 888–96.

North, Stephen. "The Death of Paradigm Hope, the End of Paradigm Guilt, and the Future of (Research in) Composition." *Composition in the Twenty-First Century: Crisis and Change.* Ed. L. Bloom, D. Daiker, and E. White. Carbondale: Southern Illinois UP, 1996. 194–207.

———. *The Making of Knowledge in Composition: Portrait of an Emerging Field.* Portsmouth, NH: Boynton/Cook Heinemann, 1987.

O'Brien, Kathleen. "Romanticism and Rhetoric: A Question of Audience." *RSQ* 30.2 (spring 2000): 77–91.

Olson, Gary. "Struggling over Composition." *JAC* 20.2 (spring 2000): 454–55.

———. "Theory and the Rhetoric of Assertion." *Composition Forum* 6 (1995): 53–61.

Paley, Karen Surman. "Writing and Rewriting Racism: From the Dorm to the Classroom to the Dustbowl." *JAC* 16.2 (1996). http://www.cas.usf.edu/JAC/162/paley.html.

Perelman, C. H., and L. Olbrechts-Tyteca. *The New Rhetoric: A Treatise on Argumentation.* Notre Dame, IN: U of Notre Dame P, 1969.

Perry, Seamus. "Coleridge, the Return to Nature, and the New Anti-Romanticism: An Essay in Polemic." *Romanticism on the Net* 4 (Nov. 1996): http://users.ox.ac.uk/~scat0385/antirom.html.

Petraglia, Joseph. "Shaping Sophisticates: Implications of the Rhetorical Turn." *Inventing a Discipline: Rhetoric Scholarship in Honor of Richard E. Young.* Ed. Maureen Daly Goggin. Urbana, IL: NCTE, 2000. 80–104.

Phelps, Louise Wetherbee. *Composition as a Human Science: Contributions to the Self-Understanding of a Discipline.* New York: Oxford UP, 1988.

———. "Institutional Invention: (How) Is It Possible?" *Perspectives on Rhetorical Invention.* Ed. Janet Atwill and Janice Lauer. Knoxville: U of Tennessee P, 2002. 64–95.

Phelps, Louise Wetherbee, Mark Wiley, and Barbara Gleason, eds. *Composition in Four Keys: Inquiring into the Field.* Mountain View, CA: Mayfield, 1996.

Polanyi, Michael. *Personal Knowledge: Towards a Post-Critical Philosophy.* Chicago: U of Chicago P, 1958.

———. *The Tacit Dimension.* 1966. Gloucester, MA: Peter Smith, 1983.

Porter, Kevin. Rev. of *Post-Process Theory,* ed. Thomas Kent. *JAC* 20.3 (summer 2000): 710–14.

Poulakos, John. "Nietzsche and Histories of Rhetoric." *Writing Histories of Rhetoric.* Carbondale: Southern Illinois UP, 1994. 81–97.

———. *Sophistical Rhetoric in Classical Greece.* Columbia: U of South Carolina P, 1995.

Quirk, Tom. *Bergson and American Culture: The Worlds of Willa Cather and Wallace Stevens.* Chapel Hill: U of North Carolina P, 1990.

Rasch, William, and Cary Wolfe, eds. *Observing Complexity: Systems Theory and Postmodernity.* Minneapolis: U of Minnesota P, 2000.

Ratcliffe, Krista. "Eavesdropping on Others." *JAC* 20 (2000): 908–19.

Reynolds, Nedra. *Geographies of Writing: Inhabiting Places and Encountering Differences.* Carbondale: Southern Illinois UP, 2004.

Rice, Jeff. "The 1963 Hop-Hop Machine: Hip-Hop Pedagogy as Composition." *CCC* 54.3 (Feb. 2003): 453–71.

Rickert, Thomas. *Acts of Enjoyment: Rhetoric, Žižek, and the Return of the Subject.* Pittsburgh, PA: U of Pittsburgh P, 2007.

———. "Engaging Modernisms, Emerging Posthumanisms, and the Rhetorics of Doing." *JAC* 20.3 (summer 2000): 672–84.

———. "In the House of Doing: Ambience, Rhetoric, *Kairos.*" *JAC: Special Issue on Mark C. Taylor and Emerging Network Culture* 24.4 (2004): 901–27.

Roberts-Miller, Patricia. "Post-Contemporary Composition: Social Construction and Its Alternatives." *Composition Studies* 30.1 (spring 2002): 97–116.

Ronald, Kate, and Hephzibah Roskelly. *Farther Along: Transforming Dichotomies in Rhetoric and Composition.* Portsmouth, NH: Heinemann, 1990.

Rorty, Amelie O., ed. *Essays on Aristotle's Rhetoric*. Berkeley: U of California P, 1996.

Rutsky, R. L. *High Technê: Art and Technology from the Machine Aesthetic to the Posthuman*. Minneapolis: U of Minnesota P, 1999.

Salvan, Jacques León. *The Scandalous Ghost: Sartre's Existentialism as Related to Vitalism, Humanism, Mysticism, Marxism*. Detroit, MI: Wayne State UP, 1967.

Saper, Craig. *Artificial Mythologies: A Guide to Cultural Invention*. Minneapolis: U of Minnesota P, 1997.

Schell, Eileen E. "Tight Spaces in and out of the Parlor: Negotiation and the Politics of Difference." *JAC* 20 (2000): 919–31.

Schiappa, Edward. *Defining Reality: Definitions and the Politics of Meaning*. Carbondale: Southern Illinois UP, 2003.

———. "Neo-Sophistic Rhetorical Criticism or the Historical Reconstruction of Sophistic Doctrines." *Philosophy and Rhetoric* 23 (1990): 192–217.

———. "Sophistic Rhetoric: Oasis or Mirage?" *Rhetoric Review* 10 (1991): 5–18.

Schilb, John. "Future Historiographies of Rhetoric and the Present Age of Anxiety." *Writing Histories of Rhetoric*. Carbondale: Southern Illinois UP, 1994. 128–38.

Schrödinger, Erwin. *What Is Life? The Physical Aspect of the Living Cell*. Cambridge: Cambridge UP, 1944.

Schubert-Soldern, Rainer. *Mechanism and Vitalism: Philosophical Aspects of Biology*. Notre Dame, IN: U of Notre Dame P, 1962.

Seitz, David. "Hard Lessons Learned since the First Generation of Critical Pedagogy." *College English* 64.4 (2002): 503–12.

Shaviro, Steven. *Connected: Or What It Means to Live in the Network Society*. Minneapolis: U of Minnesota P, 2003.

Shor, Ira. *When Students Have Power: Negotiating Authority in a Critical Pedagogy*. Chicago: U of Chicago P, 1996.

Sidler, Michelle, and Richard Morris. "Writing in a Post-Berlinian Landscape: Cultural Composition in the Classroom." *JAC* 18.2 (1998): 275–91.

Sinnott, Edmund Ware. *The Bridge of Life: From Matter to Spirit*. New York: Simon and Schuster, 1966.

Sirc, Geoffrey. *English Composition as a Happening*. Logan: Utah State UP, 2002.

———. "Godless Composition, Tormented Writing." *JAC* 15.3 (1995): 543–64.

———. "Never Mind the Sex Pistols, Where's 2Pac?" *CCC* 49.1 (1998): 104–8.

———. "Never Mind the Tagmemics, Where's the Sex Pistols?" *CCC* 48.1 (1997): 9–29.

Smith, Paul. *Discerning the Subject*. Minneapolis: U of Minnesota P, 1988.

Sutton, Jane. Rev. of *Negation, Subjectivity and the History of Rhetoric*, by Victor J. Vitanza. *Philosophy and Rhetoric* 32.2 (1999): 180–84.

Syverson, Margaret. *The Wealth of Reality: An Ecology of Composition*. Carbondale: Southern Illinois UP, 1999.

Taylor, Charles. "Heidegger, Language, and Ecology." *Philosophical Arguments*. Cambridge, MA: Harvard UP, 1995. 100–126.

Taylor, Mark C. *The Moment of Complexity: Emerging Network Culture*. Chicago: U of Chicago P, 2001.

Taylor, Paul. "Social Epistemic Rhetoric and Chaotic Discourse." *Re-Imagining Computers and Composition: Teaching and Research in the Virtual Age*. Ed. G. Hawisher and P. LeBlanc. Portsmouth, NH: Boynton/Cook, 1992. 131–48.

Thacker, Eugene. *Biomedia*. Minneapolis: U of Minnesota P, 2004.

Therborn, Goran. *The Ideology of Power and the Power of Ideology*. New York: Verso, 1980.

Thompson, Roger. "*Kairos* Revisited: An Interview with James Kinneavy." *Rhetoric Review* 19 (2000): 73–88.

Ulmer, Gregory. *Applied Grammatology.* Baltimore, MD: Johns Hopkins UP, 1985.

———. *Heuretics: The Logic of Invention.* Baltimore, MD: Johns Hopkins UP, 1994.

———. *Internet Invention: From Literacy to Electracy.* New York: Pearson/Longman, 2003.

———. *Teletheory.* New York: Routledge, 1989.

Ulmer, Gregory, Robert Scholes, and Nancy Comley. *Text Book: Writing through Literature.* 3rd ed. New York: Bedford/St. Martin's, 2002.

Van Pelt, Tamise. "The Question Concerning Theory: Humanism, Subjectivity, and Computing." *Computers and the Humanities* 36.3 (Aug. 2002): 307–18.

Vatz, Richard. "The Myth of the Rhetorical Situation." Rpt. in *Rhetoric: Concepts, Definitions, Boundaries.* Ed. W. Covino and D. Jolliffe. Boston: Allyn and Bacon, 1995. 461–67.

Villanueva, Victor. Afterword. *Grading in the Post-Process Classroom.* Ed. L. Allison, L. Bryant, and M. Hourigan. Portsmouth, NH: Boynton/Cook, 1997.

Vitalisms: From Haller to the Cell Theory: Proceedings of the Zaragoza Symposium, XIXth International Congress of History of Science, 22–29 August 1993. 19th International Congress on the History of Sciences, Zaragoza, Spain. Florence, Italy: L. S. Olschki, 1997.

Vitanza, Victor J. "An After/word: Preparing to Meet the Faces that 'We' Will Have Met." *Writing Histories of Rhetoric.* Carbondale: Southern Illinois UP, 1994. 217–57.

———. "Critical Sub/Versions of the History of Philosophical Rhetoric." *Rhetoric Review* 6.1 (fall 1987): 41–66.

———. "From Heuristic to Aleatory Procedures; or, Towards 'Writing the Accident.'" *Inventing a Discipline: Rhetoric Scholarship in Honor of Richard E. Young.* Ed. Maureen Daly Goggin. Urbana, IL: NCTE, 2000. 185–206.

———. "Historiographies of Rhetoric." *The Encyclopedia of Rhetoric and Composition: Communication from Ancient Times to the Information Age.* Ed. Theresa Enos. New York: Garland, 1996.

———. *Negation, Subjectivity, and the History of Rhetoric.* Albany: State U of New York P, 1997.

———. "Notes toward Historiographies of Rhetorics; or, Rhetorics of the Histories of Rhetorics: Traditional, Revisionary, and Sub/Versive." *Pre/Text* 8.1–2 (1987): 63–125.

———. "'Some More' Notes: Toward a Third Sophistic." *Argumentation* 5 (1991): 117–39.

———. "Three Countertheses: Or, a Critical In(ter)vention into Composition Theories and Pedagogies." *Contending with Words: Composition and Rhetoric in a Postmodern Age.* Ed. Patricia Harkin and John Schilb. New York: MLA, 1991. 139–72.

———. "Writing the Paradigm." Rev. of *Heuretics: The Logic of Invention,* by Greg Ulmer. *Electronic Book Review* 2 (winter 1996). http://www.altx.com/ebr/ebr2/r2vitanza.htm.

Vitanza, Victor J., ed. *Pre/Text: The First Decade.* Pittsburgh, PA: U of Pittsburgh P, 1993.

Vitanza, Victor J., et al. "The Politics of Historiography." *Rhetoric Review* 7.1 (1988): 5–49.

Watson, Sam. "Breakfast in the Tacit Tradition." *Pre/Text* 2 (1981): 9–31.

Weidner, Hal Rivers. "Three Models of Rhetoric: Traditional, Mechanical and Vital." Diss. University of Michigan, 1975.

Weinstein, Michael A. *Structure of Human Life: A Vitalist Ontology.* New York: New York UP, 1979.

Weiss, Paul. *Morphodynamik.* Berlin: Gebrüder Borntraeger, 1926.

White, E. C. *Kaironomia: On the Will-to-Invent.* Ithaca, NY: Cornell UP, 1987.

White, Hayden. *Tropics of Discourse: Essays in Cultural Criticism.* Baltimore, MD: Johns Hopkins UP, 1978.

Wiener, Norbert. *Cybernetics: Or Control and Communication in the Animal and the Machine.* New York: Wiley and Sons, 1948.

———. *What Is Life?: A Study of Vitalism and Neo-Vitalism.* St. Louis, MO: B. Herder, 1908.

Winterowd, W. Ross. *Contemporary Rhetoric: A Conceptual Background with Readings.* New York: Harcourt, 1975.

———. *The English Department: A Personal and Institutional History.* Carbondale: Southern Illinois UP, 1998.

Wisneski, Craig, et al. "Ambient Displays: Turning Architectural Space into an Interface between People and Digital Information." *Proceedings of the First International Workshop on Cooperative Buildings.* London: Springer, 1998. 22–32.

Wolfe, Cary. *Critical Environments: Postmodern Theory and the Pragmatics of the "Outside."* Minneapolis: U of Minnesota P, 1998.

Wordsworth, Jonathan. "The Infinite I AM: Coleridge and the Ascent of Being." *Coleridge's Imagination.* Ed. R. Gravil et al. Cambridge: Cambridge UP, 1985. n.p.

Worsham, Lynn. "Eating History, Purging Memory, Killing Rhetoric." *Writing Histories of Rhetoric.* Ed. V. J. Vitanza. Carbondale: Southern Illinois UP, 1994. 139–55.

———. "The Question Concerning Invention: Hermeneutics and the Genesis of Writing." *Pre/Text* 8 (1987): 197–244.

Yarbrough, Stephen. *After Rhetoric: The Study of Discourse Beyond Language and Culture.* Carbondale: Southern Illinois UP, 1999.

Young, Richard. "Arts, Crafts, Gifts, and Knacks: Some Disharmonies in the New Rhetoric." *Reinventing the Rhetorical Tradition.* Ed. Aviva Freedman and Ian Pringle. Conway, AR: Published for the Canadian Council of Teachers of English by L&S Books, 1980. 53–60.

———. "Invention: A Topographical Survey." *Teaching Composition: Ten Bibliographic Essays.* Ed. Gary Tate. Fort Worth: Texas Christian UP, 1976. 1–44.

———. "Paradigms and Problems: Needed Research in Rhetorical Invention." *Research and Composing: Points of Departure.* Ed. Charles R. Cooper and Lee Odell. Urbana, IL: NCTE, 1978. 29–47.

Young, Richard, Alton Becker, and Kenneth Pike. *Rhetoric: Discovery and Change.* New York: Harcourt Brace, 1970.

Young, Richard, and Yameng Liu. Introduction. *Landmark Essays on Rhetorical Invention in Writing.* Ed. R Young and Y. Liu. Davis, CA: Hermagoras Press, 1994. xi–xxiii.

INDEX

Aarseth, Espen, 175
Abercrombie, Nicholas, 83
Abrams, M. H., 22, 54, 58
abstract machines, 202, 203
accident, 106, 148, 157, 255
actuality, 124–25, 163, 165, 282n15
Adams, John Quincy, 64
Adobe Photoshop, 253
Adanson, Michel, 130
Adorno, T. W., 76
affect: 41, 118–19; 255, 269–70; Internet and, 242–44; language and, 189–90; Ulmer and, 237, 239
Against Method (Feyerabend), 110–11
agency, 138, 277n11
alchemy, 128–29
Allison, Libby, 220
Althusser, Louis, 81, 196
ambience, 177–78
American Critical Idealism, 68
analogy, arguments from, 143
analysis, 113
Anderson, Virginia, 13
animism, 129
Applied Grammatology (Ulmer), 234–36
archaeology, Foucauldian, 266–67, 298n5
Arendt, Hannah, 195, 204
argument, Aristotle and, 126–27
Aristotelian epistemology, 55–56, 58
Aristotle, 6, 9, 19, 29, 60, 263; on art versus knack, 27, 28; and current-traditional rhetoric, 15, 24, 38, 55–56; and ethos, 187–88; and heuristics, 252; and pedagogy, 52; and prime mover, 151; role of, in rhetoric and composition discipline, 122–27
Armstrong, Aurelia, 119
arrangement, talent and, 43
art: body and, 105; Coleridge on, 47–48; as gift, 43–44; Heidegger on, 174; method and, 47–48, 105; methodism and, 32; mind and, 31–32; nature and, 125–26; as technê, 27–28, 43–44, 167–68; as

unique, 30; Young's definition of, 26. *See also* poetry; technê
articulation, pedagogy of, 216–17
artificial intelligence, 152
artificial life, 152–57
"Arts, Crafts, Gifts, and Knacks" (Young), 7–8, 12, 25–29, 35–38, 40, 249
assemblage, 201–3, 205
associationism, 99
astrology, 127, 129
Atwill, Janet, 39–40, 250–51
audience-based approaches, 94
Aydelotte, Frank, 68
Azyr, Félix Vicq d', 133

Bacon, Francis, 29–30, 45, 73, 102, 107, 130
Ball, Lucille, 242–43
Barfield, Owen, 73, 99
Barilli, Renato, 170
Barthes, Roland, 194, 195, 237, 271
Barthez, Paul Joseph, 131
Bartholomae, David, 13
Barzun, Jacques, 20, 89
Bassett, Sharon, 21
Baudrillard, Jean, 181, 197, 271
Baumlin, James, 187
Becker, Alton, 21, 36, 246
Bedau, Mark, 157
Bedford Bibliography for Teachers of Writing, The, 38
Beer, John, 95
Bergson, Henri, 6, 9, 96, 113–15, 120, 136, 147–51, 158, 164
Berlin, Isaiah, 5, 33
Berlin, James A., 2–3, 6, 7–10, 12, 18, 21, 34, 48, 49–88, 91, 96–98, 104, 111–15, 119–21, 166, 195–97, 201, 204–5, 211–16, 233, 244–46, 256, 259, 273, 275n3, 286n6; characteristics of work of, 50; "Contemporary Composition," 54, 57, 62, 209; "Current-Traditional Rhetoric," 50–51; "Freirean Pedagogy in the U.S.," 79; "Postmodernism, Politics, and Histories of

Berlin, James A. *(continued)*,
Rhetoric," 83; "Revisionary History," 73–76; "Rhetoric and Ideology in the Writing Class," 77, 81; *Rhetoric and Reality*, 60, 65–72, 75, 209; "The Rhetoric of Romanticism," 7, 8, 12, 52–53, 56–57, 73, 212; *Rhetorics, Poetics, and Cultures*, 119, 195, 203, 212; "Richard Whately and Current-Traditional Rhetoric," 50–52; *Writing Instruction in Nineteenth-Century American Colleges*, 59–65, 71, 73
Bernard, Claude, 137
Berndtson, Arthur, 20
Bertalanffy, Ludwig von, 139–40
Berthoff, Ann, 2, 16–18, 21, 36–37, 39, 57, 59, 65, 108, 278n1
Beyond Hegel and Dialectic (Desmond), 74
Bichat, Marie-François-Xavier, 131
Biesecker, Barbara, 182–83
Bigelow, Julian, 152
Bildersee, Adele, 69
Biographia Literaria (Coleridge), 97, 100
biology, 132–34
Bitzer, Lloyd, 182
Bizzell, Patricia, 87
Blair, Hugh, 30, 49, 51–52, 53, 60, 63–67, 71
Blanchard, Margaret, 70
bliss-sense, 237
Bloom, Lynn, 90, 92
Blumenbach, Johann Friedrich, 131
Boden, Margaret, 156, 157
body: affect and, 189–90; art and, 105; and environment, 178; ethics and, 189; Heidegger and, 173; ideology and, 83; knowledge and, 113–19, 149; method and, 104–5; pedagogy and, 119–20; situation and invention mediated by, 120; the virtual and, 117–19; without organs, 161–62
Bohr, Niels, 139
Bonnet, Charles, 132
book, Deleuze-Guattari concept of, 199–200
Bordeu, Théophile de, 131
Braddock, Richard, 91
Brahminical romanticism, 67–68
breaks, Deleuze-Guattari concept of, 159–61
Britton, James, 40, 88
Brooks, Kevin, 247
Bryant, Lizbeth, 220

Buck, Gertrude, 72
Buffon, Georges-Louis Leclerc de, 131, 137
Burke, Kenneth, 14–15, 125, 163, 271
Burton, Gideon, 3
Burwick, Frederick, 136
Butler, Samuel, 162–63

Camera Lucida (Barthes), 237
Campbell, George, 19, 30, 51–52, 60, 65
capitalism, 196
casuistic stretching, 271–72
categorization, 273–74
CATTt (Contrast, Analogy, Theory, Target, and tale), 240
causes. *See* four causes
CCCC. *See* Conference on College Composition and Communication
cell theory, 137–38
cellular automata, 153–56
chance, 2, 48, 52, 148, 184–85, 212–16, 226–29, 283n3
change: Berlin and, 58–59, 62, 71, 76–84; biological, 137–38; complexity and, 154–58, 165, 183, 192–93; Kameen and, 224–29, 232, 234; polarity and, 181; Sirc and, 216–17
Channell, David, 125, 128–29, 135, 282n12
chaos, 17, 36, 148, 155, 180, 184–85
Chora (Derrida), 238
chorography, 239–42, 246–48
Christensen, Francis, 37
Classic, Romantic, Modern (Barzun), 20
Classical episteme, 131–32
classical rhetoric, 60, 112
cleverness, 43–44
Close, Chuck, 192
cognitive mapping, 195–97, 199, 203, 296
"Coleridge: On Method" (Kameen), 96, 99, 278n1
Coleridge, Samuel T.: on art, 47–48; Berlin on, 49–53, 57, 68, 71, 96–98, 212, 213; *Biographia Literaria*, 97, 100; complexity of, 95–96; dialectical method of, 53, 57, 72–73, 99–100, 102–3; "Essays on the Principles of Method," 42; and forethoughtful query, 102–3; and genius, 32–34, 41–44; "Genius, Talent, Sense, and Cleverness," 42–43; and German philosophy, 141–42, 281n4, 281n6; and idealism, 95–96, 281n5, 281n6; on imag-

ination, 32, 53, 96–104; Kameen on, 96–
97, 103, 121, 194; on life force, 142–45,
281n4; method of, 17–19, 30–34, 42, 44–
48, 50, 93–96, 104–7, 212, 233 (*see also*
dialectical method of); "On the Origin
and Progress of the Sect of Sophists in
Greece," 44–45; on Plato and Shakespeare, 232; on poetry, 47–48, 53; and
polarity, 97–100, 106–7, 141–42, 144–45;
and rhetoric, 48, 53, 94; role of, in rhetoric and composition discipline, 7–9,
33–34, 41–44, 48, 120–21; and science, 5,
47; and Spinoza, 281n5; "Theory of
Life," 142, 281n4, 281n6; "Treatise on
Method," 45, 106; and vitalism/roman-
ticism, 1, 5, 18–20, 28–30, 33, 94, 120,
142–46, 265, 281n6
Coles, William (Bill), 21, 27, 56–57, 65, 71,
86, 250
College Composition and Communication
(journal), 13
commonsense epistemology, 51–52, 61
communication, 221–22, 253, 286n12
communications triangle, 50–51, 54–55, 58,
112–13, 205–6, 221–24
community, 204
complex adaptive systems, 169, 183, 187, 189
complex systems, 6, 154, 157–58, 163–64,
169–70; behavior in, 155–56
complex vitalism, 6, 122, 136, 139–40, 179–
80, 203–4, 229–30, 273–74 ; in humanities, 158–63; in sciences, 152–57
complexity theory, 155–56; chaos theory
versus, 184; Deleuze-Guattari and, 162;
and invention, 206; rhetoric and, 180–
85, 194
composition: literature and, 69; philosophies of, 54; versus rhetoric, 31. *See also*
rhetoric and composition discipline
Composition as a Human Science (Phelps),
108
Composition in Four Keys (Phelps, Wiley,
and Gleason), 91–92
Composition in the University (Crowley),
217–18
Composition-Rhetoric (Connors), 89
computers, and artificial life, 152–57. *See
also* digital technology; digital, the
Conceptual Theory of Rhetoric, A
(D'Angelo), 17–18

conduction, 248
Conference on College Composition and
Communication (CCCC), 13–14
Connected (Shaviro), 204
Connors, Robert, 89–90, 92, 259
"Contemporary Composition" (Berlin),
54, 57, 62, 209
Contemporary Writer, The (Winterowd), 62
context: ecology and, 223; pedagogical use
of, 249–58
Conway, John, 154
Cooper, Lane, 68
Cooper, Marilyn, 223–24
Copernicus, 129
Corpus Hermeticum, 128
Correspondences (journal), 278n1
Corson, Hiram, 68
counter-history: 260, 289n5, 289n6; meth-
ods and, 259–74
counter-method, 107–12
craft, 26
creative writing, 69
creativity, 16–17
Crisis in Modernism, The (Burwick and
Douglass), 136
Croce, Benedetto, 30, 69
Crowley, Sharon, 30–31, 38, 44, 61, 84, 217–
19, 259
cultural studies, 59, 79, 245, 246
Cultural Studies in the English Classroom
(Berlin and Vivion), 79
current-traditional rhetoric: Aristotle and,
15, 24, 38, 55–56; Berlin and, 49–52, 54;
category of, 275n2; characteristics of,
14; epistemology of, 112; Fogarty on,
14–15; institutionalism and, 84; new
rhetoric versus, 25–26; as pedagogy,
35–36; romanticism and, 31–32, 35; vitalism and, 8, 22–23; Young on, 22–27
"Current-Traditional Rhetoric" (Berlin
and Inkster), 50–51
Cuvier, Georges, 134
cybernetics, 152–53
Cybernetics (Wiener), 152
cynicism, 79–80

D'Angelo, Frank, 7, 16, 17–18, 21, 23, 25, 93
Darwin, Charles, 137
Davis, Diane, 179–80, 255, 259–60, 270–71,
286n12

Davy, Humphry, 47
De Man, Paul, 198
Debord, Guy, 197
decomposition: Coleridge and, 145; Deleuze and, 245; Derrida and, 235–37; ethics and, 256–58; life and, 136; pedagogy and, 246
Deemer, Charles, 70, 250
Deleuze, Gilles, 6, 9, 96, 112, 115, 116, 120, 141, 158–65, 179, 181, 189, 198–203, 205, 233, 245, 255–56, 268–70, 274
delivery: cleverness and, 43
Democritus, 127
Derricote, Toi, 226, 227
Derrida, Jacques, 112, 182, 235, 237–40, 279n12
Descartes, René, 29–30, 38, 44, 107, 114, 248
desire: Berlin and, 57, 79–80, 84, 115, 215, 246; Bergson and, 149–51, 153; Deleuze and, 159–65; Kameen and, 234; pedagogy and, 216–19, 249, 252, 255, 257–58; vitalism and, 5–6, 114, Young and, 41; Ulmer and, 237, 243–44, 246, 248
desiring-machines, 159–65, 202, 245
Desmond, William, 74
Detroit, I Do Mind Dying, 197–98
Dewey, John, 71
diagrams, 202–3, 245
dialectical method: Adorno and, 76; Berlin and, 50, 53, 57, 72–76, 112–13, 198, 212; Coleridge and, 53, 57, 72–73, 102–3; Emerson and, 64; Hegelian, 50, 74–75, 99, 279n12; imagination and, 99–100; Marxist, 50; Platonic, 57; post-, 112, 113, 201–2, 230, 235; Ricoeur and, 108
Diderot, Denis, 131, 132
différance, 182
digital technology: impact of, 7, 207–8; nature of, 171; posthumanism and, 175
digital, the, 118. *See also* computers
discipline, definition of, 275n1
dissoi logoi, 10, 109, 111, 180–81, 184
distributed vitality, 178–79, 190–91, 193–94, 199, 203
Dobrin, Sidney, 222–24
Douglass, Paul, 136
Doyle, Richard, 178–79
Driesch, Hans, 6, 136, 138
Duchamp, Marcel, 249–50
dwelling, 229–30, 233

ecocomposition, 222–24
Ecocomposition (Dobrin and Weisser), 224
ecology: Aristotle and, 125–26; Coleridge and, 146; Deleuze-Guattari and, 160, 163–66, 200; pedagogy and, 193, 222–34, 249–58; techné and, 169, 176; technology and, 170–75
Ede, Lisa, 21
Einstein, Albert, 139, 164
Eisenman, Peter, 238–40
Elbow, Peter, 62, 65, 71, 88
electromagnetic force, 136–37
EmerAgency, 241–44
emergence: complexity and, 156, 165, 176–77, 184–85, 190, 206; Deleuze-Guattari and, 201, 203; Foucault and, 265–67; invention and, 240, 249; pedagogy and, 225, 228, 232, 255,
Emerson, Ralph Waldo, 32, 56, 57, 59–66, 68, 71
emotion, 190
"Encomium on Helen" (Gorgias), 181
Encyclopedia of Rhetoric and Composition (Burton), 3
English Composition as a Happening (Sirc), 249–50
English Department, The (Winterowd), 3, 31
Enlightenment, 5
Enos, Richard, 21, 39, 191, 252
entelechy, 123–26, 129–30, 138, 146, 151, 163–64, 168, 170, 219, 255, 282n14
Epicurus, 127
epistemology: Berlin and, 55–58, 112–15; beyond Berlin, 112–116; commonsense, 51–52; Deleuze and, 203–5; Kameen and, 101–3. *See also* knowledge
"Essays on the Principles of Method" (Coleridge), 42
ethics: body and, 189, 255; pedagogy and, 256–58; and relations, 255–57
ethos, 187–89
Ethos (Baumlin), 187
evolution: invention and, 193–94; investigative vitalism and, 137–38; self-organization and, 157; terminology of, 284n17
exploration, writing as, 106
expressionism, 158, 200–201, 233, 276n2
expressivism, 2, 7, 35–36, 54, 56, 58, 65–72, 88–89, 112, 158, 276n2

Faigley, Lester, 87
false consciousness, 78–79
fancy, 32, 99–100
Faraday, Michael, 137
Farther Along (Ronald and Roskelly), 87
feedback, 117–18, 140, 152–53, 156–58, 161, 183–84, 187
Feyerabend, Paul, 110–11, 123
Ficino, Marsilio, 128–29
Fiedler, Leslie, 70
field, definition of, 275n1
field theory, 139
Fish, Stanley, 40
Fishman, Stephen, 88–89, 92
Florescu, Vasile, 29–30, 38
Flower, Linda, 21, 94
Fogarty, Daniel, 14–16, 21–22, 24, 29, 38, 45, 50–52, 55, 85, 89, 275n2, 275n3, 275n4
force: Harmon and, 173; Heidegger and, 174–76; historical, 82–84; polarity and, 57, 97–98, 106–9, 181, 186; sciences and, 133–51; vitalism and, 5–6, 157, 162–65, 179; *See also* polarity; "two forces, one power"
forestructure, 228, 230
forethoughtful query, 102–3
formalist approaches, 93
Foucault, Michel, 6, 81, 112, 130–35, 140–41, 146, 179, 187–88, 245, 265–67, 271, 274, 277n12, 278n13
four causes, 124–26, 138, 142–44, 147–49, 163–64, 168, 176
"Four Philosophies of Composition" (Fulkerson), 54
Fractenberg, David, 21
Frankfurt School, 78
Freire, Paulo, 78, 209, 223
"Freirean Pedagogy in the U.S." (Berlin), 79
Freud, Sigmund, 66–68, 159, 160, 162, 248
Frye, Northrup, 21
Fulkerson, Richard, 54–56, 58, 62, 80
Fulwiler, Toby, 231

Gadamer, Hans-Georg, 222
Game of Life, 154
General Semanticists, 14–15
general systems theory, 139–40
General System Theory (von Bertalanffy), 140
genius: Berlin and, 49–51, 56, 66–67;
Coleridge and, 32–34, 41–44; education and, 42, 46; invention and, 43, 51–52
"Genius, Talent, Sense, and Cleverness" (Coleridge), 42–43
Genung, John, 26, 51, 52
Gere, Anne Ruggles, 90
Gibson, Walker, 71
gift, 26–27, 34–35, 42–44, 63–64, 67, 94–95. *See also* talent
Gilbert, Allan, 69
Gilbert, William, 129
Gilles Deleuze (Marks), 119
Giroux, Henry, 210
Glas (Derrida), 182, 235
Gleason, Barbara, 91–92
Glenn, Cheryl, 232
God, 281n5, 281n6
Gorgias, 109, 181, 271
Gradin, Sherrie, 89, 92, 278n5
Grading in the Post-Process Classroom (Allison, Bryant, and Hourigan), 220
Great Chain of Being, The (Lovejoy), 263
grids, 191–92
Grossberg, Lawrence, 216
Guattari, Felix, 158–65, 179, 181, 198–203, 205, 245, 268–70
Guerrilla Metaphysics (Harman), 173

Habermas, Jürgen, 92–93
Hamann, Johann Georg, 5
Hamilton, Leo, 70
happenings, 249–50
Hardin, Joe Marshall, 211
Harkin, Patricia, 215
Harman, Graham, 173, 178, 253
Hartley, David, 99
Harvard plan, 67
Harvey, David, 195, 198
Harvey, William, 131
Hatch, James, 70
Hatchet, Charles, 47
Hawhee, Debra, 181
Hayakawa, S. I., 70
Hayes, Dick, 21
Hayles, N. Katherine, 6, 169, 175, 177, 206, 249–51
Haynes, Cynthia, 251
Hegel, G. W. F., 20, 30, 50, 74–75, 99, 279n12
Heidegger, Martin, 6, 9, 10, 158, 167, 171–79, 228, 229–30, 232, 252, 253

Heisenberg, Werner, 139
Henry, Jim, 251–52
Heraclitus, 184, 186
Herder, Johann Gottfried, 88–89, 189
hermeneutics, 221–22
Hermeticism, 128–29
heterogeneity, 185
Heuretics (Ulmer), 238–41
Heuristic Research (Moustakas), 115
heuristics: Aristotle and, 252; art and, 16–
    17; chance and, 2; complex vitalist ap-
    proach to, 254; controversies over, 2–3,
    16–17; intuition and, 115; invention
    and, 37–38, 191; method and, 120; na-
    ture of, 28; problem solving and, 16–17.
    See also method
high technê, 174–75
High Technê (Rutsky), 170–71
Hill, A. S., 51, 52
Hill, Stephen, 83
historiography: antiquarian, 261; Berlin
    and, 73–76; categorization and, 273–74;
    critical, 261–62; Deleuze and Guattari
    and, 268–70; Foucault and, 265–67;
    Lovejoy and, 262–65, 289n4; monu-
    mental, 260–62; names and dates in,
    268–70; Nietzsche and, 260–62, 288n2;
    philosophy and, 264; revisionary, 259–
    60; rhetorical, 261–63, 265, 274, 289n4;
    sub/versive, 259–60, 270–73, 288n1; tra-
    ditional, 265–66
history, Berlin and, 81–85
Hitler, Adolf, 195
Holland, John, 155
Hourigan, Maureen, 220
Hughes, Richard, 123, 126
humanities, complex vitalism in, 158–63
Hume, David, 31
hypertext, 223, 238, 240, 241, 247

idealism, 95–96, 281n5, 281n6
ideology, 77, 82, 196
*Ideology of Power and the Power of Ideol-
    ogy, The* (Therborn), 77, 81
imagination: Coleridge on, 32, 53, 96–104;
    dialectics and, 99–100; invention and,
    100–104; primary, 32, 53, 97–98, 100;
    secondary, 32, 53, 98–100, 104
In Defense of the Accidental (Marquard), 255
incorporeal transformations, 269–70

individualism: romanticism and, 30, 88;
    vitalism and, 20
individuation, principle of, 144
information, 153–55
Inkster, Robert, 21, 50–51
instinct, 44, 104–6, 114, 149
institutions: impact of, on pedagogy, 84,
    210–11, 218, 220; Ulmer and, 241–44
instrumentalism, 172–73
intelligence, 114, 117
interdisciplinarity, 264
Internet, 118, 207, 238, 241–42
Internet Invention (Ulmer), 241–44
intuition, 43, 102–7, 110, 113–16, 120, 149,
    279n11, 285n2
Inventing a Discipline (Enos), 39
invention: Berlin and, 246; communica-
    tion versus, 253; complexity theory
    and, 206; conceptualization of, 39–41;
    current-traditional rhetoric and, 22–
    24; and evolution, 193–94; genius and,
    43, 51–52; heuristics and, 37–38, 191;
    imagination and, 100–104; method
    and, 13; nature of, 2; and potentiality/
    possibility, 117; strategies for, 37; teach-
    ability of, 2, 18, 22–24, 26–27, 35, 37–38;
    Ulmer and, 238–39, 242, 246; vitalism
    and, 22–23, 25
investigative vitalism, 6, 122, 137–38, 146–51

James, William, 71
Jameson, Fredric, 196–97, 201, 203–5, 212,
    234, 241, 256
Jarratt, Susan, 273
Jay, Martin, 195, 204
Johnson, Calvin, 69
Johnson, Robert, 245
Johnstone, Henry, 21
Joyce, Michael, 247
Judy, Stephen, 65, 94
Jussieu, Antoine-Laurent de, 133

Kahn-Egan, Seth, 216
Kaironomia (White), 109, 184
kairos, 109, 183–85
Kameen, Paul, 1–2, 4, 6–10, 13, 19, 34, 48,
    86, 93–104, 106–8, 120–21, 167, 192,
    194, 208, 215, 224–34, 257–58, 287n15;
    "Coleridge: On Method," 96, 99, 278n1;
    "Rewording the Rhetoric of Composi-

tion," 7, 13, 93, 96, 100–104, 108, 229, 233, 278n1, 279n7; *Writing/Teaching*, 224–29, 233, 258

Kant, Immanuel, 30, 97, 141–42

Kelly, Lou, 70

Kennedy, George, 3–4

Kent, Thomas, 193, 221–22, 286n12

Kepler, Johannes, 129

Kerferd, G. B., 185–86

key terms, 262–63

Kinneavy, James, 21, 50, 54, 228

Kitzhaber, Albert, 22, 259, 275n2

Klee, Paul, 17

knack, 26–27

Kneupper, Charles, 21

Knoblauch, C. H., 210

knowledge: body and, 113–19, 149; in rhetorical epistemologies, 112. *See also* epistemology

Kuhn, Thomas, 22

Lacan, Jacques, 160

Lamarck, Jean-Baptiste, 133, 137

Landmark Essays on Rhetorical Invention in Writing (Young and Liu), 37, 40

Landow, George, 259

Langer, Susanne, 91, 103

Langton, Christopher, 154–55

language: affect and, 189–90; body's experience and, 114; functional versus representational character of, 200–201; imagination and, 101; phenomenological ground of, 232; and subjectivity, 119

Language and Learning (Britton), 88

Lauer, Janice, 2, 7, 16–18, 21–22, 36–37, 39–40, 191, 243, 252

law, 105, 248

Lawrence, William, 142, 143

Leclerc, Georges-Louis, 137

Leibniz, Gottfried Wilhelm, 141

liberal culture, 67–68

life: Aristotelian traits of, 163; artificial, 152–57; Bergson on, 149–50; Coleridge on, 142–45, 281n4; complex character of, 5; complexity theory and, 156; generative character of, 5; nineteenth-century views of, 6; as self-organization, 157; vitalism and, 4–5

lines of flight, 164, 170, 219, 229, 233–34, 235, 244, 245–46, 252, 255, 282n14

linking, 255–57

Linnaeus, Carolus, 131, 132

listening, 230–34, 257

Liu, Yameng, 37–38

Livingston, Ira, 203–4

Lloyd-Jones, Richard, 91

Locke, John, 31

logos, 185–87

Lovejoy, Arthur, 33, 34, 262–65, 274, 289n4

Lutz, William, 70, 250

Lynch, Kevin, 196

Lyotard, Jean-François, 198, 222, 272

machinic assemblage, 201–3

machines, Deleuze-Guattari model of, 159–65, 199, 202–3

Macrorie, Ken, 65, 70

magnetism, 129

Maillet, Benoît de, 132

mandarin romanticism, 68

manifold assignment, 172

mapping: as assemblage, 201; cognitive mapping, 196–97; local-global, 195–98, 201, 205, 213, 245; as methodology, 203–6; micro-, 198–99

marginalization, 4, 244

Marks, John, 119

Marquard, Odo, 255

Marxism, 50

Massumi, Brian, 116–19, 190, 238, 247

mathematical order, 148

McCarthy, Lucille, 88–89, 92

McCrimmon, James, 13

McCulloch, Warren, 152

McLuhan, Marshall, 171

mechanism, 131–35, 139, 147, 162

media culture, 236–38

Melville, Herman, 17

memory, 149, 239

metaphor: Coleridge and, 98–99; understanding and, 63–67

method: art and, 47–48, 105; Coleridge and, 17–19, 30–34, 42, 44–48, 50, 93–96, 104–7, 212, 233; complex vitalist, 254; counter-, 107–12; definitions of, 44–45; Greek meaning of, 45; heuristics and, 120; intuition and, 104–7; Kameen and, 120, 224–29; mapping and, 203–6; mentalism and, 31; process versus, 215; in science, 110–11; Ulmer and, 248;

method *(continued)*:
  vitalism and, 22–23, 25. *See also* dialec-
  tical method; heuristics
Methodical Memory, The (Crowley), 30, 44
methodism, 31–32
micro-mapping, 198–99
Miller, Carolyn, 184, 185
Miller, James, 27, 65, 94
Millonas, Mark, 156
mind, 31–32
Mirror and the Lamp, The (Abrams), 54
modernism, vitalism and, 130–35
molar level, 161, 164–65, 245
molecular level, 161, 164–65, 245
Moment of Complexity, The (Taylor), 169,
  181
Morphodynamik (Weiss), 139
Morris, Richard, 214, 244
Moustakas, Clark, 115–16
Murphy, Michael, 84
Murray, Donald, 71
Murray, John, 47
MySpace, 243
mysticism, 5–6, 8, 127–30
mystory, 234, 236–39, 245, 248
Mythologies (Barthes), 195

naive vitalism, 136, 281n3
nature: art and, 125–26; romanticism and,
  33; as technê, 176
Naturphilosophie, 141–42, 144–45, 281n4,
  281n6
Needham, John Turberville, 137
*Negation, Subjectivity, and the History of
  Rhetoric* (Vitanza), 186, 271–73
NEH seminar, 21–22, 49, 86
Nelson, William, 21
neo-Platonic epistemology, 55–56, 58
Neo-Platonism, 129
network logic, 186–87
new classicism, 25–27
New Criticism, 69
New Humanism, 68
new rhetoric, 3–4, 14–15, 25–27, 35, 55–59,
  65, 275n3
New Rhetoric, The (Perelman and
  Olbrechts-Tyteca), 15
new romanticism, 17–18, 25–28
Newton, Isaac, 136
Nietzsche, Friedrich, 98, 146–47, 158, 179,
  259, 260–62, 274, 279n11

nonplaces, 204
North, Stephen, 87, 90–91, 92

objective theories, 65–66
occasions, pedagogical, 27, 108, 168, 249–50,
  258
Oersted, Hans Christian, 137
Ohmann, Richard, 21
Olbrechts-Tyteca, L., 15
"On the Origin and Progress of the Sect of
  Sophists in Greece" (Coleridge), 44–45
Ong, Walter, 44
oppositional vitalism, 5–6, 122, 136–37,
  141–46
order, 148
order-words, 269
Osgood, Charles, 67–68

Palmer, Glenn, 67
Parables for the Virtual (Massumi), 116
paradigms, 22
"Paradigms and Problems" (Young),
  22–25
paralogy, 222
pathos, 189
patrician romanticism, 68
pattern, 169
pedagogy, 207–58; Berlin and, 79–81, 119–20,
  195–98, 209, 211–16, 233, 256, 286n6;
  body and, 119–20; and change, 81–83,
  212–16, 226–29; complex vitalist, 257–58;
  and context, 249–58; desire and, 216–19;
  digital technology and, 207–8; ecology
  and, 222–34; ethics and, 256–58; expressivism and, 68, 277n7; Freire and, 209–
  10; institutional impact on, 210–11, 218,
  220; Kameen and, 224–34, 257–58,
  287n15; listening and, 230–34; of 1950s–
  1970s, 69–70; open-ended, 224–34; and
  the personal, 227, 229, 231; philosophies
  of composition and, 54–55; and politics,
  59, 70, 78; posthuman, 255; posthumanist, 258; post-process, 219–24; pre-
  strategy and, 208; process pedagogy,
  208–9; reification in, 208–11; resistance
  to, 214–15, 244; social-epistemic, 78–81;
  technology and, 247; Ulmer and, 234–
  48; Whately and, 51–52; Young and,
  35–38. *See also* invention: teachability of
Pedagogy for Liberation, A (Freire and
  Shor), 210

Pedagogy of the Oppressed (Freire), 209
Pepper, Stephen, 21
perception, 114, 116–17, 143
Perelman, C. H., 15
Perry, Seamus, 95
Personal Knowledge (Polanyi), 116
personality, 81–82
Perspectives on Rhetorical Invention
   (Atwill), 39, 276n8
Petraglia, Joseph, 168, 170
Phaedrus (Plato), 63
Phelps, Louise Wetherbee, 91–92, 108, 111,
   206
Phelps, William, 68
philosophy: historiography and, 264; and
   rhetoric, 19
Physiocrats, 130
Pike, Kenneth, 36, 246
Pitts, Walter, 152
place, 204, 239–40
Plato, 47, 238, 248, 263; and concepts, 242;
   and dialectic, 45, 57, 73; dual reading
   of, 63, 70; and ethos, 187; and expressivism, 56, 58, 65, 66, 114, 232; and
   forms, 151; and truth, 107
Plotinus, 263
pneuma, 127
poetry, Coleridge on, 47–48, 53
Polanyi, Michael, 115–16, 120, 178
polarity, 97–100, 106–7, 141–42, 144–45, 181,
   184, 285n22; *See also* force; "two forces,
   one power"
politics: pedagogy and, 59, 70; rhetoric
   and, 77–81; in rhetoric and composition discipline, 39, 57–60; writer's role
   and, 58–59
Politics of Education, The (Freire), 210
Pollock, Jackson, 249
popcycle, 239
positivist epistemology, 55–56, 58
possibility: invention and, 117; potentiality
   versus, 282n15
post-consciousness, 178
post-dialectical approach, 112, 113, 201–2,
   230, 235
posthumanism: Deleuze-Guattari model
   of, 158–59; and distributed cognitive
   environments, 177; and pedagogy, 255,
   258; subjectivity and, 141; technology
   and, 169–70, 175–80
postmodernism, 140, 197, 204

"Postmodernism, Politics, and Histories
   of Rhetoric" (Berlin), 83
post-process pedagogy, 219–24
Post-Process Theory (Kent), 193, 221–22
potentiality: Aristotle and, 124–25; invention and, 117, 247; possibility versus,
   282n15
Poulakos, John, 180, 261
Practical Elements of Rhetoric, The (Genung), 51
pragmatics, Deleuze-Guattari concept of,
   202–3
praxis pedagogy, 216
Pre/Text (journal), 278n1
prima materia, 128
primary imagination, 32, 53, 97–98, 100
principle of individuation, 144
Principles of Rhetoric, The (Hill), 51
privilege, 244–45
problem solving, 16–17, 94, 192, 209–10,
   243
process, method versus, 215
process movement, 208–9
process pedagogy, 208–9
process theory, 193
Prodicus, 180
professional writing, 251–52
progressivism, 79, 84
Protagoras, 180
psyche, 127
psychological-epistemological rhetoric,
   60, 64
psychology, composition instruction and,
   16–17, 36
puncept, 235
punctum, 237
Pythagoras, 129

Ramus, Peter, 31
randomness, 169
Ray, Roberta, 63
read-arounds, 225–31
relations of law, 105
relations of theory, 105
Renaissance, vitalism in, 128–29
representation, language-world, 200–201
Research in Written Composition (Braddock, Lloyd-Jones, and Schoer), 91
retreat and return, narrative of, 14, 15, 20,
   29, 34, 41
"Revisionary History" (Berlin), 73–76

"Rewording the Rhetoric of Composition" (Kameen), 7, 13, 93, 96, 100–104, 108, 229, 233, 278n1, 279n7

rhetoric: Coleridge and, 48, 53, 94; complexity theory and, 180–85, 194; devaluation of, 14, 19, 29–30, 32, 48; philosophy and, 19; politics and, 77–81; science and, 19; teaching versus philosophy of, 14–15, 51–52; universal versus particular in, 39–40. *See also* rhetoric and composition discipline

rhetoric and composition discipline: binary oppositions in, 7, 18, 24, 37, 87; classicism/romanticism opposition in, 2, 7; Coleridge's place in, 7–9, 33–34, 41–44, 48, 120–21; concept of, 275n1; exclusion as tool for defining, 1, 3, 8, 11, 13–16, 271; mapping of, 13–15, 21–29, 35–39, 49–50, 54–55, 57–60, 64–65, 76–77, 87–93, 259–74; and narrative of retreat and return, 14, 15, 20, 29, 34, 41; 1980 in, 7, 12–13; pedagogy in, 35–38; politics of, 39, 57–60; science and, 36–39; status of, 41; vitalism and, 1–11

"Rhetoric and Ideology in the Writing Class" (Berlin), 77, 81

Rhetoric and Reality (Berlin), 60, 65–72, 75, 209

Rhetoric: Discovery and Change (Young, Becker, and Pike), 36–38

Rhetoric in American Colleges, 1850–1900 (Kitzhaber), 275n2

Rhetoric of Religion, The (Burke), 125

"Rhetoric of Romanticism, The" (Berlin), 7, 8, 12, 52, 56–57, 73, 212

"Rhetorical Invention and the Composing Process" (seminar), 21–22, 49, 86

Rhetorics, Poetics, and Cultures (Berlin), 119, 195, 203, 212

Rice, Jeff, 247

"Richard Whately and Current-Traditional Rhetoric" (Berlin), 50–52

Richards, I. A., 14–15, 57, 108

Rickert, Thomas, 177–78

Ricoeur, Paul, 108

Roberts-Miller, Patricia, 92

robotics, 156

Rohman, Gordon, 26

Romancing Rhetorics (Gradin), 89

romantic rhetoric, 60–62

romanticism: Berlin and, 52–53, 56–58, 60–65; Brahminical, 67–68; and creativity, 17; current-traditional rhetoric and, 31–32, 35; definition of, 33; in discipline of rhetoric and composition, 1–5; and the individual, 30, 88; mandarin, 68; new, 17–18, 25–28; patrician, 68; varieties of, 33; vitalism and, 1, 3, 4–5, 18–21, 23, 28, 33

Ronald, Kate, 87–88, 92

Roots for a New Rhetoric (Fogarty), 14–15

Roskelly, Hephzibah, 87–88, 92

Rousseau, Jean-Jacques, 3, 130

Rutherford, Ernest, 139

Rutsky, R. L., 170–71, 174–75, 177

salon, 284n20

Schelling, F. W. J., 142, 144

schemata, 191–92

Schiappa, Edward, 271, 272

Schilb, John, 273–74

schizoanalysis, 159, 202, 245, 282n11

Schlegel, A. W., 46

Schleiden, Matthias Jakob, 137

Schoer, Lowell, 91

Schrödinger, Erwin, 139

science: Coleridge and, 5, 47; complex vitalism and, 152–57; Hermeticism and, 129; method and, 110–11; modern, 130; and rhetoric, 19, 36–39; vitalism and, 129–40, 152–57

science fiction, 285n21

Scott, Fred Newton, 60, 65, 71–72

screens, 188–90

secondary imagination, 32, 53, 98–100, 104

self-expressivist approaches, 94

Semiotic Challenge, The (Barthes), 194

semiotics, 202–3

sense, 43–44

Shakespeare, William, 46–47, 232

Shaviro, Steven, 204–5

Shor, Ira, 78, 210–11

Sidler, Michelle, 214, 244

silence, 230–34

Simonson, Harold, 70

Sirc, Geoffrey, 35, 38, 216–17, 249–50, 252

situated robotics, 156

Smith, Paul, 83, 277n11

social constructivism, 88, 220–22